Alliance Formation in Civil Wars

Some of the most brutal and long-lasting civil wars of our time – those in Afghanistan, Bosnia, Lebanon, and Iraq, among others – involve the rapid formation and disintegration of alliances among warring groups, as well as fractionalization within them. It would be natural to suppose that warring groups form alliances based on shared identity considerations – such as Christian groups allying with other Christian groups, or Muslim groups with their fellow co-religionists – but this is not what we see. Two groups that identify themselves as bitter foes one day, on the basis of some identity narrative, might be allies the next day and vice versa. Nor is any group, however homogeneous, safe from internal fractionalization. Rather, looking closely at the civil wars in Afghanistan and Bosnia and testing against the broader universe of fifty-three cases of multiparty civil wars, Fotini Christia finds that the relative power distribution between and within various warring groups is the primary driving force behind alliance formation, alliance changes, group splits, and internal group takeovers.

Fotini Christia is Associate Professor in Political Science at the Massachusetts Institute of Technology. She received her PhD in public policy from Harvard University in 2008. Her research interests deal with issues of ethnicity, conflict, and cooperation in the Muslim world. She has done extensive ethnographic, survey, and experimental research in Bosnia and in Afghanistan. Her current Afghanistan research project, which draws on a randomized impact evaluation of a $1 billion community-driven development program, assesses the effects of foreign development aid on post-conflict governance and state-building initiatives. Professor Christia has received support for her research from the Harvard Academy for International and Area Studies, the International Growth Center, the UN World Food Program, USAID, and the World Bank, among other institutions. She has published work in journals such as *Science*, *Comparative Politics*, and the *Middle East Journal*. She has also written about her experiences in Afghanistan, Iran, the West Bank, and Uzbekistan for *Foreign Affairs*, the *New York Times*, *The Washington Post*, and *The Boston Globe*. She graduated magna cum laude with a joint BA in Economics and Operations Research from Columbia College and an MA in International Affairs from the School of International and Public Affairs at Columbia University.

Alliance Formation in Civil Wars

FOTINI CHRISTIA
Massachusetts Institute of Technology

CAMBRIDGE
UNIVERSITY PRESS

CAMBRIDGE
UNIVERSITY PRESS

32 Avenue of the Americas, New York NY 10013-2473, USA

Cambridge University Press is part of the University of Cambridge.

It furthers the University's mission by disseminating knowledge in the pursuit of education, learning, and research at the highest international levels of excellence.

www.cambridge.org
Information on this title: www.cambridge.org/9781107683488

First published 2012
Reprinted 2013

A catalog record for this publication is available from the British Library.

Library of Congress Cataloging in Publication data
Christia, Fotini.
Alliance formation in civil wars / Fotini Christia, Massachusetts Institute of Technology.
   pages   cm
Includes bibliographical references and index.
ISBN 978-1-107-02302-4 (hardback) – ISBN 978-1-107-68348-8 (paperback)
1. Civil war.   2. Alliances.   3. Civil war – Case studies.   4. Alliances – Case studies.
I. Title.
JC328.5.C57   2012
303.6′4–dc23   2012012693

ISBN   978-1-107-02302-4   Hardback
ISBN   978-1-107-68348-8   Paperback

To my parents

Contents

Figures

Tables

Maps

Acknowledgments

Having spent several months in the former Yugoslavia during my undergraduate years, I came to Harvard to write a dissertation on post-conflict reconstruction and nation building. The turn of global affairs – 9/11 was the first day of my graduate student career – instead prompted me to focus on conflict itself. There was a notable surge in academic work on violence at the time, but the discourse was still very much dominated by questions of how civil wars start and end rather than on how they are fought. In my decision to try to decipher some of the pathologies in civil conflict – namely what brings groups together and what breaks them apart – I benefited greatly from my interactions with my advisors Robert Bates, Roger Petersen, Monica Toft, and Stephen Walt. They all played instrumental roles at different times and on different aspects of this project. The imprint of their rich and diverse contributions to my scholarship is no doubt visible throughout this book.

In embarking on this project, I was very much driven by the pioneering work on civil wars by Jim Fearon, Stathis Kalyvas, David Laitin, and Nicholas Sambanis. On ethnicity I became a disciple of Dan Posner's work. Jeremy Weinstein, an advanced graduate student at Harvard at the time I was starting out, set the paradigm of how to do fieldwork in conflict-ravaged countries. His subsequent work with Macartan Humphreys directly inspired some of my research in Afghanistan and Bosnia and Herzegovina that was to follow. For hands-on chapter-by-chapter feedback at an early manuscript conference, I dearly thank Alex Downes, Jorge Dominguez, Matt Kocher, and Bob Powell. Alex Downes and Jorge Dominguez also offered invaluable mentorship throughout the publishing process. Great thanks also go to Lew Bateman and two anonymous reviewers for helping me transition this work from a manuscript into an actual book.

Researching this book, I found myself meeting conflict protagonists in pig farms and mud huts, cemeteries and incarceration facilities, forts and military barracks, presidential palaces and parliament buildings across Afghanistan and the former Yugoslavia. The quality of the meeting venue was strongly correlated with whether the individual had ended up on the war's winning or losing side. In the process, I met several people with blood on their hands (some had even been convicted for their war crimes) and was relieved when cultural norms prevented me from having to shake those hands or look them in the eye. There was an eerie banality in how both winners and losers viewed violence that made for fascinating, albeit disturbing, narratives that I am nevertheless grateful they shared. I would not have been able to hear these stories or theorize on them were it not for the support I received from Harvard University.

At Harvard, I am grateful to the Belfer Center for Science and International Affairs (especially to Steve Miller, Steve Walt, and the incredible Susan Lynch) and to the Davis Center for Russian and Eurasian Studies (especially to Tim Colton); and to the Weatherhead Center for International Affairs for support in the pre- and post-dissertation stage. Special thanks to Jorge Dominguez (again!), Steve Levitksy, and Steve Rosen and inordinate gratitude to Steve Bloomfield, Kathleen Hoover, Clare Putnam, and Larry Winnie. For instruction and assistance with Geographic Information Systems at Harvard I want to thank Jeff Blossom and Ben Lewis – I would not have been able to geo-reference and digitize my maps of Afghanistan and Bosnia and Herzegovina without their guidance. Outside Harvard's intellectual research centers, I found a home in Quincy House. I was a resident tutor there for most of my graduate student years and want to thank House Masters Robert Kirshner and Jayne Loader as well as House Masters Lee and Deb Gehrke for making me part of the community. Larry Peterson was a truly wonderful friend throughout the Quincy years and beyond, and many thanks also go to Quincy's Judith Flynn, Susan Hamel, and Sue Watts. I fondly remember all the fellow tutors I worked with but am most grateful for my intellectual friendships with Thomas Baranga, Louis-Philippe Hodgson, Chris Leighton, John McMililan, and David Singer.

My debt to Harvard is only comparable to what I owe MIT. This book was thoroughly rewritten at MIT's Political Science Department, where it turned into a manuscript from what was an admittedly ambitious and insightful but also quite tortured Harvard dissertation. I am deeply thankful to all my colleagues and the department chairs – Charles Stewart in my first two years at MIT and Rick Locke for the years since then – for their feedback and support throughout the process. Special thanks go to Roger Petersen for having been my mentor from the very start (and for never defecting from our alliance!), to Cindy Williams for inspiration and advice, and to Barry Posen and Dick Samuels for making me a member of the Security Studies Program and the Center for International Studies at MIT. It was thanks to their support – along with that by Dean Deborah Fitzgerald – that I was able to work with an array of extraordinary MIT graduate students who provided some excellent research assistance for this book. First among them is Nathan Black, who did an inordinate amount of work and coding on this book and became probably more intricately familiar with Afghanistan, Bosnia, Iraq, and the book's other fifty multiparty civil wars than he would have ever wished to. Nicholas Miller only comes second because he joined the department later! His commitment to the project and dedicated work in replicating all the results and getting it ready for the publisher were astounding. I also want to thank Daniel Altman for his initial coding work; Chad Hazlett for his ever-scrutinizing and constructive eye over the book's theory and empirics; and Alec Worsnop for his detailed work on refining the Afghan and Bosnian qualitative chapters. They are all brilliant scholars in the making, and I hope their apprenticeship on this project will be a lesson on how to write an academic book.

For my fieldwork in Bosnia and Herzegovina I am most indebted to Dušanka Sekulić. Her inquisitive mind and strong spirit helped me be resourceful in reaching out to as many wartime personalities as possible. Lucio Valerio Sarandrea was also a wonderfully supportive friend, as were Miho Radovan in Mostar and Alexandra Popić in Prijedor. I also want to extend my warm thanks to former OSCE staff from Banja Luka, Bihać, Mostar, Prijedor, Sanski Most, Sarajevo, and Velika Kladuša for their friendship during my time in the field. For unparalleled research assistance on the case of Bosnia and Herzegovina during World War II I want to thank Vujo Ilić. For wonderful commentary on my Bosnia work my heartfelt gratitude to one of the leading Balkan scholars out there – Florian Bieber. Special thanks also to Susan Woodward for her feedback on the Fikret Abdić material presented in the book. I am also indebted to a set of great women academics that I met while still an undergraduate at Columbia and then came across during my fieldwork in the former Yugoslavia – most notably Dana Burde, Lara Nettlefield, and Sherill Stroschein. Radmila Gorup will be always dear to me for having taught me Serbo-Croat, true Yugoslav style, during my Columbia College years. Ellen-Elias Bursac took up that brave role in my early Harvard graduate school years and I am greatly thankful to her, too.

For providing linguistic training for my Afghan fieldwork, I am grateful to Wheeler Thackston for his exceptional Farsi classes and his stories about life in Iran that inspired two summers of further language training at the University of Tehran. For actual work in Afghanistan, I am indebted for life to Michael Semple. It was his encyclopedic knowledge and his brilliant analysis that helped me bring together in a systematic fashion a lot of the primary material collected in the field. He, along with Mervyn Patterson, another one of the undisputed authorities on Afghanistan, were the forces behind the commander dataset, which all came to life thanks to the great research assistantship of the young Afghan scholar Abdul Malik Sahibzada. For support during my work in the field great thanks go to Hamid Gharibzadah, Majid Karzai, Musa Mahmudi, Bilal Sarwari, Rory Stewart, Lema Zekrya, and to Nancy Dupree at the Kabul University library for granting me access to their archive on the Afghan Jihad. During my work on Afghanistan, I also crossed paths with some incredibly talented journalists. Dexter Filkins shared my passion and views on that war-torn country – per his memorable quote on Afghan alliances as pickup basketball – and dragged me through the finish line when I was working on my dissertation and he on his extraordinary book. Adam Ellick and Lucian Read, loyal friends and intrepid fellow travelers, showed me Afghanistan through a different lens with their path-breaking video work.

Parts of this book have previously been published in *Foreign Affairs* in 2009 (Fotini Christia and Michael Semple, "Flipping the Taliban: How to Win in Afghanistan," *Foreign Affairs* 88 (4): 34–45, Copyright 2009 by the Council on Foreign Relations) and in *Comparative Politics* in 2008 (Fotini Christia, "Following the Money: Muslim versus Muslim in Bosnia's Civil War," *Comparative Politics* 40 (4): 461–480). I thank the editors of each publication for their permission to use this material in the book.

During this book's writing, I had the unwavering support of a set of wonderful friends and colleagues. First, Evan Liaras, a high school friend from Salonica, Greece, and a Harvard- and MIT-trained academic, offered the most committed and insightful commentary. This book would not have been written without him. Petar Momcilović, very dear to me from my Columbia College days, also contributed his intellectual clarity to this project from beginning to end. Marc Alexander, Afua (B.B.) Banful, Caty Clement, Ruben Enikolopov, Shuhei Kurizaki, Paul Staniland, and Pierre Yared gave great feedback on parts of this work during our graduate student years. My human rights lawyer friends Hillary Schrenell and Cornelia Schneider were inordinate sources of energy. Their trust and love only came second to that of my parents who stuck with me, unconditionally, throughout this journey – which ended up lasting as long as Odysseus's trip back to Ithaca! This book is dedicated to them.

Introduction

TALIBAN DECREE

[Taliban Seal]
Islamic Emirate of Afghanistan

In the name of Allah the most merciful, the most compassionate

Piece of advice to officials of the Islamic Emirate of Afghanistan and to the Taliban from the respectable *Amir al Mu'minin* [commander of the faithful, title used historically by powerful leaders in Islam that Mullah Omar also assumed]

There has been lethal activity in our midst which may result in our destruction. Taliban accuse each other behind each other's backs, . . . resorting to false and unfounded accusations. . . . There is no doubt that this backstabbing is happening. I once again appeal to you to stop this or else whoever is involved will be cursed in this world and in the afterlife, over which I have no control. These acts are damaging Islam. For God's sake, stop doing this!

With respect,
Servant of Islam
Commander of the Faithful
Mullah Mohammad Omar, *Mujahed* [freedom-fighter][1]

---

[1] Taliban decree in author's possession.

EXCERPT FROM *THE FOREVER WAR*

Men fought, men switched sides, men lined up and fought again. War in Afghanistan often seemed like a game of pickup basketball, a contest among friends, a tournament where you never knew which team you'd be on when the next game got underway. Shirts today, skins tomorrow. On Tuesday, you might be part of a fearsome Taliban regiment, running into a minefield. And on Wednesday you might be manning a checkpoint for some gang of the Northern Alliance. By Thursday you could be back with the Talibs again, holding up your Kalashnikov and promising to wage jihad forever.... Battles were often decided this way, not by actual fighting, but by flipping gangs of soldiers. One day, the Taliban might have four thousand soldiers, and the next, only half that, with the warlords of the Northern Alliance suddenly larger by a similar amount. The fighting began when the bargaining stopped, and the bargaining went right up until the end.[2]

[2] Filkins (2008), p. 51.

THE PUZZLE

In the years since the ousting of the Taliban, we have seen scores of lives, military and civilian, lost in Afghanistan. The internecine relationships between the warring actors have made the logic of the fighting hard to make sense of – so much so that it has prompted the United States to revise its counterinsurgency doctrine, shifting the strategic focus from killing the enemy to protecting the population. In that vein, the United States has sent anthropologists into the field to lead American soldiers and commanders through the maze of Afghanistan's ethnic and tribal politics. This book argues that although the importance of cultural awareness can never be overestimated, no knowledge of history and culture alone, regardless of how deep or profound, will get us to understand why warring actors fight with or against one another.

Rather, we are arguably going to be just as well off going with one rule alone: the expectation that warring groups will aim to side with the winner, so long as they can have a credible guarantee that the winner will not strip them of power once victory is accomplished. Afghan commanders, not unlike other wartime commanders in similar circumstances, are the guardians of specific interests linked to the groups from which their men are recruited. And few factors have motivated them more over the years of war than the desire to end up on the winning side. They have often switched camps mid-conflict. In doing so, their rationale was obvious: In a war that drags on, changing camps means surviving longer and holding onto power.

Indeed, Afghanistan's recent history is replete with examples of warring leaders choosing to switch sides. In the civil war that lasted from the collapse of the Soviet-backed regime in 1992 to the Taliban's capture of almost 90 percent of Afghanistan in the fall of 1998, the heads of mujahedin groups constantly shifted their allegiances. The Uzbek general Abdul Rashid Dostum was the Tajik commander Ahmad Shah Massoud's friend first, and then his foe. The Hazara leader Abdul Ali Mazari fought against the Pashtun headman Gulbuddin Hekmatyar before fighting by his side. Constantly shifting alliances meant no single group could gain the upper hand, eventually allowing the Taliban to persuade many factions to side with them. By the time the Taliban reached Kabul, their ranks were teeming with fighters once allied with someone else.

This book explains the choices behind the double-crossings in the Afghan civil war and develops a broader theory on alliance formation and group fractionalization in multiparty civil wars. It shows that changing sides, realigning, flipping – whatever one may choose to call it – is not just the Afghan way of war. Rather, the theory travels well across warring times and regions in Afghanistan, and also outside it. Indeed, apart from Afghanistan, some of the most brutal and long-lasting civil wars of our times – Bosnia, Lebanon, and Iraq, among others – are associated with the rapid formation and disintegration of alliances among warring groups, as well as with fractionalization within them. The resulting multiplicity of actors has paralyzed outsiders, who have often been unable to even follow the unraveling of the conflicts' complex trajectories.

It would be natural to suppose that the way in which warring groups align and the determinants that shape their internal splits and takeovers result from similarities and differences of identity within and between these warring groups. For example, in a multiparty war of Christians versus Muslims (i.e., Bosnia or Lebanon), we might expect the Christian groups to always ally with one another. In reality, however, this is not what we see. Instead, there appears to be no such thing as an impossible alliance in the context of a multiparty civil war: Two groups that identify themselves as bitter foes one day, on the basis of some identity cleavage, might be allies the next day, and vice versa. Nor is any group, however homogeneous, safe from internal fractionalization. Rather, I find that the relative power distribution between and within the various warring groups in a given conflict is the primary driving force behind alliance formation, alliance changes, as well as group splits and takeovers.

CONTRIBUTIONS TO THE LITERATURE

In recent years, there has been a surge of scholarly interest in civil war, as a result of the high place of internal conflict on the U.S. national security agenda following the end of the Cold War. However, the majority of these works have focused on civil war onset and termination rather than on within-conflict processes.[3] Existing works on civil war processes have predominantly taken the form of either formal models or case studies, which are, respectively, too abstract or too esoteric to capture empirical reality.[4] Most extant literature treats civil war as a contest between two coherent, unitary actors (the government vs. the rebels, the incumbents vs. the insurgents), thus overlooking internal divisions among groups and the multiparty character of many such conflicts.[5] Using a theoretical approach, along with multiple methods of empirics, this book aims to shed light on these warring group interactions that have been largely understudied, thereby relating civil war processes to onset and termination.

Other contributions of this book to the broader literature on civil war can be enumerated as well. The book speaks to the debate over whether so-called

---

[3] Examples of such work follow. On onset, see Posen (1993); Harff and Gurr (1994); Collier and Hoeffler (2000); Petersen (2002); Fearon and Laitin (2003); and Toft (2003), among others; on duration, see Elbadawi and Sambanis (2000); and Fearon (2004), among others; on termination, see Licklider (1995); Kaufmann (1996a, 1996b); Stedman (1997); Walter (1997); Hartzell (1999); Zartman (2000); and Toft (2010), among others.

[4] Examples of formal models of conflict processes include Skarpedas (1992); and Hirshleifer (1995). Exceptions to this trend include Petersen (2001); Valentino (2005); Kalyvas (2006); and Weinstein (2007).

[5] Prominent examples include Kaufmann (1996a, 1996b); Walter (1997); Fearon (2004); Kalyvas (2006); Lyall and Wilson (2009); Toft (2010).

ethnic and nonethnic civil wars should be considered separate phenomena,[6] by studying alliance and fractionalization dynamics in both contexts. Ultimately, I find that the rationale behind alliance formation and group fractionalization is the same, suggesting that certain strategic choices relating to civil war processes are independent of the conflict's character. I also engage the level of analysis issue that has become quite contentious in recent civil war scholarship.[7] Rather than studying these conflicts at a macro level (i.e., societal cleavages) or a micro level (i.e., individual incentives), I try to link the two levels analytically by focusing on the interactions between them. Specifically, I find that the key actors vis-à-vis warring group alliance formation and fractionalization are often local elites, operating at a "meso level" that links the national-level cleavages with individual-level motivations. Additionally, whereas most existing works focus only on the motivations for starting or ending civil wars, I explicitly theorize the motivations of warring actors during the conflict itself, highlighting how concerns about survival and division of postwar political control drive alliance choices and group fractionalization.

In addition to the theoretical contributions outlined earlier, a theory on civil war alliance formation is also interesting from a methodological perspective. The dynamic of interaction between three or more actors tends to be under-theorized in the field, including in theories of civil war, partly because a bipolar frame of reference is easier to conceptualize but also because many modeling approaches, including game-theoretic ones, get much more cumbersome with the addition of a third actor. A work on alliance formation and group fractionalization can provide a framework for better understanding the different dimensions of multi-actor interactions, moving us beyond binary approaches.

Apart from their theoretical and methodological importance, the questions of how groups ally and why they fractionalize have clear policy implications. In a multiethnic state at war with itself, a group's access to resources and capabilities is conditioned by the behavior of other groups and by the group's own internal stability, thus making alliance strategies and group fractionalization important. The theory presented in this book reveals the forces that determine these choices and outcomes, and in turn shows what policy instruments can be used to prevent fighting or bring an ongoing conflict to an end.

For example, a better understanding of alliance behavior and group fractionalization in the 1992–1998 Afghan civil war would have illuminated the reasons behind the coalitions between sworn enemies (such as the Pashtuns and the Hazaras), would have predicted fragmentation within the Hazara and Uzbek forces, and would have, in turn, anticipated the Taliban's victory. In Iraq, if the international community was more astute to alliance and

---

[6] See, for example, Kaufmann (1996a); Sambanis (2001); Buhaug, Cederman, and Rod (2006); Cederman and Girardin (2007); and Toft (2010).

[7] See, for example, Elbadawi and Sambanis (2000); Kalyvas (2003, 2006); Downes (2008); Fearon (2004); Humphreys and Weinstein (2006); and Valentino, Huth, and Balch-Lindsay (2004).

fractionalization dynamics, it might not have been surprised when the Sunni tribes dropped their alliance with Al Qaeda, leading to the emergence of the Sons of Iraq – an initiative among Iraqi tribal leaders that precipitated an end to mass violence. Errors in diplomacy, stemming from a faulty understanding of the origins of intergroup alliances and the causes of within-group instability, have undoubtedly led to the perpetuation of these wars and resulted in hundreds of thousands of civilian casualties. A sounder grasp of civil war alliance and fractionalization dynamics would have arguably allowed for fewer grave policy errors and faster ways to peace. The policy implications of this work therefore pertain to conflict prevention and termination, as well as postconflict state-building initiatives.

Having provided an overview of the basic goals and contributions of this book, I proceed to outline the theoretical argument, discuss the relevant definitions and scope conditions, and offer a road map for what follows.

THE ARGUMENT

In this book, I argue that alliance formation is tactical, motivated by a concern with victory and the maximization of wartime returns as anticipated in the political power sharing of the postconflict state. In principle, all groups want to be in a coalition large enough to attain victory while small enough to ensure maximum political payoffs. In practice, however, given the multitude of players and the chaos inherent in civil war, this outcome proves difficult to secure. A major reason for this is that commitment problems – the inability of actors to credibly commit not to exploit one another later – are inherent in warring group interactions.[8] More specifically, while much of the literature has focused on commitment problems as a barrier to rebel groups reaching negotiated settlements with the state, commitment problems will also make groups wary of winning the war as a weaker alliance partner. Because there is no third party that can credibly enforce the agreed-on division of political control, the weaker party will often prefer to defect and prolong the war rather than risk being double-crossed at the hands of the stronger ally upon the war's conclusion, which may involve violent purges and political subordination. The implication of this dilemma is that unless one group is powerful enough to win the war on its own, the conflict will degenerate into a process of constant defection, alliance reconfiguration, and group fractionalization, as groups maneuver in an effort to win the war while ensuring they do not get victimized at the hands of the strongest actor left standing.

Contrary to identity-based arguments, race, language, religion, or ideology do not appear to guarantee in any enduring way the formation of alliances. Instead, elites of the warring parties pick their allies based on power considerations and then construct justifying narratives, looking to their identity repertoires for characteristics shared with their allies and not shared with

---

[8] On commitment problems, see Fearon (1995, 1998); Lake and Rothchild (1996); Walter (1997); and Powell (2006).

their foes. Likewise, local elites can make a similarly instrumental use of identity narratives when justifying whether or not to stay subservient to their group's leadership. This argument, which is consistent with a large body of research in comparative politics that shows elites strategically manipulate identity categories for political purposes,[9] nonetheless suggests that identity attributes do have psychological and emotional import for the rank and file – hence the reason elites constantly invoke them. In other words, while identity factors do not determine alliance choices, the fact that leaders feel compelled to justify their choices in these terms implies identity narratives are useful for public consumption. My view is essentially an instrumentalist one: Wartime alliances, and the groups that comprise them, are not merely imagined but rather constantly reimagined communities.[10] Given that there is nothing intrinsic about these alliances, the identity narratives that appear on the surface to hold them together are simply "invented traditions" developed by elites.[11] When power considerations call for it, these communities and traditions will be cast aside and new ones imagined in their place.

More specifically, the argument of this book is that alliance formation takes place through two mechanisms, both of which rely on relative power rather than identity as the key explanatory variable. The first mechanism is the evolution of the relative power balance between groups. As groups lose battles or come out of them victorious, other groups are confronted with survival choices on whether to flock to them or abandon them. In making these choices, leaders consider their relative power both within and across alliances: While they desire to be on the winning side, commitment problems make them wary of winning the war as a weaker alliance partner. Such alliance changes occur more frequently in conflicts where relative power is more or less balanced between the various warring groups, because in these conflicts small changes in a single group's relative power can significantly alter the incentives of other groups to align with it or against it. Conversely, in conflicts where power is unevenly distributed, small shifts in the power distribution are unlikely to spur such alliance changes. The implication of this logic is that we should expect to see more alliance changes in multiparty civil wars in which there is a rough balance of power, as opposed to those conflicts in which power is unevenly distributed. In other words, conflicts involving a strong government force (i.e., Guatemala) should see less volatility in alliances than conflicts involving a weak government (i.e., Lebanon).

A second mechanism that drives alliance choice is warring group fractionalization. The uncertainty and complexity of intergroup relations in multiparty civil wars are to a certain extent mirrored at the level of intragroup relations, between the various subgroups that comprise these groups. These subgroups

---

[9] See, for example, Bates (1974); Kasfir (1979); Gagnon (2004); Posner (2004, 2005); and Wilkinson (2006).

[10] Anderson (1983).

[11] On "invented traditions," see Hobsbawm (1984); see also Brass (1974) and Wedeen (1999).

tend to be led by local elites – a critical unit of analysis in this book – and differ from each other along regional lines; they may also have leadership disputes between them that predate the war. Critically, these subgroups exist and are identifiable prior to the onset of war: They are not endogenous products of the conflict. Bonds between subgroups are stronger than bonds between allied warring groups because of a combination of increased trust, in-group bias, and institutionalized sanctioning and enforcement mechanisms. However, even the bonds between subgroups with the same identity repertoires are not immune to fractures when subgroup survival is threatened.

In this context, battlefield wins will foster intragroup cohesion by convincing local elites that they are on the winning side. On the other hand, battlefield losses, which are typically borne unevenly between the various subgroups, will shake the confidence of these local elites and will frequently encourage fractionalization along the preexisting regional or leadership cleavages. Fractionalization, in turn, is a form of relative power change, regardless of whether (1) a splinter faction joins up with an opposing group (increasing that group's power at the expense of the group it left), (2) a splinter group strikes out on its own (breaking the overall power distribution into smaller units), or (3) a group is taken over by a dissatisfied faction (decreasing that group's relative power as the turmoil rages). The resulting change in the intergroup distribution of power will spur alliance shifts, as groups seek to form updated, optimally sized coalitions.

What, then, are the observable implications of these mechanisms at work? We can observe our dependent variables – alliance choices and changes, and within-group splits and takeovers – fairly easily, and the independent variables – relative power shifts and identity cleavages – can be observed as well. But how can we know which independent variable has more explanatory power vis-à-vis the dependent variable when we expect to observe both power shifts and seemingly compelling identity narratives?

The fact that ethnic, linguistic, regional, religious, and (to a lesser extent) ideological identities are presumed to stay relatively fixed – at least given the rather short timescale of civil wars – allows this book's theory to be falsifiable. If identity commonalities or dissimilarities explained intergroup alliance choices and intragroup cohesion, then we would see relatively few alliance changes and little group fractionalization in these conflicts. Alliance patterns and groups would be fairly stable, as they would be constructed around relatively immutable cleavages. As I demonstrate, however, that is quite the opposite of what we see within the empirical scope of this book. The empirical chapters show alliances constantly shifting and groups perpetually at risk of internal splits and takeovers. Dramatic identity narratives arise in proximity to these events, but as soon as another disruption to the intergroup or intragroup equilibrium takes place, those narratives are abandoned and new narratives spring up. The capriciousness of these narratives suggests they are not a key explanatory variable, and that relative power changes are really doing the work behind alliance changes and fractionalization.

Figure I.1 illustrates two of the theory's observable implications with basic descriptive information about the multiparty civil wars that will be the focus of this book. We see that the numerous identity cleavages in these conflicts were not stable predictors of intergroup and intragroup dynamics. While these cleavages can be assumed to have remained more or less constant for the duration of the war, these conflicts saw an average of roughly 0.33 alliance shifts per year, while an average of 46 percent of the original warring parties in each conflict suffered some form of internal fractionalization.[12] Moreover, these numbers are not driven by extraordinary rates of shifting or fractionalization in just a few unusual conflicts. Rather, these phenomena are ubiquitous among multiparty conflicts. As the left panel of Figure I.1 shows, not only did the average multiparty conflict see fractionalization (at least once and oftentimes more) of about half of the original groups, but this percentage is roughly normally distributed and very few conflicts escaped some degree of fractionalization. Of fifty-three multiparty conflicts assessed here, only six (11 percent) did not experience any fractionalization. The right panel of Figure I.1 shows that alliance shifts, too, were frequent. Of the fifty-three multiparty civil wars, forty-five (85 percent) experienced at least one alliance change during their course, and twenty-seven (51 percent) experienced three or more alliance shifts during their course. These rough statistics tell us two things. First, fractionalization and alliance change are so common that a picture of war that does not include them is incomplete. Second, given that identity-based cleavages cannot change quickly enough to explain these rates of breakdown among groups, clearly something more than identity cleavages was at work in these chaotic conflicts.

The implication of this book's theory is that by closely observing relative power changes in multiparty conflicts, we can make reasonable predictions about which groups will ally with one another, and about which groups will suffer internal instability. One of the main goals of this work is to increase the feasibility and accuracy of such predictions.

DEFINITIONS

By "civil war" I mean an internal armed conflict, directed against the government of a sovereign state, which has caused at least 1,000 cumulative battle-related deaths.[13] Extending from Walt's (1987) definition of interstate alliances,

---

[12] These are simple averages weighing each conflict equally. If one weighted alliance shifts by war duration, the average would be 0.25 alliance shifts per year, and if one weighted fractionalization by number of groups at onset, the average would be 48% of warring parties facing fractionalization.

[13] The other major type of internal armed conflict studied in the academic literature is the "minor armed conflict," defined as the one that has caused between 25 and 1,000 battle-related deaths (see Sambanis (2004) on the debate over the proper death threshold). I chose the high death threshold not only because more deadly conflicts are more policy-relevant, but also because more intense conflicts are more likely to have a multiplicity of warring groups, allowing the extensive study of inter- and intragroup dynamics.

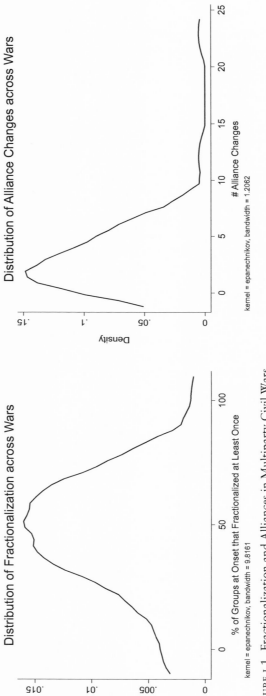

FIGURE I.1. Fractionalization and Alliances in Multiparty Civil Wars

this work considers a civil war alliance to be a formal or informal relationship of security cooperation between two or more groups, which involves commitment and exchange of benefits for both sides as well as a form of cost if the agreement is breached. Alliances are treated as a discrete rather than a continuous variable: Groups are either in an alliance or not. There is, however, a sense of temporal continuity, as alliance trajectories are examined from their inception to their termination, accounting for alliance changes over time. Warring group fractionalization, meanwhile, can take one of two forms. "Splits" involve groups in which a major faction breaks off to either form its own group or join up with an opposing group; "takeovers" involve groups in which one of the factions, instead of leaving the group altogether, successfully topples the leadership of the group.

The two main independent variables are power and shared identity. Power is operationalized through the demographic size or territorial control of each warring group at different points in the war's trajectory. In turn, shared identity is operationalized through commonalities across each warring group's identity repertoire,[14] which I define inclusively to encompass race, language, religion, tribe, social class, and ideology.[15] From a methodological perspective, this broad definition of identity is useful because it provides an easy test for the identity-based theories: If none of the above elements of groups' identity repertoires can reliably explain alliance choices, this is strong evidence against the explanatory power of shared identity writ large.

SCOPE CONDITIONS

As noted previously, some civil war scholars have come to appreciate that not all civil wars are the same, and that there is analytic value in distinguishing between different subtypes while still seeking to explain some general phenomena. The proper set of civil war subtypes remains hotly debated, but suggestions have included ethnic and nonethnic wars, old and new wars (i.e., pre– and post–Cold War conflicts), and conventional, irregular, and symmetric nonconventional wars.[16] In this work, I also advance the view that civil wars are best understood when they are disaggregated, by focusing my study of alliance behavior and warring group fractionalization within the particular scope of multiparty civil wars. By "multiparty civil wars" I mean civil wars in which there are three or more major domestic combatant groups. This is a necessary scope condition for my work, because if the conflict is binary, there are no intergroup alliances to be formed. One could rightly note that there can certainly be group fractionalization in a two-party conflict, but given that the dominant type of fractionalization is the splitting of one group into two or more, such wars become multiparty wars if they were not already. In other

---

[14] Posner (2005), p. 17.

[15] On the benefits of a broad definition of identity, see Horowitz (1985).

[16] See Kalyvas (2001); Sambanis (2001); and Kalyvas and Balcells (2010b) for such debates.

words, when a conflict does transform from binary to multiparty, it is included in the universe of cases and I expect the same dynamics to apply.

The most prominent finding on multiparty civil wars so far suggests that these wars are longer in duration because an increase in the number of actors leads to heightened informational asymmetries and shrinks the range of acceptable negotiations for the multiple parties involved.[17] My definition of multiparty civil wars, however, deviates from some existing works as it is based on three or more *domestic* actors, and does not include in the count external actors that may be supporting domestic warring groups. I choose to constrain the definition to three or more domestic parties because without this constraint, a conflict can be designated as "multiparty" either because it has more than two internal parties or because it has only two internal parties but at least one external party. While the effects of external party intervention are an interesting area of study, I did not want to conflate third-party involvement with the presence of multiple internal parties, as the two circumstances likely involve very different dynamics with different causes and consequences. Moreover, focusing on multiple internal parties alone rather than additional external parties is a much more sensible choice for an inquiry into warring group alliances and fractionalization, which looks at such processes on the level of domestic warring group protagonists. As demonstrated later, the multiparty versus two-party distinction is not only a logical one to make, but also one that appears to be statistically justified as these subtypes strongly differ on a number of covariates of both theoretical and intrinsic interest.

The first step to understanding multiparty civil wars is to identify all the cases of multiparty conflict between 1816 and 2007 meeting the definitions given earlier. The time frame was chosen in order to maximize the sample size within the constraints of data availability: Most international relations datasets begin in 1816, because the Congress of Vienna is often viewed as the beginning of the modern international system. The set of fifty-three wars so defined became the basis of a larger coding project in which extensive meso-level data were collected regarding the evolution of the number and identity of warring factions, their alliance choices, and the degree and type of fractionalization they experienced. Once these data were collected, I sought to examine how multiparty wars differ or do not differ from civil wars in the aggregate. To determine this, it was necessary to examine a dataset of all civil wars, without reference to multiparty status. Fearon and Laitin (2003) (henceforth FL) was used as this baseline dataset because their dataset has the most similar definition of civil war to mine (absent the multiparty restriction). Matching the multiparty conflicts previously identified to the wars on this list, it was possible to compare multiparty to non-multiparty wars within that single universe of cases without any risk of selection on the dependent variable. This analysis confirmed that multiparty civil wars, as defined for this book, are a

---

[17] Cunningham (2006, 2011).

TABLE I.1. *Prevalence of Multiparty Conflict in Broader Universe of Civil Wars*

	Estimate	Standard error
Percentage of conflicts that are multiparty	32.4	4.5
Percentage of conflict years attributed to multiparty conflicts	51.5	4.8
Percentage of battle deaths attributed to multiparty conflicts	29.7	4.4
Percentage of log(deaths) attributed to multiparty conflicts	35.8	4.6

Source: Data on universe of civil wars from Fearon and Laitin (2003).

sizable subsample of civil wars as defined by FL, composing almost a third of such wars and accounting for a full half of conflict years (see Table I.1).

Next, to ensure that the subset of multiparty wars in the FL dataset was relatively representative of my full set of fifty-three multiparty wars – which spanned a greater time period and had slightly different rules for the number of fatalities[18] – I compared all available covariates present in both datasets for these two sets of wars. Despite scope and definitional differences, the fifty-three cases I had identified did not differ significantly from the subset of thirty-six multiparty wars matching those in the FL dataset on any of the covariates tested, which among others included duration, mortality rates (and log transformations of these two measures), ethnic fractionalization, and year of onset.[19] Given that conflict duration, death rates, ethnic fractionalization, and time period are four of the main variables used to characterize different types of civil war,[20] this suggests that definitional differences and an expanded time frame do not alter our inferences about the attributes of multiparty conflicts.

Comparing multiparty conflicts to non-multiparty conflicts within the FL dataset, we see that the subtypes of war seem to differ systematically on a number of covariates. First, multiparty conflicts were associated with significantly longer mean durations by eight years ($p = 0.001$).[21] Multiparty conflicts also have higher fatality rates (when measured in natural logs) ($p = 0.0005$) and later years of onset ($p = 0.024$),[22] the latter reflecting the increasing rate of multiparty wars over recent decades (see Figure I.2). Indeed, in the 1940s, only

---

[18] Fearon and Laitin's (2003) definition of civil war requires that "the conflict killed at least 1,000 over its course, with a yearly average of at least 100" and "at least 100 were killed on both sides" (p. 76).

[19] The full comparison table of covariates is provided in the Appendix.

[20] See, for example, Sambanis (2001); Fearon (2004); Lacina (2006); and Kalyvas and Balcells (2010b).

[21] This is consistent with Cunningham's (2006) finding that civil wars with more "veto players" last longer.

[22] I find that a number of these variables (log *duration*, log *deaths*, and *year* of onset) remain significantly correlated with *multiparty* even when using regression to condition on all the variables that appeared to be correlated in the bivariate analyses. See Appendix for results.

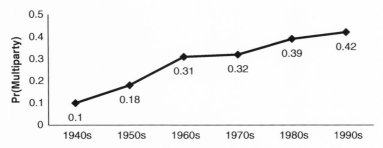

FIGURE I.2. Percentage of Multiparty Conflicts by Decade

10 percent (se = 10%) of conflicts were multiparty as compared to 42 percent (se = 9%) in the 1990s.[23]

The relationship between multiparty conflicts and conflict duration is similarly strong: conflicts lasting fewer than fifteen years were 25 percent likely to be multiparty, but conflicts fifteen years old or older were 58 percent likely to be multiparty – a statistically significant difference ($p = 0.006$). Even though we cannot infer the direction of causality in this relationship from these data alone (it could be that longer wars are simply likelier to become multiparty because there are more chances for fractionalization or for additional domestic parties to join in), the correlation between duration and multiparty civil wars makes this subsample of civil wars particularly interesting for the study of group fractionalization. In short, multiparty civil wars with three or more domestic actors are becoming more common, take longer to end, and kill more people than the average civil war, making them important for scholars and policy makers to analyze and understand. As new scholarship in the realm of civil wars advocates, such disaggregated analysis can be fruitful both theoretically and empirically in identifying processes that may be obscured in more aggregated inquiries.[24]

A final note on scope: many have written about the brutality of the several multiparty civil wars that the book references – the infamous conflicts that pitted Christians against Muslims, Sunnis against Shiites, communists against royalists, fascists, or mujahedin, be they in Afghanistan, Bosnia, or Iraq. This book, however, is about allies, not enemies. In that regard, it only aims to explain the wartime dynamics of alliance formation among groups and fractionalization within those groups. It does not aspire or claim to provide an understanding of larger civil war processes such as targeting, violence, recruitment, or civil war termination. These dynamics are highly complex in their own

---

[23] This trend is nearly linear without statistical evidence of any discontinuities at the end of the Cold War or elsewhere. For each year that passes, conflicts are on average 0.6% more likely (in absolute terms) to be multiparty.

[24] Wimmer, Cederman, and Min (2009); Kalyvas and Balcells (2010b).

right and constitute primary matters of inquiry in other works on civil war.[25] Moreover, I would like to emphasize that the role of shared identity in this work is examined in the very specific context of alliance formation among, and fractionalization within, warring groups. Hence the book does not speak to the larger questions involving the use of identity and symbols in civil war onset, targeting, or violence. These are all highly interesting and important dynamics and processes, but they run outside coalition and cohesion dynamics and are therefore beyond the scope of this study. Although identity considerations may indeed exogenously influence strategic choices in those domains, I aim to show that this is not the case with regard to alliance choices in civil war: Rather, relative power drives alliance choices, which in turn endogenously shapes identity narratives.

LOOKING AHEAD

This book is organized into four parts: one theoretical and three empirical. Specifically, Part I, comprised of Chapters 1 and 2, offers a theoretical framework to understanding alliance formation, group fractionalization, and the use of identity narratives. Chapter 1 situates this book's approach to alliances. Specifically, it frames the question in the context of existing approaches to cooperation during conflict – be it alliances between states in the international relations literature; alliances between political parties as understood in comparative politics; or cooperation between actors in the political economy literature on ethnicity and conflict. It also describes the research design and data used in this book. Chapter 2 presents this work's theory. It puts forth relative power as the main explanatory variable and lays out an alliance mechanism spurred by the evolution of relative power among warring groups. Additionally, the chapter presents a mechanism on the fractionalization of warring groups and shows how it feeds into the alliance dynamics of warring parties. Chapter 2 also discusses the role of shared identity and alliance narratives.

In Part II, Chapter 3 takes us through the Machiavellian in-group and out-group politics of the 1992–1998 intra-mujahedin war in Afghanistan. Drawing on interviews with warlords and mujahedin and on wartime primary sources that range from fatwas and religious decrees to Guantanamo Bay testimony, along with data on territorial control that capture relative power among warring parties, this chapter shows how group alliances and fractionalization, as well as the creation of narratives, unraveled in the context of this war. Chapter 4 tests the resonance of the power argument through a discussion of alliance politics and group fractionalization during the 1978–1989 Afghan Jihad of mujahedin against communists. Chapter 5 further reinforces the external validity of the theory by ascertaining whether the proposed framework only applies to warring groups or whether it holds at a more micro level of

---

[25] Petersen (2002, 2011); Kalyvas (2006); Weinstein (2007); Lyall and Wilson (2009); and Toft (2010), among others.

analysis: the local commander. A unique dataset on Afghan strongmen across Afghanistan's ideological and ethnic civil wars was collected and coded for this test.

Part III of the book is intended to show us that the proposed power-driven theory of alliance formation and change is relevant not only to the specificities of Afghanistan. In that regard, Chapter 6 takes us to a very different type of multiparty civil war in 1992–1995 Bosnia and Herzegovina, with only three groups and one main identity cleavage (religion). It illustrates the byzantine alliance choices and fractionalization patterns of that war using interviews with former military and political elites as well as convicted war criminals, and primary sources ranging from local news sources to wartime ceasefire and alliance agreements, fatwas and religious decrees, and municipal-level demographic data and data on territorial control. Chapter 7 takes us to a Bosnia of the past. Through the use of archival sources from all warring sides, this chapter shows that in the arguably ideological civil war of World War II Bosnia, much as in the Afghan Jihad of mujahedin against communists in the late 1970s and 1980s, the proposed theoretical mechanisms on warring group alliance politics and group fractionalization hold. These dynamics thus do not appear to be conditional on the character of war (ethnic or nonethnic).

In Part IV, I test the generality of the argument further by looking at other specific cases as well as the whole universe of cases of multiparty civil wars. Specifically, the validity of the theoretical framework is further probed, over time and space, in Chapter 8, through the use of an original fifty-three-case dataset of multiparty civil wars. I run a battery of statistical tests on this dataset that prove consistent with the proposed theoretical framework. The book's concluding chapter offers a short overview of alliance and fractionalization dynamics in the infamous civil war cases of present-day Afghanistan and Anbar in Iraq, and discusses in more detail the policy implications of my argument, closing with suggestions on promising avenues for future research.

PART I

CONTEXT AND THEORY

1

Literature and Research Design

Afghanistan, ethnically fractionalized and at war for much of the past thirty years, is a prime example of pernicious multiparty conflict. But it is hardly alone. The world is comprised of multiethnic states, more than half of which have three or more ethnic groups – often caught up in disputes.[1] It is thus striking to note the lack of a systematic theory on alliance formation and group fractionalization in civil wars, a gap that this book attempts to address. Although no work in the existing literature specifically theorizes the causes of such alliance shifts and the interlinked group fractionalization dynamics, a variety of works in international relations, political economy, and comparative politics have substantial bearing on these questions. Collectively, this diverse literature explains the within-conflict processes at hand as a result of power dynamics, identity politics, both, or neither. I outline these hypotheses and the literature supporting them as a way to motivate the discussion, later on in this chapter, of the research design and data I used to build and then test the proposed theory of civil war alliances and group fractionalization. This theory is then presented in Chapter 2.

RELEVANT LITERATURE

Several prominent political science theories, most of them not directly concerned with intrastate conflict, suggest that power considerations should motivate warring groups' behavior in multiparty civil wars. The first of these theories is the neorealist paradigm of international relations, which argues that alliances tend to be power-balancing – actors choose to balance against their most powerful rivals.[2] A modified version of this theory suggests that weaker actors balance against the most powerful actor only if that most powerful actor is perceived as threatening, which itself is a function of offensive power,

[1] Toft (2003), p. 17 and the Appendix.
[2] Waltz (1979).

19

aggregate power, geographic proximity, and perceived aggressive intentions.[3] Neither variant of neorealist theory sees bandwagoning – siding with the stronger power at the expense of the weaker one – as an optimal option in general,[4] although it has been argued that bandwagoning can be a preferable alliance strategy if the objective is profit rather than security.[5] Bandwagoning is also more likely, according to the literature, when an actor is particularly weak, proximate to a strong power, or when it recognizes that defeat in an ongoing war is imminent.[6] The neorealist international relations paradigm would apply to the phenomena explored in this book if, as has often been the case in the civil war literature, we suppose that substate actors in civil wars behave like sovereign states in the anarchic international system.[7] This analogy would suggest that weaker warring groups, like weaker states, will align with one another to balance against a rising potential hegemon, irrespective of identity considerations. Bandwagoning will be most unlikely because alliances in multiethnic states are security-driven rather than profit-driven, as we will see in subsequent chapters.

A look at the political economy literature on civil wars also yields rational, instrumentalist predictions about the different groups' alliance preferences and their tendency to fractionalize. The hypothesis derived from this school of thought, based on opportunity and economic viability as explanations for civil war, is practically in agreement with the international relations prediction presented earlier: Groups and subgroups will align in a way that maximizes their expected share of returns, without regard to identity considerations.[8] The political economy-inspired literature similarly explains group fractionalization with reference to rational incentives and opportunities. While selective incentives help recruitment into insurgent organizations,[9] too much resource wealth may lead to a flood of opportunistic recruits and consequently an undisciplined, fragmented fighting force.[10] Echoing the large-N work on civil war onset, recent empirical work finds that rebel fractionalization is more likely when the barriers to entry are lower (when the conflict is relatively new, when the state is weak, and when the rebellion is non-territorial in its aims), when natural resources are available to finance rebellion, and when high conflict intensity leads to strategic disagreement within rebel groups.[11] Groups may also be more likely to violently fragment when they are medium in size, as the group leadership will have the ability to maintain unity when the group is small, whereas the state will be especially wary of allowing

---

[3] Walt (1987).
[4] Mearsheimer (2001) considers bandwagoning the equivalent of capitulation.
[5] Schweller (1994).
[6] Walt (1987).
[7] See, for instance, Posen (1993); Fearon (1995, 1998); and Kaufmann (1996a, 1996b).
[8] See Collier and Hoeffler (2001); Fearon and Laitin (2003), among others.
[9] Popkin (1979); Berman and Laitin (2008).
[10] Weinstein (2007).
[11] Burch and Ochreiter (2010); Fjelde and Nilsson (2011).

violence when the group is large.[12] Finally, building on the economics literature on governance costs and principal-agent relations, theoretical work suggests that the unity of rebel groups is affected by technology and geography – where geographical distances are great and technology is primitive, monitoring costs make rebel defection, opportunism, and fragmentation more likely.[13]

Another set of theories that seems to predict the primacy of power considerations in warring group alliance and fractionalization dynamics comes from the comparative politics literature on parties and voting.[14] The literature on coalition politics in legislatures is extensive and has generated specific, conditional predictions about which political parties will align with each other. Starting with the simplest scenario, if one party has a majority of seats, it will just proceed to form a one-party cabinet. Translated to the civil war context, we would expect that if one group is powerful enough to win the war on its own, there will be little need for coalition-building. If, however, no such dominant warring group exists, more complex coalition dynamics become relevant.

In multiparty contexts, legislative coalition theory emphasizes the idea of a "minimum winning coalition," or a mix of parties that have just the right number of representatives to form a majority. The theory suggests that parties seek to form minimum winning coalitions irrespective of their ideological agenda.[15] Applied to civil war, coalition theory suggests that warring groups and subgroups seek the smallest possible partnerships that make victory appear likely, without being constrained by the identities or ideologies of their potential partners. The rationale behind minimum winning coalitions is rather intuitive: It is the coalition that ensures victory while maximizing returns, a rationale that would also make sense in the context of civil wars where commitment problems abound.[16] In particular, relatively weak warring groups will worry about joining coalitions that are too powerful because the stronger alliance partner cannot credibly commit that it will not turn on its weaker partner after securing victory.

From its origins in the study of legislative politics, coalition theory has also been applied to the study of ethnic identity construction. Constructivist scholars who study how ethnic groups are formed and defined argue that ethnic elites act as "identity entrepreneurs," stringing together sets of different identity attributes that do not necessarily have any intrinsic relationship to one another. The goal of this aggregation process, as in legislatures around the world, is to form a minimum winning coalition of individuals sufficient to wield power in

---

[12] Warren and Troy (in press).

[13] Johnston (2008).

[14] For a detailed discussion of these theories, see Przeworski et al. (2000), pp. 92–97.

[15] Riker (1962).

[16] It is important to note that minimum winning coalition theory makes a single prediction only when there is one party powerful enough to form such a coalition on its own. If there is no such party, the theory grants multiple predictions.

the state.[17] This body of work, representing the successful transfer of coalition theory from sovereign state legislatures to intrastate ethnic politics, suggests the applicability of the same minimum winning coalition logic to behavioral dynamics within multiparty civil wars. It further suggests that identities – ethnic or otherwise – are themselves the product of power-driven, coalition-building politics.

All of the theoretical works above – neorealism, the political economy theories of civil war, and legislative coalition theory and its application to ethnic politics – suggest that within-war alliance shifts and group fractionalization can be explained primarily by relative power considerations rather than identity variables. However, another diverse body of theory supports the opposite hypothesis: that alliances and fractionalization will take place on the basis of shared or unshared ethnic, linguistic, regional, religious, or ideological identities. Meanwhile, two other schools of thought – sociological/institutional theories and theories that emphasize the role of state actions – fit squarely into neither camp, highlighting the role of state repression, state conciliation, and the organizational characteristics of rebel groups in producing alliances and fractionalization.

First, there are approaches to legislative coalition politics that take ideology into account, such as theories on policy-viable coalitions, which presume that parties care first for their policies rather than for being in power. These theories in turn suggest that the closer the parties are on the ideological spectrum, the likelier they are to align.[18] Extrapolating this to warring parties, we would expect to see alliances form among groups closest to each other on the identity spectrum. Such theories seem to capture the empirical reality of cabinet coalitions better than theories that disregard ideology,[19] probably because the latter theories largely rest on majoritarian assumptions and are insensitive to institutional features that may prompt the creation of minority or oversized cabinets.[20] Yet many of these institutional features are absent in the civil war context, perhaps diminishing the applicability of policy-viable coalition theory to the phenomena of interest here.

Second, there is significant work on the role of ethnicity in civil war that seems to suggest the importance of ethnic identity to within-conflict dynamics such as alliance formation and group fractionalization. A substantial body of scholars has reintroduced the "grievance versus greed" debate in the civil war subfield by bringing ethnicity back in as a grievance variable and arguing that materialist, "greed"-based explanations for civil war (summarized earlier) are overplayed.[21] In addition to providing a base of grievance that may explain

---

[17] Chandra and Laitin (2003); Chandra and Boulet (2003); Chandra (2004); Posner (2004, 2005).
[18] De Swaan (1973).
[19] Przeworski et al. (2000), p. 98.
[20] Ibid, p. 91.
[21] Rokkan (1999); Kaufmann (2001); Buhaug, Cederman, and Rød (2006); Cederman and Girardin (2007); Cederman, Wimmer, and Min (2010).

civil war onset, ethnicity may also shape the way in which these conflicts are fought. Since the wave of ethnic conflicts in the 1990s, some scholars have argued that ethnic identities are entirely rigid during civil wars, necessitating the use of partition and population movements to prevent atrocities.[22] Even among instrumental interpretations of identity there is a general stance that identity choices are stable – if not hardened – during conflicts.[23] At least in conventional civil wars, there is evidence that preexisting identity cleavages do indeed structure violence against civilians throughout the course of war, even when the cleavage is ideological and not ethnic.[24] Meanwhile, both old and new research on communist groups suggests that ideology and organizational skills make such groups similarly disciplined, deadly, and unified.[25] If this is the case, it follows that warring groups should ally on the basis of shared ascriptive characteristics and that, given the rigidity of those identities, these alliances will remain stable.

The primordialist school of thought – arguably still the predominant school of thought among international relations scholars despite its obsolescence in comparative politics – also supports this reasoning, arguing that ethnic groups satisfy individuals' evolutionary need to belong to an in-group. This important need for belonging could well be the basis for a number of warring group alliances in ethnic conflicts.[26] In more tangible and instrumental terms, ethnicity can provide several formal or informal social institutions that encourage collective action, through the opportunity for repeated interaction and information sharing. Indeed, repeated interactions lead to an understanding of reciprocity that, along with reputation costs, facilitates in-group policing and sanctioning.[27] Moreover, political economy scholars have argued that ethnicity provides a readily available shared code for communication (be it common language, religion, shared customs and norms, etc.) that allows for easy coordination.[28] If these scholars are correct, then alliances between warring groups of the same ethnicity should be not only natural but also durable – co-ethnics, according to these works, are practically wired for cooperation. In short, ethnic identity may not only matter to civil war onset. Rather, the literature on ethnicity and civil war suggests that ethnicity or other ascriptive elements of identity, because of their importance to individuals and their rigidity in wartime, may constitute a solid base on which groups can form stable alliances.

---

[22] Kaufmann (1996a, 1996b).

[23] Kalyvas (2006, 2008) is one of the few exceptions.

[24] Balcells (2010, 2011).

[25] Selznick (1952); Pye (1956); Huntington (1968); Kalyvas and Balcells (2010).

[26] Tajfel, Billig, Bundy, and Flament (1971); Van Den Berghe (1981); Horowitz (1985); Barkow, Cosmides and Tooby (1992); Van Evera (1994, 2001); Kaufmann (1996a, 1996b); Petersen (2001, 2002).

[27] Platteau (1994); Fearon and Laitin (1996); Miguel and Gugerty (2005); Habyarimana, Humphreys, Posner, and Weinstein (2007).

[28] Bates (1983).

Third, some work on alliance politics in international relations goes against the generally dominant neorealist paradigm, arguing instead that alliance behavior is determined at least in part by variables other than relative power. Many of these variables could be construed as one form or another of identity. For example, the democratic peace literature argues that democracies are naturally predisposed to ally with one another, regardless of relative power considerations;[29] if states have identities, then regime type is undoubtedly an element of them. Several other scholars find fault with the democratic peace view of interstate alliance behavior, but still conclude that various forms of ideological affinity – another manifestation of state identity – are a key determinant of states' alliance choices.[30] Finally, the growing literature on "security communities" – which, for the purposes of this book, can be considered equivalent to alliances – also emphasizes the importance of shared identity to the formation of these communities.[31] Although identity scholars are very much in the minority in the alliance politics literature within international relations, their work suggests that alliances in the civil war context may be determined, in whole or in part, by identity considerations as well.

Thus, the substantial support for the power arguments notwithstanding, a hypothesis emphasizing the role of shared identity in civil war alliance formation is supported by some later derivatives of legislative coalition theory, as well as the more recent literature on the role of ethnicity in civil war onset and processes, and an articulate minority within the alliance politics literature of international relations. It could be that both hypotheses are right – that power considerations drive warring group alliance choices and group fractionalization, but that identity variables condition and constrain that power-based decision making. Indeed, there are some coalition theories that try to account for both power and ideology. A representative example would be the "minimal connected winning coalition" theory, which suggests that parties will be keen to form minimum winning coalitions, but will be constrained by ideology, looking first for alliance partners among their ideological neighbors.[32]

In turn, other comparative politics scholars who have studied demographically fractionalized societies in the nonviolent context, both observationally and experimentally, have appreciated the role of cross-cutting identity cleavages in facilitating coalitions, be it in the way they affect individual voting patterns or party coalitions and electoral competition more generally.[33] Recent exciting works in the literature underline the instrumental use of identity, noting convergence around different identity dimensions of political salience at different times.[34] Despite the instrumentality in the salience of cleavages that

---

[29] Doyle (1986); Risse-Kappen (1996).
[30] Barnett (1996); Hass (2003); Narizny (2003).
[31] Starr (1992); Adler and Barnett (1998); Acharya (2001).
[32] Axelrod (1970); Grofman (1982).
[33] Lipset and Rokkan (1967); Roemer et al. (2007).
[34] Posner (2004, 2005); Eifert, Miguel, and Posner (2010); Chandra (2004); Dunning and Harrison (2010).

this approach allows, it also presupposes an objective and largely unchanging perception of identity cleavages within and between warring groups. These immutable perceived cleavages are in turn considered to impose structural constraints on the power-based choice of allies.

Empirically, however, perceptions of identity cleavages in civil wars do not prove to be objective and unchanging: Unlike ideological differences on the left-right political spectrum for parties, or linguistic, religious, or even demographic-size identity differences, they are neither unidimensional nor fixed. Rather, they appear to be multidimensional and variable, understood in largely functional and contextual ways that make the possible combinations of minimal winning coalitions practically infinite. Specifically, the argument I am making on the role of shared identity in the justification of alliance narratives builds off of these findings and shows how the instrumental use of shared identity gets amplified in the context of civil war: Groups that want to find a common identity narrative employ very flexible ways of interpretation of their shared identity dimensions.

There is also a set of alternative explanations for alliance and group behavior that invokes neither power nor identity. Turning to the sociological/institutional theories, recent research finds that the network structure on which rebel groups are formed is a key variable determining their propensity to fractionalize or stay unified. Where rebel groups are built on "bonding" networks with strong horizontal and vertical ties, fractionalization is unlikely because of high levels of trust, monitoring, and institutionalization. In contrast, rebel groups built on "coalition" networks of strong vertical and weak horizontal ties are more likely to fractionalize in the course of conflict because of the absence of these same mechanisms.[35] A more holistic institutional approach to explaining group fractionalization stresses three key variables: the number of subgroup factions, the degree of institutionalization across factions, and the distribution of power among the factions. Violent fractionalization is most likely, according to this argument, when there are many factions, low institutionalization, and a diffuse distribution of power.[36]

Finally, a significant body of research highlights the role of state responses to rebels in determining the likelihood of group fractionalization. At a general level, qualitative accounts of rebel movements often emphasize the importance of state actions in precipitating fragmentation or increasing group unity.[37] Many scholars have noted that government negotiations tend to precipitate group fractionalization and spoiling, as rebel groups split apart into hawks and doves (or hard-liners and soft-liners).[38] Statistical analysis suggests that government mediation efforts tend to precede group fragmentation, and not

[35] Staniland (2010).
[36] Bakke, Cunningham, and Seymour (2011).
[37] Kenny (2010).
[38] Stedman (1997); Kydd and Walter (2002); Bueno de Mesquita (2005); Pearlman (2009).

the other way around.[39] On the state repression side of the ledger, scholarly arguments are mixed. Some scholars argue that state repression increases rebel unity and spurs rebel recruitment through a variety of mechanisms, both grievance-based (revenge) and rational-choice (the desire for protection in the face of indiscriminate targeting).[40] Others note that state repression can cause groups to fragment because of disagreements over strategy and an exacerbation of preexisting factional tensions.[41] A more nuanced argument holds that state repression amplifies whatever preexisting trends are present in the organization – internally unified groups will become more cohesive in response to repression, and internally divided groups will be more likely to fracture.[42]

Overall, the rich and diverse existing literature across political science subfields motivates this book's theory as reflected in the research design, discussed in the next section.

RESEARCH DESIGN

In an ideal (or mad) social scientific world, a researcher examining alliance formation and group fractionalization in civil wars would randomly assign levels of power and shared identity attributes to a variable number of groups and then set them out to fight, monitoring how they form alliances and experience within-group fractionalization in a context that simulated civil war. Given that the golden standard of the experimental method – which focuses on the pertinent explanatory variables while controlling for non-related variables through randomization – is clearly unrealistic for the question at hand, I looked for semblances of such settings by selecting civil war cases that were similar in some respects and different in others, and by ascertaining a relationship between the explanatory variables (power and shared identity) while controlling for factors that may be deviating from or biasing the effect of interest.

Although scholars have recently proposed additional explanations for group fractionalization – network structure, resource wealth, state repression and mediation, number and institutionalization of factions, barriers to entry, geography, and technology – I choose to focus on power and shared identity for two main reasons. First, these remain the dominant competing explanations in the literature for alliance formation and group cohesion, and for civil war dynamics more broadly. Second, the aforementioned alternative explanations are not well suited to answering the specific research question at hand, nor can they explain the puzzle of similar outcomes in Afghanistan and Bosnia. Generally speaking, these alternative explanations are better suited to addressing the likelihood of fractionalization cross-sectionally than they are at explaining the likelihood of fractionalization *within a conflict over time*. For example,

---

[39] Lounsbery and Cook (2011).
[40] Goodwin (2001); Kalyvas (2006); Kalyvas and Kocher (2007b).
[41] Lawrence (2007); Lyall (2009).
[42] McLauchlin and Pearlman (2009).

network structure, resource wealth, geography, technology, and barriers to entry are slow-moving (or stationary) variables that may help explain why particular *conflicts* or why particular *groups* are more prone to fractionalization, but they do not explain why the same conflict or group sees variation in fractionalization over time, nor do they explain the timing of splits or takeovers. Moreover, many of these explanations simply cannot account for the similar outcomes in Afghanistan and Bosnia, as different values of the independent variables led to the same outcome on the dependent variable (fractionalization). Specifically, despite Afghanistan's greater natural resource wealth, more difficult geography, more primitive technology, greater number of subgroups, and lower degree of institutionalization, Bosnia nonetheless saw similar group fractionalization dynamics. This suggests that some other variable is at play, and I argue that relative power is the best candidate. Although state repression and mediation may play a role in producing group fractionalization, I argue that this is achieved through these variables' effect on the relative power of the warring groups.

My work uses a comparative case research design of the multiparty civil wars in Afghanistan and in Bosnia across their recent histories (1978–1989 and 1992–1998 for Afghanistan; 1941–1945 and 1992–1995 for Bosnia and Herzegovina [BiH]). It then broadens the lens with an analysis of the universe of cases of fifty-three multiparty civil wars. Specifically, I rely on rich and diverse ethnographic data on warring groups, as well as on geographic data reflecting changes in territorial control in the 1992–1998 Afghan civil war and the 1992–1995 Bosnian civil war (both largely seen as ethnic civil wars), to generate a theory of alliance formation and group fractionalization. In terms of presentation, I offer the theory first and then illustrate the evidence that led to its development. I then proceed with both within- and across-case tests of the theory. Specifically, I test the predictions of the theory against the largely nonethnic civil wars in Afghanistan (1978–1989) and Bosnia (1941–1945) to see if the predictions hold irrespective of the character of war, be it primarily ethnic or nonethnic. I also construct a commander-level dataset to test the predictions for warring group alliances on the level of local commander for Afghanistan, and use municipal-level data to gauge district-level dynamics in BiH. I then examine the testable implications of my theory of group alliances and fractionalization against the entire universe of multiparty civil wars. Thus my empirical work bridges country-level, group-level, and micro-level research, through looking at alliances and fragmentation in multiparty civil wars.

The intent of this incremental and cumulative empirical discussion is to triangulate data sources and levels of analysis in an effort to gain analytic inference that is potentially greater than the sum of its parts.[43] That is arguably achieved by examining a rich and diverse set of empirics – ranging from ethnographic interview data and rich wartime qualitative sources, to data on warring groups'

---

[43] Lieberman (2005).

makeup and territorial control over the war's trajectory, to quantitative codings of dozens of conflicts besides those in Afghanistan and in BiH. The case studies allow for detailed process tracing over time, highlighting the mechanisms at work behind alliance formation and group fractionalization. The testing of both the alliance and fractionalization phenomena against micro-level and macro-level quantitative data in turn examines the correlations between variables identified as important in the theory and confirmed as such in the case studies.

The ultimate goal is to present a coherent and theoretically well-founded argument on alliance formation and group fractionalization during civil wars; to show how it was developed; to argue that it travels outside that context in other regions and types of multiparty civil wars; and to show that the theory speaks to levels that go even below the warring group and subgroup.

THEORY-BUILDING CASE SELECTION

Alliance formation and group fractionalization in multiparty civil wars, as this book has so far suggested, are complex and interconnected processes that constitute a prevalent reality in multiparty civil wars. For the theory-building part of this book, I thus opted for a comparative case design that would allow for the deconstruction of the phenomena at hand through a close interrogation of the pertinent data. More specifically, this work builds theory through controlled comparison across cases and process-tracing within cases. Though undoubtedly infamous and intrinsically interesting, Afghanistan (1992–1998) and BiH (1992–1995) were selected as the theory-building case studies of this book because they met specific methodological criteria. In terms of structural conditions, the two cases could hardly be more different. Namely, they have different intergroup cleavages. Afghanistan has four main ethnic groups varying in demographic size and military power, with multiple cross-cutting cleavages along racial, linguistic, and religious/sectarian dimensions. BiH, with three ethnic groups of variable demographic size and military power (as compared to each other and those in Afghanistan) and one notable cleavage dimension (religion), constitutes the simplest case. As a result, although we may expect to see alliance shifts and fractionalization in the Afghan case, this would be significantly more surprising in the Bosnian context.

Despite the significant structural differences, however, both cases experienced a relatively high level of alliance changes and group fractionalization. If the cases are so different on the structural level, why are their outcomes on the dependent variables so strikingly similar? This is the puzzle that motivates this book as it tries to theorize on the rationale behind alliance formation and group fractionalization in times of conflict. As shown in subsequent chapters, the intergroup and intragroup volatility in Afghanistan and in BiH can be explained by the frequent shifts in relative power balances these two conflicts experienced.

SOURCES, DATA, AND TESTS

My analysis relies on primary data collected over two years of fieldwork, including 135 interviews conducted in the respective local languages – in Afghanistan with leading Afghan experts, warlords, and mujahedin, and in BiH with wartime politicians, generals, and convicted war criminals, among others. In terms of sampling for the interviews, because the primary level of analysis is the "meso" level manifested on the level of elites with leading roles in the warring factions, these were the types of people who were generally interviewed across the groups involved in the different wars. A list of all such relevant actors was originally compiled, and a sizable number of them were eventually interviewed.[44]

The analysis also draws on wartime declarations, ceasefire agreements, fatwas, memoirs, archival documents, and propaganda materials from the different parties involved in the war, as well as articles from the local and international press. For Afghanistan, I also relied on U.S. Freedom of Information Act declassified documents pertaining to the rise of the Taliban, as well as Guantanamo Bay testimony involving detainees from the Afghan conflict. Territorial control was the main proxy for the warring groups' relative power in the theory-building case studies, along with qualitative discussions of the warring groups' respective number of arms. (Demographic size for each warring group is used as an alternative power proxy in Chapter 8, which covers part of the testing of this theory.) To capture and present the changes in territorial control over the war years and their resultant effect on alliance formation in both cases, I used Geographic Information Systems (GIS) to geo-reference and digitize prewar Yugoslav municipal maps for BiH, as well as Soviet declassified provincial maps for Afghanistan, to spatially project the territorial changes over time in these conflicts.

As difficult as it may be to effectively operationalize power, it is just as difficult to conceive of how to define and measure shared identity. The first measures that probably come to mind are the various ethnolinguistic fractionalization and polarization indices.[45] Although these measures capture the number and proportion of different ethnic groups in a country, they do not capture any of the cultural variation between those groups. Therefore, if a researcher is trying to test a hypothesis based on the importance of shared identity or ethnic distance among groups, a fractionalization index will not do.

In an attempt to fill this gap, academics have pursued other ways of operationalizing ethnic cleavages. Some have tried to use objective and measurable

---

[44] See the References for a detailed list of interviewees. Given the realities of war, the list suffers from some inevitable selection effects as it excluded, among others, those who were dead, facing criminal procedures in international tribunals – such as Radovan Karadžić and Ratko Mladić in BiH – or at large – such as Gulbuddin Hekmatyar, Jallaludin Haqqani, Pacha Khan Zadran, or Mullah Omar in Afghanistan.

[45] Alesina et al. (2003); Fearon (2003); Montalvo and Reynal-Querol (2005).

ethnic characteristics that would allow them to code a variable of ethnic distance based on linguistic, religious, or primarily phenotypic characteristics.[46] Others, coming from the realm of comparative politics and ethnic voting, have placed more emphasis on the process that determines what ethnic cleavages become relevant in the political scene at different times – how the designation of the prominent ethnic cleavage in a society's political realm comes about.[47] The first set of works is basically trying to codify a measure of "objective" ethnic distance, seeing shared identity as something fixed. The latter set of works uses a more dynamic process, allowing for a range of different possible ethnic cleavages over time. While recognizing the limitations of the former approach and the analytic contribution of the latter, I will consider identity attributes here to be relatively fixed, given that I am considering them as variables within the context of years- or at most decades-long civil wars. (Note that this is different from considering *perceived* identity cleavages as fixed – to the contrary, my case studies suggest that these perceptions are ever-changing.) Hence, in each conflict I study, I identify what I believe to be the objective ethnic, linguistic, regional, religious, and ideological characteristics of each warring group at the time of the conflict, and code the nature of the primary intergroup cleavage that distinguished these groups from one another.

My inferences are then further probed in the Afghan context through a unique commander-level dataset for the three Afghan provinces most known for their local-level politics (Balkh, Nangarhar, and Kandahar). These three provinces thus pose the most rigorous tests of whether the theory of group and subgroup behaviors in Afghanistan's ideological and ethnic civil wars is consistent with commander-level behavior in those areas. Similar to the warring group and subgroup-level analyses, this dataset captures the rivalries and splits these individuals had with other local elites and how those changed over the course of the conflict. I find that the commander-level dynamics correspond fairly well to the dynamics at higher levels of aggregation. In the case of BiH, I also test the convergence of the group and subgroup theory on the level of the municipality through the use of a range of prewar demographic data, including municipal-level data on arms, ethnicity, population density, and income as well as wartime data on casualties. The empirical discussion on the WWII Bosnian conflict largely draws on four archives in Belgrade, Serbia, referenced in detail in Chapter 7.

I then test my theory on a dataset of fifty-three multiparty civil wars that have occurred between 1816 and 2007, as well as 397 of the warring groups that comprised those conflicts. For each conflict, I consulted secondary sources pertaining to the conflict to identify the number of intergroup alliance changes and intragroup splits and takeovers that occurred. I also closely consulted secondary sources to code the relative power distribution within the conflict

---

[46] Caselli and Coleman (2001); Fearon and Laitin (2000a); Fearon (2003).
[47] Chandra and Boulet (2003); Posner (2005); Chandra and Wilkinson (2008); Baldwin and Huber (2010).

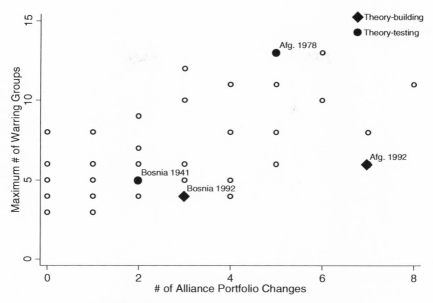

FIGURE 1.1. Case Studies for Theory Building and Theory Testing

and the primary intergroup identity cleavage that existed, and then verified my coding decisions with area experts. Basic information on conflicts by country, conflict years, and number of groups for all fifty-three cases is shown in Table 8.2 in Chapter 8, along with more detail on the dataset and the statistical findings that I infer from it. Figure 1.1 shows where the different Afghan and Bosnian cases selected for theory building or testing fit among the universe of multiparty civil war cases in terms of number of warring groups and alliance changes. In the concluding chapter, I also offer a shadow treatment of the alliance and fractionalization dynamics of the civil war in Anbar Province in Iraq and in the present war in Afghanistan. These recent cases complement the more detailed Afghan and Bosnian chapters.

Having situated my project in the context of the existing literature and described my research design, in the next chapter I present the theory of this book. My theory essentially suggests that relative power considerations dictate both alliance choices and – to a certain degree – group fractionalization in multiparty civil wars. If we accept that argument, we must also conclude that warring actor behavior in chaotic multi-actor internal conflicts may be more predictable than presently believed. The next chapter makes the formal case for that supposition, and also explains the role that we should expect identity narratives to play in warring actors' alliance behavior.

2

A Theory of Warring Group Alliances and Fractionalization in Multiparty Civil Wars

This book seeks to explain two phenomena. The first phenomenon is civil war alliances between warring groups – why they form and why they shift over the course of a conflict. I argue that civil war alliances are instrumental – they are formed by groups in order to (1) win the war and (2) maximize the group's share of postwar political control. Groups seek alliances that are powerful enough to secure victory but small enough to avoid having to share payoffs. Moreover, there is an inherent commitment problem within alliances: With no third-party enforcer, the strongest group cannot credibly commit that it will not turn on its weaker partner(s) and capture complete political control after the war's conclusion. Neither the past histories of alliances between groups nor the track records for trustworthiness of individual groups seem to have any meaningful effect on the intensity of this commitment problem – in an environment so characterized by anarchy, groups can be cheated by seemingly trustworthy partners, so long as the relative power conditions are right. The result of this commitment problem is that the weaker alliance partner, *even when it appears to be on the winning side*, will often prefer to defect to a balancing alliance and prolong the war if this gives them a chance to be a relatively stronger group within a winning alliance. These complex dynamics, exacerbated by the fog of war, make it very difficult for the multitude of warring parties to determine which side to be on. The result is a process of constant defection, alliance reconfiguration, and group fractionalization.

Meanwhile, identity – be it racially, linguistically, religiously, or ideologically defined – appears to have no sustained causal role in the formation of alliances. Rather, elite-constructed identity narratives that arise in justification of alliance choices are a mere product of tactical preferences. Identity matters in that it provides the building blocks from which warring groups are formed, but it does not drive alliance choices. Instead, elites of the warring parties pick allies whose support will result in optimizing their wartime returns, and then look to their identity repertoires for characteristics shared with their allies while not shared with their foes. The resulting identity narratives, while epiphenomenal to elite power considerations, serve as important signals to the rank and file, signals that resonate more strongly than unmasked references to relative power.

The second phenomenon to be explained is the fractionalization of individual groups into subgroups along fault lines that predate the conflict. I will argue that the specific trigger for fractionalization is an asymmetric loss experienced by a group's constituent subgroups. The theory predicts that groups will fracture along prewar cleavages, be they regional differences or preexisting leadership disputes. It is important to note that subgroups comprising a warring group – even though they may appear as an alliance at a lower level of organization – do not behave the same way as allied groups. Although generally instrumental, subgroups, unlike allied groups, have identity ties to their groups that they only sever in times when the group's survival is at risk. Relatedly, trust is more strongly shared between members of a given group than between members of an alliance in general, and thus commitment problems that are central to alliance decisions – particularly in the context of fear of betrayal of weaker alliance members from stronger ones – are not relevant to dynamics of group fractionalization. Commitment problems are also mitigated by preexisting institutions (whether formal or informal) that can enforce agreements within identity groups; even in weakly institutionalized states, identity groups tend to have strong internal institutions and enforcement mechanisms.[1] Such institutions do not exist to the same degree in cross-group alliances formed as a result of temporary wartime exigencies. Almost by definition, civil war implies the breakdown of state and cross-group institutions; as a result, once conflict is under way, these institutions are incapable of enforcing agreements between groups – even in states with previously high degrees of institutionalization.

For any warring group confronted with alliance choices during a civil war, there are two main competing considerations: winning the war and maximizing postwar political control. This means that each group wants to be part of a coalition that is large enough to win the war but also small enough to maximize the group's share of postwar power.[2] In making those alliance choices, the distribution of power among groups is a determining factor, and it is in every group's interest to be part of a *minimum winning coalition*. While in parliamentary terms this translates into a legislative majority,[3] in the case of groups in civil war it means the smallest possible alliance powerful enough to make victory appear likely. Although uncertainty about the war's outcome may lead groups to focus exclusively on being on the winning side at the outset of the conflict, as the war progresses and more information is revealed about the war's probable outcome, they are likely to worry more and more about

[1] See Migdal (1988).
[2] See Riker (1962), p. 121.
[3] Riker (1962).

commitment problems and revert to a minimum winning coalition logic in making alliance choices.

More specifically, fear of betrayal drives groups to also worry about their relative power compared to other alliance members – in other words, warring groups will ally or affiliate with the weaker side in an anarchic all-out civil war to balance the distribution of power.[4] By contrast, they realize that if they bandwagon – side with the more powerful actor – they will be on the losing end of a significant commitment problem. Even if it has behaved in a trustworthy manner in the past, the more powerful group cannot credibly commit to dividing power fairly; thus smaller groups are better off balancing in hope of improving their chances when it comes time to divide up postwar political control.

The rationale behind a minimum winning coalition strategy is clear, but creating such an intergroup coalition during civil war is very hard a priori; there can be no true commitment to an alliance if there is uncertainty whether a higher return could be gained from switching to the other side. This uncertainty is particularly high under the balancing dynamic proposed here (unless a single hegemonic group already exists), because balancing coalitions ensure that victory cannot be predicted with certainty in either direction and thus predictions of who will be victorious are easily upended by small distortions in perceived power.

War is therefore an extension rather than an alternative to the bargaining process.[5] Given that perceptions about the relative power of groups are variant and often conflicting, fighting can reveal information about the groups' actual capabilities. And because alliance choices are instrumental and a result of strategic interactions among the warring parties, a group's optimal coalition strategy will change as the revealed power dynamics among groups change. In this power-determined context, the first-order interaction among groups at war is the change in their relative power that in turn prompts alliance shifts. This fluidity is a result of dominated payoffs – groups can get a higher share of postwar political control by joining a different alliance that promises to offer more.

Realignment prompted by changes in or revelation of information on the warring groups' relative power is further exacerbated by the fact that warring actors cannot be treated as unified actors as they fractionalize throughout the conflict – the second phenomenon that this theory seeks to explain. The proliferation of warring actors, brought on by poor battlefield performance and groups' asymmetrically borne battlefield losses, in turn leads to a change in the distribution of relative power among groups and to new alliances.

What falsifiable predictions does this framework generate? Under this model, we would expect to see very little alliance reconfiguration only when there are no commitment problems – that is, when one warring group is powerful enough

---

[4] Schelling (1960), Chapter 3; Elster (1989), Chapter 14.
[5] Wagner (2000).

to constitute a minimum winning coalition on its own. If that is the case, the group will rise up to defeat the others, leading to victory and to an overall shorter war. Similarly, multiparty conflicts in which there is a strong state government should be less prone to frequent alliance shifts than conflicts in weak states, where intergroup power balances are more or less at parity and the government, if present at all, is merely one of many warring actors. A strong government experiencing multiparty civil war may not hold a true minimum winning coalition sufficient to end the conflict, but at least its preponderance of power reduces the incentive of warring groups to switch alliances in the wake of small power changes (they could switch alliances, but the government side would still be dominant). Weak governments have no such advantage, and we should expect to see the most volatile alliance configurations there.

This framework, described in full detail later in the chapter, puts forth power as the main explanatory variable and lays out two interconnected mechanisms that explain how power determines alliances among warring groups and fractionalization within them. I start by laying out the first mechanism, which captures the relative power change among and within alliances and the prompting of alliance shifts. Groups make alliance choices based on a desire to win the war, but also a desire to be the strongest party within the winning alliance. I then present the second mechanism: that of group fractionalization, the proliferation of actors during the war's trajectory, and the second-order effect these phenomena have on alliance formation. I argue that group fractionalization is triggered by poor battlefield performance and asymmetric losses across subgroups. Next, I proceed to discuss the role of shared identity in the construction of alliance narratives. Although shared identity proves endogenous to the group's power considerations and is therefore not an independent variable, these narratives are nevertheless an integral part of the civil war process. Their content plays a role in the justification of wartime alliances and their allegiances, serving as a signal to group followers as to who is an enemy and who is a friend that is more acceptable than undignified references to relative power. Moreover, identity groups provide the building blocks from which warring actors are formed; within these groups, identity is indeed a powerful bond, with subgroups only splitting off when their survival is at stake. In the final section of this chapter, I summarize the theory and derive discrete hypotheses from it. I also discuss my theory's relationship to the neorealist international relations paradigm, with which there are notable parallels but also some key differences.

FIRST MECHANISM: EVOLUTION OF RELATIVE POWER AMONG ALLIES

This section presents the mechanism of the evolution of relative power among coalitions in civil war. It highlights the rationale as to why a minimum winning coalition is more desirable than the strongest alliance: Groups will tend to ally with the side they think can win the conflict, but will also defect from that side if they believe it is growing *too* powerful. The expectation will be for alliances with a closer distribution of relative power to be more stable. By examining the simplest case, that of two alliances at war – in which the alliances contain the entire set of warring actors – this section outlines why and how alliance shifts take place. Although the complexity would inevitably increase with the number of coalitions, the intuition informing the simple illustrative model that follows remains the same.

Let us assume we have two coalitions, A and B, and that these coalitions are at war. For simplicity, war is considered to be equally costly for all groups comprising these coalitions.[6] The objective to win the war while maximizing one's share of political control – understood as the power share at the end of the war – is what drives this interaction. The metric of interest is relative power rather than overall power – because war is costly and overall power will inevitably diminish over time as a result of the fighting – and is normalized between 0 and 1. The war ends either in outright victory, with one of the sides' relative power being 1 or close to 1, or in negotiated settlement, with all sides agreeing over the share of relative power.[7]

Let us also assume that the power of coalition A is p, and that p evolves in time. By p_t we denote the power of coalition A at time t. Assume that the conflict between A and B starts at time $t = 0$. The relative power of A at the beginning of the conflict is p_0 and that of coalition B is in turn $1 - p_0$. Additionally, a change in the level of relative power dp during a small time interval dt has two components: a deterministic component and a stochastic component, as indicated in Equation 2.1 below.

$$dp = (\delta(p) \times dt) + (\sigma(p) \times dB_t) \qquad\qquad \text{Equation 2.1}$$

Let us first consider the deterministic component to ascertain how it affects the level of relative power p. The change in relative power is given by $dp = \delta(p) \times dt$, where $\delta(p)$ is the drift that depends on the current level of power p, which in the absence of any randomness is the derivative of p over time. This function is symmetric around $p = 0.5$, non-decreasing, and $\delta(p) \geq 0$ for $p > 0.5$, $\delta(p) \leq 0$ for $p < 0.5$, and $\delta(p) = 0$ for $p = 0.5$.[8]

Based on the deterministic component of Equation 2.1, if one were to know the level of p at time t_0, one could ascertain how p would evolve. For example,

---

[6] For simplicity, the war is assumed to be equally costly. If it were to be less costly for a group, its relative power would increase, whereas if it were to be more costly, the group's relative power would decrease. If needed, a discount rate could be added to these models. If one presumed the discount rate to be equal for everyone (a fair assumption given that alliance switches occur when relative power is close to $p = 0.5$, i.e., when the probability of losing and winning the war in the next period is roughly the same), then time does not influence the relative value attached to victory by the different warring sides.

[7] The end of the conflict can be exogenous to the within-conflict processes and a result of outside intervention.

[8] The three properties of $\delta(p)$ can be summarized as follows:
Property 1:

$$\delta(p) \geq 0 \quad \text{for} \quad p > 0.5, \ \delta(p) \leq 0 \quad \text{for} \quad p < 0.5, \ \delta(p) = 0 \quad \text{for} \quad p = 0.5$$

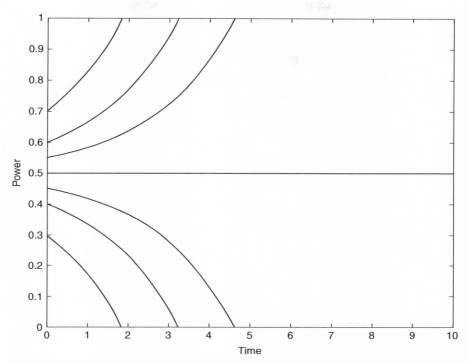

FIGURE 2.1. Relative Power Changes for Different Levels of Initial Power, ranging from $p = 0.3$ to 0.7, assuming $\delta(p) = 0.5(p - 0.5)$ and $\sigma(p) = 0$.

and as indicated in Figure 2.1, an alliance for which $p > 0.5$ would eventually be expected to win because it would keep increasing its power, ultimately reaching $p = 1$. Similarly, if we were to merely look at the deterministic component of the model, it would suggest that if a coalition were to start at $p = 0.5$, the conflict would go on forever, whereas if it were to start with $p < 0.5$, the coalition would eventually lose. Clearly, the winning alliance would prefer to have a higher δ for every $p \geq 0.5$ because that would bring the alliance to a quicker

Property 1 suggests that if $\delta(p) > 0$, the coalition will gain more power over time and thus the change in the relative level of power will be positive. Similarly, if $\delta(p) < 0$, the change in the relative level of power will be negative, and if $\delta(p) = 0$, there will be no change in the relative level of power.

Property 2:

$$\delta(p) = -\delta(1 - p)$$

This property captures the notion of symmetry.

Property 3:

$\delta(p)$ is a non-decreasing function, implying that the higher the values of p the higher the $\delta(p)$ – as the level of relative power increases, the drift also increases. The increase does not have to be linear. It could be exponential, or any specification that is symmetric and non-decreasing.

victory.[9] As also suggested by Figure 2.1, smaller relative power differentials between the two alliances result in longer civil wars – a notion that makes intuitive sense and that will be revisited later.

However, the evolution of power in time is not just deterministic; if it were – and assuming complete and symmetric information – rational parties would never go to war because they would be able to accurately ascertain the outcome in advance and act accordingly.[10] As suggested in the second term of Equation 2.1, there is also a stochastic component that captures randomness. This component captures battlefield mistakes as well as exogenous factors such as changes in external support, unexpected weather conditions, disease, or other factors beyond the control of the actors involved. The random change during a small interval dt is given by $\sigma(p) \times dB_t$, which is modeled as a standard Brownian motion.[11] Parameter σ determines the amount of randomness in the power change dp. The lower the σ, the lower the random component, with no randomness if $\sigma = 0$. Figure 2.2 on the left panel shows the anticipated result for $p = 0.55$ if dp were to only have a deterministic component, and Figure 2.2 on the right panel if the random component is also taken into account. Whereas in the first case victory is certain, in the latter case, which maps five different simulations, this is not always true. Victory may be quicker (first case) or slower to attain (three consecutive cases) than in the deterministic case, and it is also possible for the coalition that starts out more powerful to actually get defeated at the end (fifth and final case). Intuitively, this trajectory could be described as a "biased" random walk – that is, at each point in time there is a step in a direction of increased or decreased power that is random in part but also influenced by the power asymmetry.

As suggested earlier, groups shift alliances if they feel that their expected return from the division of postwar political control will increase in the context of a new alliance. Relative power changes across alliances thus lead to new alliance formations, which could in turn lead to further alliance changes. An example is presented in Figure 2.3, where the drop in the relative power of alliance A motivates an alliance switch from a group in alliance B.

Each alliance change is a tipping point in the distribution of relative power, with groups updating their probability of expected returns and choosing whether to shift alliances. These alliances can at best be seen as temporary local optima, susceptible to change as the probability of victory changes. But how is winning and the division of wartime returns understood in this context? Is it maximization of per capita payoffs over something divisible, such as political control, or is it mere survival that is at stake? In this anarchic context of civil

---

[9] A higher δ implies a faster evolution of relative power (upward if $p > 0.5$, downward if $p < 0.5$), which could in turn suggest very ruthless tactics such as ethnic cleansing or genocide.

[10] The assumption of complete and symmetric information is relaxed later in the chapter.

[11] The standard Brownian motion is an established way to model randomness. Its properties are such that the value of B_t is distributed as a normal random variable with mean 0 and variance t.

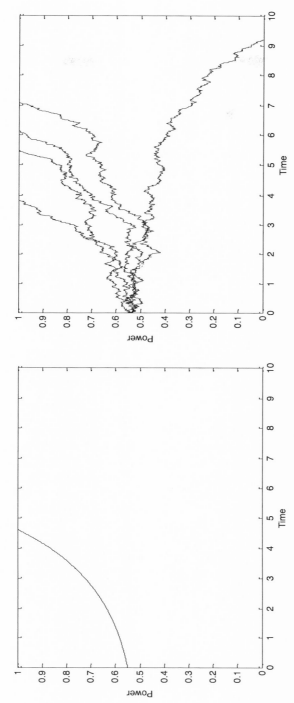

FIGURE 2.2. Relative Power Changes for Different Levels of Randomness: Initial Power Level $p - 0.55$ and assuming $\delta(p) = 0.5(p - 0.5)$ and $\sigma(p) = 0$ for left panel and $\sigma(p) = 0.5$ for right panel.

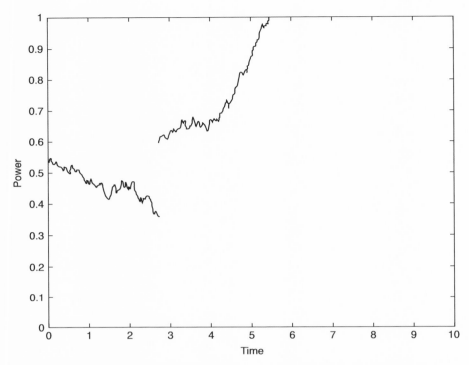

FIGURE 2.3. Relative Power Changes over Time Leading to an Alliance Switch, assuming initial power $p = 0.55$ and assuming $\delta(p) = 0.5(p - 0.5)$ and $\sigma(p) = 0.5$.

war, the primary aim is one of preservation. Each group's notion of winning entails its survival as an autonomous entity. It is an outcome-oriented conflict, with losses and gains understood in terms of survival and quantified using temporal assessments of casualties and territorial control. (Territorial control and number of casualties emerged throughout my field interviews with leaders of warring groups as their rule-of-thumb measures for power and control.) Also, one could argue that bigger actors are trying to gain control and maximize their gains, whereas smaller actors are more concerned with minimizing their losses. Regardless of the way one chooses to put it, the calculus is ultimately one of maximizing expected returns – whether those are rooted in survival or power. As a result, once the minimum winning threshold is either largely surpassed or remains unmet (i.e., p_t is far from 0.5 in either direction), groups switch sides.

The model outlined here assumes complete and symmetric information across groups. The only unknown is the stochastic element. In actuality, however, groups only have incomplete information on each other's relative power and every group is working off its own reference model. So it is not just the random component that groups are unclear about. They also have incomplete information pertaining to the deterministic component, and thus often make mistakes in the relative power assessment, pursuing alliance switches (or decisions not to switch) they would not have chosen given perfect information. Let us consider an illustration of this misperception. Assume that a group is in a winning coalition that temporarily starts to lose in the short run, but retains more than half the relative power objectively. Because the group has incomplete information, it may think that the relative power of the coalition has fallen below $p = 0.5$ and as a result may switch alliances. This switch would be suboptimal, as the group is actually still on the winning side. Imperfect information is more likely to lead to incorrect decisions when alliances are of largely comparable power – for example, when they find themselves in the $p = 0.5$ range. If groups hover around that stalemate range, small misperceptions are sufficient to drive errors in decisions regarding switching behavior.[12]

The model presented earlier examines the simplest case – that of two alliances at war. In this context, a single relative power scalar p determines the interaction.[13] The complexity increases with the number of coalitions, but the intuition informing the model remains the same. The equation capturing the change in relative power will still have a deterministic and a stochastic component; there will still be a drift $\delta(p)$, which will be a symmetric, non-decreasing function with the properties outlined earlier; and the smaller the difference in power between coalitions, the longer the war will last. Moreover, in the case of three or more coalitions, it is likely that they form supra-coalitions – coalitions of coalitions – in turn collapsing the case to a two-coalition dynamic similar to the previously described model.

Conflict duration largely depends on the power differential between the opposing coalitions. If we were to assume unified warring actors, then one alliance or the other would eventually win and the power differential between alliances would determine the length of fighting, with smaller power differentials implying longer war duration.[14] However, the situation in actuality is considerably more complicated, because the groups who were constituent members of coalitions in the earlier analysis are themselves non-unitary and prone to fractionalization. Their breakup leads to a change in the distribution of relative power among warring parties that in turn prompts alliance changes. Group fractionalization tends to prolong the conflict, as it leads to the proliferation of actors, and thus a less "lumpy" distribution of possible alliances. Given the claim of balancing behavior, this results in the creation of minimum winning coalitions whose relative power is closer to $p = 0.5$ in the two-alliance case (or otherwise more equal in the multi-alliance case), resulting in more prolonged wars. Thus on average, group fractionalization is predicted to lead

---

[12] A set of simulation graphs on actual versus perceived power as a way to illustrate the possibility of unwarranted alliance switches among groups is provided in the Appendix.

[13] With three coalitions, the model gets more complex, with scalars p_1 and p_2 representing the respective powers of groups 1 and 2, and $1 - p_1 - p_2$ reflecting the relative power of group 3.

[14] If one looks just at the deterministic component, the length of the conflict is longer if p is closer to 0.5. If one looks at both the deterministic and the random component, the duration of conflict is longer in expectation.

to longer-lasting civil wars. I turn to the discussion of group fractionalization next.

SECOND MECHANISM: GROUP FRACTIONALIZATION

This discussion on group fractionalization analyzes how and why warring groups break up during the war's trajectory – the second outcome of interest in this theory – and also examines the second-order effects of the proliferation of warring groups on civil war alliances. Although several civil war theories, inspired by the international relations literature on interstate warfare, treat the main warring factions as largely homogeneous units with a set of common preferences, recent systematic critiques highlight the importance of internal group dynamics, as well as individual incentives and preferences.[15] This new line of work highlights the problem of ecological inference in the context of civil wars, suggesting that individual choices are dynamic and strategic – "purposive" and "contingent" – and do not allow for simple aggregation or extrapolation.[16]

While identifying the local dynamics of conflict is highly important, it is equally necessary to focus on the set of interactions between the micro and macro level. In the context of civil war, political and military elites are macro-level actors, whereas individuals – be they combatants or civilians – are micro-level actors. Even in the most democratic of cases, the two are not directly linked, and there are usually meso-level actors, such as local elites, who act as intermediaries.[17] The mechanism on group fractionalization presented later takes this meso-level approach and looks at the role of local elites, as well as their interactions with national elites, in civil wars. This is arguably a level of analysis that has been highly understudied and offers ample opportunity for inference, as it gives agency to what proves to be a set of meaningful, yet neglected, actors.

The mechanism on group fractionalization rests on the premise that groups are susceptible to fractionalization at times of sustained war-related losses in the context of a largely stalemated conflict. The mechanism takes as a given the empirical reality that warring groups – ethnic or otherwise – are rarely homogeneous in composition. They tend to be comprised of a set of subgroups that can vary in size and can be predetermined on largely structural elements that predate the fighting. In the case of ethnic groups, subgroup differences are manifested through differences – among others – in regions, tribes, or dialects. For instance, in the case of the 1992–1998 Afghan civil war, the fighting happened along ethnic lines and the groups were Tajiks, Pashtuns, Uzbeks,

---

[15] Kalyvas (2003, 2006); Brubaker (2004); Downes (2004); Valentino, Huth, and Balch-Lindsay (2004); Humphreys and Weinstein (2006, 2008); Balcells (2010).

[16] Schelling (1978), p. 17.

[17] The term "local elites" does not strictly refer to local elected officials, but should rather be interpreted loosely to include other local stakeholders, be they warlords, chieftains, or sheikhs.

and Hazaras, with respective subgroups of (among others) Herati Tajiks versus Panjshiri Tajiks; Durrani Pashtuns versus Ghilzai Pashtuns; Faryabi Uzbeks versus Jowzjani Uzbeks; and Kabul Hazaras versus Hazarajat Hazaras. Such subgroup cleavages are common in many ethnic groups, informing preferences, in-group leadership struggles, and relations with other groups, and are often manifested at the level of local elites.

Naturally, the desires of national elites and local elites are not always compatible and can actually diverge.[18] Local elites play a critical role in deciding whether the war fought will be the locally relevant war or the centrally relevant war. So long as the national group elites are strong, the local elites allow for the central cleavage to trump all else – individuals may be motivated by private incentives and not necessarily group concerns, but their actions stay in accordance with the central cleavage. With increased uncertainty over the group's central power, however, the relevant arena of the conflict shifts from the group to the subgroup, and collective action problems arise. Once local actors realize that they can no longer rely on the center for backup and protection, and particularly when they believe their survival may be at stake, they proceed to fight their locally relevant wars. All else being equal, warring parties with larger numbers of constituent subgroups should be more likely to fractionalize in the face of battlefield losses because of the greater opportunities for disagreement and defection. The war thus turns into a conglomerate of subgroup fights that often work in dissonance rather than in a coordinated fashion compatible with the macro-cleavage. Aside from being a dependent variable in itself, this group fractionalization is a key second-order cause of intergroup alliance shifts, as discussed in more detail later.

The group fractionalization mechanism thus relies on the assumption that each group consists of a set of constituent subgroups that, much like groups, also calculate their expected returns. Critically, the group-level dynamic is different from the alliance-level dynamic because within a group, the constituent subgroups anticipate sharing in postwar political control, and as a result of stronger in-group bonds, they do not fear that their group-mates will betray them when it comes time to divide postwar political power. Thus subgroups do not follow the "minimum" aspect of the "minimum winning coalition" logic in deciding whether to remain in a given group or not. However, groups are vulnerable to fractionalization when shifts in relative power result in a change to the strategy that will ensure them victory. Specifically, severe battlefield losses can cause a breakdown in group cohesion as subgroups begin to fear that survival is at stake, and as the group's poor performance leads to

---

[18] Kalyvas notes the disjunction between central and local incentives and highlights the fallacy in assuming common preferences between local and central actors. Rather, local conflicts are linked to the overarching conflict – which Kalyvas terms as the master cleavage – through an "alliance" between central and local actors that promotes their respective interests: the central actors' desire for overall control and the local actor's desire for local dominance. Kalyvas (2003), pp. 475–486; Kalyvas (2006), p. 14.

disputes over strategy that map on to preexisting subgroup cleavages. These subgroups, which differ from each other along regional lines and may also have leadership disputes that predate the war, are faced with a choice to (1) stay subservient to a group's leadership, (2) split off from the group, or (3) take over the leadership of the group. This choice is motivated primarily by subgroups' assessments of their group's relative power. Battlefield wins will foster intragroup cohesion by convincing subgroups that they are on the winning side. While such successes can actually lead to shifts at the alliance level (to restore the balance), the subgroups that make up a group do not, in this model, worry about their share of postwar political control within the group. Considerable battlefield losses may, however, put the efficacy of the group into question and are also typically borne unevenly between the various subgroups because of their frequently variable geographic distribution across the country or their various sub-relationships with other opposing actors. In response to these developments, local elites often fractionalize along the preexisting regional or leadership cleavages. In other words, presented with new information about their group's power, a subgroup will stay with the group if its power is on the rise, but will either abandon the group or topple its leadership if the group's standing is being seriously compromised as the conflict progresses. Whether it is asymmetric losses across subgroups or simply declining battlefield performance more broadly, subgroups often come to believe either that (1) a change in strategy is needed, leading them to topple the leadership and take over the group; or (2) that the group's relative power is declining, leading them to break off and join the opposing alliance in an effort to be on the winning side.

Fractionalization, in turn, is a form of relative power change, regardless of whether (1) a splinter faction joins up with an opposing group (increasing that group's power at the expense of the group it left), (2) a splinter group strikes out on its own (breaking the overall power distribution into smaller units), or (3) a group is taken over by a dissatisfied faction (decreasing that group's relative power as the turmoil rages and those loyal to the previous leadership leave or are purged). The resulting change in the intergroup distribution of power will spur alliance shifts, as groups seek to form updated minimum winning coalitions. In that context, we can see how a group (or a coalition) would have an incentive to accept a defecting subgroup into its ranks if it is not powerful enough to win the conflict outright on its own.

What is it about poor battlefield performance that drives fractionalization? The driving factor is that in-group opinions could be split on who is going to win. This uncertainty is further compounded by the likely asymmetric losses among a group's constituent subgroups, which cast more doubt on whether the group is really making optimal choices and on whether it can convince subgroups that their survival is not threatened. This is what justifies a decision to split at a time of weakness, a choice that on its face appears counterintuitive, but which allows a subgroup to ensure its own survival by defecting and joining the opposing alliance.

It is important to note that fractionalization is a distinct phenomenon from the bandwagoning that the theory predicts will only occur at a conflict's end, when one side is clearly winning the war and other warring groups seek to join it to ensure survival. In contrast, fractionalization happens at a time of high uncertainty, when it is unclear which way the war is going to turn. If the winner could be safely predicted, and this was a typical case of bandwagoning, then there is no reason for us to expect the group to split – we would rather expect it to join the winning side intact.

As described earlier, group fractionalization can take two forms: splits and takeovers. In the context of asymmetric losses, whether the in-group transformation will be a split or a takeover depends on the amount of loss that each subgroup has faced. If one of the subgroups has been seriously compromised while the other is still powerful, there will be a takeover by the more powerful group.[19] If both subgroups have managed to retain a solid power base among their respective constituents, there will be a split. This means that there is a minimum amount of power required for the leadership of each subgroup to sustain its hold over the group, and if that minimum threshold is not met, the leadership loses its credibility and the other subgroup takes control of the group as a whole. (The latter case is basically an internal coup. An *external* takeover – by the state government or by another warring group – is a different phenomenon outside the scope of this book.) The exact threshold is of course case-specific – it depends on the conflict and warring group size – but it generally requires the maintenance of control over enough constituents, resources, and territory for the group to maintain its viability.

THE ROLE OF SHARED IDENTITY AND NARRATIVES

The theoretical framework presented so far suggests that alliances and group fractionalization are tactical and power-driven. The mere fact that allies turn into foes and then friends again suggests that alliances and group fractionalization cannot be strictly motivated by shared identity. If that were the case, and presuming hardened (or at least slow-changing) identities at time of conflict – which is the standard assumption in the field – all alliances and groups would follow a predictable pattern dictated by specific identity considerations, often related to the primary cleavage of the war, which would in turn be maintained throughout the conflict. Yet, although notions of shared identity do not dictate alliance formation or group fractionalization, they play an important role in this theory in two ways.

First, while identity does not determine alliance behavior, at the group level it is critical because subgroups are bound to each other by strong notions of shared identity. Until a cause for fractionalization comes along – generally only

---

[19] For simplicity, I choose to stick to the fractionalization term, but in actuality, a takeover is an in-group transformation that leads to a subgroup getting subsumed by another rather than fractionalized per se.

in the extreme circumstances when a group's survival is threatened – subgroups see themselves as belonging to in-groups that define all other groups as out-groups. These groups that comprise the initial warring parties are characterized by high levels of trust, as well as formal and informal institutions that can enforce agreements and thereby render commitment problems irrelevant. The bonds within the group are strong enough that the component subgroups are willing to jointly pursue the superordinate goal of achieving victory, and thus they do not worry much about being exploited by more powerful subgroups within the group. Put differently, while these subgroups seek to be part of a winning coalition, they do not worry about the "minimum" part because they do not fear double-crossing. Thus in-group identity does play a key role at the group level that is absent at the alliance level.

Second, and central to the thesis of this book, notions of shared identity are not causes of alliance behavior but are employed instrumentally to justify the power-driven alliance decisions that are actually made by elites. Elites, acting as identity entrepreneurs, broadly employ the language of shared identity – ethnic or otherwise – as a way to rationalize their alliances. These narratives not only provide signals to followers about who is an enemy and who is a friend; they also resonate more strongly with them than justifications based on relative power. Notions of shared identity thus prove endogenous to alliance preferences: Elites pick their allies first based on tactical dictates, and then look to their identity repertoire for characteristics they share with their friends – and at the same time do not share with their enemies – that would allow for the construction of justifying narratives.[20]

My discussion of these narratives builds on existing literature on instru-mentalism and identity construction that sees elites as constructing minimum winning coalitions on a certain identity dimension that promotes political inter-ests. Even though these theories (as referenced in more detail in Chapter 1 of this book) are not directly transferable to the civil war context, their dynamic element, allowing for the construction of different possible coalitions around different cleavages, is consistent with the variability of alliances and group fractionalization during civil wars, and in that regard informs the analysis that follows.

My analysis argues that the relevant identity dimensions in civil war alliance narratives are both ethnic and nonethnic, with the latter being largely ideo-logical, or economic. Within those ethnic and nonethnic dimensions there are specific defining attributes. For ethnicity, per Horowitz's (1985) definition, the defining attributes would include: race, language, religion, tribe, nationality, and caste. Each of these attributes in turn takes different values. Looking at the Afghan case as an example, and accounting for the four dominant ethnic groups, the respective values for these attributes would broadly look as follows: *race:* South Asian (for Pashtuns and Tajiks), Central Asian (for Uzbeks and Hazaras), or mixed; *language:* Pashto-speaking (for Pashtuns), Dari-speaking

---

[20] See Oren (1995) for an analogous argument on narratives relating to the democratic peace.

(for Tajiks and Hazaras), Uzbek-speaking (for Uzbeks), or multilingual; *religion:* Sunni (for Pashtuns, Tajiks, and Uzbeks), or Shi'a (for Hazaras); *tribe:* Ghilzai, Durrani, Independent (for Pashtuns), or non-tribal (for Tajiks, Uzbeks, and Hazaras), and so forth.

As far as nonethnic dimensions are concerned, in the civil war context there can be ideological as well as economic dimensions. The relevant ideological dimension could have a party attribute with values such as communist, socialist, democratic, republican, or fascist; and a beliefs (or moral values) attribute with values such as progressive, conservative, or fundamentalist. The economic dimensions could include aspects such as class, with values like working class, middle class, or upper class; as well as other income-determining aspects with values such as urban or rural, pastoral or agricultural, and so forth. For example, in the 1992–1998 Afghan Jihad, some of the relevant values for ideological attributes were former communist, or mujahedin, and some of the relevant values for economic attributes were urban/rural or nomadic/agricultural.

I assume that every group has one and only one value for each of its ethnic and nonethnic attributes.[21] I also assume that the values in the "identity repertoire" of each group – its portfolio of various identity values – are rank-ordered in decreasing order of ascriptiveness. This means that the value for an attribute such as race – arguably the "stickiest" of characteristics – would rank first on the list, followed by characteristics of lesser stickiness such as language or religion. Most of these characteristics are likely to be ethnic, but that is not always the case. If there are ideological or economic attributes that have assumed a level of stickiness in the society that approximates ascriptiveness, then those could easily end up ranking higher than attributes that are traditionally considered ethnic.[22]

Elites willing to form a narrative in justification of an impending alliance or group allegiance first look for shared values at the top of their group's or subgroup's identity repertoire (i.e., start off with the higher values on the stickiness scale) that are shared with their desirable partner(s), while at the same time not shared with their foes. The elites move down the identity repertoire until they identify the value that meets this requirement, and move to suppress all the higher-ranking preceding values that fail to satisfy it. Leaders therefore choose to emphasize some aspects of their identity repertoire at times and different aspects at other times, depending on power-dictated alliance choices.

The rank-ordering of each group's attributes varies from one societal context to another, but is presumed to be common knowledge for all groups residing in the same state at the time of civil war onset. The mechanism also assumes that each group's rank-ordering of values in its identity repertoire does not change during the war. The mechanism of justifying narratives requires high degrees

---

[21] For instance, if a group speaks both Dari and Uzbek, this is entered as one value for the attribute language, the value being bilingualism in Dari and Uzbek.

[22] The notion of stickiness comes from economics (sticky prices) but is defined and used in ethnic terms in Chandra (2006).

of coordination, which would be impossible to attain if the rank-ordering of values were to shift. It is important to highlight that the mechanism behind these narratives allows for alliance switches during civil wars, prompted by and consistent with changes in the relative power among the different competing groups. There is therefore no sense of stickiness in the alliance narratives that would prevent any power-dictated alliance from taking place. Elites can find narratives to disassociate themselves from former friends as well as narratives to connect themselves with former enemies. Thus a broad range of proximity and distance narratives appears throughout the war, reflecting the fluid nature of alliances.

Given this rather counterintuitive finding on the role of shared identity in civil war, it is important to strike a cautionary note. This work looks at the role of shared identity in alliance formation and group fractionalization in multi-party civil wars. In that very specific context, it examines how shared identity is understood and whether it is perceived as fixed or variant, unidimensional or multidimensional; and although this dynamic could arguably be at work in other conflict and non-conflict contexts, this analysis makes no broader claims. It is therefore not meant as a general discussion of whether identity matters or not in civil wars or what the broader role of identity and symbols may be in civil war onset, violence, or termination.[23]

Rather, the discussion focuses on the more nuanced questions of when and how shared identity matters in the context of civil war alliance formation and group fractionalization. It would be a grave mistake to infer that my findings suggest that the role of identity in civil war is epiphenomenal. As we clearly see in the role of subgroups, identity works in ways that assuage commitment problems: Subgroups only break off in contexts of poor battlefield performance – that is, only when their survival is at stake. What my findings rather suggest is that in the very specific context of multiparty civil war alliances and group fractionalization, shared identity proves to be multidimensional, variant, and largely endogenous to power considerations.

But why discuss the identity construct in such detail if narratives are actually endogenous to power considerations – why bother with shared identity if it generally does not affect alliances or group fractionalization? First, to show that shared identity does not determine alliances and group fractionalization, one must examine how identity narratives – that feature prominently in civil wars – get constructed and how they work. In that regard, one needs to look at their intricacies through process tracing and figure out if they are driving alliances and group fractionalization or if they are *being driven* by these phenomena. Such analyses are presented in more detail in the empirical chapters of this book. Second, assuming that these narratives do indeed work in the way presented earlier, one wonders: Are there not any credibility concerns between

---

[23] For works discussing the importance of identity in these contexts, see Wedeen (1999) and Petersen (2001, 2002).

the actors that devise the narratives and their constituents, given that the narratives change so much? How convincing are the narratives if they keep on changing all the time?

Although they are perhaps not "convincing" in the traditional sense of the word, for the calculating power-driven elites, narratives seem to serve an informational purpose in the context of war: They are an easy way to communicate which side their constituents should be on today. Narratives ensure and enhance compliance with the new alliance or group allegiance, and act as a short-term mobilization and commitment device. Meanwhile, elites cannot simply voice the logic of relative power to justify new alliances because they would seem craven and it would suggest an immediate willingness to double-cross new alliance partners when conditions change. In addition, for smaller groups, discussing the reasons for alliances will often emphasize that group's weakness in the field, which could be detrimental to the group's chances for success, given that this is an environment with incomplete information about relative power. By contrast, focusing on the most salient and ascriptive sources of shared identity, however constructed, suggests a reason for allying that does not overtly signal weakness, and perhaps a willingness to commit to their new partners as a result of this newfound bond of shared identity, together with an expectation that such loyalty will be reciprocated.

ALLIANCES AND CIVIL WAR TERMINATION

This theoretical framework has so far suggested that war either ends in victory, if one group constitutes a minimum winning coalition on its own, or, in the absence of such a case, it degenerates into a process of constant realignment and fractionalization with all warring groups aiming to be part of a minimum winning coalition. In the latter context, often characterized by a highly fractionalized landscape of warring actors, the conflict does not resolve itself unless one group musters the power to win on its own or a negotiated settlement gets brokered.

Civil war termination is, along with civil war onset, one of the most studied phenomena pertaining to civil conflict. Some of the more robust findings in that voluminous literature suggest that civil wars are more likely to end in outright victory than negotiated settlement, although there have been more of the latter since the end of the Cold War. In the cases of negotiated settlements, external interveners – if not necessary to broker them in the first place – are required in some capacity to do away with the commitment problems among warring factions that may have caused the fighting.[24] In civil wars, external intervention – be it by the international community or a third state – can come in two ways: (1) it can either prop up the winning side and allow it to attain a decisive victory, or (2) it can prop up the losing side to get the winning side to agree to a negotiated settlement. The type of intervention can often be linked

---

[24] Licklider (1995); Walter (1997); Fearon and Laitin (2007); Toft (2010).

to the type of intervener: Kin states usually (but not exclusively) intervene for a decisive victory, whereas the international community usually aspires to a negotiated settlement. In turn, civil war duration appears to be a critical determinant of civil war termination, with longer civil wars being more likely to end in negotiated settlements.[25]

It is beyond the scope of this work to focus on civil war termination, an important subject matter in its own right. Ultimately, civil wars are decided on the battlefield or at the bargaining table, and this is neither a theory of battlefield performance nor of conflict mediation. A whole host of exogenous shocks outside the realm of this book's theory may break a battlefield stalemate and trigger a military victory – for example, the introduction of new technologies, external intervention on the part of the stronger party, a loss of foreign support for a warring party, or the death of a leader.[26] Similarly, exogenous shocks may lead groups to come to the bargaining table, most prominently in the form of external mediation or intervention to prop up the losing side. However, once it becomes clear which outcome is likely (military victory vs. negotiated settlement), the theory makes predictions about the warring parties' alliance behavior. The expectation is for warring parties to start bandwagoning if they see one party heading toward a decisive victory that no opposing alliance could block. Specifically, small groups on the losing side face the reality that unless they switch alliances, they will have no say in the division of postwar power, so they are better off hedging their bets and trying to join in as a junior partner on the winning side.

Similarly, if the outcome is expected to be a negotiated settlement, the warring parties are likely to maintain their balancing posture until the end of the civil war as a way to get the highest negotiating leverage. Thus the claim being made here as it pertains to alliances is that an expectation of a decisive victory will lead to bandwagoning, with smaller parties wanting to join on the side of the winner, whereas an expectation of negotiated settlement or of continued fighting with no clear winner will perpetuate a balancing configuration among the warring parties until the end of hostilities. There are thus three possible outcomes: (1) no prospects for settlement or no obvious winner, leading to balancing; (2) prospects for negotiated settlement, also leading to balancing; or (3) an obvious winner emerging, leading to bandwagoning behavior.

COMPARISON TO NEOREALISM

This theory should resonate with readers acquainted with international relations scholarship – it is essentially a neorealist account of group behavior in multiparty civil wars.[27] Like neorealists, I posit that alliance choices are driven

---

[25] Mason, Weingarten and Fett (1999); Fearon (2004).
[26] On the latter two factors and civil war termination, see Fearon and Laitin (2007).
[27] Waltz (1979).

by relative power considerations, and that in their search for security, smaller groups balance against more powerful adversaries. Just as neorealist tendencies in the international system of states are sometimes tempered by other variables, such as regime type or ideology,[28] it could well be that variables such as identity temper the relationship between relative power and alliance formation in multiparty civil wars (see Chapter 1). In both cases, however, power is the primary determinant of behavior and the best predictive tool that social scientists and policy makers have at their disposal. Neorealism, though arguably the dominant paradigm in international relations, has drawn criticism on a variety of fronts, many of them legitimate. Interestingly, however, four of the most prominent critiques of the paradigm do not apply to a neorealist view of warring group alliance behavior in multiparty civil wars. These critiques are reviewed and discussed in this section.

First, neorealism is faulted on the grounds that state death is rare. According to the theory, states must play by the rules of the international system – they must balance – or they will be eliminated from the system, much as a firm that does not efficiently pursue profit will go bankrupt.[29] In practice, however, states do not die very often, particularly since the end of World War II, and when they do die it is largely a function of an unfortunate geographic location rather than their refusal to play by the rules of the system per se.[30] On the other hand, in multiparty civil wars, the actors – warring groups – die regularly. Consider the Tamil conflict in Sri Lanka, which gradually evolved from a multiparty to a binary civil war as the groups known as EROS, TELO, PLOTE, EPRLF, and JVP were dramatically eliminated (leaving only the Sri Lankan state and the LTTE from about 1990 to 2004). Thus the quasi-Darwinian logic of neorealism seems to fit the civil war context more closely: If warring groups do not form alliances tactically and balance against more powerful adversaries, there is a good chance they will be wiped off the map.

Second, the predictions of pure neorealism are sometimes simply wrong. For example, during the Cold War, the Western European states balanced against the Soviet Union rather than the more powerful United States. These empirical pitfalls have led to attempts to refine the paradigm – for example, some scholars consider threat, rather than power, as the motivating variable behind state behavior.[31] These refinements are unnecessary in the civil war context because a state in internal conflict is in many ways more anarchic than an international system. There is, for instance, virtually no institutionalization of relationships between warring groups, while some such institutionalization is provided in the system of states by treaties and intergovernmental organizations. Because any warring group can be any other warring group's mortal enemy, and can

[28] Doyle (1986); Haas (2003).
[29] Waltz (1979), pp. 76–77.
[30] Fazal (2007).
[31] Walt (1987).

switch from friend to enemy at any time, threat is not a major factor in groups' calculations; instead, threat is assumed and power is the main variable driving alliance choices (granted, power can be misperceived).

Third, states do not always balance against adversaries even when threatened; sometimes they "buck-pass," or free-ride on the balancing behavior of another threatened state.[32] This further complication of neorealism seems quite unlikely to apply to multiparty civil wars. In civil wars, the threats to a group's survival are immediate, as discussed earlier, and "buck-catchers" (groups willing to take on the balancing burden unilaterally) are generally in short supply. This trend should be heightened in conflicts with generally equal balances of relative power as groups are unable to free-ride.

Finally, it has been argued that not all states are motivated by security. The implication is that states will behave in different fashions given different motivations. For example, some states, such as Italy in the 1930s, may instead be motivated by greed, and as a consequence may choose to "bandwagon" with stronger powers rather than balance against them so as to share in the spoils of expansionism.[33] The theory in this book steps around this critique by arguing that warring groups are motivated by both security *and* greed. Indeed, during civil conflict, security and greed are often tightly intertwined for substate actors for which political and economic control is intricately tied to group security. Without access to political and economic resources, groups are unable to guarantee protection and ensure group viability vis-à-vis other groups. This is why substate actors seek to form minimum winning coalitions: They want the security of being on the winning side, but they also want to ensure that the winning side is as small as possible so they get the largest possible share of political control.

These four prominent critiques of neorealism, which have generated substantial debates among international relations scholars, simply do not travel well to the multiparty civil war context on which this book focuses. Thus, ironically, in some ways a neorealist, power-centric view of actor behavior seems better suited to the study of multiparty civil war than it is to the study of international politics.

THE THEORY IN SUM

The theoretical framework presented in this chapter allows us to make specific hypotheses about group behavior, subgroup behavior, and overall outcomes in multiparty civil war. These hypotheses, which are illustrated and then tested (qualitatively as well as quantitatively where data are available) in the empirical parts of the book, follow in this section. The expectation is that they hold

---

[32] Mearsheimer (2001).
[33] Schweller (1994).

across multiparty civil wars, irrespective of their character, be they ethnic or nonethnic.

GROUP BEHAVIOR HYPOTHESES

1) As a given alliance increases in perceived relative power, past the point of being a minimum winning coalition, groups will defect from the alliance and try to form a smaller winning coalition (in the hopes of maximizing their share of postwar political power).
2) When alliance composition changes over the course of a war, the identity-based justifications for alliances put forth at one point in time will often be contradicted by alliance composition at another point in time. Shared identity will thus not determine alliances among warring groups. Warring groups will rather form shared identity narratives to correspond to their power-determined alliance choices.
3) If the war either appears likely to end in a negotiated settlement or to continue on without foreseeable victory by either side, the balancing alliance tendencies will persist. If outright military victory appears to be the likely outcome, groups will bandwagon with whichever group appears most powerful.

SUBGROUP BEHAVIOR HYPOTHESES

1) As a given group's perceived relative power decreases, it will have an increased risk for fractionalization, either as a result of disagreements about strategy or an asymmetric distribution of the perceived relative power loss among its constituent subgroups, which threatens the group's survival and which leads to divergent opinions among subgroups as to which side is likely to win.
2) Group leaders who lose perceived relative power, but who still retain enough power to control the group, will suffer a group split. The splinter faction may join up with an opposing group, or it may strike out on its own.
3) Group leaders who lose enough relative power to lose control over the group will suffer an internal takeover by a stronger subgroup.
4) Groups that split are likely to fracture along regional lines or leadership disputes that predate the conflict.

OVERALL OUTCOME HYPOTHESES

1) Multiparty civil wars in which the intergroup distribution of power is more uneven will see fewer alliance changes than wars in which the distribution of power is more balanced. In power-balanced conflicts, small changes in relative power will substantively alter what constitutes a

minimum winning coalition, incentivizing warring groups to change alliances frequently. In power-skewed conflicts (referred to as "hegemonic" conflicts in Chapter 8), only large – and therefore less common – changes in relative power will alter the optimal alliance configurations. (Generally, conflicts are hegemonic because the government is significantly stronger than the various rebel groups.)

2) Multiparty civil wars will last longer than binary civil wars.
3) Conflicts with more fractionalization will have more alliance changes.

Having laid out this book's theory, I now turn to the empirical illustrations and tests of that theory. In Chapter 3, I introduce one of the two cases that informed the development of the theory: the 1992–1998 intra-mujahedin civil war in Afghanistan. The trajectory of that bewildering conflict illustrates in detail the theoretical predictions made in this chapter.

PART II

AFGHANISTAN

3

The Afghan Intra-Mujahedin War, 1992–1998

The idea that large groups of armed men bent on killing each other can be persuaded to change sides may seem fanciful at first. It is this book's primary objective to show that it is not fanciful at all. Specifically, in Afghanistan's intra-mujahedin civil war, which lasted from 1992 to 1998 and is the motivating case of this book, the heads of mujahedin groups constantly changed their allegiances as shifts in the balance of power demanded a strategic realignment. More than the fighting, it was this flipping that decided major outcomes – it kept people alive while allowing their groups to stay in power. Meanwhile, these elites came up with vivid stories to justify their behavior.

The analysis of the 1992–1998 Afghan civil war that follows brings the mujahedin's civil war machinations to life by drawing on a diverse set of mostly primary data collected in the field. These range from semi-structured interviews with Afghan warlords and mujahedin who took part in the conflict to wartime fatwas, declarations, and Taliban decrees; coverage in the local and international press; and U.S. Freedom of Information Act declassified documents – including Guantanamo Bay testimony of Afghan detainees and U.S. diplomatic wires. Afghan culture is largely an oral one, compounding the typical data scarcity that characterizes civil wars. This was particularly a challenge in trying to systematically capture the changes in power over the war years and their resultant effect on alliance formation and group fractionalization. For that I rely on interviews and other pertinent primary and secondary sources to territorially trace the power and alliance/group shifts throughout the civil war's trajectory. In that regard, I use Geographic Information Systems (GIS) to geo-reference and digitize Soviet declassified maps on the provincial level for the whole of Afghanistan. I use these maps to quantify and spatially project territorial changes over time as a way to test the extent to which the empirical evidence corresponds to the proposed theoretical framework, complementing the rich qualitative data analysis. The stories of alliance switches and group fractionalization, and the ensuing victories and defeats, are told on the level of the various warring groups/subgroups and their leaders that were in the heart of this ethnic conflict. The theory is then put to the test in a nonethnic Afghan civil war of the past, the Afghan Jihad between communists and mujahedin (Chapter 4), as well as against a micro-level dataset of wartime commanders in three of Afghanistan's arguably most contested provinces other than Kabul (those being Balkh, Kandahar, and Nangarhar) across both of Afghanistan's civil wars (Chapter 5).

The Afghan intra-mujahedin conflict is a highly complex case. The objective of this chapter is to focus on the alliance and fractionalization dynamics among and within Afghan warring parties and is therefore largely divorced from the macro-politics around them. Even though the role of Pakistan's involvement is referenced in a separate section later in the chapter, this is not a work on the involvement of regional players in civil wars, which is a worthy matter of inquiry in its own right. Rather, external meddling – which varied across actors, intensity, and time – is indirectly accounted for by the way these external actors projected power through their local allies, be they the Pashtuns, Tajiks, Uzbeks, or Hazaras. This chapter starts off with a brief overview of Afghanistan's ethnographic makeup and warring actors during the intra-mujahedin war, and offers a timeline of the civil war and the relative power and alliance changes that transpired. The discussion then shifts to the various civil war narratives that arose in justification of the ever-changing tactical alliances, and concludes with the fractionalization dynamics that plagued some of the warring parties.

ETHNIC MAKEUP AND WARRING FACTIONS

Although Afghanistan is broadly known for its multiethnic makeup, which spans various racial, linguistic, and sectarian cleavages, the prominent ethnic groups are arguably four: the Pashtuns, the Tajiks, the Uzbeks, and the Hazaras. Given the decades of civil war that have ravaged the country, there exist no reliable statistics on the demographic size of each group, estimates of which vary considerably. The general consensus is that the Pashtuns are the biggest group, followed by the Tajiks and the similarly sized Hazaras and Uzbeks. A rough demographic division based on the natural barrier of the Hindu Kush mountain range suggests that the south is populated predominantly by the Pashtuns, the north by the Tajiks and the Uzbeks, and the Hazaras are mainly situated in the central area of Hazarajat.

The Pashtuns have been Afghanistan's dominant ethnic group, both in size and political power, since the mid-eighteenth century. Primarily Pashto-speaking and overwhelmingly followers of the Sunni Muslim faith, Pashtuns generally fall under three major tribal lines that are in turn conglomerates of smaller tribes and tribal elements going all the way down to the family unit.[1] The Tajiks mainly reside in Afghanistan's urban centers and constitute

---

[1] These are: (1) the Durrani tribal line – the tribal line of the Afghan royal family, located in the north and west of Kandahar; (2) the Ghilzai tribal line – located in the eastern part of the southern Pashtun belt and in some areas in the north; and (3) the "independent tribes" – located

a majority in the Panjshir valley, in the northern province of Badakhshan, and in Afghanistan's western provinces. Like the Pashtuns, they are also predominantly Sunni but speak Dari, a dialect of Farsi. The Uzbeks, concentrated in the northern areas of Afghanistan, are a Sunni Muslim group that is primarily Uzbek-speaking but largely bilingual in Dari. Lastly, the Hazaras, the most numerous Shiite population in Afghanistan, are considered to be descendants of the Mongols and speak Dari. They are primarily situated in Afghanistan's central highlands, but considerable Hazara populations reside in Afghanistan's main urban areas such as Kabul and the main northern city of Mazar-i-Sharif.

On the eve of the 1992–1998 intra-mujahedin war, Afghanistan was just emerging from a decade-long bloody conflict. As detailed in Chapter 4 of this book, violence had erupted in 1978 as a reaction to the rise of the Afghan communist party, known as the People's Democratic Party of Afghanistan (PDPA), and their attempts to impose land collectivization and other radical social and cultural reforms. Initial opposition to PDPA rule consisted of a series of local rebellions. After 1979, it was dominated by the seven Sunni-led mujahedin parties whose leadership benefited from a safe haven and aid pipeline mostly out of Peshawar in Pakistan. The leaders of the up to nine different Shiite Afghan parties, which were mostly comprised of ethnic Hazaras and whose fighting was largely confined to the central Afghan region of Hazarajat, found refuge in Iran. The war between the communist and the mujahedin sides raged strong until February 1989, which marked the Soviet withdrawal from Afghanistan. The mujahedin then demanded the establishment of an Islamic government. Instead, the collapse of the communist government in April 1992, after a three-year interlude of relative calm, marked the commencement of a new phase of conflict, the intra-mujahedin war.[2]

The protagonists of the intra-mujahedin war belonged to the largely ethnic parties that were formed during the Jihad. The strongest political actor was Hizb-i-Islami, one of the leading two of the seven Afghan Sunni mujahedin parties. Headed by Gulbuddin Hekmatyar, a Ghilzai Pashtun from the north, Hizb-i-Islami had a predominantly Pashtun leadership and support base. Having been the primary recipient of U.S. and Pakistani training and aid during the Jihad, Hizb-i-Islami entered the intra-mujahedin war in 1992 as the militarily strongest group.

The second leading mujahedin group during the Jihad was Jamiat-i-Islami. Unlike the other Jihadi parties, which were largely Pashtun-dominated, Jamiat-i-Islami's leadership cadres were mostly Tajik, featuring individuals such as legendary commander Ahmad Shah Massoud from the Panjshir Valley and Burhanuddin Rabbani, who served as Afghanistan's president from 1992 until 1998 when the Taliban overran most of Afghanistan. Junbish-i-Milli was the majority ethnic Uzbek party of General Rashid Dostum. Having served as the

to the east and north of the Durranis and Ghilzais. Examples of independent tribes are the Afridi, Mangal, Zadran, and Orakzai.

[2] Goodson (2001), pp. 57–73.

TABLE 3.1. *Afghan Intra-Mujahedin War Alliances*

Year	Alliance One	Alliance Two
1992	Pashtuns	Tajiks + Uzbeks + Hazaras
1993	Pashtuns + Hazaras	Tajiks + Uzbeks
1994	Pashtuns + Hazaras + Uzbeks	Tajiks
1995–96	Pashtuns (Taliban) + Hazaras (Mazari/Khalili) + Uzbeks	Tajiks + Hazaras (Akbari) + Pashtuns (Hekmatyar)
1996	Pashtuns (Taliban)	Tajiks + Uzbeks + Hazaras
1997	Pashtuns (Taliban) + Uzbeks (Malik)	Tajiks + Hazaras
1997	Pashtuns (Taliban) with defectors	Remaining Tajiks + Uzbeks + Hazaras
1998	Pashtuns (Taliban) military victory with defectors from all other sides	

leader of the communist regime's northern militia during most of the Jihad, Dostum mutinied against the communist government, securing control over a considerable amount of arms and ammunition. Although Junbish-i-Milli had a notable military presence in Kabul, its area of control was the north, primarily the provinces of Jowzjan, Faryab, Balkh, and Samangan.

Lastly, the main Hazara party was Hizb-i-Wahdat. Founded in 1989 in an effort to unite all nine Jihad-era Shiite parties, it was led by Abdul Ali Mazari and its support base rested exclusively with Afghanistan's Hazara community. Though strongest in Hazarajat, Hizb-i-Wahdat also had a notable presence in some urban centers, particularly in the Afghan capital and in the northern city of Mazar-i-Sharif.

THE EVOLUTION OF POWER AND ALLIANCES AMONG
WARRING PARTIES

The Afghan civil war witnessed a complex set of ever-changing alliances. As indicated in Table 3.1, there were seven instances of alliance shifts. Although the two main warring sides were the Pashtuns versus the Tajiks, each warring group ended up forming an alliance with every other group at some point during the war's trajectory. While acknowledging that alliance members shifted, for the purpose of clarity I label the Pashtun-led alliance as Alliance One and the opposing, generally Tajik-led alliance as Alliance Two.

The mere fact that allies became enemies, and then allies again, clearly suggests that shared identity considerations alone could not have been the determining factor, as they would have precluded some alliances from ever forming. The alternative explanation put forth later in the chapter – along the lines of the theory presented in Chapter 2 – suggests that the groups' relative power considerations motivated alliance preferences. More specifically, groups looked at the distribution of relative power among the warring actors and decided whom to join.

The following section details the alliance changes that occurred from 1992 until the Taliban victory in 1998. For each alliance change, it relates the relative power distribution of the major actors involved and presents how the varying balances of political, economic, and military power translated into new coalitions or caused groups to fractionalize. Given the scarcity of micro-level data in civil wars, and specifically in the Afghan context, there are no exact numbers on the guns and casualties of the warring sides so as to systematically gauge the shifts of military power throughout the war's trajectory. Still, it is feasible to observe changes in relative power between the groups in terms of their access to government resources, ability to fend off challenging groups, and capacity to financially provide for the warring efforts, whether through internal taxation or external support. Following the detailed timeline, an additional robustness measure is used by proxying power through territorial control (a proxy for power that warring actors in the field referenced in their interviews) and evaluating the changes in alliances based on relative changes in territory. The Afghan story, as presented here, is indeed largely a story of balancing alliances, with constant shifts and breakdowns until the Taliban victory in 1998.

TIMELINE[3]

1992: Tajiks + Uzbeks + Hazaras vs. Pashtuns
(Jamiat-i-Islami + Junbish-i-Milli + Hizb-i-Wahdat vs. Hizb-i-Islami)

The 1989 Soviet withdrawal led to a marked reduction in hostilities, but this lull came to an abrupt end on March 20, 1992, a day after Mohammad Najibullah, the last communist leader of Afghanistan, announced his imminent resignation. With the dissolution of the communist regime, military resources – both troops and equipment – were absorbed by the various mujahedin parties. There was general parity in spoils between Dostum's Junbish-i-Milli, Rabbani's Jamiat-i-Islami, and Hekmatyar's Hizb-i-Islami, but in terms of numbers, Junbish-i-Milli was the clear winner.[4] Although not as large, the Hazara forces also absorbed two tribal army units, were bolstered by Iranian support, and were the only active organization in Hazarajat.[5] However, the distribution of power was also influenced by two additional factors: access to the state and economic viability, dependent on either foreign support or the revenue-generation capabilities of each group.

Although Junbish-i-Milli and Jamiat-i-Islami had greater military resources, Hizb-i-Islami was well positioned in terms of political, financial, and external resources. This was a result of Hekmatyar's adept management of the narcotics

---

[3] This chronology, which largely draws from field interviews, is also consistent with Davis (1993); Rubin (1995a); Adamec (1996); Rashid (2000); Goodson (2001); Human Rights Watch Report (2005).

[4] For numbers, see table in the Appendix; Davis (1993); Giustozzi (2004); interview with Wahidullah Sabawoon.

[5] Sinno (2008), p. 217.

trade in contrast to the other groups[6] and a consistent supply of funding from Saudi Arabia and Pakistan – as detailed in Chapter 4, Hizb-i-Islami was Pakistan's preferred mujahedin ally and the primary recipient of military aid throughout the Jihad. Hizb-i-Wahdat and Junbish-i-Milli were also well supported by Iran and Uzbekistan, respectively. Jamiat-i-Islami was the only power without a major external patron until later on in the conflict, although it had received major arms transfers from the United States in 1991.

In addition to its slight economic advantage, Hizb-i-Islami appeared to be the strongest political actor on the ground.[7] In particular, non-Pashtun groups saw the transition from the communist government as unduly focused on Pashtuns, who had been politically dominant since the inception of the Afghan state.[8] This prospect seemed heightened by the tight ties between Hizb-i-Islami and certain Pashtuns within the communist regime, and by Hizb's consistent communication with the Pashtun contingent in the military.[9] This fear seemed to play out after Hekmatyar was able to infiltrate Hizb-i-Islami troops into the capital directly following the communist government's collapse.[10]

Despite Dostum's military assets, Jamiat-i-Islami was seen as the strongest political rival to Hizb-i-Islami. Jamiat-i-Islami commander Ahmad Shah Massoud was popular with Tajiks throughout Afghanistan, as he, the "Lion of Panjshir," had led the most successful operations against the Soviets, turning back a number of Soviet offensives and inflicting severe damage on their forces. Junbish-i-Milli, by contrast, was constrained by its regional character – it was mainly confined to the Northwest – as well as continued antipathy toward Dostum for his allegiance to the communist government.[11] As such, given the perceived political advantage of Hizb-i-Islami – fortified by its continued support from Pakistan – the Uzbeks, Tajiks, and Hazaras allied to prevent a Hizb-i-Islami coup. In line with this book's theoretical framework, the three groups united in order to balance against the strongest group – in this case the Pashtuns of Hizb-i-Islami.

After allying, the Tajik forces under the leadership of Rabbani and Massoud (Jamiat-i-Islami), Uzbek forces under the leadership of Dostum (Junbish-i-Milli), and Hazara forces under the leadership of Mazari (Hizb-i-Wahdat) worked on joint strategies to gain control of the Afghan capital, Kabul. On April 18, 1992, representatives of the three groups signed an agreement in Jabal Seraj in Parwan province to enter Kabul as a joint force.[12] Although Massoud had promised not to enter the capital before the Afghan mujahedin leaders in Peshawar had reached an agreement on an interim government, on April 25, 1992, his Northern Alliance nevertheless took over the city in an effort to

[6] Rubin (1995a), pp. 118–119; Rupert and Coll (1990).
[7] Isby (1992), pp. 463–464.
[8] Rubin (1995b), pp. 130–132; Dorronsoro (2005), p. 235.
[9] Dorronsoro (2005), p. 237.
[10] Rubin (1995b), p. 133; Dorronsoro (2005), p. 238; Maley (2009), p. 160.
[11] Giustozzi (2009), p. 154.
[12] Interview with Mohammad Akbari.

preempt a similar move from the Pashtun forces of Hekmatyar's Hizb-i-Islami. The Pashtuns, taken by surprise, were forced to remain on the outskirts of the capital.

On April 26, 1992, Afghan mujahedin leaders in Peshawar reached an agreement on an interim government created to serve for the eighteen months preceding elections. The agreement had designated Hekmatyar as prime minister, but he refused to recognize it, allegedly on the grounds that it had given unwarranted power to the Tajiks by assigning Massoud as minister of defense. Jamiat-i-Islami, on the other hand, readily embraced the agreement and quickly gained the allegiance of the majority of forces that were affiliated with the Tajik wing of the communist party, solidifying its control over the security apparatus and over most ministries in Kabul.[13]

1993: Tajiks + Uzbeks vs. Hazaras + Pashtuns
(Jamiat-i-Islami + Junbish-i-Milli vs. Hizb-i-Wahdat + Hizb-i-Islami)

By June 1992, Rabbani, the political leader of Jamiat-i-Islami, had taken over the position of president in the mujahedin government while his military counterpart, Massoud, was firmly in place as minister of defense. Following Hekmatyar's refusal to join the government, Jamiat-i-Islami became the central actor in the emerging political system. Emphasizing their goal of a unitary Islamic state, Rabbani and Massoud worked to bolster their political and military power. Dorronsoro observes that Hizb-i-Wahdat and Junbish-i-Milli expected Massoud to "convert" to "ethnic realism" and "legitimate the division of the country on a politico-ethnic basis." Instead, Jamiat-i-Islami opted for a united Islamic state. For Hizb-i-Wahdat in particular, a unified state posed a real danger to the autonomy of Hazarajat and the governance preferences of the Hazara Shiites.[14] Thus, as the power of the Tajik-controlled government was markedly on the rise, the relationship with their junior allies – the Hazaras and the Uzbeks – became increasingly tense.[15] As the theory would predict, divisions emerged among these erstwhile allies as the weaker alliance partners – in this case, the Hazaras and the Uzbeks – began to worry that the dominant partner, the Tajiks, was not willing to cede significant political power.

This division reached a head in December 1992. First, after assembling an unrepresentative nationwide shura – composed mainly of Jamiat-i-Islami and Junbish-i-Milli representatives – Rabbani was elected for an additional eighteen-month term on December 29 of that year. Concomitantly, Massoud aggressively targeted Hizb-i-Wahdat positions in western Kabul in an attempt to disarm the group, which Jamiat-i-Islami had accused of attacking the civilian population. Many observers described this action as geared toward expanding Jamiat-i-Islami's power and political reach by sidelining the Shiite

---

[13] Davis (1993), p. 135.
[14] Maley (2009), p. 168.
[15] Davis (1993), p. 136; Giustozzi (2009), p. 73.

Hizb-i-Wahdat to facilitate the entry of Sunni groups into the government.[16] Indeed, by December 1992, Rubin observed that most actors on the ground held an "assumption of a near monopoly over the central government by Jamiat."[17] This sentiment was supported by Jamiat-i-Islami's increasingly coordinated and expansive military efforts across Kandahar, Helmand, and Herat, combined with Jamiat-i-Islami's and Junbish-i-Milli's entrenchment in northern Afghanistan.[18] Further, Jamiat-i-Islami was receiving increased foreign support from the United States, India – which was providing spare parts for aircraft – Iran, and even Saudi Arabia – despite the latter's continuing strong support for Hekmatyar – and was benefiting, at least to a small extent, from the central government's financial assets.[19] During this same period, Hekmatyar's Hizb-i-Islami faction was suffering declines in political, economic, and military power. First, in terms of military power, even though Hekmatyar had acquired a number of army units, as noted earlier, many of the units in eastern and southern Pashtun areas disbanded or did not join Hizb-i-Islami, as opposed to the north and west of the country where most army units were integrated by Junbish-i-Milli or Jamiat-i-Islami.[20] Further, Hekmatyar faced losses near Kabul and around the country. In Kabul, Massoud and Dostum's forces effectively pushed Hekmatyar's militants from the city in April 1992 and reached as far as Sarobi. These losses also affected Hekmatyar's economic stability. For example, the loss of the truck road from Herat to Kandahar to forces aligned with Jamiat-i-Islami cut off access to the Shindand airport, while Jamiat-i-Islami forces were taking larger portions of Kandahar province, disrupting transfers from Pakistan.[21] Similarly, the idea from 1992 that Hizb-i-Islami was politically dominant deteriorated quickly. First, with Jamiat-i-Islami's central role in the government, Hizb-i-Islami lost many of its bureaucratic connections, most importantly at the Ministry of the Interior. Following Hekmatyar's rejection of the 1992 agreement, the stakeholders in Kabul violated its terms, forming a thirty-two-member government with no Hizb-i-Islami representation.[22] This separated Hekmatyar from any official state functions, such as interactions with foreign leaders or the issuing of banknotes. As noted previously, this exclusion was heightened with Massoud's appointment as minister of defense, eliminating any Hizb-i-Islami influence on military units that remained loyal to the central government.[23]

Perhaps most importantly, Hizb-i-Islami was unable to mobilize extensive Pashtun support, especially in the tribal belt of southern Afghanistan. In particular, as Hekmatyar was a Ghilzai Pashtun from northern Afghanistan,

---

[16] Dorronsoro (2005), pp. 242–243; Maley (2009), pp. 168–169.
[17] Rubin (1995b), p. 134.
[18] Davis (1993), p. 134; Gall (1993).
[19] Khalizad (1995), p. 152; Ahady (1998), p. 125.
[20] Davis (1993), p. 134; Rubin (1995a), p. 277.
[21] Gall (1993), p. 19.
[22] Dorronsoro (2005), p. 239.
[23] Ahady (1995), pp. 624–626.

southern Durrani Pashtuns did not accept him as representative of the Pashtun cause and largely opted not to participate in the nationwide civil war.[24] This ineffectiveness began undermining Pakistan's support of Hekmatyar as well. Still, in 1993, it was providing arms, logistics, and financial support, including restocking an arms depot at Spin Boldak – which would be taken by the Taliban – that was thought to be able to support thousands of fighters.

Seeking to address these relative declines and the rising power of Jamiat-i-Islami, Hekmatyar had been flirting with Mazari on a potential Pashtun-Hazara alliance, while continuing his indiscriminate artillery attacks aiming to force the Tajik-dominated government into some form of political compromise. Mazari's group, as noted earlier, felt that it was being under-appreciated in the coalition, given its increasingly strong support from Iran and general monopoly over the central Afghanistan area of Hazarajat. Following the escalation of the Hazara-Tajik fighting in December 1992, Hekmatyar was able to formally ally his Pashtuns with Mazari's Hazaras, who were keen to join forces despite a long history of repression from the Pashtuns. In spite of ethnic antagonisms, relative power dictated that the two groups ally in order to balance against the growing power of the Tajiks.

1994: Tajiks vs. Uzbeks + Hazaras + Pashtuns
(Jamiat-i-Islami vs. Junbish-i-Milli + Hizb-i-Wahdat + Hizb-i-Islami)

Fighting in the city of Kabul between Tajiks and the now allied Pashtuns and Hazaras flared up in mid-January 1993, to the continued detriment of Mazari's forces. Indeed, the Tajiks gained even more ground against the Hazaras in Kabul – including in the infamous operation Afshar that resulted in the death of hundreds of Hazaras in Kabul.[25] Nonetheless, the extent of violence prompted the restart of negotiations in Islamabad. The talks concluded with an agreement between the major actors, stipulating that Rabbani would complete his eighteen-month term while Hekmatyar took over as prime minister and Massoud stepped down from his position as defense minister. Though Hekmatyar was sworn in with a cabinet in June 1993, he continued to attack Kabul, leaving the government effectively in the hands of Rabbani and Massoud.[26] Indeed, this continued dominance of Jamiat-i-Islami estranged their other junior partner, the Uzbeks.

Despite the relative advantage of the Junbish-i-Milli-Jamiat-i-Islami alliance, Junbish-i-Milli's military and political influence within the alliance was declining. First, Jamiat-i-Islami systematically refused to give Dostum a significant position within the government.[27] Illustratively, Jamiat-i-Islami

[24] Davis (1996), p. 184.
[25] Operation Afshar is recounted in detail in a Human Rights Watch Report (2005) and in Mousavi (1997).
[26] Goodson (2001), p. 74.
[27] Wyllie (1994), p. 273.

would not recognize Junbish-i-Milli as a political party and Dostum was not given a spot in the Islamabad deal introduced earlier.[28] Given that exclusion, there were no signs of this situation being ameliorated. As such, during the entire year of 1993, Dostum was hesitant to support Jamiat-i-Islami in military operations against Hizb-i-Islami and Hizb-i-Wahdat, often asserting neutrality.[29]

At the same time, Junbish-i-Milli was facing potential declines in military efficacy vis-à-vis Jamiat-i-Islami. First, Dostum was unable to establish centralized control of the major forces absorbed with the fall of the communist regime. He was rarely able to mobilize more than 5,000 troops and could not field more than 20,000 at the same time.[30] Illustratively, in a major fight for Sher Khan Bander, a key area near the border with Tajikistan, in November 1993, Junbish-i-Milli's forces were cleanly defeated by a mujahedin force indirectly aligned with Jamiat-i-Islami.[31] Even though Jamiat-i-Islami denied knowledge of the attack, a clear message was sent of Junbish-i-Milli 's relative military weakness versus those forces allied with Massoud. Not only was this Dostum's first major military defeat after 1992, but Jamiat-i-Islami refused to return the city directly to him.

In response to this turn of events, Dostum met with representatives of Hizb-i-Islami and of Hizb-i-Wahdat in Azerbaijan in December 1993. Despite the ethnic and ideological differences between Junbish-i-Milli and Hizb-i-Islami in particular – the latter was calling for a strongly Islamic centralized state, whereas the former sought a more secular, regionalized government – they agreed to an alliance in late 1993 and launched a fight against Massoud's government in January 1994. Conforming to the theory's expectations, the junior alliance partner defected from the leading alliance when it became evident that the dominant partner would not share political power – thus, it was its relative power within the alliance that dictated the Junbish-i-Milli decision to join the opposing side. While Junbish-i-Milli appeared to be on the winning side with the Tajiks, the Tajiks could not credibly commit to sharing power.

However, this alliance was unable to unseat Jamiat-i-Islami and instead resulted in serious losses for Dostum – who had boasted that defeating Jamiat-i-Islami militarily would be easy, and that the "politics" would be the hard part. Dostum's forces quickly lost control of the Kabul air base and became bogged down in fighting on the outside of the city, resulting in the loss of up to 1,000 troops and 11 aircraft in sorties over northern Afghanistan.[32] Indeed, in its first six months of existence, the new Pashtun-Uzbek-Hazara alliance made no gains and the war largely stalemated, with uncertainty over which side had the advantage. It was at that time, specifically on May 28, 1994, that the war

---

[28] Davis (1994), p. 323; Goodson (2001), p. 74.
[29] Davis (1994), p. 324; Giustozzi (2009), p. 153.
[30] Giustozzi (2009), p. 166.
[31] Giustozzi (2009), p. 167; Davis (1994), p. 324.
[32] Davis (1994), p. 324.

witnessed its first instance of a group split. While Hazaras in the Hazarajat area of Afghanistan had maintained control of their stronghold, they were highly embattled in Kabul and experienced a leadership and geographic split. (The Hazara split is discussed in detail in the section on group fractionalization later in the chapter.)

Following that split, the situation on the ground pitted the Tajiks and the Hazara splinter group of Hizb-i-Wahdat (led by Akbari) against the joint forces of Pashtuns, Uzbeks, and the core group of Hizb-i-Wahdat (led by Mazari).[33] Intense fighting continued and in July 1994, the alliance of Hekmatyar, Mazari, and Dostum formed a commission to negotiate with Tajik President Rabbani. The negotiations had no tangible results and the fighting further stalemated through late 1994. At that point a fundamentalist Pashtun force called the Taliban made their appearance, increasingly marginalizing Hekmatyar's Hizb-i-Islami. (The rise of the Taliban is discussed in detail in the section on group fractionalization later in the chapter.)

1995–1996: Pashtuns (Taliban) + Hazaras (Mazari/Khalili) + Uzbeks vs. Tajiks + Hazaras (Akbari) + Pashtuns (Hekmatyar) (Taliban + Hizb-i-Wahdat-Mazari/Khalili + Junbish-i-Milli vs. Jamiat-i-Islami + Hizb-i-Wahdat-Akbari + Hizb-i-Islami)

In the initial years of the war (1992–1994), the fight over the capital was the determining factor of the power struggle between groups, and a reliable barometer of their relative power. However, things changed with the appearance of the Taliban, which made the conflict spill over to the broader Afghan stage. On November 5, 1994, the Taliban took over Afghanistan's second biggest city, Kandahar, and within three months – by February 15, 1995 – the movement ended the stalemate in the Afghan civil war. Importantly, the operations in Kandahar and Ghazni were described as quite advanced vis-à-vis former mujahedin activities. In particular, they exhibited a high degree of command and control and swift force movements, as well as an affinity for attacking at night.[34]

The result was the defeat or defection of a number of Pashtun mujahedin who had, as noted earlier, remained neutral on the national scene and – as will be discussed in depth in the group fractionalization section later – were keen on balancing against the strength of the Jamiat-i-Islami forces described earlier.[35] As such, the Taliban were also able to win over a number of Pashtun mujahedin who had been under Hekmatyar. In a further blow to Hekmatyar, this trend of ethnic affinity also included Pashtuns from the Khalq branch of

---

[33] The latter were also joined by other Pashtun side actors such as Gailani, Mojadidi, and Muhammadi. These actors had a highly limited role and for reasons of parsimony they are left out of the main chronology of events.

[34] Davis (1998), p. 54.

[35] Rashid (2000), pp. 32–35.

the Communist Party, who took over the skill-requiring sectors of mechanics, tank operators, and pilots.[36] Within a mere few months since their inception, the Taliban had captured twelve of Afghanistan's then thirty-two provinces and had effectively risen as the new Pashtun force.

However, all these were Pashtun areas in the south and east of the country, and until late 1994, the Taliban were still not seen as a national actor. Indeed, Massoud intentionally avoided conflict with the group and even sought nego-tiations with them because they were targeting Hekmatyar – the capture of Ghazni was purportedly carried out to protect the Jamiat-i-Islami-supported governor from a Hekmatyar offensive.[37] For example, following the Taliban's capture of Charasyab, government mechanics from Bagram provided assistance in repairing damaged aircraft in Taliban possession.[38] However, this attitude was quickly transformed as the Taliban made clear their national aspirations. The Taliban now wanted to move to territories in the west and north of the country – where Tajiks and Uzbeks had been in control – and also had their eyes set on the capital.

In mid-1995, the Taliban had 200 tanks and armored vehicles, as well as a 220-mm Uragan multiple rocket system – all left behind by Hekmatyar's forces. They also had twelve MiG 23s and more than a dozen helicopters, as well as twelve additional aircraft and a great deal of heavy ammunition, brand-new AK-47s, RPGs, and light machine guns.[39] Moreover, they had developed a new communications network and boasted an army of 15,000 that was to grow to 25,000 by early 1996. Meanwhile Massoud had three corps commands: the Central Corps based in Kabul, which was the best organized and had 15,000–20,000 men, the 6th Corps (Kunduz) covering the northeast, and the 5th Corps (Herat) covering the west.[40]

After taking over Hekmatyar's positions in Charasyab in February 1995, the Taliban were on the outskirts of the capital. But Kabul, which had been the main point of contention during the Jihad and the present intra-mujahedin war, was to prove a much harder target. The tricks of the trade that worked in the Pashtun south were not necessarily transferable to the type of warfare demanded in the capital, as Massoud's troops were highly skilled and battle-tested.[41]

In March 1995, the Taliban struck a deal with Mazari's Hazaras, who wanted to maintain a Pashtun ally against the Tajik forces and who were

[36] Davis (1998), p. 54; interview with Shahnawaz Tanai; interview with Abdul Malik.

[37] Azoy (2003), pp. 146–148.

[38] Ibid.

[39] The Taliban would disarm the forces in the areas they took over and thus their stockpile of weapons increased with their victories, especially in areas that had served as arms caches for Hekmatyar such as Spin Boldak and Charasyab. National Security Archive, Freedom of Information Act, Taliban File, Document 6, p. 7; Davis (1998), p. 61; Matinuddin (1999), pp. 49–50.

[40] Davis (1995), p. 317.

[41] Ibid.

willing to cut a deal with the Taliban in place of the marginalized Hekmatyar. The Taliban agreed to move into west Kabul and assist the Hazaras who were besieged by Massoud, under the condition that they hand over all their heavy weapons. Fighting continued and the Tajik forces repulsed the Taliban in what was to be their first major defeat.[42] In a disagreement that followed the Taliban's defeat in western Kabul, the Taliban killed Hazara leader Mazari. Karim Khalili, a Mazari disciple, rose as his successor.[43] By the end of 1995, the Taliban had been fully pushed back and the Afghan capital and northern territories were still under Tajik control.[44] At this moment, given the defeat of the Taliban and the improved force structure noted earlier, Jamiat-i-Islami seemed dominant, with analysts even predicting the potential disintegration of the Taliban at the time.[45]

In response to Jamiat-i-Islami's apparent strength, and in accordance with theoretical expectations, Dostum sought to maintain the Uzbek-Pashtun-Hazara alliance (known as Shura-i-Hamahangi – Coordinating Council) to balance against the triumphant Tajik-dominated government that had now also taken over the Hazara positions in western Kabul. With Hekmatyar discredited, Dostum flirted with the Taliban, considering them as the potential new Pashtun power in the alliance. Meanwhile the Taliban, undeterred by their defeat – and heavily supported by Pakistan – shifted their forces to the west (to Nimroz, Farah, and Herat provinces), as well as the east (to the city of Jalalabad and in Nangarhar province more broadly).[46] In the fight for control over west Afghanistan, and more specifically in the fight for Herat province, Dostum allegedly cooperated with Taliban forces. One of his generals, Rasul Pahlawan, assisted the Taliban in driving out Tajik government forces, providing air support from Shindand to the Taliban as they faced the Jamiat-i-Islami-allied forces of Ismael Khan.[47] Khalili, the new leader of the Hazaras, also assisted the Taliban from Bamyan province in central Afghanistan.[48] The Taliban took Herat in September 1995 after being pushed back in April. This victory gave them nearly 50 percent of the country, covering much of western and southern Afghanistan.[49] As a result, the threat against Tajiks was increasing with constant Taliban advances toward Kabul, although Massoud was able to turn back a number of advances at the end of 1995 and early 1996. At the time, Jamiat-i-Islami was receiving increasing support, including cash, arms, training resources, and transport planes from Russia, Iran, and the United States. Still, the Taliban were heavily financed by Pakistan and Saudi

---

[42] Interview with Mohammad Akbari; interview with Haji Mohammad Mohaqeq; Mousavi (1997), p. 200.
[43] Interview with Mohammad Akbari; interview with Haji Mohammad Mohaqeq.
[44] Davis (1996), p. 185.
[45] Ahady (1995), pp. 623–624; Davis (1995).
[46] Interview with Wahidullah Sabawoon.
[47] Davis (1998), p. 62; Griffin (2001), p. 45.
[48] Matinuddin (1999), p. 83.
[49] Goodson (2001), p. 77.

Arabia, the former of which, according to some reports, was bussing in tens of thousands of soldiers, refurbishing air strips, providing spare parts and arms, as well as providing resources such as food, fuel, pickup trucks, and rockets.[50]

Despite Hekmatyar's defeat at the hands of the Taliban, he pursued negotiations with the group to contain Jamiat-i-Islami. Talks between Hekmatyar and the Taliban held in January 1996 had no tangible results because the differences between the Pashtun factions ran too deep to allow for any compromise. Furthermore, they were vying over the same constituency, meaning that Hekmatyar's weakened, nonrepresentative party did not provide any incentive for the Taliban to ally with him.[51] As such, the Taliban continued its advances in late 1995 and early 1996, driving Hekmatyar out of his strongholds around Kabul. Indeed, the sweeping Taliban advance made Hekmatyar realize that his only option would be to join forces with the Tajiks, an alliance that he formally announced on March 9, 1996.

1996: Pashtuns (Taliban) vs. Tajiks + Uzbeks + Hazaras
(Taliban vs. Jamiat-i-Islami + Junbish-i-Milli + Hizb-i-Wahdat)

Despite the new addition to the Jamiat-i-Islami alliance, Kabul fell to the Taliban on September 27, 1996. This victory set the Taliban apart as the most powerful actor on the scene, opening the door to the Taliban's northern offensive.[52] During this march north, the Taliban made clear that they would not respect an autonomous region for Dostum: they had now obtained a great deal of airpower and thus did not need Dostum's air force.[53] The Taliban's increase in relative power, and indications that they were uninterested in sharing it, led to the reemergence of the Northern Alliance.[54] This alliance of all of Afghanistan's minority groups (Tajiks, Hazaras [both factions], and Uzbeks) was formalized as the Shura-i-Ali-i-Difa (Supreme Defense Council) on October 10, 1996, as a balancing act against the ascendant Taliban.[55] Dorronsoro aptly notes that the "conquest of the north... within the grasp of the Taliban, which already controlled around two-thirds of the country... obliged Jamiyat, Hezb-i-Wahdat, and Jombesh to form an alliance to counter the Taliban's thrust."[56] Just as the theory would predict, defections caused a balancing alliance to emerge against the Taliban, who because of their increased relative power could not credibly commit to sharing power with their junior alliance partners.

After the Northern Alliance was re-formed on October 10, it launched a full-on assault against the Taliban on October 12. It appeared that the new balance of power was fairly even. Indeed, in terms of numbers, by the end

---

[50] Rashid (2000), pp. 44–46, 200; Coll (2004), p. 345.
[51] Rashid (2001), p. 34; Rasanayagam (2003), p. 151.
[52] Davis (1998), p. 68.
[53] Rashid (2000), p. 52; Maley (2009), p. 192.
[54] Rashid (2000), pp. 49–51.
[55] Davis (1996), p. 553; Maley (2009), pp. 191–192.
[56] Dorronsoro (2005), p. 254.

of 1996, the Taliban were thought to have around 35,000 troops whereas both Massoud and Dostum had 20,000–25,000 troops each.[57] Further, the equality in armor and airpower was demonstrated by stalemate battles along the Salang highway, as well as the significant air battle that took place in Herat and Baghdis provinces.[58] As a result, through the end of the year and the beginning of 1997, the frontline oscillated between 25 and 75 kilometers north of Kabul.[59]

1997: Pashtuns (Taliban) + Uzbeks (Malik) vs. Tajiks + Hazaras (Taliban + Junbish-i-Milli-Malik vs. Jamiat-i-Islami + Hizb-i-Wahdat)

In early 1997, however, the momentum shifted back toward the Taliban, who had taken Parwan and Laghman provinces and overran the capital of what until then had been the Dostum-controlled province of Badghis. The Taliban advance was marked by severe economic consequences for the Shura-i-Ali-i-Difa. Indeed, by May 1997, Dostum was faced with food and supply shortages and had not paid his troops for five months.[60] The coming Taliban attack, combined with Dostum's alleged assassination of Rasul Pahlawan, precipitated what amounted to an Uzbek takeover – Dostum got sidelined by one of his headmen, Pahlawan's brother, Abdul Malik Pahlawan, who was serving as the head of the party's foreign affairs department.[61] (A detailed discussion of the Uzbek takeover follows in the group fractionalization section later in the chapter.)

Rumors about Malik cooperating with the Taliban started surfacing as early as October 1996 (i.e., soon after the Taliban takeover of Kabul). In particular, a number of observers argue that Pakistan played a central role in this defection, noting that Malik may have been promised control of Junbish-i-Milli and a substantial chunk of northern Afghanistan – including his base of Faryab – with the removal of Dostum.[62] On May 19, 1997, Malik raised the Taliban's white banner in Faryab's provincial capital of Maymana. Other disaffected Dostum commanders soon followed suit. Dostum fled to Uzbekistan on May 24, 1997, mere hours before the Taliban marched into Mazar-i-Sharif.

As the Taliban forces entered Mazar-i-Sharif on May 25, 1997, people in the northern provinces of Samangan, Baghlan, Kunduz, Takhar, and Badakhshan also raised the Taliban's white banner. Malik had the impression that the cooperation protocol he signed with the Taliban would involve extensive power-sharing with his forces in the north, because Taliban leaders had made statements to the effect that they intended to form a central government

---

[57] Davis (1998), p. 69.
[58] Rashid (2000), pp. 53–54.
[59] Goodson (2001), p. 78.
[60] Rashid (2000), p. 58.
[61] Davis (1997), p. 360.
[62] Maley (1998), p. 11; Rasanayagam (2003), p. 153; Maley (2009), p. 192.

in which all Afghan nationalities and ethnic groups would be respected.[63] Thus, Malik defected from the Northern Alliance and joined the Taliban in an effort to win the war while guaranteeing his group a significant share of postwar political power, in accordance with theoretical expectations.

1997: Pashtuns (Taliban) + defectors vs. Remaining Tajiks + Uzbeks + Hazaras
(Taliban + defectors vs. Remaining Jamiat-i-Islami + Junbish-i-Milli + Hizb-i-Wahdat)

The honeymoon, however, only lasted two days – until Malik understood that the Taliban's pledge to share power was just talk. At a meeting the Taliban commanders convened with Malik and his men in the Imam Ali shrine in Mazar-i-Sharif, they offered Malik the post of deputy foreign minister in the Kabul government – a lesser post than that of foreign minister, which he had held under Dostum's government – and demanded that Malik hand over 15,000 guns.[64] In his effort to ascertain the coalition's relative power, Malik had miscalculated. Fighting broke out in the Hazara neighborhoods first, and Malik quickly turned against the Taliban, cooperating with the local groups of Tajiks and Hazaras.[65] These forces succeeded in repulsing the Taliban three days after their entry into the city – with hundreds of bodies of Taliban fighters lying on the streets of Mazar-i-Sharif – and soon after regained control of four northern provinces (Takhar, Faryab, Jowzjan, and Sar-i-Pol).[66] Fighting was more intense in the northern provinces that had a strong Pashtun presence (Balkh and Kunduz).[67] Malik fled to Iran as Dostum returned in October of that year.

Nonetheless, a month later, in June 1997, the Taliban reasserted their power in the northern province of Kunduz, where local Pashtun chieftains had switched their allegiances to the Taliban.[68] Although Hizb-i-Wahdat and Massoud continued to fight, Junbish-i-Milli was significantly weakened by the 1997 takeover. As such, given the Taliban's successes against the joint forces of Hizb-i-Wahdat, Jamiat-i-Islami, and Junbish-i-Milli – and despite the temporary setback in Mazar-i-Sharif – the Taliban now appeared to be the clear winner, and the smaller warring actors bandwagoned on its side. By July 1998, the Taliban had taken over Faryab province, entering Balkh on July 31. In August 1998, the northern capital of Mazar-i-Sharif fell to the Taliban. The central Afghanistan area of Hazarajat followed suit in September 1998.[69]

---

[63] "Defecting general says Afghanistan won't threaten Russia, Central Asia," May 27, 1997, BBC Monitoring Service: Asia-Pacific, from ITAR-TASS news agency (World Service), Moscow (in English); interview with Abdul Malik.

[64] Rashid (2000), p. 58.

[65] Interview with Abdul Malik.

[66] Interview with Abdul Malik; Davis (1997), p. 362; Pratt (1998); Rashid (2001), p. 58.

[67] Rashid (2001), p. 59.

[68] Interview with Wahidullah Sabawoon; Davis (1997), p. 363.

[69] Davis (1998), pp. 20–22.

Akbari, the leader of the splinter faction of Hizb-i-Wahdat that had allied with the Tajiks since the Hazara split of 1994, now went into hiding, practically surrendering Hazarajat to the Taliban. By late 1998, the Taliban had control of roughly 90 percent of the country. Massoud's remaining forces withdrew to the northern provinces of Takhar and Badakhshan. They were to form the backbone of the American-assisted operation in October 2001, which expelled the Taliban from Kabul and Kandahar in mere months.

PAKISTAN'S INTERVENTION AND THE TALIBAN'S OUTRIGHT VICTORY

No analysis of the Taliban's outright victory in 1998 would be complete without some reference to Pakistan's intervention. After the 1989 Soviet withdrawal, Pakistan had claimed to be interested in supporting a power-sharing government for Afghanistan that would be representative of all mujahedin groups. Its policies on the ground, however, suggested that its true interests lay with a Pashtun victory.[70] That is why, much like in the time of the Jihad, Pakistan continued to support Hekmatyar and his party in the first period of the intra-mujahedin war. However, as Hekmatyar started losing, Pakistan had a change of heart. As suggested by Rashid: "[B]y 1994 [Hekmatyar] had clearly failed, losing ground militarily while his extremism divided the Pashtuns, the majority of whom loathed him. Pakistan was getting tired of backing a loser and was looking around for other potential Pashtun proxies."[71]

The late Benazir Bhutto, then in her second term as Pakistani prime minister, was interested in pursuing a policy on Afghanistan that would reconcile divergent views of the Pakistani army and the army's intelligence organization.[72] The Pakistani army, working from Peshawar, wanted to continue supporting Hekmatyar and Hizb-i-Islami, pursuing the safer policy of sticking with the devil they knew. On the other hand, the Pakistani intelligence agency ISI and their offices in Quetta and Kandahar had picked the Taliban as their new proxy of choice. The ISI view prevailed, and Pakistan shifted from its traditional and committed support to Hekmatyar – their partner of preference throughout the Jihad – to the Taliban, which had solid Pashtun credentials and no political baggage. There is no clear evidence that Pakistan was involved in the Taliban's inception per se, but it certainly featured in the Taliban's transformation from a movement of clerics from within the Jihad driven by their local agendas and supported by their peers to an organized political unit with countrywide objectives.[73]

Pakistan always argued that the aid it provided to the Taliban was of a non-lethal military nature – arguably only relief efforts and support with logistics

[70] Davis (1998), p. 18.
[71] Rashid (2001), p. 26.
[72] Coll (2004), p. 290.
[73] National Security Archive, Freedom of Information Act, Taliban File, Document 29, p. 4. Also Coll (2004), p. 292.

and communications.[74] However, the Taliban were known to have received both financial and military support from Pakistan. Rashid reports that "in 1997/8 Pakistan provided the Taliban with an estimated US$30 million in aid. This included 600,000 tons of wheat, diesel, petroleum and kerosene fuel which was partly paid for by Saudi Arabia, arms and ammunition, [aerial] bombs, maintenance and spare parts for its Soviet-era military equipment such as tanks and heavy artillery, [and] repairs and maintenance of the Taliban's air force."[75] Indeed, the movement exhibited notable financial solvency within months of its inception. U.S. officials reported in January 1995, "All visitors to Kandahar have told us they believe that the Taliban must have access to considerable funding.... Ex-communist militia officers ... reported the Taliban were able to offer salaries 'three times' that which commanders could pay."[76] Mullahs heading the cause consistently argued that the organization raised its funds through legitimate taxation over the populations under its control, even though there were no signs that any such taxes were actually being levied.[77]

Moreover, several members of the Taliban had studied in Pakistani madrasas in the North West Frontier Province bordering Afghanistan and therefore had clear connections with Pakistan. The Taliban were getting most of their training from former Jihadists and communist army officers in their ranks, but the Pakistanis also made a contribution in terms of logistical capacity and training. When it came to assistance, the Taliban certainly proved open to anyone willing to support their movement. As noted by a member of the Taliban shura: "All can help advise us."[78]

One should keep in mind that at the time of the Taliban's ascendance in late 1995–early 1996, the other warring parties were also getting material help from a range of different actors. All the different parties to the Northern Alliance were receiving assistance from states that saw the Northern Alliance as a last bastion against the spread of Taliban Islamism: Russia, Iran, India, and Uzbekistan were all allies.[79] Nevertheless – and as these other warring groups well understood – Pakistan's assistance to the Taliban was of a much greater magnitude.[80] With the decline of power of Hekmatyar and his party, Pakistan opted for a clear intervention to achieve shifting toward "a winner-takes-all-strategy."[81] As suggested earlier, support to the Taliban went beyond the

---

[74] National Security Archive, Freedom of Information Act, Taliban File, Document 14, p. 5; National Security Archive, Freedom of Information Act, Taliban File, Document 15, p. 3.

[75] Rashid (2000), pp. 183–184.

[76] National Security Archive, Freedom of Information Act, Taliban File, Document 6, p. 6.

[77] National Security Archive, Freedom of Information Act, Taliban File, Document 7, p. 5; National Security Archive, Freedom of Information Act, Taliban File, Document 6, p. 6.

[78] "Religious leaders gave broad policy direction to the Taliban while engineers and technocrats dealt with practical matters." National Security Archive, Freedom of Information Act, Taliban File, Document 7, p. 6.

[79] Rashid (2001), p. 200. Also see Coll (2004), p. 345 for discussion of source of money, arms, and other support.

[80] Davis (1998), pp. 70–71; Khalilzad and Byman (2000), p. 74.

[81] Davis (1997).

standard military assistance that was typically directed to client parties during the Jihad. Pakistan's intervention to achieve an all-out victory for the Pashtuns was also noted by the Northern Alliance forces, who observed the massive influx of Pakistani militants throughout the conflict, and in particular during the conquest of the north. For example, following the Taliban's expulsion from Mazaar in May 1997, hundreds of Pakistanis were captured by Northern Alliance forces.[82] This trend was also noted in U.S. intelligence reports, and the American ambassador had openly confronted the Pakistanis on the issue.[83]

But the Taliban, riding high on their victories, had no interest in a negotiated settlement. As suggested in declassified documents from the time:

Ghaus [member of the Taliban shura] said... war would not end until [Massood and Dostum] were disarmed. Taliban would continue to fight until all Afghans were dis-armed and the country secure.... The [US] ambassador replied that it was difficult for him to see how peace can be established when the Taliban were essentially demanding that the other side give up its arms to the Taliban and thus surrender on their terms. When Mullah Ghaus spoke of negotiation, he seemed to be speaking of negotiated sur-render. Ghaus shot back that "Dostam and Masood will have [to] submit to the will of God and the will of the people which are manifested in the Taliban movement." "We are the majority," he continued, "and in democracies minorities must always submit to the will of the majority".... The ambassador rejoined that democracies worked only if the rights of the minorities were protected and if there were rules to assure peaceful working out of conflict over interests. He concluded that it is not enough to provide other Afghans the opportunity to surrender through negotiations; so long as the Taliban believe they can win everything and control all of Afghanistan, the war will continue.[84]

There is therefore strong evidence to suggest that Pakistan's massive military aid and clear intervention on the part of the Taliban – with the objective of a Pashtun outright victory – were what allowed the Taliban to achieve their victory against other warring parties in 1998.

CAPTURING RELATIVE POWER CHANGE

The discussion so far of relative power changes in terms of the political, eco-nomic, and military standing of the involved factions suggests that Afghan civil war alliances were motivated by tactical considerations. Alliances were driven by a desire on the part of the groups to maximize their chances of victory while staying as strong as possible within the winning alliance. Given the fog of civil war, and the sizable informational uncertainties involved, war-ring groups, which used the battlefield as an extension of the bargaining pro-cess (as indicated in the previously presented timeline), had to update their views of the distribution of relative power, switching alliances as the fighting unfolded.

---

[82] Rashid (2001), p. 59.
[83] National Security Archive, Freedom of Information Act, Taliban File, Document 19, p. 10.
[84] Ibid, pp. 13–14.

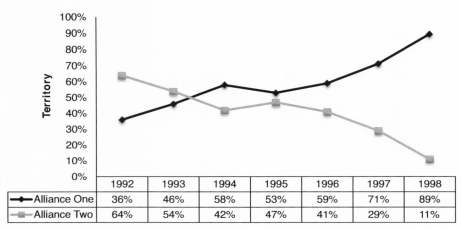

	1992	1993	1994	1995	1996	1997	1998
◆ Alliance One	36%	46%	58%	53%	59%	71%	89%
▣ Alliance Two	64%	54%	42%	47%	41%	29%	11%

FIGURE 3.1. Changes in Territorial Control among Warring Alliances in the Afghan Intra-Mujahedin War

Because of data constraints that preclude the collection of granular longitudinal political, economic, and military measures for this period of the Afghan conflict, this section takes a different approach to verifying the robustness of the earlier findings. In this section, power is operationalized using data on territorial control. Territorial changes among the warring groups over time were coded by triangulating information from primary sources of each of the competing sides for each year and district and were also cross-referenced in the secondary literature. These territorial changes are calculated in square kilometers and spatially presented in GIS (see relevant maps at the end of this section). Territorial wins and losses are also consistent with the (limited) information on the military assets of each warring side, loosely defined to include weapons, communications, logistics, and so on as referenced in the preceding section.

As indicated in the timeline of the war, warring groups largely formed balancing coalitions. Moving from the level of group to the more aggregate level of alliance, this balancing dynamic becomes even clearer. Figure 3.1 presents the power distribution among the two alliances over the war's trajectory, as proxied by territorial control. The figure clearly indicates that power was largely shared (i.e., fluctuated around 50%) for the first five years of the war, until there was decisive external intervention by Pakistan. Once the external intervener clearly signaled the winner, bandwagoning behavior among warring parties became apparent.

This finding is also apparent from the maps on territorial change, which graphically capture the cyclical dynamic of alliance formation and breakdown until outside intervention occurred. The purpose of these maps is to show that alliances appear to have been largely balancing from 1992 to 1996 (Maps 3.1–3.5), with instances of bandwagoning only becoming apparent in 1997 (Map 3.6) – with the forceful and determinant Pakistani intervention on the side of the Taliban, which resulted in victory in 1998 (Map 3.7).

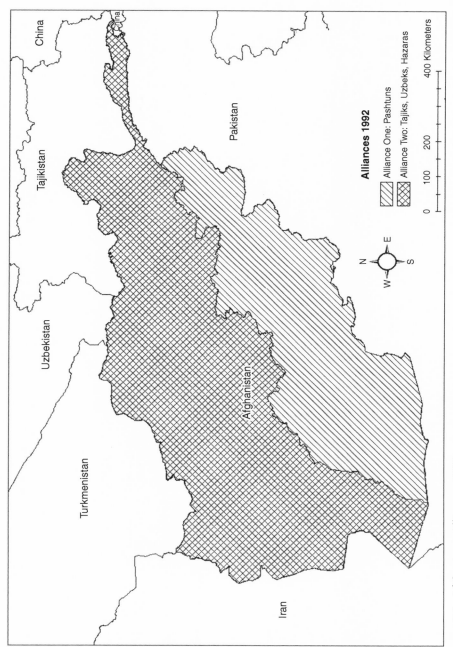

MAP 3.1. Afghanistan Alliances, 1992

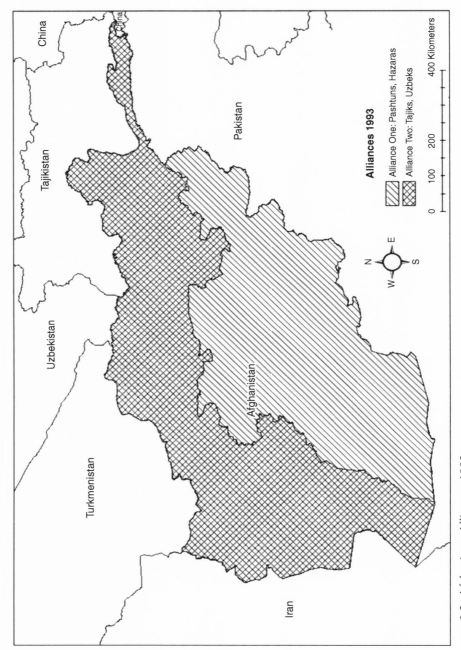

MAP 3.2. Afghanistan Alliances, 1993

Alliances 1993

Alliance One: Pashtuns, Hazaras

Alliance Two: Tajiks, Uzbeks

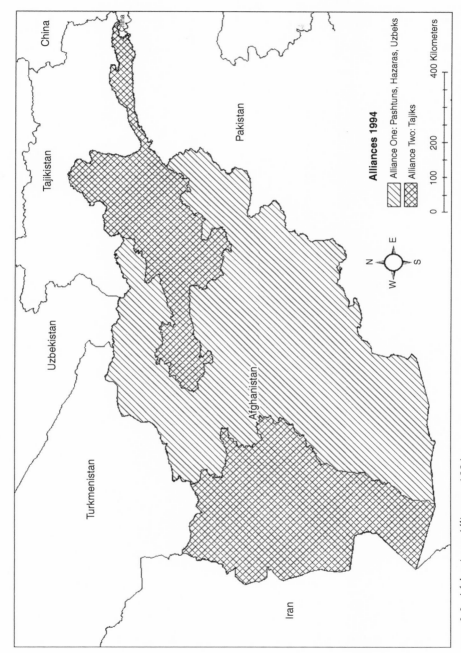

MAP 3.3. Afghanistan Alliances, 1994

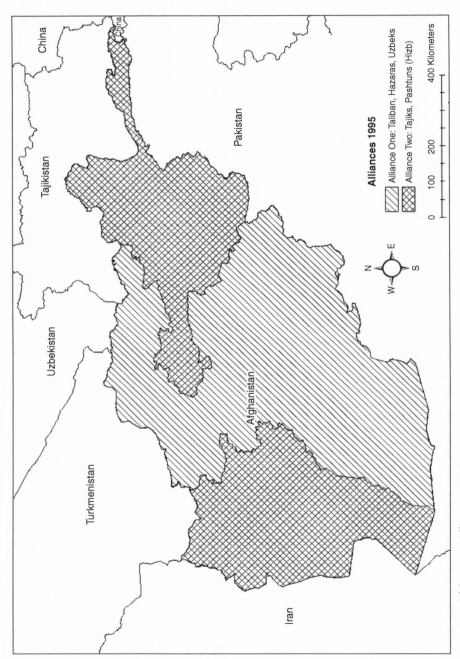

MAP 3.4. Afghanistan Alliances, 1995

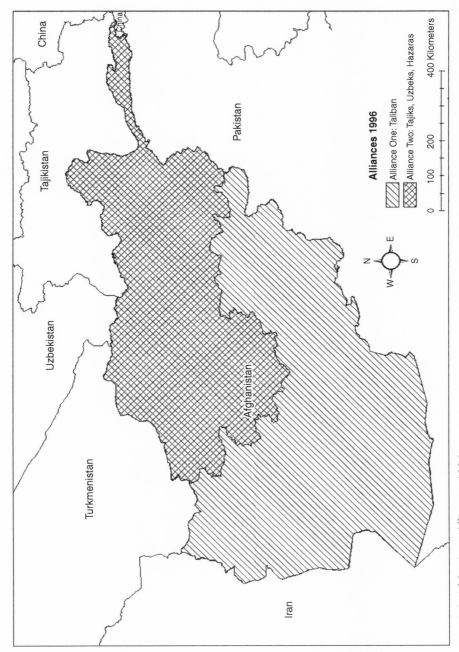

MAP 3.5. Afghanistan Alliances, 1996

81

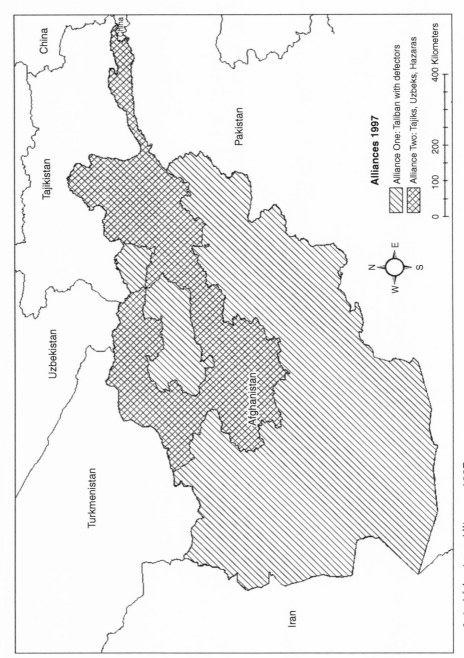

MAP 3.6. Afghanistan Alliances, 1997

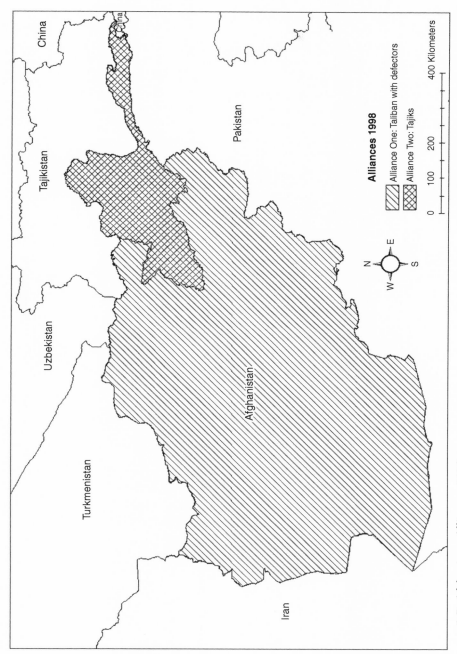

MAP 3.7. Afghanistan Alliances, 1998

Alliances 1998

Alliance One: Taliban with defectors

Alliance Two: Tajiks

0   100   200   300   400 Kilometers

China

Tajikistan

Uzbekistan

Turkmenistan

Iran

Afghanistan

Pakistan

China

CIVIL WAR ALLIANCE NARRATIVES: THE STORIES THEY TOLD

In the more than 8,000 pages of declassified Guantanamo Bay testimony, one finds references to an array of cleavages that appear to have played a role in the Afghan civil war.[85] According to one detainee, the Afghan civil war "was an ethnic war between the North and the South, Farsi and Pashtu."[86] Another argues that "the Afghanistan people were fighting for money."[87] Yet a third, detainee 1004, suggests that "the purpose was fighting Massoud and Dostum and helping Muslims... Dostum is known for helping and cooperating with the Russians.... [He] is not a Muslim, he is a communist."[88] Indeed, the stories with the most adherents appear to fall in three categories: stories suggesting that the war was fought for economic reasons,[89] others suggesting that it was fought for ascriptive reasons (as determined by linguistic or religious/sectarian divides),[90] and still others proposing ideological reasons.[91]

In the midst of it all, there were some detainees who claimed that the long cohabitation among groups and their years of interaction had created an array of differences and commonalities on a range of issues, be those ethnic, ideological, or economic. As stated by detainee 1154: "It is necessary to mention that from long before and especially because of war and killings there are numerous differences. Conflicts and fanaticism based on tribal, language, and religious, ideological, political and territorial differences exist."[92] This suggestion is consistent with the extensive gamut of narratives that surfaced in justification of the various Afghan civil war alliances.

Drawing from interviews conducted in Afghanistan with personalities who experienced the intra-mujahedin war in leading capacities, this section presents the various sets of narratives that accompanied the war's divergent alliances. The array of ethnic cross-cutting cleavages in Afghanistan allowed for a wide range of ethnic narratives that were pursued first. Where inadequate, they were in turn supplemented by ideologically and economically inspired vignettes. If no ethnic, ideological, or economic shared narrative could be recalled, shared-enemy narratives, demonizing the common foe, would take center stage. These narratives, discussed in chronological order in this section, provide interesting insights into the Afghan intra-mujahedin war, showing the instrumental use of shared identity by all sides in the conflict.

---

[85] Through Freedom of Information Act requests, the U.S. government has declassified named testimony of Guantanamo Bay Detainees (hereafter "Guantanamo Bay Named Testimony") and documents submitted on their behalf to the Combatant Status Review Tribunal and the Administrative Review Board (hereafter "ARB Transcript").

[86] Guantanamo Bay Named Testimony, Set One, p. 68.

[87] ARB Transcript, Set One, p. 144.

[88] Guantanamo Bay Named Testimony, Set Four, pp. 26, 28.

[89] ARB Transcript, Set Eleven, p. 247.

[90] ARB Transcript, Set Three, pp. 81, 96; Guantanamo Bay Named Testimony, Set Four, p. 40.

[91] ARB Transcript, Set One, pp. 166, 169; Guantanamo Bay Named Testimony, Set Two, p. 54.

[92] ARB Transcript, Set Eleven, p. 266.

1992: MINORITIES UNITE

The first wartime alliance sprang up in March 1992 and brought together the Tajiks, the Uzbeks, and the Hazaras. This was seen as a unique opportunity for the minority groups to rise up against the historically dominant Pashtuns.[93] Drawing from an entrenched Pashtun-versus-non-Pashtun cleavage prominent in Afghan history and politics, the minority group identifier served as the lowest common ethnic denominator connecting the Tajiks, the Uzbeks, and the Hazaras, who do not collectively share any racial, linguistic, or religious characteristics. As Mohaqeq, the local chieftain of the Hazaras of the north who played a leading role in the fighting in the Mazar-i-Sharif area, told me in an interview, "All of us minority people of the north came together in a natural alliance."[94]

Hekmatyar in turn came up with a set of reasons in justification of his choice for opposition. He rejected cooperation with the Uzbeks on the grounds that they had been communists, proclaiming that Hizb-i-Islami's proud Pashtun mujahedin fighters would never cooperate with groups that allowed former communists in their ranks. In a now-infamous phone communication between Massoud and Hekmatyar before the 1992 takeover of Kabul, Hekmatyar told Massoud how he would not allow communists "to pollute our victory," and how he "must enter Kabul and let the green flag fly over the capital" – a clear reference to the Islamic color of green as juxtaposed to the communist red.[95] The rejection of the Uzbeks on the grounds that they had been communist is particularly ironic, given that Hizb-i-Islami had previously welcomed all ethnic Pashtuns who were communists. More specifically, and as referenced in detail in the earlier timeline, there were complete garrisons and battalions of ethnic Pashtuns from the communist militias who joined the Hizb forces en masse. Meanwhile, Hekmatyar's objection to allying with the Hazaras was, according to his vocal statements, largely sectarian. For example, he was openly opposed to a "Shi'a system of law."[96]

1993: HAZARAS (HIZB-I-WAHDAT) JOINING PASHTUNS (HIZB-I-ISLAMI), THEIR HISTORIC ARCHRIVALS

Despite former claims of adamant opposition to the implementation of a Shiite system of law, Hekmatyar had to put his foot in his mouth in January 1993, ten months after the war's breakout, when he was confronted with the strategic value of an impending Pashtun-Hazara alliance. He struck a deal with Mazari,

---

[93] Interviews with Abdullah Abdullah, Mohammad Akbari, Nur Mohammad Atta, Haji Mohammad Mohaqeq, Yunus Qanooni, Sima Samar, Thomas Ruttig, Eckhart Schiewek, and Michael Semple, among others.
[94] Interview with Haji Mohammad Mohaqeq.
[95] The original transcript of this communication is in the author's possession. This communication is also recounted in Coll (2004), p. 236.
[96] Roy (1995), p. 99.

in what amounted to the most surprising wartime alliance. Indeed, the Pashtuns and the Hazaras differ on three main ethnic characteristics: race, language, and religion. Moreover, in terms of their position in the ethnic power hierarchy, Pashtuns have almost exclusively been Afghanistan's ruling group, whereas Hazaras have always been the country's most disenfranchised and exploited group.[97]

Given the lack of any ethnic links between Pashtuns and Hazaras, all ethnic references were suppressed. The narrative that emerged was predominantly anticommunist, building on the groups' shared past as mujahedin during the Jihad. Hekmatyar argued that Pashtuns and Hazaras had a history of good cooperation that was solidified during the Jihad and their heroic fight against the communists. A commander affiliated with Hekmatyar recalled that "we told our Pashtun people to remember how their Hazara brothers had, like us, strongly resisted against the communist enemies."[98] An interesting anecdote on the Hazara-Pashtun alliance, related by an expert on Afghanistan who lived in the country during the intra-mujahedin war, highlights the comfort of Hekmatyar's Pashtuns in their alliance with the Hazaras and their fear of other Pashtun forces (those of Abdul Rasul Sayyaf's Ittihad-i-Islami), who were at the time allied with the Tajiks:

Very soon after the Hizb-i-Islami and Hizb-i-Wahdat alliance [in January 1993], I traveled on the road from Beshud through to Maidanshahr, a route which had been closed for most of the time up to that alliance, since it was lying on the ethnic fault line of what up to now had been opposing forces [Pashtuns and Hazaras]. I arranged for some Hizb-i-Islami Pashtuns to come up to the last secure Hazara area and they escorted me down as far as Maidanshahr. Once there, I was in a solidly Pashtun, Hizb-i-Islami area. Interestingly enough, while in transit, the Hizb-i-Islami people were worried for their personal safety vis-à-vis the Ittihad-i-Islami actors [who are also ethnic Pashtuns but allied with the Tajiks]. You had the intra-ethnic factional worry [Pashtuns being afraid of other Pashtuns], while they were quite happy and comfortable in Hazara-land![99]

The Hazara side also sustained this alliance narrative and devised further ways to reinforce it. For instance, they made sure to honor Pashtun commanders for their courage on the battlefield. Mazari [the Hazara leader] even went as far as to honor Zardat Faryadi, one of the most infamous Hizb-i-Islami commanders.[100]

---

[97] Dupree (1980); Poladi (1989); Mousavi (1997).

[98] Interview with Wahidullah Sabawoon; interview with Haji Mohammad Mohaqeq; interview with Mohammad Mangal.

[99] Interview with Michael Semple.

[100] There are allegations that Hizb-i-Islami commander Zardat was involved in incidents of murder, rape, and torture, as well as looting of United Nations and Red Cross aid and medical convoys. "Afghan Ex Warlord Living in London," *The Tribune, India, On-Line Edition*, July 28, 2000, http://www.tribuneindia.com/2000/20000728/world.htm, accessed May 23, 2006.

1994–1995: THE COMMUNIST UZBEKS (JUNBISH-I-MILLI) ON THE SIDE OF THE MUJAHEDIN

The Jihadist narrative lasted for almost a year, until the embattled Pashtun-Hazara alliance realized that it was in a precarious position against the steadily rising Tajiks. The Uzbeks, dissatisfied with their junior partner status into which the increasing Tajik power had relegated them, switched sides and joined the Pashtun and Hazara alliance camp in January 1994. The mujahedin were now forming an alliance with the communists they had claimed to revile. Even though Hekmatyar had vocalized his contempt for the Uzbeks' communist past, in January 1994 he proceeded to welcome them in the alliance. Now the Jihadist narrative and rhetoric of the Hazara-Pashtun alliance was suppressed, as it could not accommodate the newly initiated Uzbek allies, who were former communists. There were no commonly shared ethnic or ideological narratives that could be readily used to justify the new Pashtun-Hazara-Uzbek alliance, so the narrative that took center stage was one targeted against the shared enemy, the Tajiks.

According to Dostum's leading advisor, Faizullah Zaki, the Uzbeks, Pashtuns, and Hazaras formed the Shura-i-Hamahangi (Coordinating Council) "to counter Tajik repression and arrogance."[101] Hazara rhetoric from the time also focused on the exploitative nature of the present Tajik-dominated government, completely burying the issue of past Pashtun domination. As indicated in one of Mazari's fiery speeches against President Rabbani's Tajik-dominated government: "We simply want to crush the monster of monopoly."[102] In turn, Tajik wartime President Rabbani, commenting on the Hazara decision to break up with them and join Hekmatyar's Hizb-i-Islami, stated:

I told him [Mazari] that he should be with the government and he said "No, I have guns and I will fight for the Hazaras with these weapons and these guns".... And they [Pashtuns, Uzbeks, and Hazaras] accused us that the government was all Tajik. Only the Defense Ministry and the President were in the hands of Tajiks – all other ministries were with others, Pashtuns, Hazaras, Uzbeks and others. Some people only think about themselves, and some people think about the national interest...those with us were people of principle... Mazari, Dostum and Hekmatyar were people of interest.[103]

Meanwhile, Junbish-i-Milli – the main Uzbek party led by General Dostum, who took great pride in the party's pan-Turkic identity – developed slogans and symbols emphasizing cooperation with all ethnic groups, conveniently shifting

---

[101] Interview with Faizullah Zaki.
[102] Mazari wartime speech. Text available at http://www.hazarapress.com/best_choice_of_politics/mazari.htm, accessed May 1, 2008.
[103] Interview with Burhannudin Rabbani.

narratives away from former allies to newly attained ones.[104] According to an Afghanistan expert commenting on the Uzbek-Pashtun alliance:

I talked with Pashtun officers who served with Dostum throughout that Uzbek-Pashtun alliance period [starting in January 1994]. They all stressed that Dostum himself personally and consistently took a stance just to demonstrate the possibility of ethnic cooperation between Uzbeks, Hazaras, and Pashtuns.... Many of these officers served very loyally because they believed that this was what he was doing.... He would do crazy things like send his plane down to Logar [in Pashtun-dominated southeastern Afghanistan] to pick up commanders and bring them to Sheberghan [in Uzbek-majority northwestern Afghanistan] just for dinner, to stress how well the Uzbeks are doing with the Pashtuns.... So you've got the Junbish-i-Milli political and military leadership bending over backwards on one level of its politics to stress that the different ethnicities all love each other based on who it is allied with.... The fact that they have these multiple levels of identity proved very convenient for re-alliance purposes.[105]

The Coordinating Council remained in alliance even after the Pashtun takeover prompted by the appearance of the Taliban. The Hazaras and Uzbeks, though originally wary of their new Pashtun ally, decided to give the alliance some more time. And time proved them wrong: The Taliban started to rise aggressively in power, in ways that resulted in sizable violence and threatened them with complete subordination.

1996: ALL AGAINST ONE: THE TALIBAN

The continuous increase in the Taliban's power, as indicated in the sacking of Kabul in September 1996, prompted the balancing realliance of Tajiks, Uzbeks, and Hazaras. The Tajiks, who had been fighting the Hazaras and Uzbeks for years, found themselves reunited in light of the new Pashtun threat. The narrative was again a narrative of northern minorities against Pashtuns of the south, the latter supporting the Taliban in droves. The minority narrative, which became popularly known as the Northern Alliance, was buttressed with stories of Taliban ethnic and racial intolerance and religious fundamentalism. Interviews with minority opposition leaders from the time reference the Taliban's fundamentalism and lack of cultural sensitivity, their inability to speak the Dari language, and their desire to implant their own southern Pashtuns as administrators in certain of the minority areas they would take under their control.

1998: TALIBAN VICTORY

The anti-Taliban alliance narrative was sustained until the Taliban received decisive and forceful support from Pakistan in late 1996. This resulted in a surge in Taliban power that led to more territorial gains and a clear trajectory for victory. The leaders of the Northern Alliance either took refuge in the

---

[104] Interview with Faizullah Zaki; Williams (2006), p. 16.
[105] Interview with Michael Semple.

intractable Panjshir valley (such as the Tajik leader Massoud) or escaped to neighboring countries (such as Dostum, who took refuge in Uzbekistan and Turkey). The Tajik, Uzbek, and Hazara local leaders who bandwagoned on the side of the Taliban suggested to their constituents that they were doing so because the Taliban were a force that could bring peace and prosperity to the war-torn country.

Akbari, who had split from the main Hizb-i-Wahdat Hazara faction and had fought on the side of the Tajik government against the Pashtuns of Hekmatyar, was a strange bedfellow for the Taliban. As late as January 1997, he was staunchly proclaiming that the Islamic parties in the north would never cooperate with the Taliban, given the latter's extreme Wahabi positions and intolerance toward Shiites.[106] This intolerance was further manifested in massacres perpetrated by the Taliban against the Hazaras in northern Afghanistan, close to the Mazar-i-Sharif area.[107] However, in late 1998, when the Taliban were on their victorious march, Akbari changed his mind. This unlikely alliance further highlights the primacy of relative power considerations over notions of shared identity and underlines wartime alliances' lack of integrity and persistence.[108] In an interview in his Karte-Se office in Kabul, Akbari recounted the rationale behind his decision:

In the year 1377 solar [1998], Kandahar, Herat, Kabul, and the north had already been captured by the Taliban and 95 percent of Hazarajat was surrounded. Hazaras had only two options: either to continue the war and the resistance or let the Taliban become their master. But I didn't think resistance was possible. We had neither weapons nor power for resistance, and six years of fighting had brought people to their knees . . . I stopped resisting and . . . joined the people [reaeyat] of the Taliban and Mullah Omar. . . . Before the Jihad Hazaras had a legacy of good cooperation with Pashtuns in Hazarajat . . . I was thinking we could find a way of mutual understanding for peace and prosperity.[109]

Indeed, local Hazara elites, who one might have expected to fight hard to keep out the Taliban, instead reinvented themselves, stressing how their respective Hazara and Pashtun grandfathers had known each other for years and had always cooperated: "The Hazaras as the loyal tenants and the Pashtuns as the local lords. . . . You got a narrative of economic solidarity between the Hazara peasants and the Pashtun landlords in these nomad areas."[110]

GROUP FRACTIONALIZATION

Apart from the effect on alliances, the shifting fortunes of war, fought both in the national capital and the provinces, confronted warring groups with episodes

---

[106] Rashid (2000), p. 74; Rashid (2001), p. 69.
[107] The bloody Hazara-Taliban fight in May 1997 in Mazar-i-Sharif, won by the Hazaras, is one of those infamous fights. Another is the Hazara massacre, perpetrated outside Mazar-i-Sharif in the fall of 1998 in retaliation for the May 1997 lost battle in that area.
[108] Interview with Thomas Ruttig.
[109] Interview with Mohammad Akbari.
[110] Interview with Michael Semple; interview with Mohammad Akbari.

TABLE 3.2. *Group Fractionalization in the Intra-Mujahedin War*

Year	Group Fractionalization	Manifestation
1994	Hazara Split	Mazari and Akbari leadership dispute
1994–1995	Pashtun Takeover	Taliban marginalize Hizb-i-Islami
1997	Uzbek Takeover	Malik mutinies against Dostum

of power loss. But despite the waxing and waning of power among the different warring factions, only a subset of these episodes led to group fractionalization, arguably the ones that seriously compromised the standing of the group in the war effort. Indeed, after qualitatively evaluating all warring groups on the level of losses sustained and the degree of subgroup control maintained for each year in the Afghan civil war's trajectory, I identified three instances of group fractionalization – one amounting to a group split and two to takeovers – summarized in Table 3.2. This variation offers a notable degree of richness that in turn allows for the illustration of the mechanisms and processes behind group fractionalization.

In each subcase of group fractionalization discussed, I identify (1) whether a warring group is comprised of distinct prewar subgroups; (2) whether a warring group is facing notable or unequal losses among its subgroups that seriously undermine the group's power base; and (3) the extent of subgroup control the warring group has maintained following a split or a takeover. To do so, I rely heavily on primary sources and interviews with personalities directly involved in the events leading up to their group's fractionalization. I then triangulate my information by looking at journalistic coverage as well as secondary source accounts from the time.

The 1994 Hazara (Hizb-i-Wahdat) Split

As discussed in detail in the timeline presented earlier, in the first stage of the Afghan intra-mujahedin war, in April 1992, the Hazaras expanded their power base by occupying much of western Kabul and securing a place in the ruling coalition. Starting in June 1992, as conflict in Kabul escalated, the Hazaras found themselves on the defensive. The Hazara-Uzbek-Tajik alliance, which was the main military power behind the new regime in the capital, collapsed a mere few months after its inception over internal disagreements on the sharing of control in Kabul.[111] Initially alienated by their more powerful ally – the Tajiks – and then directly attacked by them, Hizb-i-Wahdat had fought hard to hold their ground. Their losses were notably asymmetric. The Hazara enclave in west Kabul was under constant attack, a siege symbolized by the infamous Afshar massacre. Meanwhile they suffered no more than brief raids in their main hinterland in Hazarajat. The heavy Hizb-i-Wahdat losses in the capital were effectively described in the party's official bulletin:

---

[111] Davis (1993), p. 136.

February [1994] marked the first anniversary of the Afshar massacre.... The intervening period has unfortunately shown that the episode was but an example of what was to follow.... The government [Jamiat-i-Islami] has since relentlessly attacked various areas of Kabul under the control of its rivals.... The massacre was a well planned assault, introducing a new dimension to the government's relentless decimation of its Shi'a opposition.[112]

During a speech on the anniversary of the massacre, Abdul Ali Mazari, Hizb-i-Wahdat's Secretary General at the time, confirmed the high losses sustained since in the broader Kabul area: "During the last 18 months [we have had] 2,000 martyrs, 16,000 injured, over 700 captives taken and over 4,000 homes destroyed."[113] Meanwhile, Hazarajat was facing no such losses, with the Hazaras in that area and period of time living in peace, as further corroborated by a UN traveling mission.[114] Because of the notable asymmetry in losses, Hizb-i-Wahdat proved susceptible to in-group fractionalization over disagreements on the party's alliance choices. This resulted in a split among the Hazaras into two subgroups under different leadership, each of which maintained control of its respective constituents in Kabul and Hazarajat through distinct political and military organizations.[115]

The split's geographic dimension (Kabul versus Hazarajat) was compounded by a preexisting leadership dispute between Abdul Ali Mazari and Mohammad Akbari. Mazari and Akbari had notable differences dating back to the days of the Jihad against the Soviets, when each of them headed separate Hazara factions, Sazman-i-Nasr (Victory Organization) and Sepah-i-Pasdaran (Revolutionary Guards), respectively. Both parties had roughly 1,500 members in their cadres, but Sazman-i-Nasr had a higher support base of 4,000 as compared to the 2,000 members of Sepah-i-Pasdaran.[116] In 1989, both Mazari and Akbari had agreed to the creation of Hizb-i-Wahdat as a way to unify the nine Shiite mujahedin parties that had existed during the Jihad, and Hizb-i-Wahdat entered the political scene with a single, reconciliatory ideology.

The split materialized in September 1994 after tense leadership elections. Each side wanted to hold the elections in its respective power center, Hazarajat for Akbari and Kabul for Mazari. Mazari prevailed not only in his choice of venue, but also in the elections, receiving forty-three votes to Akbari's thirty-three. Mazari was elected Secretary General and Akbari Chairperson of the party's Central Committee. At that meeting, Mazari defended his view that Hizb-i-Wahdat should stay in the present alliance with Hizb-i-Islami and Junbish-i-Milli, while Akbari, citing severe Hazara losses in west Kabul, was in favor of aligning with Jamiat-i-Islami.[117] Right after the elections, Akbari was accused of planning a coup with the intent to take over the Hazara leadership

---

[112] *Wahdat News Bulletin* (March 1994), pp. 2, 4.
[113] Ibid., p. 8.
[114] *Wahdat News Bulletin* (August 1994), p. 4.
[115] Interview with Haji Mohammad Mohaqeq; interview with Mohammad Akbari.
[116] Interview with Haji Mohammad Mohaqeq; interview with Mohammad Akbari.
[117] Interview with Sarwar Jawadi.

and was preemptively rebuffed by Mazari.[118] Within weeks of the elections, Akbari was heading his own Hizb-i-Wahdat ranks and was in full alliance with the ruling Tajiks.

After the split, Mazari retained the allegiance of most of the Hazara fighting units in West Kabul, Yakaolang, Hazara parts of Wardak province, and in Mazar-i-Sharif, and was generally successful in maintaining recognition as the official leader of Wahdat. Meanwhile, Akbari ran a splinter group under the same name across the Hazara hinterland, with the support of commanders who had previously been active in his Sepah-i-Pasdaran faction. Akbari could count on the loyalty of the two districts of his home area, Panjab and Waras, and on Hazara enclaves of Uruzgan, Helmand, and Saripol provinces. In terms of resources, Akbari's group was receiving supplies from his alliance with Massoud, while Mazari was receiving significant donations from wealthy Hazara businessmen and from his alliance with Hekmatyar and later on with Dostum.

Even though the two Hazara groups that surfaced after the split had distinct power bases, there were no clear sub-ethnic differences between their supporters – in other words, no divergent local identities or tribal differences. The respective subgroups thus devised narratives to justify the split to their constituents. Akbari, who was affiliated with the Tajik-led government, claimed to be fighting for national unity and cast himself as a multiethnic leader.[119] In turn, Mazari, whose followers called him Baba (father), claimed to be on a crusade for equal rights for the Hazaras and labeled Akbari's Hazaras as traitors who were bowing down to the Tajik rulers and were motivated by personal interest.[120] Commenting on the intra-Hazara fighting, Akbari attacked Mazari's credibility and ethnic leverage by claiming that Mazari had usurped the rights of the Hazaras, was not interested in the Afghan nation, and was not a good Muslim. In Akbari's own words from the time:

Dear long-suffering citizens of Kabul and tragedy-stricken people of west Kabul.... Unfortunately, we are witnessing outbreaks of fighting in the west of Kabul, where the hungry and tragedy-stricken people have suffered the pains of fighting in the past two and a half years.... Who set alight the flames of war? Naturally, it is Mr. Mazari who has set alight the flames of war. The fighting is no one else's fault. The main reason for past clashes, during which we suffered and sustained casualties, as far as I know, was the obstinacy and ambition of Mr. Mazari.... This conflict was a coup d' etat by Mr. Mazari and his special gang against the majority of Shiite and Hazara people.... My request from our ulema ... is to have a feeling of responsibility and organize a delegation to come to the country, to the capital, to the west of Kabul, to see how Mr. Mazari is playing with Islam, the fate of people and the nation. To see how he and his associates have taken people hostage. How they have shed the blood of their people savagely. How they plunder people's homes and properties. They even plunder the homes of ulema [legal scholars].[121]

---

[118] Interview with Sarwar Jawadi.
[119] Interview with Mohammad Akbari.
[120] Emadi (2006).
[121] "Hezb-e-Wahdat Official Blames Mazari for West Kabul Fighting," September 22, 1994, BBC Monitoring Service: Asia-Pacific, Radio Afghanistan, Kabul, in Dari.

In turn, Mazari's faction called the opposing Shi'ite camp reactionaries, blaming them for the Kabul attacks: "Reactionary Shi'ism, servile by nature and essence... kissed the hand that shed the blood of our people's sons.... Following the utter failure of fascism's assaults on our people, it was the forces [of] reactionary Shi'ism which continued to encourage the enemy to [attack] and conquer West Kabul."[122]

After their west Kabul defeat and Mazari's assassination by the Taliban, Khalili managed to reassemble the Hizb-i-Wahdat forces and by mid-1995 had reasserted his control over Bamyan province, moving his center from Kabul to Hazarajat. Akbari attempted compromise talks with Khalili in Bamyan in May 1995. The talks, however, proved fruitless, and on June 21, 1995, Akbari's faction, backed by Massoud's government forces, took over Bamyan by force. In the meantime, the Taliban was on the rise, and the original overtures for what ended up being (a year later) the Hazara-Tajik-Uzbek alliance (known as Shura-i-Ali-i-Difa) were being put into place. Various efforts were made to reunite the Hazara groups, and reconciliatory narratives surfaced. According to statements made in Iran on August 23, 1995 by Mostafa Kazemi, chief of the military committee of Akbari's Hizb-i-Wahdat faction:

He [Kazemi] said that Hezb-e Wahdat-e Eslami should isolate the warmongers within that party and said some party members dragged the Shi'i community to fratricide rather than take revenge on the murderers of Abdol Ali Mazari [leader of alternate Wahdat party who died on 13th March 1995 while in Taliban custody]...

We have no choice but to create the atmosphere of brotherhood and unity within Hezb-Wahdat-e Eslami for the sake of the Muslims' dignity and national solidarity.... The mission of the representative of the Islamic Revolution, Hojatoleslam Ebrahimi, has served to convene representatives of the two factions.... They are studying ways of establishing ceasefire and reconciliation...

He also indirectly linked the reunification of the two Hazara parties with a broader alliance for peace in Afghanistan.[123] There were several other speeches that sprang up in the same spirit, arguing that the broader reconciliation of the Hazaras would contribute to the reconciliation among other Afghan groups. According to another Akbari deputy, Rahmatullah Murtazawi, in testimony before the U.S. Congress:

[D]ifferent ethnic groups, as well as Sunni and Shiite groups in Afghanistan, all consider themselves as united and sharing common destiny and having the same wishes for the prosperity of Afghanistan. The majority of the Wahdat Party are indeed Hazara Shia's, because of geographical and historical reasons. We are, however, sure that the only way

---

[122] "The Great 'Ustad' Mazari," http://millatehazara.tripod.com/mazari.html, accessed May 25, 2006.

[123] Statements made in Iran on August 23, 1995 by Mostafa Kazemi, chief of the military committee of Akbari's Wahdat faction; confirmed in interview with Akbari.

for all of us to live in peace and security is to consolidate our good relations with the Sunnis and the non-Hazaras.[124]

But it was not until after the fall of Kabul to the Taliban in September 1996 that the Hazara forces would reunite.[125]

The 1994–1995 Pashtun (Hizb-i-Islami) Takeover

By late 1994, the fighting had stalemated – the Tajiks and Akbari's splinter group of Hizb-i-Wahdat were on one side and the joint forces of the Pashtuns, Uzbeks, and Hazaras on the other. This stalemate represented a major affront to the Afghan Pashtuns, who had consistently been the dominant political force in Afghanistan. Beyond the political situation, by 1994, Pashtuns held only two-fifths of the country, a decrease from around 50 percent in 1992.[126] At that point, a fundamentalist Pashtun force from southern Afghanistan, called the Taliban, made its appearance and quickly asserted their power as the leading Pashtun party on the scene. It was poor battlefield performance of Pashtuns writ large in the context of internecine war among the mujahedin, which had driven the country to total anarchy, that led an outside Pashtun movement, the Taliban, to take control of the Pashtun cause in the fight.

The forces that vied for leadership of Afghanistan's distraught Pashtuns between 1994 and 1996 differed in terms of their origins in Pashtun society and their involvement in the 1980s mujahedin movement. The Taliban leadership predominantly consisted of clergy or individuals with some religious education (madrasa), whereas that of Hizb-i-Islami mainly consisted of school- or college-educated Islamists. There was also a regional and tribal dimension to their difference. Both main branches of the Kandahari Pashtun tribes played a leading role in the Taliban. Mullah Omar himself was a Hotak-Ghilzai, the tribe that had provided the first rulers after Afghans rebelled against Persia in the early eighteenth century. Many of his peers were from the Kandahari Durrani tribes, which had provided the leadership after the founding of the modern state in 1747. Hekmatyar, on the other hand, was from a low-status eastern Ghilzai tribe, the Kharoti, and his party of Hizb-i-Islami mainly consisted of eastern Pashtuns with no place in the politics of the Kandahar tribes. As Davis states:

[Hekmatyar] proved conspicuously unable to rally Afghanistan's Pashtuns as a whole behind him. That there would be a Pashtun backlash against the control of Kabul by Tajik and Uzbeks was inevitable. What Pakistan and others failed to realize was that Hekmatyar was never the man to lead it. A radical Islamist from a minor Ghilzai tribe born in northern Afghanistan, Hekmatyar was generally disdained among the conservative Durrani tribes of the southern Pashtun heartland.[127]

---

[124] Testimony by Rahmatullah Murtazawi, a deputy in Akbari's Wahdat faction, in front of the U.S. Congress; confirmed in interview with Akbari.

[125] Magnus (1997).

[126] Ahady (1995), p. 623.

[127] Davis (1996), p. 184.

As previously noted, the Pashtuns experienced losses between 1992 and 1994 that went far beyond simple battlefield losses and amounted to what they saw as loss of control of the Afghan state. Burhanuddin Rabbani's assumption of the role of president, the emergence of Ahmad Shah Massoud as the leading military strongman, and his success in confining Hizb-i-Islami to the capital's southern suburbs marked military defeat for the Pashtuns in the main battlefields in Kabul and the surrounding provinces of Logar, Wardak, Parwan, and Laghman. Not only were the Pashtuns not in control, but the whole country was largely plagued by anarchic violence. The Pashtuns around Kandahar stayed aloof from the post-1992 administration. They played no part in the first two years of factional fighting, when Hizb-i-Islami suffered its losses, but were acutely aware of the losses of state power and autonomy that contributed to their rise as a movement and resulted in the subsequent Pashtun takeover by the Taliban.

The fight that put the Taliban on the map happened on October 12, 1994, at Spin Boldak, a Hekmatyar-controlled central arms post near the Afghan-Pakistan border that, among other items, included Western rockets, artillery, and ammunition from the pre-1992 Afghan war.[128] A group of 200 Taliban fighters attacked and seized the area, along with a large cache of arms and ammunition including some 18,000 Kalashnikov assault rifles and several artillery pieces and vehicles.[129] This battle signified the tensions within the Pashtuns, with a new force rising as a reaction to Hekmatyar's poor battlefield performance in the intra-mujahedin fighting and the anarchy that had ensued as a result. On November 5, 1994, less than a month after the Spin Boldak victory, the Taliban took over Afghanistan's second-largest city, Kandahar, which had been contested territory among several local chieftains with Jamiat-i-Islami or Hizb-i-Islami affiliations.[130]

In December 1994, within a month of the fall of Kandahar, two adjacent southern provinces, Uruzgan and Zabul, fell into Taliban hands, and Helmand followed suit thereafter.[131] By the end of January 1995, the Taliban had also taken over the eastern provinces of Ghazni, Paktia, and Paktika.[132] The advance, which had been relatively easy across the Pashtun heartland, continued unabated in February 1995, with the Taliban weeding Hizb-i-Islami out of the provinces of Wardak and Logar as well as Charasyab, an area that constituted Hekmatyar's headquarters and was a mere 24 kilometers from Kabul. The fall of Charasyab dealt another serious blow to Hekmatyar's forces, some of whom defected to the Taliban. By February 15, 1995, Khost province was also under Taliban control. Within three months from the fall of Kandahar to Taliban control, the movement had "broken the stalemate in the Afghan

---

[128] Ibid, p. 46.
[129] Rashid (2000), p. 28.
[130] Davis (1998), pp. 46–47.
[131] Ibid, pp. 51–52.
[132] Ibid, p. 52.

civil war" and had captured twelve of Afghanistan's thirty-two provinces.[133] The Taliban had effectively marginalized Hekmatyar's party, subsuming Hizb-i-Islami leaders and territorial control under its command and effectively rising as the new Pashtun force.[134]

The narrative that arose in justification of the Taliban among the Pashtuns broadly rested on the Taliban's capacity to serve as a dominant force for peace against the anarchy, while reestablishing Pashtun primacy. As a Pashtun Guantanamo Bay detainee who had allegedly served as head of Taliban security in Baghlan province told his interrogators: "There were so many powers fighting against each other in Afghanistan, Islamic powers. . . . When [the] Taliban came, they wanted to establish one central government. We thought we would [be able to] get rid of those powers and there will be one government . . . I wanted one group to be able to bring peace to the country."[135]

The 1997 Uzbek (Junbish-i-Milli) Takeover

In September 1996, the Taliban solidified itself as the leading Pashtun movement by taking over the capital Kabul, thus accomplishing the feat to which Hizb-i-Islami had aspired since the commencement of intra-mujahedin hostilities in April 1992. The rise of the Taliban propelled a consolidation of forces against them: In October 1996, as discussed in detail in the timeline earlier in the chapter, the main Uzbek, Tajik, and Hazara parties formed a new alliance, Shura-i-Ali-i-Difa. At that time, the Taliban started making headway in the north. In the months leading up to the Taliban northern campaign, the economic situation in that area had become precarious. Rumors and fears of an imminent Taliban attack were escalating and the Uzbeks were feeling threatened. The Taliban attack capitalized on the tense internal politics of the Uzbek party of Junbish-i-Milli, prompting the May 1997 mutiny of one of Dostum's generals, Malik Pahlawan.[136] This takeover, like the Taliban takeover before it, was triggered by poor battlefield performance that caused disagreements over strategy and occurred along preexisting fault lines within the warring group as the strongest out-of-power faction overthrew the leading subgroup.

The mutiny occurred in the context of an already fractionalized Uzbek movement that, although led by Dostum at the center, had many power sources. Junbish-i-Milli was formed at the time of the PDPA collapse and became the party of choice for all Uzbeks as well as some northerners who had been with the former regime. The pattern of factionalism within Junbish-i-Milli was complex, as there was strong clan rivalry and its military strongmen had built up rival patronage networks. Specifically, although primarily led by Dostum, who hailed from Afghanistan's Jowzjan province, Junbish-i-Milli had a few other prominent deputy figures who had enjoyed considerable local support, such

---

[133] Rashid (2001), p. 31.
[134] Davis (1998), p. 54.
[135] ARB Transcript, Set One, pp. 166, 169; ARB Transcript, Set Two, p. 54.
[136] Interview with Abdul Malilk; interview with Faizullah Zaki; Matinuddin (1999), p. 97.

as Rasul Pahlawan from Faryab province. The disagreements between Dostum and Pahlawan predated the creation of Junbish-i-Milli and were broadly known in Uzbek circles. During the Jihad, Rasul had been a supporter of the Khalq (Masses) branch of the Afghan Communist Party, while Dostum was affiliated with Parcham (Banner), the competing and ruling branch.[137] After Dostum's ascendance as the leader of Junbish-i-Milli, Rasul withdrew to Faryab province, where he consolidated his rule with the help of his half-brother Abdul Malik, who was serving as the head of Junbish-i-Milli's foreign affairs department.[138] On June 25, 1996, Rasul Pahlawan was gunned down in Mazar-i-Sharif, and his brother Malik took over political control of the Pahlawan clan and Faryab province.[139] In the summer of 1996, a few months after Rasul's death and right before the Taliban's takeover of Kabul, Malik is said to have suggested to Dostum that Junbish-i-Milli stay allied with the Taliban. Dostum had instead chosen to fight against them and signed a ceasefire agreement with Massoud on August 13, 1996, joining the Tajik-Hazara alliance.

The coming advance of the Taliban marked a point of particular weakness and danger for the Uzbek forces. Mazar-i-Sharif, which had served as an "Oasis of Peace" during the civil war, appeared to now be facing an imminent attack.[140] This reality, combined with the fall of a Junbish-i-Milli field headquarters at Jabul Seraj in January, reduced some of the "impunity" of Dostum and ensured mass casualties, given the losses taken by Massoud during the month of January and the lack of a further northern "retreat."[141] Moreover, the Taliban was threatening Junbish-i-Milli beyond the north, as there were significant operations against Junbish-i-Milli territory in the west.[142] The Taliban-imposed blockades had also caused food scarcity and had increased inflation, creating a sense of economic uncertainty.[143] This panic was illustrated by the extreme fluctuations of the Junbish-i-Milli Afghani and Dostum's commanders' rush to convert that currency into dollars, as well as Dostum's inability to pay his soldiers and civilian bureaucrats on time. Dostum's lack of strict control over his commanders had also led to a great deal of extortion of the northern populations through intimidation and corruption. And his ruthless treatment of his soldiers damaged their morale and his support among the broader set of fighters.[144]

Given this weakness, Malik, along with another set of resentful Dostum commanders, proceeded with a well-organized mutiny within the Junbish-i-Milli forces stationed in Faryab and Badghis. Dostum had thousands of men under his command – and several tanks and Scud missiles – and believed that

---

[137] Davis (1997), p. 360.
[138] Johnston (1997).
[139] Davis (1997), p. 360; Williams (2006), p. 21.
[140] Cooper (1997a).
[141] Ibid.
[142] Thomas, Christopher, "Seizure of Key Pass Puts Defiant North at Taleban's Mercy," *The Times*, February 26, 1997.
[143] Interview with Abdul Malik; interview with Faizullah Zaki; Rashid (2001), p. 55.
[144] Cooper (1997a); Giustozzi (2004), pp. 11, 16.

he could negotiate with Malik. However, Dostum's four envoys to Faryab were kept captive, and in Badghis province, Malik's men arrested and disarmed all of Dostum's commanders. On May 19, 1997, as Taliban forces were moving to the north, Malik forces also killed Dostum's governor in Samangan.[145] By May 21, Dostum was faced with enemy fire in Sheberghan, the capital of his home province Jowzjan, which was now hotly contested. Conscripts, who had heard of the fall of Faryab and had not been paid for months, readily betrayed Dostum. He fled to Uzbekistan on May 24, 1997, mere hours before the Taliban marched into the northern city of Mazar-i-Sharif. Allegedly he had to pay his own soldiers at checkpoints along the way to let him pass through the Afghan-Uzbek border.[146] According to a Western journalist reporting on the incident at the time, Dostum's men took away his vehicle and he was forced to cross the Russian-manned bridge over the Oxus river from Afghanistan into Uzbekistan on foot.[147]

The narratives of the Uzbek takeover were cast in terms similar to those of the Hazara split. Abdul Malik, who mutinied against Dostum, was accused of being bought off by the Taliban and a traitor to the Uzbek people. Meanwhile, Malik argued that he switched sides to protect the unity of Afghanistan. Both Malik and Dostum created a narrative as to why their respective competitor was not a true Uzbek leader. For Dostum, Malik could never be the ruler of all Uzbeks because he was part Pashtun. He attributed Malik's preference for cooperation with the Taliban to his Pashtun roots and bilingualism in Pashto.[148] He also suggested that Malik was a mere opportunist who would not hesitate to betray the Uzbek people, saying, "Abdul Malik received $200 million from Pakistan, the Taliban's main supporters, and sold his people, the Uzbeks, the Turks."[149] In response to Dostum's accusations, Malik had this to say:

If you watch Aina, which is a TV that is supported by Dostum, you will hear rumors against me. The first rumor was that since my mother was Pashtun I sold the north to the Pashtuns. The second rumor was that I massacred the Pashtuns in the north. Third they said that I got lots of money. Where is this money? Which bank? If I had money what would be the necessity for the protocol [with the Taliban]?[150]

Meanwhile, Dostum himself had fraternized with the Pashtuns: He had several Pashtun commanders and had made an alliance with Hekmatyar's Pashtuns in January 1994, and with the Taliban in their advance to the west in 1995; moreover, one of Dostum's wives is Pashtun.[151] In turn, Malik also questioned

---

[145] Gannon (1997).
[146] Rashid (2000), p. 58.
[147] McGirk (1997).
[148] Interview with Faizullah Zaki; interview with Abdul Malik; Williams (2006).
[149] Dostum quoted in "Key Defection Hastens Ultimate Taliban Triumph," *The Australian*, May 27, 1997.
[150] Interview with Abdul Malik.
[151] Interview with Faizullah Zaki.

Dostum's Uzbek identity and Muslim faith. He also accused Dostum of criminal and secessionist tendencies:[152]

In Afghanistan there are two Uzbek tribes. One is the local, original Uzbeks of Afghanistan and the others are the immigrant Uzbeks who came from Uzbekistan during the Soviet revolution. My father is an original Afghan-Uzbek.... The strategy of the Uzbekistan Uzbeks is that they want to disintegrate Afghanistan. Mr. Dostum's father is originally from Uzbekistan and came as an immigrant to Afghanistan. His whole family immigrated and they have a very small tribe.... His grandfather still does not have Afghan identification. So his desire has always been to integrate the Afghan and Uzbekistan Uzbeks together. In the name of federalism, he wants to disintegrate Afghanistan and join the Afghan Uzbeks to the Uzbekistan Uzbeks. This is one of the several reasons for my disagreement with Dostum.[153]

The Taliban had even issued a religious order (fatwa) against Dostum, who was known for his communist past and boisterous drinking habits, proclaiming him a nonbeliever (*kafir*). In separate announcements, they had made clear that an amnesty offered to their opponents if they surrendered would not apply to Dostum.[154] Echoing the Taliban's statements, Malik himself had called Dostum a "bad Muslim" and presented him as the main obstacle to peace in Afghanistan.[155]

Moreover, Malik emphasized how Dostum had himself cooperated with the Taliban before joining the Northern Alliance. Malik's justification for aligning with the Taliban was allegedly for the sake of national unity:

Dostum collaborated with the Taliban in the fall of Kabul [October 1996]. He was united with the Taliban in the fall of Jalalabad. He was with the Taliban in the fall of Herat.... His technicians were helping the Taliban with their planning. Dostum's planes bombed Ismail Khan [the Tajik Jamiat-i-Islami leader in Herat] on behalf of the Taliban.... Then Dostum, Massoud, and Khalili were in one coalition against the Taliban.... This is the time that Afghanistan was [on] the verge of separation. And there was agreement between countries that Afghanistan has to be partitioned. At that time I stood up and broke this alliance... I announced my opposition against the separation of Afghanistan. I said that whether I exist or not there should be one Afghanistan. In order to end the war and have one government I signed a protocol with the Taliban. The protocol indicated that there would be one national government and Pashtuns and Uzbeks would have their share, and the fighting would stop and separation would not take place.[156]

---

[152] Interview with Abdul Malik. "I have staged the rebellion because Dostum was against a united Afghanistan." Malik, quoted in "Situation Tense in North Afghanistan amid Reports of Revolt," *Agence France Press*, May 19, 1997.

[153] Interview with Abdul Malik.

[154] Salahuddin (1997).

[155] Thomas (1997b).

[156] Interview with Abdul Malik.

CONCLUSION

This chapter used empirical evidence from the Afghan civil war to illustrate the tactical nature of alliance and warring group fractionalization dynamics. In the context of the emerging anarchy of Afghanistan's intra-mujahedin war, alliances proved to be in constant flux. Based on the relative power changes across alliances, groups recalculated their expected political returns and updated their alliance choices. With regard to identity, national and local elites of all warring groups, acting as identity entrepreneurs, broadly employed narratives – ethnic or otherwise – as a way of rationalizing their alliance or group allegiance preferences. The mechanism behind the construction of these narratives allowed for alliance and group allegiance switches during civil wars, prompted by and consistent with changes in power among competing groups.

This chapter also highlights that group fractionalization, though less likely than realignment across warring groups, is an important empirical reality in civil wars. There were three instances of in-group transformations in the Afghan civil war: the Hazara split into the Akbari and Mazari factions; the Pashtun takeover with the Taliban marginalizing Hekmatyar; and the Uzbek takeover with Malik driving out Dostum. All three were cases in which poor battlefield performance and asymmetrically borne losses across subgroups resulted in the fracturing or takeover of a group along the lines of a regional or leadership dispute. Overall, the observations in this chapter are consistent with the theory proposed in Chapter 2. The following chapter moves to test the applicability of the proposed theoretical framework in the context of a nonethnic civil war, that of the Afghan Jihad of mujahedin against communists. Its intent is to show that the alliance and group fractionalization dynamics at work in that conflict were also power-driven; in other words, irrespective of the character of war – which in this context had ideological undertones – these processes remain largely the same.

4

The Afghan Communist-Mujahedin War, 1978–1989

So far we have witnessed the unraveling of the civil war among Afghan muja-hedin factions and the dramatic rise of the Taliban. That war – which started with the collapse of the Afghan communist regime in 1992 and ended with the Taliban's takeover of 90 percent of the country in 1998 – was fought along more or less perfectly overlain lines of ethnicity and party, which had been drawn just prior to the war's outbreak. Hence one might rightly wonder how these parties, which had appeared in much more ethnically integrated versions in the days of the Afghan Jihad (1978–1989), made partners and enemies in that earlier iteration of civil war on Afghan soil. Were those alliances also power-determined? Could alliance changes be accurately traced around rela-tive power changes? Were there instances of group fractionalization during the Afghan Jihad and were they prompted by severe or asymmetrically borne losses among a group's constituent subgroups?

One might argue that the civil war in Afghanistan (1978–1989) that was cast in communist-versus-mujahedin terms is an easy first test of this book's theory. Given that it was fought along largely ideological rather than ethnic lines, one would not be surprised to see less salience placed on shared ideological charac-teristics. After all, they are not as ascriptive as ethnic characteristics, and we can see why a group may be less constrained by them. The existing literature, how-ever, has no conclusive predictions on the matter. Scholars cannot even agree on whether the ethnic/nonethnic distinction is analytically meaningful. Indeed, most civil wars have gone down in history with a label: Those dating from the start of the twentieth century to the end of the Cold War tend to be coined as "ideological," whereas those in the post–Cold War era are seen as "ethnic." And even though no unique and systematic characterization appears to exist – some scholars make a new-versus-old civil wars distinction, whereas others a distinction between ethnic-versus-nonethnic civil wars – such identifiers are nevertheless often employed as heuristic descriptors.[1]

---

[1] Kaufmann (1996a, 1996b); Kalyvas (2001); Sambanis (2001, 2004b).

Some works in the literature underline the need to differentiate between ethnic and nonethnic civil wars because ethnic organizations are mobilized to support violence in some cases and not others – a potentially meaningful variation.[2] Nevertheless, most cross-national statistical analyses on civil war onset – which pool all cases of civil war assuming that no theoretical distinction can be drawn between them – find no notable correlation between measures of ethnicity and the onset of conflict.[3] And looking beyond civil war onset to measures of civil war process such as violence, ethnic wars do not have distinctively different casualty rates; they are not more intense than nonethnic ones; nor are they less likely to be terminated by negotiated settlements.[4] The ethnic camp has been keen to discount these results, suggesting that ethnic fractionalization measures may not adequately capture the relevant ethnic cleavages at hand. Alternate measures of ethnicity, however, have not fared much better.[5]

Other scholars strike a conciliatory note of sorts by arguing that while there are meaningful distinctions to be made between civil wars, the ethnic-nonethnic distinction is not one of them. More specifically, the broad labeling of civil wars as ideological versus ethnic is often based on mischaracterizations and ignores the micro-level mechanisms and cleavages that explain many civil war processes.[6] This school of thought purports that the exogenous cleavage thesis – the idea that violence is a direct result of the character of war, be that ethnic or nonethnic – does not hold.[7] Rather, an approach that sees civil war not merely as a result of the preexisting cleavages leading to the onset of hostilities, but also as a result of the cleavages created during the war is the right analytic lens. In that regard, differences such as the type of warfare (i.e., irregular versus conventional) can be much more informative.[8]

Although the claim that the character of war should be seen as endogenous to the conflict is arguably strong, in the context of this book it would be tautological to assume that character of war is endogenous to civil war and then show that an exogenous definition of character of war proves irrelevant to alliance preferences. I therefore take the character of war as exogenous and then proceed to show – through empirical evidence from the 1978–1989 largely ideological civil war in Afghanistan (and later, in Chapter 7, through the 1941–1945 arguably ideological civil war in Bosnia) – that the rationale behind alliance formation remains the same regardless of what was presumed as the conflict's character.

This inquiry will show that the character of war does not affect alliances, but comes short of verifying the assertion that it is endogenous to the conflict.

[2] Sambanis (2004b), p. 266.
[3] Collier and Hoeffler (2000); Fearon and Laitin (2003).
[4] Licklider (1995); Walter (1999); Fearon (2004); Toft (2010).
[5] Fearon and Laitin (2003); Cederman and Girardin (2007). Cederman, Wimmer, and Min (2009) are an exception.
[6] Kalyvas (2001, 2003, 2006), among others.
[7] Kalyvas and Kocher (2007a); Kalyvas (2008).
[8] Kalyvas and Balcells (2010b).

Evidence for that argument is more readily found in the discussions of alliance narratives in each of the empirical chapters, which, as described in Chapter 2, show that national and local elites, acting as identity entrepreneurs, broadly employ a vast array of ever-changing shared identity narratives as a way to rationalize their tactical alliance preferences. Shared identity in the context of alliance narratives therefore proves to be driven by alliance preferences, lending credence to the argument for an endogenous dimension to the war's character.

The empirical evidence from the ideological civil war in Afghanistan, presented in this chapter, aims to show that the dynamics behind alliance formation are such as those theoretically outlined in Chapter 2 and empirically discussed in the context of the ethnic civil war in Afghanistan (Chapter 3) and subsequent empirical chapters (Chapters 5–8). Specifically, whereas the Afghan intra-mujahedin war discussed in Chapter 3 offered a kaleidoscope of ethnic warring actors allowing for a range of possible fighting combinations if one wished to invoke shared identity attributes, the Afghan Jihad only had one readily available cleavage – the one that pitted the mujahedin against the communists and that appeared hard to reconcile. But reconciled it was. This chapter presents the range of warring actors during the Afghan Jihad and offers a sense of their allies and enemies, as well as of the instances of their internal fracturing. What we see is that during the Jihad, just like in the intra-mujahedin war, groups formed and broke alliances in an effort to win the war while maximizing their share of postwar political power. Moreover, as the theory would predict, fractionalization occurred along preexisting subgroup divisions in response to poor battlefield performance and asymmetric losses across subgroups. In addition to analyzing the alliance behaviors of warring groups and their subgroups, this chapter concludes by referencing two important alliance and fractionalization contexts of commander-level mobilization: the Afghan communist government's recruitment of tribal militias and their secret ceasefire agreements with mujahedin commanders known as protocols. This discussion in turn motivates the next chapter of this book, Chapter 5, which looks at whether the proposed theoretical framework on alliances and fractionalization holds for a lower level of analysis than the group and subgroup – that of the wartime commander.

Much like in the empirical chapter that preceded this one and the ones that follow, the discussion and analysis here focus on the domestic warring actors. This will not be an empirical treatment of how great power politics of the United States and the Soviet Union played out in the Afghan Jihad (a topic that has been covered extensively by other scholars both through American and Russian primary sources).[9] Rather, the involvement of external actors, which varied in intensity and over time, is treated as an extension of the power of their local allies – be they the Afghan Communist Party or the different mujahedin factions.

---

[9] Coll (2004) and Bradsher (1999), respectively, among others.

WARRING ACTORS

The 1978–1989 Afghan civil war was a result of popular disdain toward the reform policies pursued by the Soviet-backed Afghan communist government, compounded by a resentment toward the government's socialist and un-Islamic ideology. To an outsider, the conflict may have appeared as having two warring sides, the communists and the mujahedin, but there were actually a multitude of warring actors within those ideological camps. Their internal politics and fragmentation shed ample light on the importance of local power-balancing dynamics and their effect on alliance formation in civil wars.

One of the warring sides was the Afghan communist government, officially known as the People's Democratic Party of Afghanistan (PDPA). The PDPA was founded in 1965 and by 1967 had already split into two subgroups named Khalq (Masses) and Parcham (Banner). The party was united on the eve of the April 1978 coup that brought it to power, but remained plagued by constant tensions of underlying factionalism (as described in detail later in this chapter). The PDPA enjoyed only limited support among the Afghan population – and that only among urban residents – but it had managed to largely infiltrate the officer corps of the Afghan military, enabling the successful April 27, 1978 coup that overthrew Mohammad Daoud's government and led to the onset of the Afghan civil war.[10] The communists cast the war as a fight of liberation against feudalism, an armed opposition to powerful landowners (*khans*) who were exploiting the poor peasant-serfs (*dehqan*). The latter were, according to that narrative, subdued by religion and could not put up a fight for their rights.[11] There was also a broader story as to how the Afghan communist movement was standing up to the preexisting regime's abuse and predation. That narrative is eloquently captured by Shahnawaz Tanai, a Khalqi general:

In the last period of Zahir Shah there were . . . economic problems including famine. People were selling their children to make ends meet. . . . There was oppression of women and peasants. Forced marriage was rife. Peasants mortgaged their land. There were the problems of *khan* and *malik* and *uluswal* and *commandant askari* [different local power brokers]. They all used to oppress people. There were political prisoners. People would be sacked from service. . . . In the army there was a lot of bribery. . . . As a result of these problems the military officers started to think politically in search for solutions. When I reflected on this I started to get involved politically. From 1971 I joined *Khalq*. . . . In those days politics were about class struggle against oppression within Afghanistan, against Zahir Shah. Also there was the factional conflict, Left versus Right. . . . The Islamic parties were weaker than *Khalq*. Officers mainly went to the *Khalq* partly because they tend to have a progressive outlook. . . . There had been propaganda that *Khalqis* are good, they represent the poor and are lovers of the nation.[12]

[10] Goodson (2001), pp. 52–55.
[11] Roy (1990), p. 85.
[12] Interview with Shahnawaz Tanai in Semple (2010).

On the opposing side were the mujahedin. They resisted what they perceived as a movement of forced modernization aiming to undermine Afghanistan's religion, culture, traditions, and family structure. They vehemently opposed a score of reforms the communists had tried to introduce, ranging from policies on land reform to education to family law. People were upset not only with the nature of the changes, but also with the style of their implementation. They joined the opposition willingly and in droves. According to a mujahedin fighter, Qazi Satar:

No particular person invited me [to join the Jihad]. I just joined naturally. Our activities were religious, including discussions on how to deal with governmental and social corruption and how to encourage a spirit of Islam in the people. Much of the focus was on opposing the communists. . . . The communists had propagated the slogan that religion is the opiate of the people and our main mission was to oppose this."[13]

Notably, the mujahedin did not exhibit any more unity than the communists. Rather, by 1980, within a year or so since the start of the war, there were seven Sunni mujahedin groups. Among these seven parties, two dominated the scene: Hizb-i-Islami, led by Gulbuddin Hekmatyar, a Ghilzai Pashtun from the north, and Jamiat-i-Islami, led by Burhannudin Rabbani, a Tajik religious scholar. Both these parties had their roots in the Organization of Muslim Youth (Sazman-i-Jawanan-i-Musulman), an Islamic movement that was created in 1972 to counterbalance the increasing influence of the PDPA. This organization was headed by Rabbani and had Hekmatyar in its ranks.[14] By 1977, the organization was in exile in Peshawar, Pakistan, and was split between the two parties, a division that remained relevant throughout the Jihad.[15] Although the rank and file of the aforementioned groups spanned Afghanistan's ethnically fractionalized mosaic, the higher echelons of Hizb-i-Islami were largely Pashtun, whereas those of Jamiat-i-Islami were mostly manned by Tajiks.[16]

There were two more groups that, along with Hizb-i-Islami and Jamiat-i-Islami, aspired to the creation of an Islamic Afghan state and were called fundamentalist: Maulavi Yunus Khalis, who left Hekmatyar's Hizb-i-Islami in the early days of the war, led a small but very militarily effective party (known as Hizb-i-Islami-Khalis) with appeal in the south and east; the other was led by Abdul Rasul Sayyaf, a mujahed known for his conservative Islamic education, and was called Ittihad-i-Islami Barayi Azadi Afghanistan (Islamic Union for the Freedom of Afghanistan). Sayyaf's primary support base was in the area of Paghman, outside Kabul.[17]

Apart from the four fundamentalist parties, there were also three so-called traditionalist political parties that wanted to see the return of the Afghan king.

---

[13] Interview with Qazi Satar in Semple (2010).
[14] Interview with Burhanuddin Rabbani; Rubin (1995a), p. 83; Bradsher (1999), p. 14.
[15] Interview with Burhanuddin Rabbani; Bradsher (1999), p. 18; Goodson (2001), p. 62.
[16] Interview with Burhanuddin Rabbani; Ewans (2002), pp. 213–214.
[17] Interview with Abdul Rasul Sayyaf.

These parties held influence among prescribed localized constituencies, mostly in the south of the country, and their appeal was tightly linked to the individuals leading them. For instance, Professor Sibghatullah Mojaddidi, known for his family's Naqshbandiyya Sufi linkages, established Jebha-i-Milli Nejat Afghanistan (Afghan National Liberation Front or ANLF), which had isolated support among some Durrani Pashtuns.[18] Maulavi Mohammad Nabi Mohammadi headed a traditional party of his own, known as Harakat-i-Inqilab-i-Islami (Movement of the Islamic Revolution), which had attracted a considerable following at the beginning of the war and mostly in the south, but its prominence was short-lived. The third and last traditional party was Mahaz-i-Milli-Islam-i-Afghanistan (National Islamic Front Afghanistan or NIFA), led by Pir Sayed Ahmed Gailani, whose constituents were Qadiriyya Sufi followers.[19]

The high number of parties that crystallized in the early days of the Jihad is attributed to ample resources and low barriers to entry. However, material support given to the Shiite groups – whose numbers reached up to nine active groups – was negligible. As a result, Shiite activity was largely concentrated in the central Afghan region of Hazarajat, on the sidelines of the Jihadi theater. (The internal politics of the Shiite groups will nevertheless be discussed in a separate section later in the chapter).

The unraveling of the Jihad involved conflict not just between communists and mujahedin, but also within them. The exposition that follows attempts to highlight the intense factionalism within the PDPA among Khalq and Parcham. For the mujahedin, the most infamous conflict on the national level was that between the two biggest mujahedin parties, those of Hizb-i-Islami and Jamiat-i-Islami. Unlike those two groups, the appeal of which reached across Afghanistan, the remaining five Sunni groups enjoyed mostly local support.

All accounts of events from the time, along with the protagonists who were interviewed, sketch out a power-driven rationale behind alliance politics during the Jihad. According to Sibghatullah Mojaddidi, leader of the ANLF mujahedin group: "The mujahedin were lovers of power. I called them profit-insurgents."[20] Such sources also insisted that the ethnicization of the conflict only took place on the eve of the intra-mujahedin war. After all, during the Jihad, co-ethnics were fighting against each other, with Pashtuns, Tajiks, Hazaras, and Uzbeks straddling the communist and mujahedin divide. Also, six of the seven Sunni mujahedin parties were largely ethnically Pashtun in leadership, further showing the lack of unity among co-ethnics. Ahmad Shah Ahmadzai, an influential figure in the Ittihad-i-Islami party, insisted that ethnicity was not a cleavage during the Jihad, even though it came to dominate the intra-mujahedin civil war that followed. He referenced the frequency in cases of co-ethnics turning on each other during the Jihad: "On the communist side [the PDPA], Amin killed Taraki and they were both Pashtuns and Khalqis. On the mujahedin

18 Interview with Sibghatullah Mojaddidi.
19 Goodson (2001), pp. 61–62.
20 Interview with Sibghatullah Mojaddidi.

side... one man would belong to *Hizb-i-islami* another to *ittihad*, but they would all be Pashtuns. There was no ethnic element in this."[21]

Another Jihadi commander, interviewed by a journalist closely covering the Jihad, also highlighted the lack of ethnic consideration in terms of mujahedin recruitment:

In 1984, Hamid had defected from an army transport division in the southern city of Kandahar and joined Yunus Khalis's Hizbi-i Islami, which is how Haq had met him.... He had the same qualities that help make a good intelligence agent, and that was why Haq recruited him.... The fact that Hamid was a Tajik meant little to Haq. "I don't give a shit," Haq told me. "I'll take a hardworking Tajik or Turkoman any day over a lazy, stupid Pathan [Pashtun]." Haq's chief accountant, who handled all the money for the Kabul underground, was also a Tajik.[22]

TIMELINE AND POWER-BALANCING WARTIME ALLIANCES

By the end of 1978, months after the April coup, there were protests in twenty-four out of Afghanistan's then thirty-two provinces, as the largely rural and illiterate Afghan population felt their culture and tradition were under serious threat.[23] But the outbursts of violence against the communist regime and all ensuing protests were stifled with the Soviet invasion, which led to the solidifying of the Communist Party's control across Afghan urban centers.[24] The Afghan army, nevertheless, continued to be confronted with a high number of deserters, and by the end of 1980 its ranks had been depleted to approximately 30,000 men, less than half of its original strength of 80,000. Haji Malik, a Hizb-i-Islami commander who had spent six months as a pro-mujahedin element in the government's army before joining the Jihad, related his experience with defecting soldiers:

The company commander, Lieutenant Fazl Haq was from Maidan and I from Paghman so we were neighbors and Fazl Haq used to warn me, in a friendly way not to be seen praying.... Initially there were sixty-eight men in the company. I brought the company numbers down to twelve people. I did this by approaching men whom I saw saying their prayers. I encouraged them to desert when they got leave. Basically everyone went on leave and failed to come back.[25]

Meanwhile, the existing mujahedin parties had already allied to deal with the communist enemy and in turn had broken that alliance.[26] In line with the theory, by mid-1980, as the relative power of the mujahedin groups increased and balancing the communists became less urgent, defections from the mujahedin alliance began to occur. In the first instance, Hizb-i-Islami and

[21] Interview with Ahmad Shah Ahmadzai.
[22] Kaplan (2001), pp. 60–61.
[23] Bradsher (1999), pp. 41–42.
[24] Arnold (1983), pp. 117–118; Goodson (2001), pp. 56–58.
[25] Interview with Haji Malik in Semple (2010).
[26] Adamec (1996), p. 294.

Jamiat-i-Islami tried to create a joint movement, called Harakat-i-Inqilab-i-Islami, under the leadership of Maulavi Mohammad Nabi Mohammadi. A power struggle among the parties led to that alliance breaking up. Another similar effort, led by Abdul Rasul Sayyaf and his movement of Ittihad-i-Islami, had the same fate.[27] These initiatives foreshadowed the fickle pattern of alliance formation and breakup among the mujahedin parties and the competition between them. Coll offers a vivid description of intra-mujahedin interactions from the time:

[I]n 1980, the Organization of the Islamic Conference, an alliance of Muslim governments, held a major summit in Saudi Arabia, in the resort town of Taif. The Saudis wanted the conference to condemn Soviet interference in Afghanistan. Yasser Arafat, then backing many leftist causes, planned to speak in Moscow's defense. Afghan rebel leaders flew in from Peshawar to appeal for their cause. Ahmed Badeeb was assigned to select just one of the mujahedin leaders to make a speech, right after Arafat, attacking the Soviet invasion as an affront to Islam. Several Afghan rebel leaders spoke passable Arabic, but Badeeb found that Sayyaf, then an assistant to another leader, was by far the most fluent and effective. "We chose him to give the speech," Badeeb recalled later. Immediately, however, the Afghan leaders began to "fight among themselves. Unbelievable guys... everyone was claiming that he represents the Afghans and he should give the speech." The scene became so unruly that Badeeb decided to lock all of them in a Taif prison until they agreed on a single speaker. After six hours of jailhouse debate, the Afghans accepted Sayyaf.[28]

While the Afghan mujahedin groups' shared ideology, and the shared communist enemy, proved entirely insufficient to maintain cohesion, the communists tried to get tribal allies on their side. One such effort to gain support of Afghan tribes in the staunchly anticommunist countryside resulted in the killing of Frontier Affairs Minister Faiz Muhammad in the fall of 1980.[29] That did not faze the communists, who continued even more forcefully to reach out to tribes by revising the government's land policies. Specifically, instead of moving ahead with strict collectivization, they lifted restrictions on the number of acres that tribal and religious leaders were allowed to own. Moreover, they also created a national policy that recognized all groups and languages. Although that may have increased the PDPA's stature among the minorities, it at the same time antagonized the dominant Pashtuns. More specifically, the unprecedented May 11, 1981 appointment of a Hazara, Sultan Ali Kesthmand, as prime minister seemed to have particularly shocked the Pashtuns, while not swaying the Hazaras to come to the support of the PDPA.[30]

The conflict was still raging in July 1981, when mujahedin were reportedly fighting communists in the Kabul suburb of Paghman, less than twenty miles from the city. And on August 22, 1981, in a notable sign of unity aimed to

---

[27] Interview with Ahmad Shah Ahmadzai.
[28] Coll (2004), pp. 82–83.
[29] Adamec (1996), p. 295.
[30] Mousavi (1997), p. 219.

balance against the Soviet-backed communist government, the power of which was in ascendance, the (at the time) five Afghan mujahedin groups formed a coalition and a fifty-member advisory council, reminiscent of the traditional Afghan councils known as shuras or jirgas.[31] In turn, in what appeared to be a response to mujahedin unity (which proved to be fleeting), the communists pursued an intense recruitment program to lure in new members so as to strengthen their cadres.[32]

Meanwhile, by January 1982, U.S. reports suggested that communist forces in Afghanistan had reached the level of 110,000–120,000 troops. This was a strong year for the PDPA, as exhibited by the May 16, 1982 gathering of 841 PDPA delegates who vowed to continue with their land reform program and with dissident purges, despite mounting popular opposition.[33] In 1983, with the struggle having spread across Afghanistan, the communists were holding strong, pursuing bombing campaigns over the cities of Herat in the west, Kandahar in the south, and Mazar-i-Sharif in the north, while the mujahedin were still disorganized.

By the end of 1983, however, things began to look increasingly more difficult for the communists. The huge population displacement of more than 3 million refugees to Pakistan and more than 1.5 million to Iran had by now markedly increased the mujahedins' recruiting capacity.[34] According to estimates from the time, the mujahedin had solidified their support in more than 60 percent of the Afghan rural areas.[35] Indeed, in late January 1984, because of his dissatisfaction with progress on the military fronts, PDPA President Karmal removed his three highest-ranking military advisors. The communists nevertheless maintained control of the major cities and military assets, and were effectively countering attacks from the mujahedin who still remained unable to mount a strong offensive. Jamiat-i-Islami commander Ahmad Shah Massoud, talking about the communist fighting capacity at the time, stated: "Their commandos have learned a great deal about mountain guerrilla warfare and are fighting much better than before."[36]

In the early months of 1985, the communist regime continued to push hard on the mujahedin, whose circumstances remained rough. On January 26, Khan Gul, a local mujahedin leader, was executed in Paktia Province. Another local leader of Jamiat-i-Islami died in a mine accident a mere three days later. The communists, meanwhile, had become more serious in their effort to gain popular support and on April 23, 1985, President Karmal held a national tribal assembly (Loya Jirga). Popular will did not seem to sway to his side, however, and in October of that year he mandated the conscription of

[31] Adamec (1996), p. 296.
[32] Arnold (1983), pp. 117–118.
[33] Goodson (2001), pp. 60–64.
[34] Ewans (2002), pp. 219–220.
[35] Coll (2004), p. 89.
[36] Ibid, p. 122.

three-year military service of all males up to the age of forty. In an effort to balance against the increasing communist military power, the Afghan mujahedin parties formed a coalition less than a month later, on May 16, 1985 in Peshawar. This move led to a marked improvement in their battlefield performance that allowed them to capitalize on the economies of scale of their interaction. The communists, however, kept up their fight, and in absolute terms probably remained marginally ahead in terms of military power.[37]

They were to lose that power advantage in 1986. By May of that year, President Karmal had been replaced by Najibullah, a former head of the Afghan secret police. Najibullah in turn formed a "collective leadership," which featured him as party leader, former president Babrak as head of the Revolutionary Council, and Sultan Ali Keshtmand as prime minister. This lineup represented a Pashtun, a Tajik, and a Hazara. Najibullah also promised the holding of elections and the formation of a bicameral parliament within a few months' time. Declaring that none of the underlying grievances of the people of Afghanistan have been or could be resolved in the fratricidal war, Najibullah announced the National Reconciliation Policy on December 31, 1986.[38] That policy consisted of four main elements: the cessation of fighting; the convening of talks among all fighting sides; the creation of a transitional government; and the holding of elections.[39] In adherence with the tenets of the policy, Najibullah abandoned all Marxist rhetoric and proceeded to change the name of the People's Democratic Party of Afghanistan to Party of the Homeland (Hizb-i-Watan). The party was now open to "believing and practicing Muslims," and Najibullah put mullahs on the civil servant payroll.[40] He tried to promote individuals from outside the party into the political establishment and offered his enemies positions in important ministries if they were to denounce the fighting – offers that the mujahedin declined.[41]

Though the regime did away with controversial social policies such as the limitation on the bride's price and the mandatory literacy program, reconciliation was largely being waged on the economic front, where aid provision had encouraged many Afghans to join the government side. The government offered a set of economic benefits to people considering reconciliation, including salaries for village heads and imams, land holdings, seeds and fertilizers, and enrollment of former mujahedin in the militias where they would make 4,000–10,000 Afs a month (in 1989 currency). There were also offers to withdraw the army from places that had been successfully reconciled, largely allowing for local strongmen to rule so long as they pledged allegiance to the central government.[42]

[37] Goodson (2001), pp. 65–66.
[38] Grau (1996), p. 8; Maley (2009), p. 101.
[39] Marshall (2006), p. 3.
[40] Rubin (1995a), p. 166.
[41] Weitz (1992), p. 31; Goodson and Johnson (2011), p. 3.
[42] Giustozzi (2000), pp. 164–172.

Nonetheless, going into 1987, the mujahedin, who had broken up their alliance again, had moved directly on the offensive.[43] As the theory would predict, alliance defections occurred precisely as the relative power of the mujahedin was increasing – as victory seemed probable, groups began to worry more about their own power and survival instead of their alliance. Najibullah continued with his policy of rapprochement. He declared a unilateral ceasefire in January 1987, which he then extended for an additional six months and tried to buttress with a national reconciliation government in May of that same year. The ceasefire did not really contribute to the dying down of the fighting, because it still allowed for retaliation on the part of the regime. As a result, the mujahedin did not abide by it.[44] On October 10, 1987, Najibullah ordered the purchase of weapons from mujahedin who wished to disarm, and a mere month later he announced on Kabul Radio a decree approving the formation and registration of political parties. At the end of November, he convened a tribal gathering (Loya Jirga) to approve a new constitution and to confirm him as president. By now, all seven mujahedin parties were in alliance once again in an attempt to balance against communist gains and ensure that Najibullah's efforts would fail.[45]

Indeed, despite the public opposition to Najibullah's efforts, his policy of rapprochement and encouraging defections among the mujahedin proved quite successful. By 1989, more than 70 percent of mujahedin commanders had ceased military operations against the government, 25 percent of opposition armed units had signed reconciliation agreements with the government, and 40 percent had ceasefire agreements with the government. Also, the number of villages under government control almost doubled in the period between 1986 and 1989 as compared to between 1980 and 1986, with 11,265 villages under government control.[46] Figure 4.1 indicates the number of provinces under the pacification process over the course of the war as well as the number of districts – be they contested, controlled by the government, or in mujahedin hands.[47] Consistent with the book's theoretical framework, defections from the mujahedin to the government increased precisely as the relative power of the mujahedin increased and groups began to worry about their relative position within the alliance and access to postwar political power.

The largely power-balancing alliance pattern shifted in 1988, once the Soviet withdrawal was imminent, making a mujahedin victory appear highly likely. This triggered a wave of defections from the communist side and a bandwagoning process whereby elites scrambled to ensure that they would be on the winning side and have access to postwar political control. After years of internecine conflict, on February 23, 1988, the mujahedin alliance announced the formation of an interim government, with the leaders of the seven groups

[43] Harpviken (1996), pp. 52–53; Goodson (2001), pp. 68–69.
[44] Gvosdev (2009), p. 1; Maley (2009), p. 102.
[45] Adamec (1996), p. 303.
[46] Minkov and Smolynec (2007), p. 23.
[47] Data from Giustozzi (2000), pp. 192, 283.

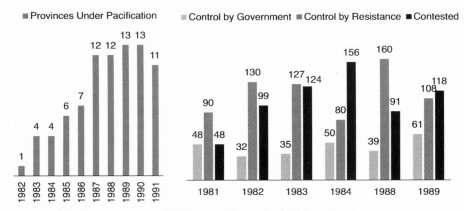

FIGURE 4.1. Government and Resistance Control of Afghan Provinces

successfully rotating in the position of alliance spokesman. Indeed, as the withdrawal was proceeding in the second half of 1988 and in early 1989, there was a dramatic reduction in the number of mujahedin groups willing to reconcile with the government. Najibullah stated at the time that "nobody wants to discuss things with the government any more."[48] The number of government-controlled villages dropped from 11,265 before the withdrawal to 6,100 after, which was lower than the number of villages under government control before the national reconciliation process had started.[49]

Meanwhile, in light of the impending Soviet force withdrawal and the likely associated undermining of the communist Afghan government, President Najibullah was trying to broker a power-sharing arrangement with the mujahedin. On March 29, 1988, he offered 54 of the 229 lower house seats and 18 out of 62 in the Senate to mujahedin groups if they were to agree to take part in parliamentary elections.[50] He also offered Massoud the post of Minister of Defense. The mujahedin were quick to reject the offer, as was Massoud.[51] Najibullah also tried to make a religious rapprochement, by hiring 20,000 mullahs in some sort of civil service capacity to intensify his claim of being a pious man.[52] It was easy for the mujahedin to reject any offers from the other side as they were clearly gaining the upper hand in the conflict. As vividly captured in an anecdote from the time:

The roll of events in Kabul told Haq [a mujahedin leader] that, given the fragility of Najib's [the last communist leader of Afghanistan] regime, the time had come to do what he had done when he first set up the Kabul network: meet with people, argue, negotiate, and persuade. On weekends... Haq began disappearing from Peshawar,

[48] Ibid, p. 178.
[49] Minkov and Smolynec (2007), p. 23.
[50] Adamec (1996), p. 304.
[51] Coll (2004), p. 186.
[52] Ibid, p. 190.

traveling with his bodyguards over roads the guerrillas controlled, to meet with regime army commanders who wanted to defect.... Haq also met with disgruntled Communist Party members who were Khalqis [ethnic Pashtuns]. Such meetings were not difficult to arrange. The level of treachery between Khalq and Parcham was so deep that for one to conspire with the mujahidin against the other was natural.[53]

Indeed, defections away from the communists to the side of the mujahedin intensified after the commencement of the Soviet withdrawal on May 15, 1988. That year alone witnessed the defection of a major general of the Afghan army, a deputy foreign minister, a deputy director in the foreign ministry, and a brigadier general, as well as a chief of the Afghan secret service.[54] Najibullah arrested 100 Khalqis (i.e., PDPA members of the faction opposed to Najibullah's Parcham) in December 1989 on charges of plotting to overthrow the regime, and thwarted an actual coup by a Khalqi General Shahnawaz Tanai on March 6, 1990, which almost cost Najibullah his life.[55] The Soviet withdrawal was completed in 1989, leaving roughly 2 million Afghans dead, the country's infrastructure devastated, and its population divided. A lull of peace descended on Afghanistan. But the lack of a credible alternative for a government among the resistance forces led to the next civil war, now among the mujahedin (as discussed in detail in Chapter 3 of this book).

The narratives that developed throughout the war's trajectory, much in line with the alliances, were purely tactical. Even though the mujahedin groups shared Islam and the notion of Jihad, they proved to be as likely to fight each other as the Soviets.[56] For instance, Hekmatyar, the ruthless leader of arguably the strongest mujahedin party, was infamous for his relentless attacks against Massoud, prompting CIA analysts to think that he was secretly working with the Soviets – a mole pursuing his objective to dominate all mujahedin groups by spreading havoc and disruption.[57] Indeed, depending on the time and context, an agreement between communists and mujahedin – in the form of a protocol as discussed later in the chapter – would often be justified on tribal or ethnic lines, with elites switching between tribal and non-tribal modes as the circumstances dictated.[58] Religious narratives were sometimes invoked as well, as in this excerpt from a 1988 editorial of the traditionalist NIFA mujahedin party, which targeted Islamist mujahedin and essentially conflated them with the communists: "All totalitarians, [be they] Islamic or non-Islamic, theist or atheist, follow the same modus operandi with only different mottos and maxims."[59] Nine years earlier in 1979, when NIFA was more closely

---

[53] Kaplan (2001), p. 176.
[54] Adamec (1996).
[55] Rubin (1995a), p. 253; Marshall (2006), p. 8; Maley (2009), p. 144.
[56] Ewans (2002), p. 156.
[57] Coll (2004), p. 120.
[58] Rubin (1995b), p. 10.
[59] "Fundamentalism in Islam," *The Front*, Vol. 1, No. 6 (1988), p. 4, quoted in Rubin (1995a), p. 203.

aligned with the other mujahedin groups, the narrative in its party program had been markedly different, seemingly blaming only the communists – "a group of traitors who have sold out their country [and] who have no roots or basis among the Muslim people of Afghanistan... [acting with the] military, political, and economic support of a foreign country."[60] Notably, defecting communists would join Hizb-i-Islami, the mainly Pashtun mujahedin party, if members of the Khalq faction, and Jamiat-i-Islami, the mainly Tajik mujahedin party, if members of the Parcham faction.[61]

GROUP FRACTIONALIZATION

The timeline has so far given us a sense of the power dynamics between the enemies – those being the communist government and the seven mujahedin parties – and how they prompted alliance formation and alliance breakdown among the mujahedin. In a truly balancing fashion, the mujahedin would tend to come together when the communists were strong, and break apart over disagreements on leadership when the communists were weak. The section that follows offers a closer sense of the fractionalization *within* the communist government and the mujahedin. As the theory predicts, fractionalization generally occurred as a result of a group's poor battlefield performance and asymmetric losses across its constituent subgroups.

The PDPA Takeover and Counter-Takeover

The main instance of group fractionalization in the government party, the PDPA, involved a takeover and a counter-takeover. In the roughly two decades from its launch to its demise, the PDPA was plagued by internal unrest that mostly manifested as factional war between its subgroups of Khalq and Parcham. The party was initially taken over by Khalq and then by the resurgent Parcham. For a proper understanding of the intragroup dynamics that played out during the 1979–1989 Afghan civil war, it is important to note the tensions and leadership disputes that predated the conflict.

The factions that by 1967 were to be known as Khalq and Parcham were the main two out of the five leftist study groups that were created in the late 1950s and 1960s, and their differences were apparent from the time of their inception.[62] Khalq's headman was Nur Mohammad Taraki, a Pashtun from the Afghan countryside who came to Kabul to study. His party attracted people similar to him, becoming the Pashtun flank of the PDPA. Parcham's leader

[60] *Mahaz-i Milli-yi Islami-yi Afghanistan: Maramnamah* [National Islamic Front of Afghanistan: *Program*] (probably Peshawar, 1979), pp. 21–23, quoted in Rubin (1995a), p. 203.
[61] A known example is that of Pashtun Khalq member Tanai, who after his unsuccessful coup against President Najibullah joined Hekmatyar's forces in Pakistan.
[62] The three other minor groups were headed by Ghulam Dastagir Panjshiri, Mohammad Taher Badakhshi, and Mohammad Zahir Ofaq; Arnold (1983), p. 26; Bradsher (1999), pp. 3–5.

was Babrak Karmal, a Dari speaker with greater appeal to upper-middle-class Afghan city dwellers and non-Pashtun urbanized constituencies.[63]

Khalq and Parcham had decided to join forces and launch the PDPA ahead of the parliamentary elections scheduled for September 1965.[64] The party's central committee – elected in Taraki's living room among twenty-seven men – selected Taraki as secretary general and Karmal as party secretary (i.e., second in command). The factionalism that was to undermine the party was manifest even then in the division of the seats in the Central Committee of seven full members and four candidate members.[65] In less than two years, with no more than 500 or so members in its ranks, the PDPA would split into its two main constituent groups, with the Central Committee members split; each party retained the PDPA name, calling the other the splinter group.[66] It took another five years for some semblance of party unity to emerge, which was prompted by General Daoud's July 17, 1973 coup. Daoud went after communists and Islamists alike, and confronted with the threat of extermination, the two PDPA factions tried to bridge their rift. After unity talks and a covert unification conference, the PDPA was formally unified by 1977, with Taraki and Karmal reclaiming their original posts of secretary general and party secretary, respectively, ahead of the PDPA-orchestrated coup that was to take place a year later.[67]

Tensions between Khalqis and Parchamis arose within less than a month of the April 27, 1978 coup that ousted (and killed) Daoud and propelled the PDPA to power. The Khalq faction, which boasted more people in its ranks than its competitor, and comprised an alleged 20–25 percent of the army's officer corps, rose as the leading power within the party.[68] Whoever was not publicly with Khalq was considered against it, and top Parchami leaders were fired, jailed, or sent into exile, solidifying Khalq's takeover.[69] While Khalq ensured that the leading cadres of the party and the military echelons remained largely staffed by its cronies, Parcham leader Babrak Karmal was assigned to be the Afghan Ambassador to Czechoslovakia, and a committed Khalqi, Hafizullah Amin, took his place as party secretary.[70]

However, the performance of the PDPA in the year following the coup was notably weak, so much so that the regime was facing imminent collapse. The whole country apart from the cities, which at the time constituted roughly a tenth of the Afghan population, was literally up in arms against the PDPA's "socialist" policies.[71] The Khalqis, who were largely from the countryside, as opposed to the Parchamis who were urban, had failed to bring the periphery

[63] Arnold (1983), pp. 21–22, 29; Bradsher (1999), p. 12; Ewans (2002), p. 172.
[64] Arnold (1983), p. 32.
[65] Ibid. p. 25; Bradsher (1999), p. 7.
[66] Arnold (1983), pp. 26–28, 35; Bradsher (1999), pp. 11–12.
[67] Arnold (1983), pp. 45–53; Bradsher (1999), pp. 20–21.
[68] Arnold (1983), pp. 56–60; Bradsher (1999), pp. 30–31.
[69] Arnold (1983), p. 63; Bradsher (1999), pp. 34; Ewans (2002), pp. 190–191.
[70] Arnold (1983), p. 68; Bradsher (1999), pp. 35–36, 41–42.
[71] Arnold (1983), pp. 76–77; Bradsher (1999), p. 89.

under their control – as manifested by the massacre in the western city of Herat of Afghan government forces in March 1979.[72] Moreover, they had failed to maintain control of the army, which among the PDPA factions was also a Khalqi affair. The rank and file was deserting the army in droves, with only half of the army's officer corps (8,000) still in place.[73] The party was reviled, having killed 12,000 political prisoners during the twenty-month reign of Taraki and Amin – a stark 1,000–4,500 of these deaths within the PDPA itself.[74] Party secretary Hafizullah Amin blamed all failures on Taraki and by the end of July 1979 had claimed control of the party and armed forces.[75]

As predicted by the theory, fractionalization was spurred by the poor battle-field performance of the Khalqis, with the out-of-power-group, the Parcham, taking control in an effort to redress the military situation. Specifically, the Parcham takeover was effected through a decapitation strategy – the assassination of Khalqi president Hafizullah Amin. The assassination brought about the return of Babrak Karmal, a Parchami, and his ascension to the presidency. The Parchamis had accused the Pashtun Amin, who had been a Khalqi and the leader of the PDPA, of having been an agent of American imperialism, of having cooperated with the CIA, and of even aspiring to form a government with Pashtun mujahedin leader Gulbuddin Hekmatyar.[76] The Parchamis proceeded with purges that further entrenched them as the leading faction within the party. Some notable examples of the purges included the execution of six Central Committee members from the Khalq-dominated PDPA administration and the disappearance of an additional seventeen. The PDPA ranks were in turn replaced by nineteen Central Committee and thirty-four new Revolutionary Council members from the Parcham side.[77] Anti-Khalq purges continued well into June 1981 in the bureaucracy and military alike.[78]

Shura Sar Ta Sari: The Commanders' Council

The communist government was undoubtedly plagued with divisions, but the mujahedin camp was also deeply embattled. Apart from boasting up to seven different Sunni parties, it was also confronted with notable infighting. In the mid-1980s, fighting among the mujahedin parties was at an all-time high. Hizb-i-Islami appeared to be at war with everyone, be it Jamiat-i-Islami or the

---

[72] Arnold (1983), p. 82.
[73] Ibid, p. 92.
[74] Ibid, pp. 116–117; Bradsher (1999), p. 62.
[75] Amin had attempted to assassinate Taraki but failed the first time around. The incident was enough to make Taraki step down for "health reasons." Amin managed to finally kill off Taraki – he allegedly ordered his killing that involved having him tied in bed and smothered with a pillow. He was pronounced dead from ill health on October 10, 1979; Arnold (1983), pp. 78, 83, 93; Bradsher (1999), pp. 55–60.
[76] Arnold (1983), pp. 98, 101; Bradsher (1999), p. 98.
[77] Arnold (1983), pp. 102–103.
[78] Ibid, pp. 111–113.

Hazara parties. Mujahedin fighters could not travel from the south to the north of the country without getting ambushed by fighters from another insurgent party, with allegations that they were at times more scared of fellow mujahedin fighters than the communists. The human toll was heavy and the effect on morale notable. In light of the resistance on the part of the mujahedin leadership to put an end to factional fighting and to forge a united front, a set of influential regional commanders decided to take matters into their own hands. Their objectives were straightforward: They would convene a Commanders' Council, known as Shura Sar Ta Sari, to stop factional fighting and coordinate their attacks in order to balance against the common enemy – the PDPA government.

The known players in the council were Jamiat-i-Islami commanders such as Amin Wardak, Abdul Haq, and Mullah Malang. They, in turn, were in charge of recruiting other commanders in their areas of influence. Amin Wardak was responsible for the central area of Afghanistan known as Hazarajat; Abdul Haq was responsible for the east; Mullah Malang for the southwest; and all worked on their respective networks in the north and west. The most conspicuous absence was the lack of representation for Hizb-i-Islami, which did not come as a surprise given the intensity of the factional conflicts among the commanders. It did, however, make it harder to attain the goal of cooperation as Hizb-i-Islami remained on the other side.

The formation of the Commanders' Council underlined the tensions between the party leaders, who were mostly waging the war from Pakistan by courting money for their cause, and the commanders, who were actually fighting on the Afghan front. The commanders who joined the council were of the opinion that no victory would be possible without unity. The party leaders were of a different mind, and induced compliance on the part of their commanders by redirecting money away from them and toward new figures such as Gul Agha Shirzai and Mullah Naqeeb. In line with theoretical expectations, the creation of the Commanders' Council was a manifestation of the strong tension between (1) the desire to form an effective alliance and be on the winning side and (2) the desire to maximize power within the mujahedin alliance.

A founder of the Commanders' Council, Mullah Malang, elaborated on the opposition the council faced and the factors that led to its demise:

I was very worried about the dangers of lack of coordination among the field commanders. I went and talked to Khalis [leader of Hizb-i-Islami Khalis] and all the *tanzeem* [party] leaders. I explained our objectives to them. . . . Some got angry at us. The others agreed but not with their heart. Khalis tried to prevent us from forming this shura – one of his eyes went blind because of the pressure he was under over this. He argued with me at length – but I did not agree. We commanders faced opposition. . . . No one helped us. Finally the reserves that we had were finished in a year or two and we could not sustain the shura. All the logistics were cut off – only some commanders who agreed to follow the line of their party leaders continued to be supplied. Massoud was supported by Rabbani [leader of Jamiat-i-Islami]. Ismail Khan likewise. Our shura's commanders in the south – we had our supplies cut. They supported new commanders instead – which had no result. This was the situation which helped Dr. Najib's [Afghan communist] government to survive.[79]

GOVERNMENT EFFORTS TO BREACH MUJAHEDIN UNITY

The Afghan communist government, aware of the conflict and resulting tensions among the mujahedin parties, had tried to amplify them in its favor through both overt and covert ways. Specifically, it tried to expand on its strength by getting tribal leaders to join its side in the form of militias and by striking secret agreements, known as protocols, with mujahedin commanders.

The Militias

In search of allies, leaders of the PDPA regime, starting with Babrak Karmal, reverted to a strategy that dated back to Durrani kings: They extended privileges to certain tribal chiefs in return for security and loyalty. This strategy was employed throughout the Jihad but was particularly pronounced in the later years, when Najibullah took the reins of the PDPA. As expected by the theory, these alliance decisions were made based on considerations of power and survival, not ideology or ethnicity. Capitalizing on the rich underlying set of intra-tribal competition and disputes, the PDPA would get tribal chiefs who had rivals in the ranks of the mujahedin to strike an alliance with the government. In terms of the narrative used to justify this association, as a regional expert vividly attests: "There was never any serious pretense that the tribal figures who sided with the government brought with them any ideological commitment. Instead the government provided and the tribal allies endorsed a nationalist façade."[80] The main service of the militia was to protect government positions near urban centers and strategic passages, but it never won grassroots support. At best it allowed for protection of certain critical areas and exacerbated the internal division among its mujahedin opponents.[81]

An example of such an arrangement was with Malik Firdous Khan Mohmand, who was given a seat in the senate and whose sons, Mohmand and Feridun, were commissioned army officers who led militias in Mohmand territory bordering Goshta District. In an interview, one of the sons, Feridun, said that the family tradition of serving in militias was power-driven: "During the British period (in Peshawar) our tribe had a role on the frontier. The tribe had armed men who were responsible for solving any problems on the frontier. They did not use to sit there permanently. They could be mobilized as necessary."[82]

The strategy on selecting militias was quite standard: The government would identify the ethnic or religious minorities in the regions of interest, as they were

---

[79] Interview with Mullah Malang in Semple (2010).
[80] Semple (2010), p. 46.
[81] Dorronsoro and Lobato (1989), pp. 98–99, 104.
[82] Interview with Feridun Mohmand in Semple (2010).

likely to be the aggrieved populations most interested in striking a deal as a means of increasing their relative power. Indeed, the PDPA proved anthropologically astute in identifying the relevant antagonisms that, for instance, made the Uzbek minority prime targets for militia conscription. The most famous militia was undoubtedly that of the northern Uzbek strongman, General Dostum – a militia that would feature prominently in the mutiny against Najibullah that led to the onset of the intra-mujahedin war, described in the previous chapter, and that in turn played a prominent role in the commencement of intra-mujahedin hostilities. Other famous militia leaders included Rasul Pahlawan, the future Dostum commander, who was killed under dubious circumstances and whose brother Malik orchestrated the anti-Dostum mutiny described in Chapter 3 of this book. Rasul Pahlawan had originally been affiliated with the Harakat-i-Inqilab-i-Islami mujahedin party until 1982, when factional fighting with Jamiat-i-Islami drove him into the arms of the government.[83] A famous religious minority turned militia involved Kayan Ismaili, located between the North Salang and the Kelagay army base. Their strategic position earned them this government intervention to serve as a militia, which they saw as a way to retain their autonomy and increase their power.[84] That, of course, did not prevent them from also dabbling with the mujahedin.

Many had feared the lack of loyalties of these tribal militias. And the rift within the PDPA was so deep that some elements saw the militia strategy as not targeted against the mujahedin but rather as an effort to strengthen one PDPA faction against another. Shahnawaz Tanai, a known Khalqi general infamous for attempting a failed coup against Najibullah's regime, was opposed to the creation of militias:

I was against forming the militia units. They were without discipline and were a threat to our regime.... There were 70,000 militia [fighters] eventually. Many of them had contacts with the Jihadis as well as with the government. They could be killed by either side or by their allies.... In general they were loyal to no one.... The militias also split into two pro-Khalq units and pro-Parcham units. We would not give assistance to the wrong side! However, Najibullah was more prejudiced against Khalq than against the mujahedin.[85]

In other words, both sides – the government and tribal leaders themselves – recognized that power and survival, and not ideology or ethnicity, were the ultimate determinants of alliance decisions.

The Protocols

The protocols were cooperation agreements between local Afghan commanders and the Afghan communist government. Although they were supposed to be

---

[83] Dorronsoro and Lobato (1989), p. 101.

[84] Ibid, p. 102.

[85] Tanai in his interview attributed his failed coup to the internal party divisions. Interview with Shahnawaz Tanai in Semple (2010).

covert, as indicated in oral narratives from commanders and fighters at the time, the cessation of hostile activity by government forces (be it bombing, shelling, and so forth) and the flow of resources were good indicators of the signing of such an agreement. For instance, Haji Malik, a commander who himself had signed one of the early protocols with the government, reports that he knew which of his fellow local Paghman commanders were *protocolis* – that is, had signed such agreements with the government.[86]

Syed Irkam, who was a fighter in late Jihad, described the manifestation of the protocols on the front:

Haji Hamdai, a commander of Dr. Sadiq, took forward the representational work of the protocol. When he first went to Kabul there was a rumor that he had negotiated a protocol. People did not really believe the stories initially. But when the weapons arrived people realized what had happened. No one dared ask Dr. Sadiq about it. He would have shot anyone or arrested them if they mentioned the word protocol . . . After the protocol, weapons used to come by the container load . . . There used to be flour and other foodstuffs in the front and then weapons stacked behind . . . When commanders fell out, each accused the others of being *protocolis*.[87]

Protocols also appear to have been at least fully tolerated, if not officially condoned, by the mujahedin party leaders whose commanders were involved in such agreements. The protocols were a pragmatic, power-driven exchange. The PDPA government wanted to put a stop to mujahedin activity in certain strategic areas, while the mujahedin wanted access to resources and a respite from the fight with the government that would allow them to regroup, rearm, and address their factional fights for superiority over other mujahedin parties. Neither ideology nor ethnicity, but rather concerns about relative power – this time in comparison to other alliance partners – drove the decision to sign protocols. As a regional expert attests: "Intensified factional conflict between the mujahedin factions was a key driver behind the protocols. . . . This allowed the government to buy off the mujahedin, . . . gradually establishing a balance of power, at the price of a large subsidy to the armed groups."[88]

A case in point is offered by Sher Zaman Kochai, who discussed the government's protocol with a Harkat commander, Abdul Hakeem Akhundzada, as a way to protect the critical Naghlu Dam. This dam was on the target list of the commander's factional opponent, a Hizb-i-Islami commander. The government understood that the protocol would allow Akhundzada to marginalize his factional enemy and would in turn extend protection to the valuable infrastructure of the dam.[89]

The fact that even Ahmad Shah Massoud, the leading commander of Jamiat-i-Islami, had allegedly signed a protocol is suggestive evidence of why such agreements were tolerated by the party leadership. In the initial years of the

---

[86] Interview with Haji Malik in ibid.
[87] Interview with Syed Ikram in ibid.
[88] Semple (2010).
[89] Interview with Sher Zaman Kochai in ibid.

civil war the mujahedin were all on the defensive, facing severe casualties, but there was no doubt that Panjshir, the area under Massoud's control, was among the hardest hit. Coll writes, "By the end of 1982 more than 80 percent of the Panjshir's buildings had been damaged or destroyed... with their crops in ruins, their livestock slaughtered, and no end to the fighting in sight, it was unclear how much more hardship the valley's population could bear."[90] It is suggested that Massoud signed his protocol in the spring of 1983 when faced with an acute shortage of arms and military supplies.[91] According to Coll, "Massoud's truce with the Soviets... was his first public demonstration that in addition to being a military genius, he was also willing to cut a deal with anyone at any time and in any direction if he thought it would advance his goals."[92] Meanwhile, Massoud continued his fight against the Hizb-i-Islami forces of Hekmatyar. The rationale behind the protocol that Ahmad Shah Massoud had signed with the government is vividly captured in an account of the events by Kareem Hashimi, a fighter and resistance official:

Massoud sent Abdul Rahman to Panjshir in his capacity as deputy to establish links with the government. This was also the period in which Massood signed a protocol.... In the towns they organized links with anti-government forces. They started working in the jails and managed some important prisoner exchanges. They formed a group to work inside *Hizb-i-Islami* in each neighborhood of Kabul and inside the PDPA army.... Tanks and massive depots with food supplies and logistic materials were captured. Massood was now successful in securing his rear and had all the supplies he could use.[93]

SHIA ALLIANCE FORMATION AND FACTIONALISM

Apart from the seven Sunni parties discussed earlier, the Jihad also prompted intense political and military interactions among the Hazaras, the largest Shia community in Afghanistan. Their politics, however, remained largely distinct from those of the Sunni mujahedin parties and were largely confined to the central Afghan area of Hazarajat. The discussion that follows offers an overview of their factionalism and alliance politics and how it all fit in the context of the broader conflict.

Much like other Afghan urban dwellers, some Hazaras were part of the Communist Party and were affiliated with its Dari-speaking Parcham faction.[94] In the egalitarian spirit that the PDPA liked to claim it fostered, and in the context of its general nationality policy – which had intended to elevate the status of Afghanistan's non-Pashtun population – some Hazaras even managed

---

[90] Coll (2004), p. 118.
[91] Ibid, pp. 118, 124.
[92] Ibid, p. 121.
[93] Interview with Kareem Hashimi in Semple (2010).
[94] Bradsher (1999), p. 49.

to rise to the party's higher echelons: Most prominently, Sultan Ali Kesht-mand served as prime minister. But the PDPA was largely seen as unable to break from the pro-Pashtun bias that had characterized Afghanistan's earlier governments.

The PDPA also tried to win over more Hazaras in 1984, as part of a broader concerted effort to drive fighters away from the ranks of the mujahedin opposition. As the most politically underrepresented group, the Hazaras were considered more likely to be swayed than the other warring factions. In that regard, the government started publishing a sociocultural magazine for the Hazara community, called *Gharjestan*, which became popular among Hazara intellectuals in the capital. It also established a Hazara council (shura) as a way to signal the political relevance of the group and tried to woo its elements in a later reconciliation process.[95]

However, most Hazaras were not members of the communist establishment, and rather formed their own Shia Afghan mujahedin groups in reaction to policies that the PDPA tried to implement in the central Afghan region of Hazarajat in the late 1970s. Even though those Hazara parties were also in opposition to the PDPA, there were no formal links between them and their Sunni mujahedin counterparts, excluding them in turn from the main body of the resistance. Despite being localized, the Hazara mujahedin opposition reacted strongly to government policies that targeted existing elites and their patronage networks.[96] Religious elites were first to be targeted, with the traditional local elite structures following soon after. The idea behind the policy was simple – for the educational and modernization policies to succeed, the PDPA needed to do away with religious elements that opposed them. Similarly, for land collectivization to work, the PDPA would need to do away with the feudal landowners and break the bond between them and their serfs working the lands.[97] This view distorted the patron-client relations that informed the interactions between landowners (*mir*) and farmers in Hazarajat without offering some sort of alternative sustainable leadership.

In an attempt to balance against the communists, the resistance came together under the leadership of Sheikh Sayed Ali Behesti and his Shura-i-Inqelab-i-Ittefaq-i-Islami-i-Afghanistan (Revolutionary Council of the Islamic Union of Afghanistan), also known as Shura-i-Ittefaq, in September 1979.[98] That organization included both landowners (*mir*) and religious leaders (both traditionalist *seyed* and more radical *sheikhs*), with the *seyed* being the dominant center. By mid-1981, the PDPA government had effectively been driven out of the region.[99] Governance decisions were now in the hands of the Shura-i-Ittefaq.

[95] Harpviken (1996), p. 81.
[96] Ibid, p. 48.
[97] Roy (1990), p. 85.
[98] Harpviken (1996), p. 71.
[99] Ibid, p. 62.

The withdrawal of the PDPA brought about a change in the balance of power, resulting in an internal rift in Hazarajat. As the theory would predict, the declining power emanating from the communists led to infighting among the Hazara, as groups began to worry more about their relative power *within* the alliance. In the first stage, the traditionalist religious elites targeted the landowners, with the *seyed* turning against the feudal *mir*. The latter had lost the resources from which they leveraged power and were easily marginalized.[100] But the primacy of the *seyed* was itself short-lived, as by 1982 Hazarajat became engulfed in civil conflict. This time around, more conservative religious elements among the *seyed*, along with Islamist *sheikhs* from Sazman-i-Nasr-i-Islam-i-Afghanistan, known as Sazman-i-Nasr (the Islamic Victory Organization of Afghanistan, which was created in 1979 and inspired by the fervor of the Iranian Revolution), vied for power. Their rise was in reaction to what they saw as an increasingly repressive administrative apparatus that the Shura-i-Ittefaq, under traditionalist *seyed* leadership, had put in place. With the implementation of mandatory conscription to the Shura's militia and a 20 percent tax on production across the former PDPA administrative units that the Shura had chosen to maintain, the "revolutionary" regime put in place felt as predatory as the one the people had fought to oust.[101]

Through popular support, the Islamists finally asserted their control two years later.[102] The Islamists promoted a political role for religion and did not shy from using violence to attain it. Their popular appeal relied on their service provision and their stance to protect the people from the Shura's predation. It was easier for them to assert their control in areas where they had a preexisting local network. In other localities, they had to resort to coercion.[103] And they succeeded. While in 1982 they only controlled 15 percent of Hazarajat, by 1984 the Islamists controlled two-thirds of the territory.[104] The religious side had ascended to political power, marginalizing the former local elites, first the feudal *mir* and then the traditionalist *seyed*. The takeover by the Islamists lowered the intensity of the conflict, but the fighting did not cease. Now there was low-intensity conflict across Islamist parties. Echoing the pattern in the Hazara territory more broadly, and confirming the theory's expectations, balancing alliances held together until victory seemed likely and then broke apart as formerly allied groups began to worry about their relative power within the alliance. Sepah-i-Pasdaran (Army of the Guardians), which was created in 1982 and first worked in alliance with Sazman-i-Nasr to overthrow the *seyeds*, later turned against it. Sepah-i-Pasdaran was more radical than Sazman-i-Nasr and even closer in ideology to the teachings of Imam Khomeini.[105]

[100] Ibid, pp. 59–70.
[101] Ibid, pp. 70–73.
[102] Ibid, pp. 68, 86.
[103] Ibid, pp. 87–89.
[104] Roy (1995), p. 96.
[105] Emadi (1995), p. 377.

Factional conflict only really ended with the formation in July 1989 of Hizb-i-Wahdat (Party of Unity), an umbrella organization for all the Shiite parties. Hizb-i-Wahdat acted as a reconciliatory coalition, bringing together Islamists, traditionalists, landowners, and even a notable number of former communist Hazaras before the onset of the intra-mujahedin conflict.[106] The common narrative that united them all was one of Hazara ethnic identity.[107] But splits in the Hazara front were witnessed again a few years into the intra-mujahedin war (as discussed in detail in the previous chapter), with Hizb-i-Wahdat splitting along the lines that were identifiable as the Sepah-i-Pasdaran vs. Sazman-i-Nasr rift.

CONCLUSION

The Afghan Jihad, much like the intra-mujahedin war, was riddled with strife and factionalism linked to concerns about relative power. The warring sides fought among themselves nearly as much as they fought against their nominal ideological enemies. They switched sides, they split apart, and they took over their respective party's leadership. Consistent with this book's main argument, alliances tended to hold together when the opposing force was strong and would break apart over issues of strategy and postwar political control when the opposing force was weak. In other words, exactly as the theory would predict, groups maneuvered in order to (1) be on the winning side and (2) maximize their share of postwar political power. This latter imperative meant that groups often worried about their relative power within their alliance, particularly when the enemy was weak and victory seemed possible. Instances of fractionalization also were in line with theoretical predictions – splits and takeovers occurred along preexisting subgroup fault lines, and were generally triggered by poor battlefield performance and asymmetric losses across subgroups.

During this war we also witnessed three instances of commander-level decisions: the recruitment of tribal leaders into militias; the signing of the protocols; and the creation of the Commanders' Council (Shura Sar Ta Sari). Whereas the militias constituted outright defection away from the mujahedin and into the hands of the government, the protocols and the Commanders' Council – for different reasons and with different degrees of tolerance – actually remained consistent with warring party politics. In the instance of the protocols, the party leadership was willing to tolerate this form of government co-optation of their commanders as a way to extend further resources to them, which would allow them to pursue the factional politics for dominance in the intra-mujahedin competition. In the case of the Commanders' Council, however, the party showed no tolerance. The unity exhibited by the commanders was opposed to factional politics and threatened the leadership of the party. As a result, the party withheld resources, starving the commanders who refused to comply

---

[106] Ewans (2002), pp. 215–216.
[107] Harpviken (1996), p. 100.

with party policy. Chapter 5 goes on to examine in more detail the degree to which warring tribal leaders and commanders acted in accordance with group demands or deviated from them. The chapter also examines whether alliance choices on the level of the warring group and subgroup converged at a lower unit of analysis, that of the Afghan local strongman. Chapter 5 does so for three Afghan provinces that were most notorious for their local-level politics – the provinces of Balkh, Nangarhar and Kandahar – during both the Jihad and the intra-mujahedin war periods.

5

The Theory at the Commander Level in Afghanistan, 1978–1998

Thus far, this book has examined the relationship between relative power and identity cleavages in terms of alliance formation and group fractionalization in the Afghan Jihad and the intra-mujahedin war. Actors have included alliances, warring groups, and their subgroups. The book's decision on the relevant level of analysis was made based on an argument about minimum effective actors – an argument that a unit of analysis aggregated at the levels of warring groups and their subgroups would adequately capture alliance shifts and group fractionalization throughout the conflict's trajectory. That approach is fully consistent with the general historiography on the Afghan Jihad and intra-mujahedin war, which has been almost exclusively presented on the level of mujahedin parties and their elites.

The intent of this chapter is to see whether the anticipated behavior, as reflected in the theory, also holds for a lower level of analysis than the subgroup. As referenced in the first chapter of this book, there is a strong trend in the civil war literature of focusing either at the macro (state or rebel group) or micro (individual or village) level with little attempt to link the two. Having examined the macro-level of warring groups and then the lower level of subgroups, the goal of this chapter is to move another level lower and to explore whether local level behavior indeed matches the macro-level predictions of the theory. To the extent that the theoretical predictions hold at multiple levels of analysis, we have greater confidence in the theory's explanatory power and specified mechanisms. In the Afghan context, the relevant lower level is arguably that of the wartime commander.

Assuming reasonably strong central leadership of warring groups, antici-pated differences between the center and the periphery should be subtle. But given that the degree of control of the warring group's central leadership varied over time, we would expect to see some deviation in local behavior, particularly so in Afghanistan where there are several competing as well as cross-cutting cleavages and multiple layers of identity: the extended family (*qawm*), the sub-tribe, the tribe, the ethnic group, and the political party (*tanzeem*) to name a few. Did commanders really act in accordance with group demands or did they pursue competing strategies? Using an original commander dataset that covers Afghanistan's three most important provinces other than Kabul – which is thoroughly discussed in the qualitative case treatments that have preceded this chapter – I show that on the whole, commander behavior tends to converge with the alliance choices made by warring groups. Furthermore, whatever splits or rivalries occur among commanders (of which there are a notable number) are generally consistent with those on the group and subgroup level. In a large majority of cases in both the Afghan Jihad and intra-mujahedin war, leaders either did not have local rivalries or had rivalries consistent with the macro-level cleavages. As a result, though behavior that deviates from such patterns certainly exists, it tends to be contained enough so as not to affect the broader alliance patterns at play.

Because of the scarcity of available information and the labor-intensive nature of the data collection process, data were collected for district commanders in three purposively sampled Afghan provinces.[1] (A detailed description of the methodology behind this data collection enterprise is offered in the Note on Sources at the end of the book). The rationale for selecting Balkh, Kandahar, and Nangarhar provinces is that they pose the hardest test. As described in detail later, these are provinces that are very different from each other in terms of geographic location and ethnic makeup, and arguably had the strongest and most distinctive local politics in Afghanistan for the periods under inquiry. For these three provinces, all of the major commanders in any one (or both) of the civil wars – a total of 141 of them – were identified. For each individual commander, descriptive information was collected on ethnicity, tribe, language, sect, education, and party affiliation. The relative power of each commander was assessed using information about the number of fighters he controlled, his battlefield performance, and his source of influence.

An important disclaimer is that this book does not seek to explain the incentives and behaviors of individual commanders. It recognizes that these motivations can be multidimensional and highly complex. The fact that local rivalries and alliance choices may manifest themselves in a way that maps up closely against warring group cleavages does not say anything about why individual commanders made those decisions. Commanders may have joined competing factions because they were enemies to begin with, or they may have become enemies after joining the factions, or both. The potential endogeneity of individual-level motivations has been compellingly addressed by other scholars and is beyond the scope of this book.[2] To the extent that commanders sort themselves into factions and alliances on the basis of personal rivalries and grievances, or that factional rivalries subsequently produce personal grievances, that literature and this book are compatible. What this chapter aims to see

[1] Afghanistan now has thirty-four provinces, after the addition of Panjshir and Daikundi as provinces in 2004.

[2] Kalyvas (2003, 2006, 2008).

is simple and specific: whether alliances in the Afghan Jihad and the intra-mujahedin war were more or less mirrored at a level below the group and the subgroup – that of the commander. So long as this is the case, the theory is supported, regardless of individual-level motivations.

What are the expected outcomes in terms of commander behavior that would be consistent with the theory? Enemies and rivalries, as well as friendships and alliances, on the local level should be consistent with those on the warring-group level. Splits should also mirror those predicted by group fractionalization, and should converge with subgroup behavior – in other words, commanders belonging to the same subgroups should act the same way. Commander behavior that betrays tensions between commanders belonging to the same warring group or groups in the same alliance, as well as splits inconsistent with those predicted on the subgroup level, would be deviating from the proposed theory. Similarly, cooperation between commanders whose parties are national-level enemies would also be considered incompatible with the theory's predictions. This does not preclude local level rivalries or alliances. It just anticipates that those rivalries and alliances will be forged along lines that are largely consistent with the group-level alliances.

COMMANDER DESCRIPTIVE STATISTICS

Figure 5.1 employs a flowchart to portray the entry and exit of commanders in the two civil wars – the Afghan Jihad and the intra-mujahedin war – across the three provinces under study. It is interesting to note the degree of continuity between the two conflicts, with 102 out of the 131 commanders who participated in the Jihad continuing on to be strongmen in the intra-mujahedin war, in which only 10 new commanders surfaced. This continuity is also clear when looking at each of the three provinces separately, with Balkh having forty-three out of its forty-eight Jihad commanders continue on to fight the intra-mujahedin war and Nangarhar thirty-seven out of forty-one. The case with the least continuity in commanders between the two civil wars is Kandahar. As described later in the chapter, Kandahar saw many commanders withdraw from fighting altogether in the intra-mujahedin war, with only twenty-four commanders being prevalent in that war as opposed to forty-two during the Jihad. Only two of those were new players.

Commander Identity Characteristics

As expected, because of the high degree of overlap in terms of commanders between the Jihad and the intra-mujahedin war, the general descriptive statistics presented here – be it their ethnicity, language, sect, or educational levels – do not differ markedly from one war to the other. In terms of ethnic makeup (Figure 5.2), the provinces of Kandahar and Nangarhar (which also happen to be the epicenters of the present-day insurgency in the south and east) are almost exclusively Pashtun, and the commanders, both during the Jihad and during

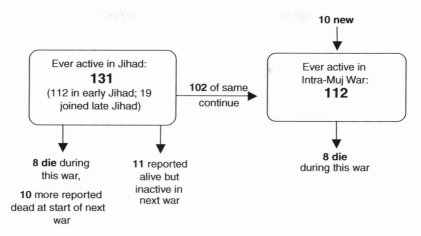

Kandahar Only

Balkh Only

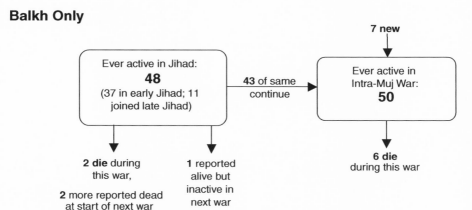

FIGURE 5.1. Number of Commanders Active in the Afghan Civil Wars

Nangarhar Only

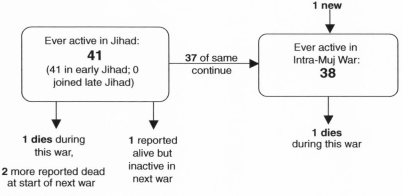

FIGURE 5.1 (*continued*)

the intra-mujahedin war, were ethnic Pashtuns. On the other hand, Balkh, the central region of political activity in the north, is the heartland of minorities, with Tajik, Uzbek, Hazara, as well as Pashtun representation, and commanders more or less reflected the demographics of those constituencies across the two conflicts. Similarly, the commanders also appear to be representative of a broad set of tribal demographics in the majority Pashtun provinces of Kandahar

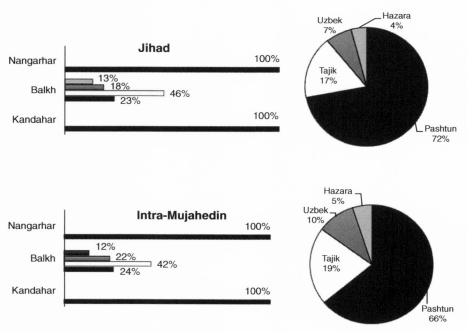

FIGURE 5.2. Afghan Commander Ethnicity

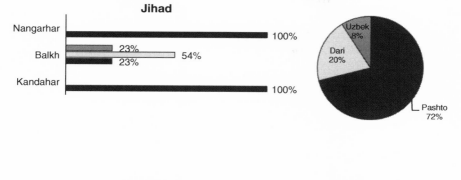

FIGURE 5.3. Afghan Commander Language

and Nangarhar.[3] In Kandahar, the more highly represented tribes were the Noorzais, Alokozais, and Popolzais (the tribe of president Hamid Karzai), whereas in Nangarhar they were the Mohmands and the Khogyanis.[4]

As far as primary language is concerned (Figure 5.3), all the Pashtun commanders spoke Pashto, with Tajik and Hazara commanders speaking Dari, and Uzbek commanders Uzbek.

Similarly, in terms of sectarian affiliation, all the Pashtun, Tajik, and Uzbek commanders were Sunni, whereas the Hazara commanders were Shiites. All the commanders in Kandahar and Nagarhar had Pashto as their first language and were Sunni, whereas in Balkh half were Dari-speaking, with the rest evenly split between Uzbek- and Pashto-speakers. Roughly 15 percent of Balkh commanders (the Hazara ones) in both the Jihad and the intra-mujahedin conflict were Shiites.

There is also notable variation among the commanders in terms of their educational levels both within and across provinces (Table 5.1). Looking at the whole sample, only roughly a fifth of them are illiterate (with levels being higher in Balkh than in Kandahar or Nangarhar during the intra-mujahedin war); roughly a third of them had religious education (with numbers being considerably higher in Kandahar, where more than half received religious education, and lowest in Balkh, where only a fifth did); 10 percent had some

---

[3] No such breakdown is available for Balkh, which is overwhelmingly minority-populated, with the Pashtuns residing there belonging almost exclusively to Ghilzai tribes.

[4] See Appendix for a table with a complete tribal breakdown.

TABLE 5.1. *Afghan Commander Education*

	Jihad				Intra-Mujahedin War			
	All N = 131	Kandahar N = 42	Balkh N = 48	Nangarhar N = 41	All N = 112	Kandahar N = 24	Balkh N = 50	Nangarhar N = 38
Illiterate	22%	24%	23%	20%	22%	17%	26%	21%
≤6 yrs. Religious	15%	33%	8%	2%	13%	42%	8%	3%
>6 yrs. Religious	18%	21%	13%	20%	17%	21%	12%	21%
Primary (≤6 y)	11%	2%	27%	2%	14%	4%	28%	3%
Secondary (6–12 y)	21%	5%	23%	34%	21%	4%	22%	32%
Tertiary (>12 y)	12%	10%	6%	22%	12%	13%	4%	21%
Missing	2%	5%						

primary education (with only 2 percent of the sample in Kandahar and Nangarhar falling into this category, as opposed to more than a fourth in Balkh); 20 percent had some secondary education (with Nangarhar having more than a third of its commanders with secondary education during the intra-mujahedin war, Balkh roughly a fourth, and Kandahar a mere 5 percent); and another roughly 10 percent had university-level education (the most highly educated being in Nangarhar, where more than a fifth had university education, as opposed to roughly 10 percent in Kandahar and 5 percent in Balkh between the two conflicts).

Commander Power Characteristics

Afghan commanders get their influence from a range of sources that can be tribal/ethnic, religious, or political (Table 5.2). Tribal or ethnic influence stems from a commander's position in the hierarchy of a descent-based group (i.e., a tribal chief or leader); religious influence flows from a commander's Islamic learning, credentials, or charisma (i.e., a cleric or imam); and political influence derives from a leadership role in a party or other political organization. Any combination is theoretically possible, and in fact all eight combinations are observed in the data. In the Jihad, 83 percent of commanders had some form of political backing, of whom 50 percent had political backing alone and another 44 percent had tribal/ethnic and political backing together. The numbers are similar for the intra-mujahedin war. Exceedingly few commanders relied solely on tribal backing or solely on religious backing. Most had either political backing alone or some combination of sources of influence. This is strongly suggestive of the financial connections that come from political backing linked to parties, and the influence that parties had over their field commanders through the control of resources. (This was also apparent in the discussion of the shura sar ta sari, the Commanders' Council, in the previous chapter, where parties quelled a commander-level initiative by cutting off

TABLE 5.2. *Afghan Commander Sources of Influence*

	Jihad N = 131	Intra-Muj N = 112
Tribal/Ethnic only	6%	3%
Tribal/Ethnic and Religious only	2%	1%
Tribal/Ethnic, Religious, and Political	3%	3%
Tribal/Ethnic and Political only	34%	43%
Religious only	5%	2%
Religious and Political only	8%	13%
Political only	38%	33%
Missing/None	4%	3%
Marginals		
Tribal in any combination	44%	50%
Religious in any combination	18%	19%
Political in any combination	83%	92%

(*continued*)

TABLE 5.2 (continued)

	Kandahar		Balkh		Nangarhar	
	Jihad N = 42	Intra-Muj N = 24	Jihad N = 48	Intra-Muj N = 50	Jihad N = 41	Intra-Muj N = 38
Tribal/Ethnic only	14%	13%	2%	0	2%	0
Tribal/Ethnic and Religious only	5%	4%	0	0	0	0
Tribal/Ethnic, Religious, and Political	0	0	2%	0	7%	8%
Tribal/Ethnic and Political only	19%	0	38%	62%	44%	45%
Religious only	17%	8%	0	0	0	0
Religious and Political only	12%	38%	0	2%	15%	13%
Political only	26%	29%	54%	34%	32%	34%
Missing/None	7%	8%	4%	2%	0	0
Marginals						
Tribal/Ethnic, any combination	38%	17%	42%	62%	54%	53%
Religious, any combination	33%	50%	2%	2%	22%	21%
Political, any combination	57%	67%	94%	98%	98%	100%

their funding or diverting it to party-compliant commanders.) Looking at the provincial level, the density of penetration of political parties is clearly evident in Balkh and Nangarhar, and considerably less so in Kandahar, where the religious influence was an important factor. It was no accident that the Taliban movement sprang up in that province.

As far as battlefield performance is concerned, commanders were either political figures or facilitators with no battlefield role, or had a battlefield role that ranged from an active one to one that had made them leading figures. The overwhelming majority of commanders – be it in the Jihad or the intra-mujahedin war – were active on the battlefield and evenly split in terms of distinction, as judged by their performance across wartime periods and reported in Figure 5.4 and Table 5.3.

Looking at the maximum number of fighters available to a commander over a particular war and reporting the means of that statistic broken down by battlefield performance – even though not much can be reliably said about the relationship between force size and battlefield activity for those who did no fighting, or even among those engaged in low-level fighting – I can conclusively say that those who engaged in high levels of fighting had far larger forces both in the Jihad ($p < 0.000$, $t = 5.56$) and the intra-mujahedin war ($p = 0.0036$, $t = 3.07$), a fact attesting to their leadership roles (Figure 5.5).[5]

[5] Two-tailed p-values. T-test with unequal variances.

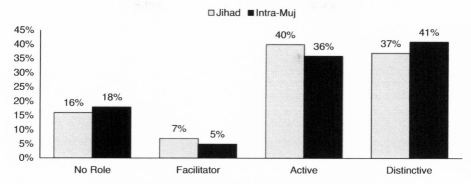

FIGURE 5.4. Afghan Commander Battlefield Performance

TABLE 5.3. *Afghan Commander Battlefield Performance by Province*

	Kandahar		Balkh		Nangarhar	
	Jihad *N* = 42 (%)	Intra-Muj *N* = 24 (%)	Jihad *N* = 47 (%)	Intra-Muj *N* = 49 (%)	Jihad *N* = 40 (%)	Intra-Muj *N* = 38 (%)
No discernible battlefield role	24	38	11	8	13	18
Facilitator off the field	17	13	0	2	5	5
Active on battlefield	43	21	51	45	25	34
Distinctive action on battlefield	17	29	38	45	58	42

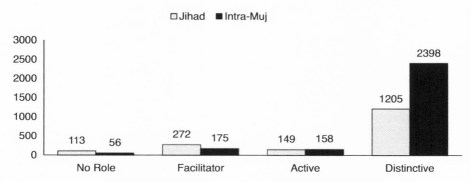

FIGURE 5.5. Mean "Maximum Number of Fighters" by Effectiveness

COMMANDER COMPLIANCE

Now that we have a sense of the identity and power characteristics of Afghan commanders for both the Jihad and the intra-mujahedin war for each of the three provinces of Balkh, Kandahar, and Nangarhar, I discuss commander behavior as it pertains to alliances. The question, again, is the extent to which a commander's behavior converged with that of his respective group's alliance. To capture within-war variation – as these wars were lengthy affairs, with the Jihad lasting for eleven years and the intra-mujahedin war for six years – I code commander behavior for historically analytically relevant periods for each war. Those periods, based on the general literature on Afghanistan's conflicts, are two periods for the Afghan Jihad – the early years of 1978–1985 and the later years of 1986–1989, as determined by the communist leadership phases discussed in Chapter 4 – and three periods for the intra-mujahedin war – the intra-mujahedin party conflict years of 1992–1994, the early Taliban years of 1994–1996, and the late (post-capture of Kabul) Taliban years of 1996– 1998. Coding these five periods was the only realistic and analytically tractable way to try to get at within-conflict variation. Commander-level data are very difficult to collect as it is, and particularly so if one tries to add longitudinal dimensions.

One test on variability of behavior is to see how many commanders keep the same enemy, or change enemies, during a conflict. It is not immediately clear how to aggregate data from the periods within each war so as to come up with an *enemy* variable for each commander, given that some actually change enemies and this is a change that I am interested in observing. A way to address this issue is to track how many commanders keep the same enemy or change enemies within wars. By "enemy" I mean a party with which the commander in question had an active violent conflict. For each war, I count only commanders present in all periods, as this is the only meaningful subsample of commanders to be considered (given the nature of the coding, a commander needs to be around for more than one period for change to be observed). For the Jihad, among 114 commanders who were around for both periods of that war, the People's Democratic Party of Afghanistan (PDPA) – i.e., the communist government – was the primary enemy. We have three instances of commanders who left the mujahedin and joined the government and two instances of commanders who left the government and joined the mujahedin. Among the remaining 109 commanders, 105 of them were against the communist government from beginning to end and 4 were against the mujahedin from beginning to end (Table 5.4).

One may find it surprising that there were so few commanders on the side of the communist government. But given the Afghan context, this makes sense. The periphery (other than some urban centers) was never in the hands of the government. The main actor on the government side was the army. In addition – and as explained in the previous chapter – there were two other ways for the government to exert control in the periphery: through militias, which were

TABLE 5.4. *Enemies in the Afghan Communist-Mujahedin War*

	N = 114
PDPA as enemy in both periods	105
PDPA as enemy first, then Mujahedin	3
Mujahedin as enemy both periods	4
Mujahedin as enemy first, then PDPA	2

selectively employed (and this is the case of the commanders coded here as pro-government), and through protocol agreements. As discussed in Chapter 4, militias sprung up where the communist government awarded monetary benefits to certain disaffected tribal chiefs in exchange for security and loyalty. The main cases of militias were limited but well known. Protocols, on the other hand, as discussed in Chapter 4, did not involve commanders formally changing sides and joining the government. They were "secret" agreements that resulted in the cessation of government hostile activity or in resources in the form of food and weapons.

Although known and informally condoned by the mujahedin leadership – as it allowed them to place the fighting with the government on hold while they pursued their own rivalries – protocols were not particularly extensive (Figure 5.6). In the three provinces covered in the dataset, 15 out of 112 Jihadi commanders (13 percent) had signed a protocol. Most of them were in Kandahar, as this was the only way for the government to exert influence in the rebellious and intractable south; one was in Nangarhar, where a more educated and politically developed mujahedin cadre was better at preventing protocols than in Kandahar; and five were in the northern province of Balkh, the diverse area that also featured the most established militias. Overall, then, commander behavior vis-à-vis alliances during the Jihad was fairly consistent with the group-level cleavage.

Looking at the intra-mujahedin war – and examining only the commanders who were active throughout the three periods of that conflict to leverage

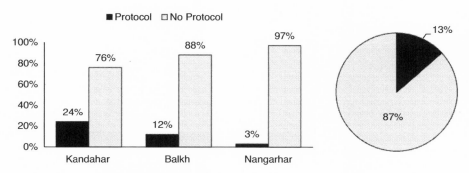

FIGURE 5.6. Commanders' Signing of Protocols

within-war changes – the enemy sides in the first part of the war were Jamiat-i-Islami on one side, fighting Hizb-i-Islami (and its allies of Junbish-i-Milli and Hizb-i-Wahdat in the later years of that period). In the second and third periods, the enemy was either a mujahedin alliance or the Taliban. Among the warring commanders in the first period of that war, twenty-eight were fighting against Jamiat-i-Islami and twenty-four against Hizb-i-Islami and its allies. These fighting patterns indeed reflect the main cleavage of the intra-mujahedin war as captured in Chapter 3. The remaining twelve commanders were Nangarhar commanders in the collaborative shura of that province who for the most part stayed out of the intra-mujahedin fighting (with some exceptions).

In the second period of that war, twenty-six out of the twenty-eight commanders who were fighting Jamiat-i-Islami turned their weapons against the Taliban, and so did twenty-two of the twenty-four commanders who had been fighting Hizb-i-Islami and its allies, as well as eight of the twelve commanders in the Nangarhar shura. These switches were consistent with the national-level anti-Taliban alliance that formed among former warring mujahedin parties. The remaining eight commanders (overwhelmingly from Kandahar) joined the Taliban in that early stage of its appearance. The third period reflects a certain degree of bandwagoning that happened on the side of the Taliban as it became clear that the Taliban would win the conflict. Sixteen commanders were now on the side of the Taliban, with nine commanders switching away from the mujahedin and into Taliban ranks (five from Jamiat-i-Islami, one from Hizb-i-Islami's alliance, and three from the Nangarhar shura). This move is also largely consistent with expected behavior, based on the national-level alliance changes.

Besides national-level enemies, there were also local rivalries between commanders. The rivalries either manifested themselves in cleavages that mirrored the party-level cleavage or they went counter to it, constituting deviations from group and subgroup alliance politics. As stated earlier, having rivalries that were observationally equivalent with the macro-level cleavage does not mean they were motivated by that cleavage. Local level politics most likely inspired many commanders to side with competing camps in the first place. The theory is thus agnostic as to individual-level motivations of commanders; it simply holds that once leaders sort themselves into factions (regardless of their motivations), they will tend to behave consistently with the national-level dictates of that faction.

In Table 5.5, a commander is coded as having a rivalry in a given war if he had a violent clash with another commander during any phase of that war. Commanders are coded as having "inconsistent" rivalries if they had a rivalry that was deviant from their warring group's enemies during any period of the respective war. Finally, in each period I also show what portion of rivalries are inconsistent. These last two measures differ slightly. One is based on commanders, and codes whether they have any inconsistent rivalry in either

TABLE 5.5. *Afghan Commander Consistent and Inconsistent Rivalries*

	Jihad N = 131	Intra-Muj N = 112
Commanders with rivalries	54% (4.4%)	21% (3.8%)
Portion of commanders with rivalries of which at least 1 was inconsistent	48% (6.0%)	70% (9.8%)
Portion of *all* commanders (with rivalries or not) with inconsistent rivalries	26% (3.8%)	14% (3.3%)
Portion of rivalries inconsistent in phase 1	43% (7.3%)	65% of 20 (10.9%)
Portion of rivalries inconsistent in phase 2	52% (6.3%)	100% of 2
Portion of rivalries inconsistent in phase 3	NA	100% of 3

	Kandahar		Balkh		Nangarhar	
	Jihad N = 42	Intra-Muj N = 24	Jihad N = 48	Intra-Muj N = 50	Jihad N = 41	Intra-Muj N = 38
Commanders with rivalries	55% (7.8%)	8% (5.8%)	69% (6.8%)	10% (4.3%)	37% (7.6%)	42% (8.1%)
Portion of commanders with rivalries of which at least 1 was inconsistent	35% (10.1%)	100% (NA)	45% (8.8%)	100% (NA)	73% (11.8%)	56% (12.8%)
Portion of *all* commanders (with rivalries or not) with inconsistent rivalries	19% (6.1%)	8% (5.8%)	31% (6.8%)	10% (4.3%)	27% (7.0%)	24% (7.0%)

Note: Standard error in parentheses

phase of the war, meaning it reflects the likelihood that a given commander is involved in an inconsistent rivalry (given that they were involved in at least one rivalry). The other measure reflects the likelihood of any particular rivalry being inconsistent with the higher-level order. More than half of commanders had some form of local rivalry during the Jihad, but only roughly half of those – which means approximately a fourth of overall commanders – had an inconsistent rivalry. The numbers are considerably lower for the intra-mujahedin war, which lasted roughly half as long as the Jihad and had far fewer warring parties. About 21 percent of commanders had some form of local rivalry, with about 70 percent of these rivalries being inconsistent with the higher-level cleavage. That means about 14 percent of the commanders in the intra-mujahedin war at some time were involved in a fight that was against the dictates and patterns of the general war – quite a low proportion.

Balkh had the highest level of rivalries, which is unsurprising given the number of active groups in the province, but it is Nangarhar that had the higher rate of inconsistent rivalries. A short qualitative discussion on the provinces later in the chapter describes how these rivalries manifested themselves. The important thing to take away from this analysis is that even in Afghanistan, which is renowned for the importance of its local politics, and even in the arguably most fractionalized and locally political provinces within Afghanistan such as Balkh, Kandahar, and Nangarhar, the rivalries that deviated from those in the center occurred only a fourth of the time in the Jihad and less than a sixth of the time in the intra-mujahedin war. This means that in the large majority of cases, local rivalries (or lack thereof) were consistent with the national-level cleavages – a finding that lends significant support to the theory.

What really stands out in Table 5.5 is how few local rivalries there are in the second and third parts of the intra-mujahedin war. There are so few local rivalries in these cases that I cannot say much about their likelihood of being inconsistent (they tend to be 100 percent inconsistent, but this is on the basis of only two rivalries in the early Tailban and three rivalries in the late Taliban periods). This immediately suggests that (a) there may be something different about the Taliban phases in terms of generating local rivalries, and that (b) there does not appear to be any increase in the likelihood of local rivalries as a war goes on. (Quite the contrary in this case, though certainly other differences may explain this non-effect.) The explanation for this phenomenon, per the theoretical framework in Chapter 2, is that the conflict shifted from one in which relative power was relatively balanced to one in which it was skewed toward one actor over the course of the intra-mujahedin war. This phenomenon, referred to by area experts as *Pax Talibana*, was a result of the increased control of the Taliban of both towns and the countryside. As predicted, power-skewed or "hegemonic" conflicts saw fewer alliance shifts and splits than power-balanced ones. Since the intra-mujahedin conflict had an ethnic character from its very beginning, fewer deviations in its later stages cannot be attributed to character of war. An attempt to further explain the deviation in commander alliance behavior – both through a discussion of the non-effects in the data and through a short qualitative treatment of the Balkh, Kandahar, and Nangarhar provinces – follows.

EXPLAINING DEVIATIONS IN COMMANDER ALLIANCE BEHAVIOR

Given that there are only two wars, the Jihad and the intra-mujahedin war, there is not much computational analysis one can do on the war level. One can only acknowledge that the Jihad was almost twice as long and featured almost twice as many groups, and possibly attribute the higher degree of deviant commander behavior during that war to those factors. After all, the yearly rate of inconsistent rivalries per commander is virtually identical in the two conflicts

(0.024 in the jihad, 0.025 in the intra-mujahedin war).[6] A contrarian, however, may argue that the outcome is overdetermined – it may be that the higher number of groups or the longer duration explains the higher magnitude of deviance, but it may very well also be that the difference in the character of war (ideological Jihad versus ascriptive intra-mujahedin war) explains the difference in deviance. The qualitative discussion of the Jihad and intra-mujahedin wars in Chapters 3 and 4 should have put such arguments to rest. The section that follows in any case offers a certain degree of qualitative background for the respective conflicts in each province, as a way to further buttress the argument that the number of groups and the war's duration, rather than the character of war, explain the degree of deviance, and when such deviations happen they seem to be an idiosyncratic and often esoteric local power scramble that a national-level warring party could not account for.

Looking at the commanders during the Jihad, where these inconsistencies are most common (there are too few rivalries to be of much statistical use in the intra-mujahedin war), there do not appear to be any systematic predictors of deviation from alliance behavior. Even with an increased possibility of false-positives because of multiple comparisons, after several different tests, nothing approaches a statistically significant result. (That of course can be partially attributed to the relatively low number of incidents of deviation to begin with). Specifically, one of these tests looks at the mean number of fighters and finds it to be similar among those commanders who did and did not sign a protocol – 512 for non-signatories versus 642 for signatories ($p = 0.63$). Similarly, those who have inconsistent rivalries have 520 fighters on average, whereas those with no rivalry or with consistent rivalries have 559 fighters ($p = 0.81$). Likewise, those with any local rivalries, consistent or not, are similar to those without any local rivalries – 542 versus 557 ($p = 0.93$). Commanders who switched between PDPA and non-PDPA parties also showed no statistically significant difference according to a t-test – 965 fighters for those who switched versus 514 fighters for those who did not (with only 10 switchers, $p = 0.39$).

Additionally, there are also no clear differences in relation to battlefield performance. Comparing protocol signatories to non-signatories, there is no difference in their likelihood of having some battlefield activity (be it distinctive or not) – 67 percent of signatories have such involvement as compared to 79 percent of non-signatories ($p = 0.35$). Looking instead at only distinctive performers on the battlefield, protocol signatories are 40 percent likely to be distinctive on the battlefield, whereas non-signatories are 36 percent likely ($p = 0.80$). Similarly, those who are highly engaged on the battlefield are no more likely to have local rivalries (60 percent) than those who are less active (51 percent) ($p = 0.28$), nor are they significantly more likely to have inconsistent rivalries (48 percent for distinctive performers, 33 percent for others, $p = 0.14$).

---

[6] These figures were calculated by dividing the number of inconsistent rivalries in each conflict by the number of commander-years in each conflict. For the jihad: (34)/(11 years*131 commanders) = 0.024. For the intra-mujahedin war, (17)/(6 years*112 commanders) = 0.025.

Finally, the probability of switching sides (from PDPA to non-PDPA or vice versa) is no higher among those who are highly active on the battlefield (6 percent) than among those who are not (9 percent) ($p = 0.61$).

A qualitative glimpse of the relevant cleavages and rivalries in the respective provinces during the Jihad and the intra-mujahedin offers an illuminating backdrop to the discussion of these non-results. Starting with Balkh, the most ethnically heterogeneous of the three provinces with Tajik, Pashtun, Hazara, and Uzbek commanders, among others, one needs to note that this is an area that exhibited major shifts in political alignment – there were relatively more commanders and people with influence from this area who sided with the government during the Jihad. The Jihad period saw multiple cases of factional conflict, but the main rivalry in the province matched the national alignment. Hizb-i-Islami, whose primary support base was among the Pashtuns of Balkh district, clashed with Jamiat-i-Islami, whose main support base was Tajik. Local Pashtun rivals of the leading Hizb-i-Islami commanders joined Jamiat-i-Islami, in a move that gave them a platform to rival their neighbors. However, this rivalry is fully consistent with the rivalry of these parties on all fronts throughout the war. The rivalry between Harakat-i-Inqilab and Hizb-i-Islami was also consistent with that across the country. But any rivalry between Jamiat-i-Islami and Harakat-i-Inqilab commanders would be considered deviant behavior, as there was no such fight on the national level.

Indeed, the vast majority of cases of deviation we see in Balkh are cases of Jamiat-i-Islami commanders against Harakat-i-Inqilab commanders. This is directly attributable to local power dynamics. Specifically, an Uzbek cleric, Abdul Rahman Haqani, helped establish a network of commanders in northern Balkh, affiliated with Harakat-i-Inqilab, by appealing to their position as Uzbeks and Sunni clerics. In the power play between minority groups in the North, many of them waged a prolonged fight against Jamiat-i-Islami in the area and eventually affiliated with the Uzbek party of Junbish-i-Milli after the end of the Jihad. Looking at the intra-mujahedin war, Junbish-i-Milli was the dominant power in Balkh and rapidly formed a coalition with Jamiat-i-Islami in 1992–1993. By 1993, Jamiat-i-Islami was fighting Hizb-i-Islami and Hizb-i-Wahdat and by 1994 also Junbish-i-Milli – all changes that were manifested in a more or less fully consistent fashion on the local level in Balkh. Deviations were mostly observed at the 1997 Junbish-i-Milli takeover by Malik (detailed in Chapter 3), which offered an occasion for realignments with the Taliban and then against the Taliban soon after.

In Nangarhar, given the underlying tribal structure in the province, the two dominant parties were Gulbuddin Hekmatyar's Hizb-i-Islami and the party of the same name led by Yunus Khalis. The Mahaz-i-Milli party as well as Ittihad-i-Islami, led by Abdul Rasul Sayyaf, also emerge as relevant parties. The competition among these parties is positive – that is, they are competing over recruitment of fighters, but there are no instances of violence among them or any rivalry that would be quoted as inconsistent. The main deviations are seen in the context of militias – the PDPA relied on its regular army to hold the urban areas and a corridor through the main Jalalabad Valley toward the border post with Pakistan at Torkham. As the regime consolidated, it achieved some success in winning over border tribes to form pro-government militias. For example, and as cited in Chapter 4, one of the leading families of the Mohmand tribe, under Firdous Khan, initially cooperated with the mujahedin before allying with the Kabul government to run a border militia. In the intra-mujahedin war, a general council among the mujahedin commanders across all parties (shura) became the dominant alliance in Nangarhar. The intent of the shura was to prevent conflict among its members. There were, however, some rivalries that were related to the emergence of four major local power brokers – Hazrat Ali, Shomali Khan, Haji Munjai, and Haji Zaman Khogyani – that went against the shura's aspirations for abstinence from intra-mujahedin fighting.

In Kandahar, during the Jihad, the bulk of deviant alignments occurred as vertical splits rather than horizontal splits. A normal seeding process occurred within the fighting parties, in which junior commanders saw little opportunity for advancement in the area of operation of their original front. They thus chose to split off to found their own fronts, leaving the original front intact and often maintaining cordial relations with its commander, who became a mentor figure. This is not considered as inconsistent behavior in terms of alliance choices, as it did not result in any violence or acrimony. However, there were instances of deviation in which several fronts experienced hostile splits, with the original commander proving unable to maintain the loyalty of his sub-commanders. When the sub-commanders took large numbers of men with them and succeeded in obtaining patronage from the Pakistan-based parties, they entirely overshadowed the parent front. One such split, which generated some of the prominent figures of the Jihad in Kandahar, was that in the Arghandab front of Mawlvi Akhtar Mohammad Agha. His junior commanders, such as Akbar Agha, split off to form separate fronts, leading to a terminal decline in Akhtar Mohammad's armed activities. He eventually retired to his madrassah. In Spin Boldak, one of the most prominent and successful commanders of the early Jihad, Faizullah, experienced similar splits. Sub-commanders from the Nurzai tribe split from and eclipsed the commander who had originally mobilized them.

The most famous case of deviant alliance formation and splitting among the Kandahar mujahedin was that of Commander Ismat Muslim. He was one of the early prominent mujahedin commanders in the province. Uniquely, he succeeded in founding and sustaining a political grouping (Fedayin Islam) that received patronage from Pakistan and avoided being absorbed by the seven main Sunni parties. In the early years of the Jihad, Muslim's party maintained an alliance with the other Sunni mujahedin, but Muslim tried to leverage himself into being recognized as the foremost Kandahar commander. This eventually led to a power struggle and armed clash between Muslim and a grouping of the other mujahedin commanders. Having badly miscalculated, Muslim ended up defecting to the government, the senior-most Kandahar commander to do so during the Jihad. But the calculation for Muslim, as the head of his commander network, was different from other members of the network. Thus he was able to bring some but not all of his commanders over to the government. Muslim suffered defections while he made his shift. Mullah Ismail, for example, calculated that it was neither viable nor palatable for him to follow Muslim into the PDPA camp, and he aligned with Ittihad-i-Islami and won recognition as a commander in his own right.

During the intra-mujahedin war in Kandahar, most commanders withdrew from activity. The main ideological driver for the conflict, that being resistance to a communist regime they had labeled as alien and un-Islamic, disappeared. Furthermore, the centralized supply of resources to commanders to maintain their men dried up. The decision to stay in the field entailed either maintaining an alliance with one of the factions still in the field or establishing a roadside checkpoint to extort money from the population. (In some cases, commanders chose both.) The majority of commanders who stayed active after 1992 did indeed adopt a stance that was aligned with that of their faction at the national level. Jamiat-i-Islami-aligned commanders, such as Mullah Naqeeb, became part of the new regime at the provincial level. Hizb-i-Islami ended up in opposition in Kandahar, matching their position at the national level.

However, a handful of commanders adopted alliances at variance with their national alliances, as not all local politics could be accommodated within the factional alignments straddling the national and provincial levels. For instance, one of the leading Ittihad-i-Islami commanders, who followed his faction's line at the center (aligned with the Jamiat-i-Islami led government against Hizb-i-Wahdat), in Kandahar chose to support Hizb-i-Islami in its fight against Jamiat-i-Islami. This was a case of a clash between factional obligations and Kandahar tribal alliances and obligations. Ustad Haleem, as a Nurzai, allied with Ghilzais (Hizb-i-Islami) against Alakozais (the main Jamiat-i-Islami fighters in the province).

CONCLUSION

This chapter has made an important clarification to the theory of this book. It has demonstrated that by and large, it is appropriate to measure the dependent and independent variables of the theory at the level of the warring group or the subgroup. Below that level of aggregation, actors appear more or less compliant with the dynamics taking place over their heads. Even though commander-level local rivalries were abundant, deviations from party-level alliances and cleavages were notably rare in both of the multiparty civil wars in Afghanistan, even in the three locally minded provinces where one would expect those deviations to most likely occur. When those deviations did occur, they were over local scrambles for power. Hence, although the individual level of analysis is important to many strands of the recent civil war literature, it appears that it is safe to operate above that level of analysis while examining alliance and group fractionalization dynamics in multiparty civil wars.

Having now built and tested a theory of warring group alliance and fractionalization behavior in multiparty civil wars through the lens of the Afghan civil wars, it is time to gauge that theory's external validity on a more substantive level. Put simply, is this a theory about Afghanistan, or can it explain group- and subgroup-level conflict processes in multiparty civil wars more generally? Chapters 6–8 seek to answer that critical question. We begin with Chapter 6, which covers the other theory-building case in this book: the gruesome multiparty ethnic civil war in 1990s Bosnia.

PART III

BOSNIA AND HERZEGOVINA

6

The Bosnian Civil War, 1992–1995

This book has so far made the claim that alliances in multiparty civil wars are power-determined, motivated by concerns for victory and the maximization of postwar political control. It has illustrated the theory through the 1992–1998 Afghan intra-mujahedin war, which was largely fought along ethnic lines, and has showed it to hold in the 1978–1989 Afghan civil war, which pitted communists against mujahedin. The theory has also proved robust to different levels of analysis: It is relative power – rather than shared identity – that largely drives alliances, be they among groups or district-level actors, with a notable overall convergence to group directives. What this chapter aspires to do is show that this is not just a story about Afghanistan. Taking us through the 1992–1995 civil war in Bosnia and Herzegovina (BiH), we will witness the alliances and intragroup dynamics at play in this very different context, while recognizing their consistency with the proposed framework. This, in turn, begins to suggest that the theory at hand can offer insight on alliances and group fractionalization in multiparty civil wars more broadly.

The Bosnian conflict was bloody and intense, but it was not selected for examination merely because of its infamy. Rather – as argued in Chapter 1 – it offers interesting variation in alliance patterns, while constituting the simplest case to examine civil war alliance formation. It had three ethnic groups of different demographic sizes and military power, and one notable identity cleavage, that of religion.[1] If there is any case where identity cleavages should determine alliance choices, it would be Bosnia. This case in turn allows for an examination of the role of character of war, because Bosnia also experienced a war from 1941 to 1945, fought along lines with ideological dimensions, as

---

[1] Bosniacs, Bosnian Croats, and Bosnian Serbs are largely Caucasian and speak essentially the same language, but have different faiths – Muslim, Catholic, and Christian Orthodox, respectively. The idea that there are three different languages took hold during the dissolution of Yugoslavia and was entrenched after the end of the 1992–1995 civil war.

discussed in Chapter 7. The analysis of the Bosnian civil war (1992–1995) that follows draws closely from primary sources collected over nine months in the field, which include semi-structured interviews with local political and military elites and convicted war criminals; wartime alliance agreements, declarations, and memoirs; articles from the local and international press; prewar demographic data; and data on wartime casualties and territorial control. I also closely consult the extensive secondary literature on the conflict.

The recent Bosnian civil war was undoubtedly a gruesome affair with strong ethnic undertones. As clearly indicated in *The Bosnian Book of Dead*, a rigorous effort to systematically compile evidence on the war's dead and missing, the overwhelming majority of violence was interethnic. This chapter starts out with a disclaimer in recognition of that indisputable fact – that it does not aspire or claim to provide an understanding of the dynamics and processes that pertain to the targeting and violence during the Bosnian conflict, but rather focuses on a different aspect of the war altogether: the wartime dynamics of alliance formation among groups and the fractionalization dynamics within them. In that regard this will not be a discussion of the massive ethnic cleansing and massacres perpetrated on the orders of infamous Serb wartime leader Radovan Karadžić or his General Ratko Mladić and their cronies. Neither will there be discussion of the counteroffensives of Croat and Muslim forces that finally brought the opposing factions to the negotiating table. Moreover, in a similar vein to the empirical chapters so far, and true to this book's theoretical emphasis on domestic actor interactions, this chapter does not discuss the interventions – be they overt aggression or covert assistance – of external actors such as Serbia, Croatia, or the United States. Indeed, this is a discussion of BiH in which the then-Serb leader Slobodan Milošević and his Croat counterpart Franjo Tuđman do not feature. These personalities, their actions, and general wartime events have been systematically documented in the proceedings of the International Criminal Tribunal for Yugoslavia (ICTY) and in numerous compelling journalistic accounts, academic books, and memoirs.[2] Rather, this chapter focuses on the complex and often brutal interactions among allies, as well as the clashes among co-ethnic rivals in the same warring factions. It exposes the intensity of internal competition and the banality and construction of distance among warring groups.

I should also note that by attempting to explain the infighting between wartime alliances and by observing the associated cooperation between different ethnic warring groups at different times, I am not seeking to justify any such behavior. Nor am I seeking to imply that interethnic cooperation in the name of mass violence is in any way excusable. The violence committed by all parties to this civil war was atrocious, and a small fraction of the perpetrators – most prominently Ratko Mladić and Radovan Karadžić – are laudably in the

---

[2] Gutman (1993); Maass (1996); Silber and Little (1997); Rohde (1997); Sudetic (1998); Cohen (1998). For the most widely acclaimed academic accounts, see Woodward (1995) and Burg and Shoup (1999).

process of being brought to justice by the ICTY. This is a book that describes the conduct of civil war as it is, not as it should be. (In any case, the cooperation of warring groups proved fleeting, and past cooperation did not dissuade warring groups from brutalizing one another at other points in the war.)

On a related note, while this work looks at the role of shared identity in alliance formation during civil wars, it does not speak to the larger identity questions in Bosnia's civil war onset, targeting, or violence. As highly interesting and important as these dimensions of the conflict may be, to the degree that they do not pertain to alliance and group fractionalization dynamics they remain beyond the scope of this study. As noted in the introduction, this is not meant to suggest that identity did not matter in the Bosnian conflict – I only argue that identity did not seem to matter much to the intergroup dynamics under study here.

This chapter traces out the relative power changes over the civil war years and their effect on alliance formation. After an overview of Bosnia's warring actors and a chronology of events, it offers a presentation of the warring groups' relative power changes through shifts in territorial control, which are in turn presented on GIS maps that capture the territorial control of wartime alliances. A discussion of the variant alliance narratives that sprang up in justification of the different alliances follows, along with a detailed exposition of instances of fractionalization among warring actors, examining the cases of the political takeover in Croat ranks and the intra-Muslim conflict. The chapter closes with a section that uses prewar municipal-level data on demography and arms availability, as well as violence and territorial control, as a segue into a discussion of whether the framework holds for levels of analysis more nuanced than the group and subgroup.

ETHNIC MAKEUP AND WARRING FACTIONS

This book is concerned with the civil war in BiH rather than the overall breakup of Yugoslavia, which also precipitated conflicts in Slovenia and Croatia. The conflict in Slovenia was short and contained, resulting in a very small number of deaths, whereas that in Croatia was longer and more substantial but mainly involved only two warring groups – Croats and Serbs. The case of BiH, on the other hand, had three main domestic warring groups, and the fighting was of considerable duration and produced considerable casualties to allow for – if not warrant – an examination of alliance dynamics. In its recent history – the roughly seventy-five years preceding the onset of civil war – BiH was part of Yugoslavia.[3] Although BiH's three ethnic groups of Croats, Muslims, and Serbs spoke essentially the same language, they were of three distinct religions (Catholic, Muslim, and Orthodox Christian, respectively), and had conflicting views on whether their heritage amounted to an idea of a

---

[3] Burg and Shoup (1999), pp. 20–21.

shared Bosnian nation.[4] Despite their differences, BiH's Muslims, Serbs, and Croats did not just reside in purely mono-ethnic areas but rather often lived in highly ethnically mixed contexts. Urban centers tended to be overwhelmingly more ethnically heterogeneous than the countryside. According to the 1991 census, Muslims accounted for 44 percent of the population, Serbs for 31 percent, and Croats for 17 percent, but Serbs tended to populate more rural areas, inhabiting 56 percent of BiH's territory according to the municipal cadastre.[5]

The war in BiH was the most tragic result of the 1991 dissolution of Yugoslavia. In the years leading up to the conflict, BiH's political terrain had become increasingly ethnicized. Muslims founded the Party of Democratic Action (Stranka Demokratske Akcije-SDA) in May 1990; the Serbs launched the Serbian Democratic Party (Srpska Demokratska Stranka Bosne i Hercegovine-SDS) in July of that same year; and the Croats also established their own ethnic party, known as the Croatian Democratic Union (Hrvatska Demokratska Zajednica Bosne i Herzegovine-HDZ), soon after. These nationalist parties came out victorious in the November 1990 republic-level elections, ethnically polarizing BiH.

A few months later, in June 1991, Croatia and Slovenia simultaneously and unilaterally declared their secession from Federal Yugoslavia. After a short-lived and mostly bloodless conflict in Slovenia, and a considerably more violent stand-off between Croats and Serbs in Croatia, the European Community (EC) – the predecessor of the EU – proceeded to recognize them as independent states in January 1992. The proposal for a referendum for independence for BiH in February–March 1992 was supported by the Republic's Muslim and Croat citizens but was opposed by its Serb constituents, who had set up their own parliament and had held their first separate plebiscite in November 1991. The February 29–March 1, 1992 referendum came out 62.68 percent in favor of independence, an anticipated outcome given that the Serbs – who constituted 31 percent of the republic's population – were

---

[4] Given this book's focus on domestic warring actors and their interactions, Bosnian Serbs and Bosnian Croats will, for simplicity, be referred to as Serbs and Croats. In the case where a specific reference needs to be made to Serbs from Serbia and Croats from Croatia, it will be made explicit. This book also refers to Bosnian Muslims as Muslims rather than Bosniacs because the events described predate the recent adoption of the latter term. The term "Muslim" dates from the Austro-Hungarian reign over BiH, and though in broad use, it was only elevated in status in 1971, making Muslims Yugoslavia's sixth constituent nation along with Serbs, Croats, Slovenes, Macedonians, and Montenegrins. The term "Bosniac," which came into popular use during the 1992–1995 war, was originally meant to refer to all people residing in BiH irrespective of nationality. It was espoused by individuals such as Adil Zulfikarpašić, a Muslim leader of the largely secular Muslim Bosniac Organization (MBO) founded in 1991. However, the term Bosniac failed to capture the notion of a true civic identity and instead came to be identified with BiH Muslims. Bosniac was formally codified as the newly espoused term for Muslims in the March 18, 1994 Washington Agreement on the constitution of the Bosnian-Croat Federation. See Woodward (1995), p. 315; Burg and Shoup (1999), pp. 19–20, 36, 41–42, 68, 195–196.

[5] Burg and Shoup (1999), p. 28.

boycotting while the Muslims and Croats had come out in favor.[6] Within a mere two days after the referendum, on March 3, 1992, Alija Izetbegović, the Bosnian Presidency's Muslim president, declared BiH's independence. The results of the pro-independence referendum encouraged the already defiant Serbs to initiate the conflict.[7] War broke out across the country in early April of that year. A detailed timeline and discussion of the conflict, to the degree it relates to wartime alliances, follow.

THE EVOLUTION OF POWER AND ALLIANCES AMONG
WARRING PARTIES

The Bosnian civil war has been largely cast as a war of stark ethnic divisions.[8] It is thus startling to note that all warring parties were both foes and allies at different times throughout the conflict: Serbs against Muslims and Croats, Serbs with Muslims, Serbs with Croats, Muslims against Croats. In a war of all against – and with – all, shared identity considerations alone could not have been the determining alliance factor, as such considerations would have precluded some unions from ever forming. Rather, instrumental considerations manifested in a desire for victory and the optimization of political returns actually dictated alliance preferences.[9] Evidence from the BiH civil war indeed highlights a story of alliances shifting around the balance-of-power nexus until the negotiated settlement that brought peace in late 1995.

1992: Serbs vs. Muslims and Croats
(VRS vs. ABiH and HVO)

The localized ethnic clashes that BiH had experienced in the days leading up to the April 7, 1992 EC and U.S. recognition of BiH as an independent state soon turned into all-out war.[10] By May 1992, all warring groups had formed official armies.[11] However, there were clear delineations in the strength of the

---

[6] "Members of all political parties, except the SDS, supported the referendum." "Bojazan od kantona, Interview with Dr. Ejup Ganić," *Oslobođenje*, February 26, 1992, p. 5; see also Burg and Shoup (1999), p. 118.

[7] "SDS organizator barikada [SDS is the organizer of barricades]," *Oslobođenje*, March 3, 1992, p. 1; "Pucnji u narodnu volju [Shooting at people's will]," *Oslobođenje* March 3, 1992, p. 2; Silber and Little (1997), pp. 205–206.

[8] Glenny (1993); Ignatieff (1998); Petersen (2002).

[9] Susan Woodward, one of the leading academics on the former Yugoslavia, also identifies the tactical nature of the military activities among warring groups in BiH: "The description of the Yugoslav wars as ethnic conflict is most misleading, however, as a predictor of military activity. Military strategy in this case was not driven by ethnic hatred, class conflict or historical aspirations for territory but by the geopolitical and institutional preconditions of sovereignty: obtaining the strategic and economic assets and borders of a secure future state, destroying those of one's enemies, and building (in the course of war) the armies and foreign alliances of a new defense"; Woodward (1995), p. 272.

[10] Goldsmith (1992).

[11] The Croat Defense Council (Hrvatsko Vijeće Obrane – HVO) was established on April 8, 1992; the Army of Bosnia and Herzegovina (Armija Republike Bosne i Hercegovine – ABiH) was

three actors in terms of overall power. The most powerful group in BiH was the Serbs, estimated at 67,000–80,000 troops. Further, they had inherited a considerable number of arms and firepower after the Yugoslav People's Army (Jugoslovenska narodna armija, JNA) withdrew from Bosnia in early May 1992.[12] As such – as would be the case for much of the conflict – they were the best armed in terms of tanks, armored personnel carriers, artillery, rocket launchers, mortars, and infantry fighting vehicles.[13]

The Muslims and Croats were less prepared. The Muslims were slow to establish a concerted fighting force, lacking weaponry and a unified command structure. But they were still presumed to have between 30,000 and 60,000 troops at the start of the war, with many estimates noting that their actual force figures were probably higher given their larger population share.[14] Croat Defense Council (Hrvatsko Vijeće Obrane – HVO) forces were estimated at 45,000–50,000 troops. Although they had more effective organization and command-and-control mechanisms than the Muslim army, the Croatian forces were nearly all static, allowing them to defend territory but not to proactively prevent offensives or take territory.[15]

Thus, upon the onset of hostilities, a Muslim-Croat alliance was formed in order to balance against the militarily stronger Serbs. As predicted by the theory, given the balance described here, the war raged strong throughout Bosnia for months, with notable territorial gains on the part of the Serbs and massive displacement of mostly Muslims into Central Bosnia and other Muslim-majority areas. However, with infusions of troops and equipment, by October 1992 fighting between the Serbs and the Croat-Muslim coalition had largely reached a stalemate.

Croat-Serb (HVO-VRS) and Muslim-Serb (ABiH-VRS) Alliances (1993)

At the end of 1992 and into early 1993, as much of the fighting against the advancing Serbs had reached a stalemate, there were notable breakdowns in communication between Muslims and Croats reflecting increasing tensions and lack of trust.[16] Bosnian Serb leaders gladly exploited this turn of events, as they had been trying since mid-1992 to "[break] up the [Muslim]-Croat alliance, realizing that this would significantly strengthen their [the Serbs'] military position." (These efforts mainly took the form of trying to "woo" the Croats.)[17] These developments soon led to an onset of hostilities between Croats and Muslims throughout Central Bosnia, as well as in the Herzegovinian

---

established on April 15, 1992; the Army of the Serb Republic (Vojska Republike Srpske – VRS) was formed on May 12, 1992.

[12] See Sudetic (1992a, 1992b); Woodward (1995), pp. 262, 292.

[13] Shrader (2003), pp. 59–60.

[14] Ibid, p. 22.

[15] Ibid, p. 29.

[16] For instance, the Muslims had openly accused the Croats of failing to help them out during the siege of Sarajevo. For more, see Burns (1992b); Judah (1999), pp. 206–207.

[17] Caspersen (2010), p. 154.

capital of Mostar. As the theory would predict, when the relative power of the Croat-Muslim alliance increased – and outright elimination by the Serbs no longer seemed likely – the Croats and Muslims began to fight. This was prompted by the increased relative power of the Muslims within the alliance, which signaled to the Croats that the Muslims could no longer credibly commit to sharing postwar political power.[18] And although several Croat and Muslim units had fought in mixed army formations, this changed in the days leading to their confrontation, when they chose to join their respective ethnic armies, the HVO and the Armija BiH – ABiH, respectively.

In many places, the start of the Muslim-Croat infighting was a result of the change in the balance of power when Serb forces withdrew from certain areas where they were a minority, leaving Croats and Muslims to divide power. This led to Muslim-Croat squabbles and skirmishes that culminated with the fall of the city of Jajce into Serbian hands. Neither HVO nor ABiH defended the city, which in late October 1992 was taken by the Serbs, who had surrounded it since the early days of the war.[19] Signs of increasingly strained relations also manifested themselves in early 1993 in the area of Gornji Vakuf and its environs from Bugojno to Jablanica (on the border of Central BiH), where fighting broke out between Croat and Muslim forces. The ceasefire agreement that was reached was short-lived.[20] These hostilities would turn into a "total" war by the spring of 1993, inspiring new alliances in response to local balances of power.

Given the presence of what had been broadly perceived as the advancing common enemy, the Serbs, it was surprising to see the Croat-Muslim allies turn into foes. This reality was driven by the nature of the conflict in 1993, which created varying balances of power across the country as discussed in more detail later in the chapter. As such, the alliances formed during 1993 were highly regionalized, though still driven by the dynamics of the national leadership of each faction. For example, in the Central Bosnian city of Fojnica, the Croat leadership in Mostar, in opposition to the wishes of many local Croats, chose to fight the Muslim forces in the city, eventually resulting in a major fight between HVO and ABiH forces late into 1993. A similar process took place in Vareš, where local HVO leaders were ordered to take the city, precipitating a drawn-out fight.[21] Consistent with this book's theory, what we see on the ground were alliances built on the balance of forces in particular areas under contest, as dictated by the broader interests of their factions. The following sections outline the localized military balance in Central BiH that provoked separate instances of Croat-Serb and Serb-Muslim cooperation.

[18] Silber and Little (1997), p. 294. The Army of BiH consisted at that time of five corps – in Sarajevo, Mostar, Tuzla, Bihać, and Central Bosnia. Two more brigades would be added in the late spring of 1993 to the third corps. The soldiers manning them were the displaced populations who had found themselves in Travnik and Zenica for protection from the advancing Serbs.

[19] Burns (1992c); Silber and Little (1997), p. 295; Burg and Shoup (1999), p. 134.

[20] Shrader (2003), pp. 74–75, 80.

[21] Hoare (2004), pp. 96–97.

The Military Balance in Central Bosnia. Despite the regional nature of the balance of forces, if there was a general tendency in 1993, it was the expansion of the Muslim forces, supported by increased arms transfers, more men (be they internally displaced Muslims or foreign mujahedin), and an overall improved force structure. Specifically, there was a clear increase in the organization of Muslim ranks resulting from an influx of internally displaced men from Eastern Bosnia. As far as weapons are concerned, the Muslim Army, ABiH, started domestic production of weapons in Zenica, increasing its arsenal by 2,000 weapons each month. There are also several references to violations of the military embargo such as through the founding in Zagreb of NGOs – such as the "International Organization for the Help of Muslims in Bosnia-Herzegovina" – that smuggled in guns and money. During the Croat-Muslim cooperation, these smuggling operations were called "Convoy of Joy."[22] It was the increase in relative power on the side of the Muslims that prompted changes in the relationship between the former allies in Central Bosnia, precipitating the Croat-Muslim war. Indeed, wartime leaders in interviews were foreshadowing this conflict, raising their concerns in balance-of-power terms. For instance, in the words of Ismet Hadžiosmanović, the local chairman of Bosnia's main Muslim party, in the late fall of 1992:

"It is simply not in the Croats' interests to make enemies of the Muslims.... The consequences for the Croats would be catastrophic.... If the Croats seek more than 50 percent of the political power, there will be terrorism against them.... A balance of terror now exists," he said, asserting that thanks to Arab money, the once poorly armed Muslims now possess firepower almost equal to that of the Croats. "Franjo Tudman and Mate Boban [the Croat and Bosnian Croat leaders, respectively] understand this."[23]

Though it is hard to get exact data on the military strength of the Croat-Muslim forces in Central Bosnia in the spring of 1993, it is clear that the ratio favored the Muslim forces. According to HVO estimates, at the time the Croat-Muslim hostilities broke out in the spring of 1993, the Croats had an 8,000-strong force in Central Bosnia. In turn, the ABiH claims to have had roughly 26,000 officers and soldiers in the area between November 1992 and April 1993.[24] The 3:1 ratio was a result of the Muslims' increasing strength, as they were replenished in manpower by the aforementioned flows from internally displaced men from Eastern Bosnia and in arms by the tacit lifting of the arms embargo.[25]

HVO's military power in Central Bosnia was comprised of thirteen brigades that were formed in late 1992, drawing from JNA territorial-defense units.

---

[22] Halilovic (1997), p. 97; O'Ballance (1995); Wilcox (1999), p. 225. Moreover, the creation of safe havens put all major Muslim military centers (aside from Zenica) under UN protection, giving a further boost to the Muslims' relative power. Wilcox (1999), pp. 228–229.

[23] Cited in Sudetic (1992c). On the increased Muslim power also see from *The New York Times*: Sudetic (1992d); Hedges (1992); Sudetic (1992e); Burns (1993).

[24] Shrader (2003), p. 22.

[25] Burg and Shoup (1999), pp. 338–339; Shrader (2003), pp. 22–23.

Even though originally reserve formations, they were relatively well organized and well equipped, but could only undertake limited local operations as they were mostly geared toward static defense.[26] Still, the Muslims had a significant armaments advantage in Central Bosnia, including thirty mortars, twelve Howitzers, and five tanks versus twenty-six, one, and zero respectively for the Croats. Further, as noted earlier, they had superior lines of communication as they controlled land routes to their forces elsewhere.[27]

In mid-April 1993, fighting broke out between Croats and Muslims throughout Central Bosnia and did so with a vengeance. Within two months, all Central Bosnian areas except for Vitez, Kiseljak, and Prozor were under full Muslim control.[28] Along with battles in the broader Travnik area, ABiH also overran HVO positions in Kakanj and Novi Travnik, soon followed in early July 1993 by the Central Bosnian town of Bugojno, which fell in Muslim hands on July 23.[29] Apart from the territorial losses, the fighting also resulted in the annihilation of four of the thirteen Croat brigades, leaving only nine active by July 1993. Nonetheless, HVO forces were often able to hold out or respond in kind, resulting in a tit-for-tat focused on gaining control of the cities and towns on the highway running from Jajce through Bugojno to Mostar.[30]

The Military Balance in Herzegovina/Neretva Valley. As the Muslims were asserting their control in the Muslim-Croat areas in Central Bosnia, the Croats were similarly mobilized in the city of Mostar in Western Herzegovina, where the demographic realities and power dynamic were reversed.[31] Mostar had witnessed an earlier phase in the war that had united Croats and Muslims against almost exclusively Serb JNA forces, 17,000 in strength.[32] The hostilities

---

[26] It was not until later, in early 1994, and after the Washington Agreement and the U.S. intervention with force training, that the HVO transitioned mobile unit-guard brigade formations. Shrader (2003), pp. 27–30.

[27] Ibid, p. 19.

[28] Sudetic (1993a).

[29] Shrader (2003), pp. 136–137.

[30] Central Intelligence Agency (2002), volume 1, pp. 198–199.

[31] This differential ratio of Muslims-Croats in Central Bosnia and in Herzegovina came up in all interviews with Muslim and Croat local elites from the area. For instance: "Croats were strong in Herzegovina but weak in Central Bosnia and the more we intimidated Muslims here the more they intimidated Croats there." Interview with Milivoj Gagro. Also: "Croats in central Bosnia were abandoned by the rest of the Croats.... Our status as Muslims here in Mostar was like their status as Croats in central Bosnia." Interview with Esad Humo.

[32] "The Muslims did not have the necessary organization. Their formations were small, far smaller than brigades, and they were just on the *mahala* (neighborhood) level. With the help of the HVO and our cooperation these Muslim formations made up one of the components of Mostar's defense.... Even Safet Oručević [the leading Mostar politician on the Muslim side] was my soldier in HVO. They were all soldiers together with us in HVO in 1992." Interview with Petar Zelenika. "You should note that in Mostar 80% of Muslims were in HVO and only 20% or so were in the ABiH. The ABiH here was weak." Interview with Zoran Perić. Also confirmed in interview with Esad Humo.

between Muslims and Croats started in early 1993, soon after the Serb with-drawal from the area, and broke out in full force in April 1993. By early June, the Croats had consolidated control in a considerable part of the city of Mostar.[33]

The Croats held the clear military advantage as the HVO headquarters was based in Mostar. Although it is difficult to ascertain precise figures given con-sistent troop movements and incomplete staffing, the HVO had five brigades, one Special Forces regiment, as well as five or so military police battalions based in the city.[34] Further, these forces were closely supported by the remain-der of the SW Herzegovina forces, including units from Ljubuški, Čitluk, and Čapljina.[35] By contrast, even though the 4th Corps of the ABiH was based in East Mostar, the only forces directly under Mostar command were in the 41st Mostar Brigade.[36]

As in the case of Central Bosnia, there exist competing narratives as to how the conflict between Muslims and Croats broke out in Mostar. The Muslims accuse the Croats of precipitating the fight, believing the Muslims could be easily prevailed upon. As narrated by Esad Humo, a leading Muslim figure in wartime Mostar:

Soon after the JNA withdrew, it appeared that the Croats wanted to control everything. Regardless of what it was, military, civilian, political life, they just wanted to control everything. . . . They started creating trouble. They would arrest and punish Muslims for no reason. Then they started giving us ultimatums, wanting to take the arms that they had given us back. . . . And this happened slowly, little by little; it didn't just happen overnight.[37]

The Croats in turn find the accusations unfounded. According to Petar Zelenika, a main Croat local commander in the fight over Mostar: "It is ridicu-lous and absurd that they accuse us of attacking them. We had armed all of them. I for one expected to get a gold medal since I had saved thousands and thousands of Muslim families and children. But all was in vain."[38]

Indeed, the Croats in turn claimed that the Muslims were the ones who had plans to take over the city. In the words of Miho, a Croat combatant in Mostar, the narrative sounded conspiratorial:

The Muslims had actually organized the war in Mostar before it broke out. There was a Muslim guy who had high connections and in 1992 he told this Croat who had been displaced from the Serbs from Jasenica and had moved into an apartment of a Serb who

---

[33] Lewis (1993).
[34] Thomas and Mikulan (2006), p. 17.
[35] Central Intelligence Agency (2002), vol. 1, p. 194.
[36] Ibid, vol. 1, p. 200.
[37] Interview with Esad Humo.
[38] Interview with Petar Zelenika.

had left town that he should move out of there because this place is theirs [Muslim]. And the Croat asked "What do you mean this place is Muslim? A Serb owned it." And the Muslim guy showed him a map with the line of division of Mostar and how that would look like. And this was in February 1993.[39]

Miho goes on to describe an ambush, his first recollection of the Croat-Muslim war in Mostar, which he rendered in largely backstabbing terms:

We were in the battle front and our positions were up above Blagaj. Croatian cannons were close to Mostar, and Muslim grenade launchers were above us, all aimed to shoot at the Serbs. All of a sudden the grenade launchers were turned towards Croat positions . . . we [Croats and Muslims] were supposed to be together. It was not clear to me what had happened, who was behind this. . . . We went back to our positions, and that night we saw machine gun shots from the Orthodox cemetery over the Croatian part of the city. We now looked less towards the front line where the Serbs were, since at that time they were quiet and did not do anything, and were more afraid about what was going to come from the Muslims behind our backs.[40]

Croats attributed the war to the military strengthening of the ABiH. According to a leading Croat commander in Mostar:

The Muslims left the HVO and created their own army. And how can there be two armies in one city? . . . This signaled that there will be conflict. And on top of that, food from Saudi Arabia started coming in along with mujahedin. . . . There were mujahedin in Mostar . . . Croats in BiH never attacked anywhere . . . there were only lines that we defended. . . . That was started by their Muslim brigades."[41]

While the Croat side was accusing Muslims of bringing foreign fighters, namely mujahedin, to Mostar, the Muslim side was in turn accusing the Croats of bringing in Croat fighters from Croatia proper. Despite the major advantages held by the HVO in Mostar, they only won minor victories, with stalemate often resulting from the back and forth between offensives from each side.[42]

Alliance Formation in Central Bosnia and in Herzegovina:

Croats-Serbs vs. Muslims (HVO-VRS vs. ABiH) and Serbs-Muslims vs. Croats (VRS-ABiH vs. HVO). The Serbs undoubtedly saw the Croat-Muslim conflict as beneficial and did nothing to stop it. On the contrary, they were accused of fanning the flames to advance their strategic interests.[43] During this time,

[39] Interview with Croat fighter in Mostar, nom de guerre Miho.

[40] Ibid.

[41] Interview with Petar Zelenika. For more on mujahedin involvement in the BiH war, see Bruce (1995), pp. 175–178; Woodward (1995), p. 338; Holbrooke (1998), pp. 51, 319–321.

[42] "33 Soldiers Die in Bosnia City as Croats Battle the Muslims," *The New York Times*, August 18, 1993. Bjelakovic and Strazzari also add that "unlike most other front lines in Bosnia, belligerents in Mostar for months stood a few meters from each other along the central 'Bulevar.'" Bjelakovic and Strazzari (1999), p. 87.

[43] "The Serbs could not fight the war with Muslims and Croats united so they fired up that fight." Interview with Stjepan Kljujić.

the Serbs remained the strongest force on the ground. Though with slightly fewer troops than the Muslims (80,000 vs. 110,000), they remained by far the best organized and equipped force, with an estimated 330 tanks, 400 armored personnel carriers, 40 fighter jets, 30 helicopters, and a wide array of artillery in use by mechanized, mountain, and regular infantry brigades.[44]

Nonetheless, as in the case of the Muslims and Croats, this military advantage was regionally variable as well. Despite holding 70 percent of the country, the key Serb objective was a viable entity bordering Serbia in eastern Bosnia.[45] For the most part, their goal in 1993 was simply to hold onto the territorial advances of 1993 and create a defensible buffer zone around those areas. In this respect, the majority of the territory they sought was in Muslim hands or disputed between Muslims and Croats. As such, the Serbs focused their efforts on solidifying and expanding their control of eastern Bosnia, in particular widening the so-called Posavina corridor in the northeast to connect the eastern entity with territorial holdings in the west.

To achieve this end, during the intense Muslim-Croat fighting, the Serbs cooperated with both Muslims and Croats. Specifically, they pursued a local balancing policy, allying with the weaker of the two sides on a case-by-case basis – that is, with the Muslims in Mostar and with the Croats in Central Bosnia. A CIA review of the conflict observes that the Serbs provided "military support to both sides... most often to the side that was in the weaker military position, thus prolonging the fighting and increasing the costs to both sides."[46] Under this scenario, they were able to regionally weaken the foe that held territory that the Serbs desired. As recounted by a leading Muslim military figure in wartime Mostar:

Serbs knew that Mostar was not theirs but rather for the Croats to claim so they'd basically say: "You go ahead and kill yourselves down there. What does it matter to us?" ... For instance, the same unit that helped us [Muslims] in Mostar helped the Croats in Konjic. The same exact unit, the exact same commander – Novica Gušić. He helped both us and them. Why? There was no love there. ... Just interest. Their interest on one side, ours on the other. And that was that.[47]

There are several more such instances in the literature suggesting Serbian cooperation with the Croats in Central Bosnia and with the Muslims in the broader Mostar area. As recounted in leading works in the secondary literature, Serb units joined Croat forces in the siege of Tešanj and Maglaj in the Bosna River valley, but worked against them in the Neretva valley where, according to the mayor of the Muslim sector of Mostar, Serbs had entered into an alliance with

---

[44] International Institute for Strategic Studies (1994), p. 84. The Muslim forces had 40 tanks, 30 armored personnel carriers, 300 mortars, and no air assets.

[45] Burg and Shoup (1999), pp. 238–239.

[46] Central Intelligence Agency (2002), vol. 1, p. 180.

[47] Interview with Esad Humo. Serb collaboration with both the Muslim and Croat sides also confirmed in interview with Gostimir Popović.

the Muslims.[48] The assistance of the Serbs to the Muslim side in Mostar is also corroborated by a Serb who lived in East Mostar (Muslim side) during the war: "Luckily, at that time, the Serbs stopped firing at the east side. It is said that Safet Oručević paid the Serbs to hit a Croat military contingent/bunker on the hill from which almost half of Mostar was being attacked and killed."[49]

In assisting the Croatian side, the Serbs helped evacuate the Croatian population of Vareš – 10,000 individuals in a single night – after Muslim encroachment on the city, much as the Croatian forces had done for the Serbian population fleeing Central Bosnia earlier in the war.[50] Judah also recounts how the Serbs and Croats celebrated their alliance at a thanksgiving mass hosted by local Franciscan monks: "Drago Šimunović, the leader of local Croatian forces, thanked the Serbs for their help and said, 'The Croatian population and army would simply have been destroyed if the Serbs had not proffered the hand of salvation.' He said that the Serbs had looked after Croatian refugees and helped with food and medical supplies, and 'we even got artillery help.'"[51] Despite attempts at a ceasefire both between the Muslims and the Croats and between the Muslims and the Serbs in September 1993, the different sides did not seem to agree on how to share the spoils – that is, on a mutually agreeable division of the requisite political power. As a result, the fighting continued.

Beyond Central Bosnia and the Neretva Valley. An important test for the theory is what happened in other parts of Bosnia, where the power distribution and exogenous constraints meant that the Serbs were the strongest player on the ground. According to theories rooted in ethnic divisions, the changing alliances of the Croats and Muslims should have been universal and constant across the country. However, this was not the case in Eastern Bosnia, where the Serbs maintained most of their forces. In this region, the Croats and Muslims, on the whole, continued fighting in tandem against the Serbs. In other words, just as the theory would predict, where the Serbs were locally powerful, the Muslims and Croats maintained a balancing alliance in order to ensure survival; conversely, where the Serbs were locally weak or absent, the Muslims and Croats fought against one another in an effort to maximize their own group's share of political power. Indeed, the magnitude of Serbian gains in Eastern Bosnia helped precipitate the end of the Croat-Muslim clashes elsewhere, as the overall national balance of power again shifted toward the Serbs, once again necessitating a Muslim-Croat balancing coalition.

Despite some animosity between the Croats and Muslims in Sarajevo, the HVO "King Tvtrko" Brigade, with 1,500 troops, continued to support the Muslim forces throughout 1993. Indeed, an attempt by the ABiH to dismantle

---

[48] Silber and Little (1997), p. 296; Burg and Shoup (1999), pp. 135, 139.
[49] Interview with Ratko Pejanović.
[50] Silber and Little (1997), p. 301; also see Judah (1999), p. 249.
[51] Judah (1999), p. 250.

this brigade was directly prevented by President Izetbegović – although that brigade would eventually be forcibly integrated into the Bosnian defense forces.[52] Further, there were a number of Croat-Muslim units fighting in the frontline neighborhoods.[53] Similarly, in the Posavina corridor, three HVO brigades continued to fight the Serbs, and Croat-Muslim forces launched joint operations near Brčko throughout 1993, although they were ultimately defeated.[54]

As a result of the challenges faced by the Muslim forces in the east, in September 1993, the Muslims of Cazinska Krajina decided to secede and to side with both Serb and Croat forces, prompting war within the Muslim ranks. As discussed in the section on group fractionalization later in the chapter, poor battlefield performance led to a split in the Muslim ranks as the Muslims of Cazinska Krajina began to worry about subgroup survival. More specifically, tensions increased when Fikret Abdić, a member of the BiH presidency and the local Muslim leader of Cazinska Krajina who had created an economic empire in the region under the name of Agrokomerc, declared the Autonomous Province of Western Bosnia (APWB) on September 27, 1993. Soon after the declaration of APWB, amid intense fighting between the Serbs, Muslims, and Croats all around BiH, Abdić signed a pact for cooperation and friendship with the Bosnian Serb Republic in October 1993 and an agreement on development of political and economic cooperation with the Bosnian Serbs and Bosnian Croats in November of the same year. Abdić maintained control of the area until January 1994, when he was overrun by the Muslim forces of President Izetbegović and signed a ceasefire.[55] The ceasefire, however, proved short-lived and the fighting continued throughout 1994.

1994 and beyond: Croats and Muslims vs. Serbs (HVO and ABiH vs. VRS)

After almost two years of intense fighting among all three parties to the conflict, the war in BiH had largely reached a stalemate. In Central BiH, despite the Muslim successes, a general equilibrium had been met and neither side was making notable advances. This was illustrated by a HVO offensive in November 1993. After sustaining losses in the summer and fall of 1993, HVO forces, with clear Serb support, moved on Fojnica and a small enclave near Kiseljak. Despite making progress, the attack was ultimately repelled by the ABiH, leading CIA analysts to observe that "[w]ith the HVO unable to take any ground with firepower alone and the Bosnian Army spent after its massive September–October offensive, the two sides were set for an impasse as

---

[52] Central Intelligence Agency (2002), vol. 1, p. 201.

[53] Burg and Shoup (1999), p. 139.

[54] Ibid; Central Intelligence Agency (2002), vol. 1, p. 183.

[55] *SPORAZUM o prekidu dejstava i neprijateljstava* [Agreement on Ceasefire and Cessation of Hostilities between APWB and the Fifth Corps], January 18, 1994.

winter [1993] began to set in."[56] By contrast, the Serb forces had made real gains during 1993, taking much of the Drina valley and expanding the Posavina corridor, as discussed earlier. Even though they were turned back by Muslim forces in late 1993 and did not fully capitalize on the Croat-Muslim fighting, the Serbs remained firmly in control of much of their eastern gains, as illustrated by their crackdown on Sarajevo in January and February 1994, as well as offensives to sever lines of communication in ABiH enclaves in Eastern Bosnia.[57]

With the fighting having no end in sight and with mounting public opinion criticizing the lack of intervention, the United States finally decided to take firm action on the Muslim-Croat conflict. It decided to give incentives to both the Croats and the Muslims to end the violence and ethnic cleansing perpetrated in Herzegovina and Central Bosnia and to agree to a new alliance.[58] The balance of forces between these two factions, illustrated by the complete stalemate induced during 1993, were important incentives for cooperation. Although the Bosnian army had "growing military confidence," it was "beleaguered" by fighting a two-front war.[59] Indeed, during 1993, the Muslims had transferred major troop installations to Central Bosnia to fight the Croats.[60] The Bosnian Croats were positioned to lose support from Croatia for fear of sanctions and were in a militarily tenuous position.[61] Similarly, as described earlier, the Serbs were making clear gains in entrenching their hold of key territories from both the Muslims and Croats.

The Washington Agreement brokered in February–March 1994 is broadly seen as instrumental in bringing an end to the conflict.[62] The intent of U.S. actions in that regard was clear – intervention to prop up one side (Croats and Muslims) as a way to get the other side (Serbs) to come to the negotiating table. All the international peace plans that had preceded this agreement – the Carrington-Cutileiro (September 1992), the Vance-Owen (January 1993), and the Owen-Stoltenberg (August 1993) – did not adequately address the existing balance of power among warring groups on the ground. As a result, their provisions could not deliver peace and do away with the commitment problems facing the warring parties.[63] According to Richard Holbrooke, the chief U.S.

---

[56] Central Intelligence Agency (2002), vol. 1, p. 206. Burg and Shoup add that by the beginning of 1994, the fighting between Muslims and Croats "had more or less already determined the territorial division of Central Bosnia and the Neretva valley." Burg and Shoup (1999), p. 293; Collinson (1994), p. 11.

[57] Burg and Shoup (1999), pp. 144–145, 207, 286; Central Intelligence Agency (2002), vol. 1, pp. 220–221.

[58] Burg and Shoup (1999), pp. 299, 409.

[59] Ibid, p. 293.

[60] Ekwall-Uebelhart and Raevsky (1996), p. 80.

[61] Burg and Shoup (1999), p. 293.

[62] Ibid, pp. 146, 408–409.

[63] Ibid, p. 257.

negotiator at the Dayton Accords: "[T]he shape of the diplomatic landscape will usually reflect the balance of forces on the ground. In concrete terms, this meant that as diplomats we could not expect the Serbs to be conciliatory at the negotiating table as long as they had experienced nothing but success on the battlefield."[64]

The local press at the time heralded the Washington Agreement as a true breakthrough in the war. In a phone interview to the newspaper *Oslobođenje* the night before the signing, Muslim President Alija Izetbegović stated: "This is a real, and not as some had earlier said, a mere change on paper.... It has brought about a serious change in the relations between powers in BiH."[65] The signing of the agreement was front-page news for days in March 1994. Muslim politician Ejup Ganić called it Pax Americana and went on to add: "The beginning of peace in Bosnia in the American way brings what is now most important – a chance for peace."[66] The Muslim chair of the municipal assembly in the Central Bosnian city of Zenica emphasized the importance of the United States acting as the third-party guarantor: "For me it is important that for the first time the guarantor for this agreement will be the greatest world power, America."[67] Similar statements of optimism were made on the Croat side: "Americans have taken matters into their own hands and now there is no return: they [Serbs] either have to conform or this will be their end!"[68] And local pundits also emphasized the role of NATO's intervention, which acted as the military enforcer of the political measures of the Washington Agreement.[69]

On the military assistance front, the United States provided arms and training to both the Muslim and the Croat armed forces through the use of private military firms as well as retired U.S. military.[70] The most notable manifestation of that support was witnessed in the Croatian takeover of Cazinska and Bosanska Krajina in an eighteen-month period in 1994–1995. As related in a note written by the late Bob Frasure, U.S. Special Envoy to BiH, to Holbrooke: "Dick: We 'hired' these guys to be our junkyard dogs because we were desperate. We need to try to 'control' them. But this is no time to get squeamish about things. This is the first time the Serb wave has been reversed. That is essential for us to get stability, so we can get out."[71]

---

[64] Holbrooke (1998), p. 73.

[65] *Oslobođenje*, March 18, 1994, cover page.

[66] "Potpis za Bosansku Federaciju" [Signing for a Bosnian Federation], *Oslobođenje*, March 19, 1994, cover page.

[67] "Volja Naroda" [The Will of the People], *Oslobođenje*, March 3, 1994, p. 3.

[68] "Herceg-Bosna ne postoji" [Herzeg Bosna doesn't exist], *Oslobođenje*, April 1, 1994, p. 2, quoting Petar Jozelić, Croat citizen from Vareš.

[69] "The NATO ultimatum and the unprecedented US engagement... changed the whole political and military climate in Bosnia within just a few weeks." See Mehmed Halilović, "Dobre Vjesti" [Good News], *Oslobođenje*, March 24, 1994, cover page.

[70] Burg and Shoup (1999), p. 340.

[71] Holbrooke (1998), p. 73.

Supplementing the training and provision of arms was the U.S. and NATO decision to move forward with the use of force and air strikes.[72] Despite the one-sidedness of the intervention, it was abundantly clear that the United States was interested in creating the conditions for a negotiated settlement. This was not only suggested in their proclamations, but also confirmed in their actions – the United States dissuaded Croat and Muslim forces from creating conditions on the battlefield that would undermine a possible negotiated settlement with the Serbs. For instance, Muslim and Croat forces were discouraged from taking the Western Bosnian Serb stronghold of Banja Luka, even though there were claims that they had the capacity to do so.[73] Moreover, the United States was willing to cater to the institutional demands of the Bosnian Serbs for a Serb Republic within BiH, which largely determined the institutional structure of postwar BiH.[74] To get to a negotiated settlement, the United States had to use force to get the Serbs to the negotiating table, while convincing the Muslims and Croats to agree to an institutional settlement that meant a de facto if not de jure partition of BiH.[75] The Muslim-Croat forces proceeded to achieve considerable victories, which brought the Serb side to the negotiating table. By October 1995, all parties to the conflict had agreed to a cease-fire and to discussions for a settlement. After twenty days of negotiations in Dayton, Ohio, a settlement was reached on November 21, 1995. It lasts to this day.

CAPTURING RELATIVE POWER CHANGE

The argument so far suggests that Bosnia's civil war alliances were motivated by tactical considerations – a desire on the part of the groups to maximize their wartime political returns by belonging to the optimally sized coalition. The sheer number of alliance changes, already enumerated in detail and summarized in Table 6.1, appears to support a power-related argument.

This section attempts to show in a more systematic fashion the relative power changes among the warring actors during Bosnia's civil war and the effect those power changes had on alliance choices. In that regard, and as discussed in Chapter 2 of this book, I use territorial control as a measure of a group's power during the civil war. Arguably other data, such as manpower and access to arms, could serve as measures. However, because such data tend to be poorly and inaccurately documented and are thus hard to reliably track over time, I argue that territorial control is the most concrete and accurate

[72] Burg and Shoup (1999), p. 317.
[73] Interview with Atif Dudaković. Also confirmed in Holbrooke (1998) p. 160, where Holbrooke, trying to get the Croats to agree not to attack Banja Luka, encourages them to take Bosanski Novi, Sanski Most, and Prijedor in the offensive but not the Bosnian Serb capital.
[74] Burg and Shoup (1999), p. 318.
[75] Ibid, p. 352. Also: "The fact that the air campaign was accompanied by significant efforts by the United States to forge a political solution that balanced Serb, Croat, and Muslim interests was vital to the emerging settlement." Burg and Shoup (1999), p. 355.

TABLE 6.1. *BiH Civil War Alliances*

Year	Alliance One	Alliance Two
1992	Serbs	Muslims + Croats
1993	Serbs + Croats (Central Bosnia)	Muslims (Central Bosnia)
	Serbs + Croats + Muslims (V. Kladuša)	Muslims (Bihać)
	Serbs + Muslims (Herzegovina)	Croats (Herzegovina)
1994	Serbs + Muslims (V. Kladuša)	Muslims + Croats
1995	Serbs	Muslims + Croats

way to proxy power in this context. Territorial control reflects the success of warring groups in an observable fashion that is arguably similarly understood by all parties to the conflict. I calculate each group's territorial control over time and visually present the results on maps that depict territorial and alliance changes.

Territorial changes among the warring groups were coded from primary sources (such as local and international press, interviews, and war memoirs) for each of BiH's 109 prewar municipalities for all 45 months of the conflict and verified in numerous secondary sources.[76] The territorial control of each warring faction was then spatially projected and calculated in square kilometers through the use of Geographic Information Systems (GIS) on a prewar BiH map that I geo-referenced and digitized. Summary data on the level of territorial control for each warring group for all the critical moments in the fight (at onset, points prior to alliance change, and at termination) are displayed in Figure 6.1.

The changes in levels of territorial control as reflected in Table 6.1, Figure 6.1, and Maps 6.1–6.4 largely sustain the minimum winning coalition

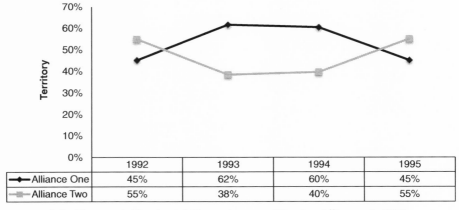

	1992	1993	1994	1995
Alliance One	45%	62%	60%	45%
Alliance Two	55%	38%	40%	55%

FIGURE 6.1. Changes in Territorial Control among Warring Alliances in BiH

[76] Woodward (1995); Silber and Little (1997); Burg and Shoup (1999); Wilcox (1999).

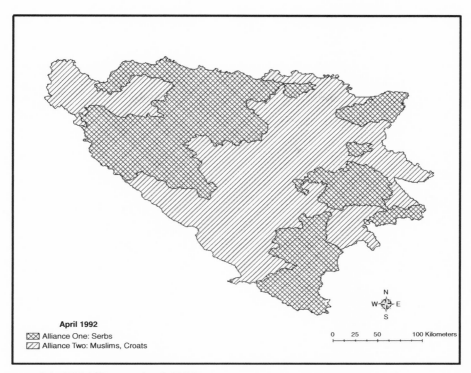

MAP 6.1. BiH Alliances, April 1992

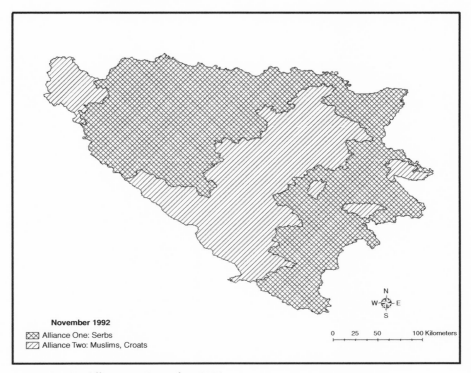

MAP 6.2. BiH Alliances, November 1992

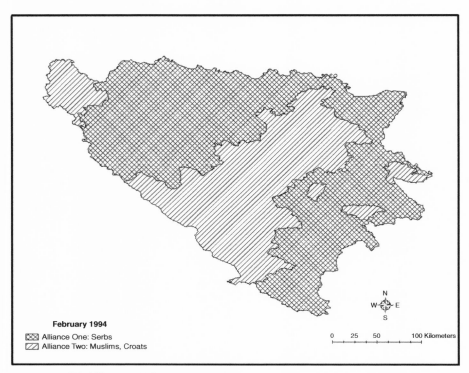

MAP 6.3. BiH Alliances, February 1994

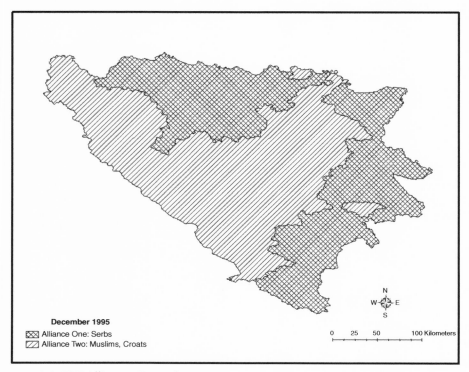

MAP 6.4. BiH Alliances, December 1995

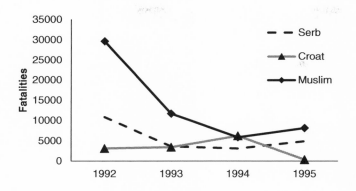

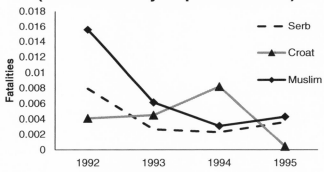

FIGURE 6.2. Fatalities by Ethnic Group by Year in BiH

argument. As the theory would predict, the balance of power generally stayed close to 50–50, as groups maneuvered and shifted alliances. At the war's onset, in April 1992, the Muslims and the Croats fought side by side in a balancing alliance against the Serbs. By the end of the year, the war had reached a stalemate. The Serbs had achieved considerable territorial victories, as discussed in the previous section, but the Muslims witnessed a relative increase in their military power. The change in relative power of the Muslims resulted in a breakdown in their alliance with the Croats, and soon after brought them to war. Meanwhile, the Serbs in 1993 were fighting to hold on to what they had won and made no notable progress, other than allying with the weaker of the Croats or the Muslims in different contexts of the conflict (with the Croats in Central Bosnia and the Muslims in Herzegovina).

The stalemate ended with external intervention on the part of the international community (mainly the United States and NATO) in 1994–1995. Consistent with the theoretical framework, given that the intervention aimed at a negotiated settlement rather than an outright victory, warring groups maintained balancing alliances to the conflict's end. The respective territorial contestations are captured in GIS maps on the alliance level from 1992 to 1995, giving a vivid spatial empirical confirmation to the balancing argument.

Aside from territory, if one were to attempt to get to balancing behavior through fatalities (Figure 6.2), looking at either the normalized or unnormalized measure by population size, the Muslims suffered the most casualties in three of the four years (1992, 1993, and 1995). The Croats sustained the most casualties in 1994. So in a loose sense, it makes sense for these two to ally against the Serbs, who were experiencing the fewest casualties (in absolute or per capita terms) in 1993 and 1994 and the second-fewest in 1992 and 1995.

CIVIL WAR ALLIANCE NARRATIVES: THE STORIES THEY TOLD

The shifting alliances in the Bosnian civil war – as discussed in detail earlier in the chapter – pitted all former allies against each other at some stage in the conflict, and often brought them back together again later on. In keeping with the theory of this book, these variant alliance patterns suggest that alliances could not have been formed based on shared identity considerations but were instead largely tactical. Despite the purely instrumental nature of alliances, identity narratives were nevertheless broadly used in justification of the variant alliance choices, suggesting that they are endogenous to changes in relative power.

The absence of cross-cutting ascriptive cleavages among the warring groups in BiH constrained the formation of ethnic alliance narratives, because race and language were commonly shared attributes across all three of Bosnia's main ethnic groups, and thus not exclusionary or restrictive in any way. Religion could not readily serve as a point of tangency either, as all three groups came from different religious traditions, namely Muslim, Catholic, and Christian Orthodox. If anything, we would expect the Croats and the Serbs to be the most natural alliance partners because both groups were Christian. However, as the preceding section illustrated, religion clearly does not explain the course of the war. Because the ascriptive characteristics often proved inadequate in offering any variation on shared identity discourse, they were in turn supplemented by local identity-inspired connections. This section presents the narratives that surfaced in justification of the different wartime alliances. In so doing, it provides interesting insights into the Bosnian civil war, showing the instrumental use of shared identity by all sides in the conflict.

April 1992–December 1992: Croat-Muslim (HVO-ABiH) Alliance

Early in the war, balance-of-power considerations mandated the alliance of the Croats and the Muslims. In the context of that alliance, a largely anti-Serb narrative emerged. While the "other" – the Serb enemy – was seen in distinctly ethnic terms, the alliance between the Croats and the Muslims was in turn cast in ethnically neutral terms, as there were no directly shared ethnic attributes. The terms that were broadly used had a historic basis and drew on identifiers that were codified during World War II, when the Croats and the Muslims had again found themselves, for the larger part of the conflict, allied against the Serbs. Chetnik (*Četnik*), the term for the World War II Serb royalists, was readopted and broadly used in reference to the Serb enemy. In turn, the Serb desire to maintain Yugoslavia by refusing to vote for BiH's independence was equated with the desire for Greater Serbia and Serb domination over the Croats and the Muslims.

An article from the leading Bosnian newspaper, *Oslobođenje*, in March 1992 – a month before the breakout of all-out war – reported on the Political Council of SDS BiH, stating that there existed overwhelming "Satanization of the Serbian people" in the Bosnian mass media.[77] For their role in trying to prevent the secession of Slovenia and Croatia, the Serbs were arguing that they were being compared to the Nazis, and presented as subhuman.[78] According to Serb propaganda – which, regardless of its empirical veracity, gives us a sense of the narratives that groups were *claiming* existed in other camps – the following dehumanizing poem had sprung up in the early days of the war in the city of Mostar:

Citizens of Mostar, evil has befallen us that is called the Serbs. Evil has befallen us that is called the army. Ignore the Serbs: on the street, in the neighborhood and door-way, at work, when going out. Don't have any relations with the Serbs, dogs – may the dogs forgive us. And with the Serbian Chetnik army. . . . Better alone than with them.[79]

One should note that whereas there is ample reference to the Serbs – four times in a sixty-word poem – there is no reference to the Croats or Muslims. They are rather subsumed under the broader identity of "citizens of Mostar," united against the Serbs who are also referenced by the negatively loaded identifier of the World War II Serb royalists known as Chetniks (*Četnici*). The civic model for alliance and Croat-Muslim coexistence, implied in the reference to "citizens of Mostar" in the poem, also arose in the context of the siege of Sarajevo, during which the calls were also directed to "citizens of Sarajevo."[80]

---

[77] "Satanizacija srpskog naroda," *Oslobođenje*, March 4, 1992, p. 6.

[78] "Ni nacisti nisu bombardovali GRAS" [Not even the Nazis bombed GRAS], *Oslobođenje*, April 21, 1992, p. 4; and "Miševi odlaze" [The mice are fleeing], *Oslobođenje*, April 14, 1992, p. 2.

[79] Newsletter of the Bosnian-Serb Army published by General Staff ("Srpska Vojska" Broj 74/75, Maj 2001), quoting a song of the *All National Resistance of Mostar*, dating to early 1992. Cited in Blažanović (2001), p. 11.

[80] As an example of references to "citizens of Sarajevo," see articles in the April 8, 1992 issue of *Oslobođenje*.

The uniting civic narrative against the shared Serb enemy lasted for roughly a year but did not prove to be a sustainable one.[81]

January 1993–January 1994: Croat-Muslim (HVO-ABiH) Conflict

All-out violence within the Muslim-Croat camp did not break out until May 1993, but tensions had started as early as November 1992. An article in *Herceg Bosna*, a local Croat paper in Herzegovina, is revealing in that regard in predicting the impending Croat-Muslim conflict in Central Bosnia:

What will remain unknown, unclear and unacceptable is the fact that the Muslim leadership asserts that the Croatian people in BiH who were truthful and blood-bound allies . . . now make an enemy worse than the Serbs. . . . From [the Bosnian government] came an order: "Kill Ustashe." There came an order . . . to clear the space between Mostar-Jablanica-Konjic-Gornji Vakuf-Bugojno-Novi Travnik from HVO – and Croats.[82]

The Croats attributed the breakup of the alliance to the increasingly Islamic stance to which the Muslims in BiH were allegedly aspiring.[83] The Muslims, in turn, accused the Croats of separatism. The tense mood between the Croats and the Muslims is succinctly captured in an article in *Oslobođenje*:

Soon after [the onset of the Croat-Muslim war] both Croats and Muslims started using amongst themselves the political language that the Bosnian Serbs had used against them. The propaganda machine of [Mate] Boban [the leader of the Bosnian Croats] started calling the Muslims *Balije* and the Sarajevo media started calling the Croats *Ustashe* (*Ustaše*).[84]

Both Balije and Ustashe are distinctively derogatory ethnic identifiers. Balije is meant to suggest crude, backward Muslims.[85] Ustashe (*Ustaše*) signifies the World War II Croat fascist movement that ruled in Croatia and part of Bosnia under the protection of the Nazis in the years of the Axis Occupation of Yugoslavia, and that committed mass violence against Serbs.[86] Indeed, whereas the Serbs had been referred to as Chetniks since the onset of hostilities in April 1992, in early 1993 such epithets were also adopted by the Muslim and Croat sides for their respective former allies-now-turned-enemies. Each side actually started comparing their respective new enemy to the Serbs, often arguing that

---

[81] Burg and Shoup (1999), p. 196.

[82] "Is the Bosnian state dying?" *Herceg Bosna*, November 1992, p. 5.

[83] "The apparent emphasis Izetbegović placed on Islam as the foundation of the new Republic of Bosnia Herzegovina was taken as a threat to the continued existence and freedom of the Catholic Croat community in Bosnia-Herzegovina." Shrader (2003), pp. 24–25.

[84] Gojko Berić, "Bolje Pakt, Nego Rat" [Better Pact Than War], *Oslobodenje*, March 10, 1994, p. 2.

[85] On the derogatory use of the term *Balija*, also see MacKinnon (1994), p. 75.

[86] The movement is infamous for their concentration camps and discriminatory policies, including extermination of Jews and Orthodox Christian Serbs. See Tomasevich (2001).

they had legitimized or facilitated Serb intentions and goals. On the Muslim side, and as argued in an article featured in *Oslobođenje*:

To dispel any doubts that in BiH there is an inter-ethnic and inter-religious civil war in which three sides participate, the Croats have opened a front against the Muslim people... supporting in this way the Serb thesis towards Europe that this is not a war of an external aggressor. The Croats have also, by marking and organizing their territory, legalized the political goals of the Chetnik aggressor."[87]

In a more direct comparison, the Muslims accused the Croats of crimes equally heinous to those perpetrated by the Serbs:

Not one Croat who has supported the vandalism of HVO [the Bosnian Croat army] in the area of Prozor and Gornji Vakuf has the moral right to complain about similar crimes that Chetnik hordes perpetrated by shelling Dubrovnik, Vukovar and other different places in Croatia and BiH. HVO units attacked Muslim people and ABiH [Bosnian Muslim Army] units at a time when that army is launching a fight against Serbian fascism.... Where are the humanists of the Croat people, the priests, intellectuals, poets, writers, photographers... who thought there were no national boundaries?... [T]he vandalistic shelling from the side of the HVO of the civilian populated areas where Muslims live created unprecedented harm in the historically good relations between Croats and Muslims, especially since the HVO uses the same warring tactics as those of the Serbian-Montenegrin Chetniks.[88]

The theme was echoed in a statement of the Islamic community of BiH: "We could not expect that the Croat armed forces would try to do to the Muslims what the Chetniks failed to do."[89] And the Muslim narratives went beyond mere facilitation of Serbian objectives. The Croats were also accused of having double-crossed the Muslims, not just by attacking them but by also directly cooperating with the Serbs on the battlefield:[90]

The interior ministry of BiH has information that certain HVO members participated in the arming of Chetniks from this area [Central Bosnia]. [They] gave semiautomatic guns and a case of ammunition... and in Slavina they gave Chetniks 20 automatic weapons, [saying] "it is better for them to protect themselves from the ABiH than to have HVO protect them."... Duževic [from the Bosnian Croat Army] on 7 January of this year [1993] organized the transit of 10 Chetnik convoys from Zenica through

---

[87] "Maske su pale" [The masks have fallen], *Oslobođenje*, March 3, 1993, p. 2.

[88] "U Bosni se brani i Hrvatska" [Croatia is also defended in Bosnia], *Oslobođenje*, January 24, 1993, p. 4.

[89] Mešihat Islamske Zajednice BiH, "Sačuvati dobre odnose" [Protect good relations], *Oslobođenje*, January 21, 1993, p. 3.

[90] "Karadžic is therefore telling the truth when he says that the Posavina corridor was 'agreed between us [Serbs] and the Croats.'" See "Otvoren pokušaj aneksije" [The effort for annexation has started], *Oslobođenje*, January 18, 1993, cover page.

Kakanj, Kraljeva Sutjeska, Kopijari, Pogar and Vareš to Okruglić and for that received DM 4,000.[91]

In turn, the Croats also accused elements of the Muslim side of being pro-Serb. Armin Pohar, a Muslim fighting on the side of the Bosnian Croat Army, accused several of the leading Muslims in the army of being "Yugo-officers." In his own words: "These Yugo-officers have more hate towards Croats than towards Serbs. They are more Serb-oriented and their targeting talk is in *ekavica* [in Serbo-Croat spoken by Serbs] the 'beautiful Serbian language.'"[92] In the Croat and Muslim local media, distinct and competing narratives started to arise, emphasizing the primordial and inevitable character of their conflict. According to an article in *Oslobođenje* from April 1993:

> The fights between Croats and Muslims in Central Bosnia, Mostar, Jablanica, Konjic, Vitez were just a matter of time.... It could not have been otherwise... everybody takes by force what he can. The Serbs did it first, we know how. The Croats did it more wisely... the Muslims just now understood this... that is why they have suffered the most losses. A while ago, at the beginning of the war, one politician with a pro-Bosnian orientation... told me: "When we defeat the Chetniks we will have to fight the Ustasha." He was not wrong. Bosnia needs to stand up against both the former and the latter.[93]

Another *Oslobođenje* article from that same time noted the deteriorating relations between Muslims and Croats: "Regardless of all politics, the relationship between Croats and Muslims in Herzegovina and Central Bosnia has its own civilizational dimension."[94] Indeed, the common thread in the narratives presented this as a "clash of civilizations," with the notion of Muslim versus Christian serving as a recurring theme. Religious identifiers were increasingly used in an opposing fashion. According to an article in a local Croat newspaper from May 1993: "Who needs weapons? It appears only the Muslims.... They say: 'The Serbs caught us off guard, the Croats will not.' Dangerous talk! It is interesting that they don't want the weapons to liberate the areas that the Serbs have occupied but rather for confrontation with the Croats who they don't call Croats but rather Ustasha, and in the best of cases Catholics."[95]

These religious identifiers also took their own dimension in wartime popular culture. An example is a short rhyming verse that was allegedly – according to HVO propaganda – sung even among young Muslim children: "Who are we? Muslims. Whose? Alija's. Who are we for? For Allah. Against who? Against

---

[91] "Pristižu bojovnici iz Hercegovine" [Warriors from Herzegovina are arriving], *Oslobođenje*, January 24, 1993, p. 3.

[92] "Ključ sukoba je u Seferu" [Sefer is the key to the conflict], *HVO Riječ*, May 24, 1993, p. 14.

[93] "Svi protiv svih" [All against all], *Oslobođenje*, April 21, 1993, cover page.

[94] "Muslimani i Hrvati: Loše i gore" [Muslims and Croats: Bad and Worse], April 20, 1993, *Oslobođenje*, p. 2.

[95] "Embargo – zamka ili čarobna formula?" [Embargo – Trap or Magic Formula?], *HVO Riječ*, May 24, 1993, p. 3.

Catholics."[96] Again, even if this propaganda distorts the truth, it gives us a sense of narratives each group accused the other of spreading.

The narrative of the Muslims wanting an Islamic state in Bosnia was what the Croats during this period recurrently cited as the formal perception of Muslim intentions.[97] Apart from the symbols of the Bosnian state being increasingly Muslim, the Croats also accused the Muslims of one-sidedness and bias in the state media[98] and of the use of mujahedin fighters from different Muslim countries in their fight against Croats.[99] Despite all the ethnic and "civilizational" narratives, observers noted the critical role of power, calling out the contradictory and inconsistent aspects of the different alliance narratives. Illustrative in that regard is an article from the Muslim local newspaper of the municipality of Maglaj in Central Bosnia:

> What happened on 24 June [1993] and why? Why did Lozančić, Jukić, Marinčić, Pera and Mostarac [Croat local elites] give their positions in Bradice, Fojnica and Crni Vrh to the Chetniks [Serbs], came to an agreement with them and robbed 2000 [of Maglaj's] Muslims of their livelihood, killing innocent people.... Why, why?... When the small stones are placed in the political mosaic it becomes crystal clear why: it is *realpolitik*.... They are not interested in the people, nor is there hatred towards Muslims nor are the [Croat] patriots instinctively bothered by their alliance with the "black devil" – the Chetniks [Serbs]. After all, the plan is simple and comprised of two elements: attack the Muslims... and then through propaganda and lies... create an image of yourself as the victim, cleansed from your territories by the Muslims.[100]

The *realpolitik* element is also clearly evident in the Serbs' stance toward the Muslim-Croat conflict, a conflict that was undoubtedly beneficial to the Serbs as it fractionalized their enemies' respective power bases. The Serb policy was summarized in a statement by Bosnian Serb General Ratko Mladić: "I will

---

[96] In the local language, the poem reads as follows: "Tko smo mi? Balije [pejorative for Muslim]! Čije? Od Alije. Za koga smo? Za Alaha. Protiv koga? Protiv Vlaha [pejorative for Catholic]." Found in: "Embargo – zamka ili čarobna formula?" [Embargo – Trap or Magic Formula?], *HVO Riječ*, May 24, 1993, p. 3.

[97] "Tuđman allows for the creation of a small Muslim or Islamic state in Central Bosnia and argues that there is 'an intention to form a larger united Islamic state in the heart of Europe,' which is as he argues the political objective of the Muslim leadership." "Maske su pale" [The masks have fallen], March 3, 1993, *Oslobođenje*, p. 2.

[98] "The Muslim propaganda made Croats look like greater criminals than the Serbs. And that came mostly from those who until yesterday were fiercely opposed to JNA, who had sent their families to Zagreb [the Croatian capital].... The 'state' media didn't once try to listen to the other side.... Croats cannot consider the [state] TV, Radio, or "*Oslobođenje*" [newspaper] as theirs." "Embargo – zamka ili čarobna formula?" [Embargo – Trap or Magic Formula?], *HVO Riječ*, May 24, 1993, p. 3.

[99] More specifically, the government of Herzeg Bosna stated that "Muslim forces, strengthened by mujahedin [foreign Muslim fighters] are terrorizing the Croatian population, perpetrating ethnic cleansing in the Zenica region.... Muslim forces much like the Serb aggressor are perpetrating the most severe genocide against the Croat people." "Vatreni okršaji i u Mostaru" [Exchange of Fire Also in Mostar], *Oslobođenje*, April 20, 1993, p. 3.

[100] H. Fermić, "Od 24. juna do danas: Hronologija jedne veleizdaje" [From 24 June to Today: Chronology of a Treason], *Maglajske Novine*, June 1993, p. 5.

watch them destroy each other and then I will push them both into the sea."[101] As discussed earlier, the Serbs pursued alliances with both the Croats and the Muslims, as they assisted the respective weaker side in each of the local warring fronts, those being the Croats in Central Bosnia and the Muslims in Herzegovina.

Indeed, as the Croat-Muslim conflict was raging, the Muslim side considered a rapprochement with the Serbs using "ascriptive" justifications. Bosnian Vice President Ejup Ganić, in a July 1993 interview to a Slovenian newspaper, stated that "the Muslims are Islamized Serbs, and the biggest mistake we made was at the beginning of the war when we concluded a military alliance with the Croats."[102] He reiterated those statements in another interview in Zagreb, adding: "We related much more closely with the Serbs than with the Slovenes and the Croats. We speak a dialect that is more similar to Serbian than Croatian. The same goes for mentality, habits and customs."[103]

While the Serbs had come to the support of the Muslims against the Croats in Herzegovina, that did not prevent them from pursuing their power interests with the Croats in other areas of the country. In Central Bosnia, where the Croats were being overpowered by the Muslims, the Serbs came to their defense. Allegedly, "[a]round this period the Serbian media even began to refer to 'Christian forces' when they meant Serbs and Croats fighting together."[104] The narrative for the Serb-Croat alliance was once again picking on the ascriptively highest-ranking common denominator, that in the case of the Serbs and the Croats being the broader category of "Christian." Indeed, the role of the Franciscan monks in promoting the "Christian" narrative for Croat-Serb cooperation was also confirmed by the then Minister of Defense of Herzeg-Bosna Perica Jukić, who highlighted the monastery of Masna Luka as the center for Croat-Serb activity coordination.[105]

January 1994–December 1995: Croat-Muslim (HVO-ABiH) Rapprochement

Starting in January 1994, and as dictated by power changes on the battlefield, there was a shift toward possible reconciliation between the Muslims and the Croats. Mirko Šagolj, a Bosnian Muslim columnist for *Oslobođenje*, suggested the need for an agreement on the cessation of hostilities between the Croats and the Muslims: "The winner in the Croat-Muslim conflict is already known: it is Karadžić [the Bosnian Serb leader]. And if the winner is already known, so are the losers."[106]

---

[101] Silber and Little (1997), p. 295.
[102] Burg and Shoup (1999), p. 269.
[103] Ibid.
[104] Judah (1999), p. 250.
[105] Wilcox (1999), p. 210.
[106] "Dogovor ili tragedija" [Agreement or tragedy], *Oslobođenje*, January 5, 1994, p. 3.

In the same spirit, Mehmed Husić, in an *Oslobođenje* piece from the same time, explored the possibility of the union of BiH with Croatia. The piece bore the title "Between (im)possible and (un)real." Discussing the relationship between the Croats and the Muslims, he noted that it is not beyond repair: "Hate and evil between these two nations, especially in Central Bosnia, it appears didn't reach proportions that cannot be healed, especially if the Croats punish their own military and civilians who encouraged them to fight their own neighbors for their own personal interests and goals."[107]

The Muslim press also made overtures to imply the presence of Croat moderates who could rise in the ranks and with whom the Muslims could actually work toward a lasting solution to the conflict. In an *Oslobođenje* piece entitled "Who is afraid of the Croat convention," the writer examines why the long-announced convention of Croats of Sarajevo was once again postponed:

At this convention one must listen to what Croats of Bosnia, Posavina and Herzegovina think about Herzeg Bosna. This convention must provide an answer as to whether HDZ is the legitimate representative of the Croatian people.... Whose interest was it to postpone the gathering and leave the resolution for a better time? Was it not changes in the cadres of the HDZ (removal of Boban) that dictated these choices? Does the new representative from Herzeg Bosna have such pull and power on Sarajevo's Croats and Croats of Central Bosnia and Posavina... to derail the political situation of the whole Croat political establishment?[108]

The narratives seemed to come full circle, returning to the time when the Muslims and the Croats were allies. Gojko Berić dedicated his January 13, 1994 column to Mostar, entitling it "Mostar for the citizens of Mostar," directly quoting Bosnian Muslim Prime Minister Silajdžić in the very same words as those in the Mostar verse from the beginning of the war.[109]

The end of the Croat-Muslim civil war was brought about by U.S. intervention and the Washington Agreement signed in March 1994.[110] The respective Croat and Muslim parties started with acts of introspection, blaming extremist elements in their midst and promoting the return of moderate individuals in their leadership. In broadly public acts, the Croat ethnic party, HDZ, removed its president, Mate Boban, and the Muslims in turn dismissed "criminal elements" from their army [ABiH]. As exemplified in a statement from the ABiH Press Center, "With this action [the removal of individuals involved in criminal

---

[107] "Union of BiH with Croatia: Between (im)possible and (un)real," *Oslobođenje*, January 11, 1994, p. 2.

[108] "Ko se boji Sabora Hrvata" [Who is afraid of the Croat Convention], *Oslobođenje*, January 15, 1994, p. 2.

[109] "Mostar Mostarcima" [Mostar for the citizens of Mostar], *Oslobođenje*, January 13, 1994, p. 2.

[110] On March 3, the leading Muslim newspaper *Oslobođenje* ran the whole text of the Framework Agreement on the Establishment of a Federation in BiH. See: "Okvirni Sporazum o Uspostavljanju Federacije u područjima Bosne i Hercegovine sa većinskim bošnjačkim i hrvatskim stanovništvom," *Oslobođenje*, March 3, 1994, p. 3.

activities within the army] our country, our army and our police show their commitment to a fight for a real state, a state where all citizens are free, have equal rights and are protected."[111]

The focus now shifted to the common enemy, the Serbs, who in all media outlets run by the Muslims or the Croats were almost exclusively referred to as Chetniks.[112] Newspapers marked celebrations of the third anniversary of the creation of the Patriotic League fighting against the Serb aggressor in Mostar, and the emphasis had shifted entirely now to "Serb aggression."[113] One article opined that "we call on you to immediately and unconditionally accept the [Washington] agreement... and to jointly form a line against the Chetniks and that you and your families return in your deserted homes.... This has all benefited the Chetniks who counted on dividing our two peoples."[114]

Sarajevo Croats publicly denounced the anti-Muslim politics pursued by Herzegovina Croats the year before, and emphasized how their moderate politics would be the future of BiH.[115] There was a narrative of "never again" and the need for the Muslims and the Croats to return to their prewar homes in Central BiH.[116] Indeed, *Oslobođenje* ran several stories encouraging Croat return to Muslim areas. One featured the return of Franciscan monks in Konjic, an area in Central Bosnia that had witnessed severe fighting between the Muslims and the Croats and that had been under Muslim control since June 1993. It reported that "the happiness of the Catholics, and all the others that see themselves as true citizens of Konjic, was not spoiled by the recent bloody wounds left by the nine month long tragic conflict between HVO and ABiH." The piece made reference to the first walk of the Catholic priest downtown in the Friday bazaar: "We walked by a school when students were coming out. Two girls approached us and said: 'We are happy that you are again with us.' I thought that the two girls were Catholic but they told me that they were actually Muslim!"[117]

---

[111] "Kriminalci s funkcijom" [Criminals with a function], *Oslobođenje*, March 1, 1994, p. 6.

[112] For example see "Četnici granatirali Zenicu i Gračanicu" [Chetniks bombed Zenica and Gračanica], *Oslobođenje*, April 6, 1994, p. 1; "Sigurna u odbranu grada" [Certainty in defense of the city], *Oslobođenje*, April 6, 1994, p. 2.

[113] "Prvi stali na branik domovine [They were the first to defend the homeland], *Oslobođenje*, April 1, 1994, p. 4.

[114] "Sačuvati jedinstvo dva naroda" [Protecting the unity of two peoples], *Oslobođenje*, March 1, 1994.

[115] Ivan Kordić, "Domovina nije drugdje" [The homeland is not somewhere else], *Oslobođenje*, February 11, 1994, p. 2.

[116] "I trust we are going to win, not just the war but also the battle over people's minds. Because now we have an even greater responsibility as individuals not to allow evil to come between us again because that was a true catastrophe." "Herceg-Bosna ne postoji" [Herzeg Bosna doesn't exist], *Oslobođenje*, April 1, 1994, p. 2, quoting Petar Jozelić, Croat citizen from Vareš.

[117] Na licu mesta-Konjic [On the spot – Konjic], *Oslobođenje*, April 2, 1994, p. 9. Also: "I want my Croats to return to Vareš to live with their neighbors again, as it was for centuries." Ibid, p. 2, quoting Petar Jozelić, Croat citizen from Vareš.

Stjepan Kljujić, the Croat member of the prewar BiH presidency and a moderate Croat, made visits to the Muslim-dominated Central Bosnian towns of Breza, Vareš, and Olovo to show the Croat support for such returns.[118] With the new U.S.-backed Croat-Muslim alliance struck, the narrative justifying the power changes on the ground was a Croat-Muslim narrative of proximity against the now-common Serb enemy.

GROUP FRACTIONALIZATION

Apart from the effect on alliances, relative power changes among the different warring factions in Bosnia's civil war also affected in-group dynamics, leading to two instances of group fractionalization: a Croat takeover and a Muslim split. As argued in Chapter 2, warring groups are susceptible to fractionalization if the group faces battlefield losses, often borne asymmetrically among the group's constituent subgroups, which put the group's survival at stake.

The shifting fortunes of war confronted groups with several episodes of power loss, which were often borne asymmetrically across their subgroups. But only some of these episodes led to group fractionalization, and once again they appear to have been the ones that severely threatened the standing of the group in the war. After qualitatively evaluating all warring groups for the level of losses sustained and the degree of subgroup control maintained for each year in the Bosnian conflict, I identified two instances of group fractionalization, summarized in Table 6.2. The following section provides empirical evidence for each of these two cases, which confirms the posited theoretical mechanisms of poor battlefield performance and asymmetric losses across subgroups.

The Croat (HVO) Takeover

The Croat takeover, which took place in late 1992–early 1993, propelled the Herzegovina Croats to the leadership of the ethnic Croat party, marginalizing

TABLE 6.2. *Group Fractionalization in BiH's Civil War*

Year	Group Fractionalization	Manifestation
1993	Croat Takeover	Herzegovina Croats displacing Sarajevo/Central Bosnia Croats; Mate Boban marginalizing Stjepan Kljujić
1993	Muslim Split	Northwest Muslims splitting off from Sarajevo Muslims; Fikret Abdić declaring autonomy from Alija Izetbegović

[118] Kljujić said he wished for the return of Croats in the area and stated: "We are on a good road and BiH is our motherland and we don't have another motherland. We are a country that has a 1000 year old tradition and we have to show love towards that tradition." He also visited Vareš and Olovo. "Kljujić na slobodnim teritorijama" [Kljujić in liberated territories], *Oslobođenje*, March 18, 1994, p. 4.

the Sarajevo Croat elite, whose power had considerably dwindled in the months following the start of the war. The Serb military operation that attempted to bridge the Serb majority areas in the east and west of the country – known as "Operation Corridor" – had resulted in the takeover of northern Croat-majority municipalities such as Bosanski Šamac, Odžak, Orašje, and Bosanski Brod.[119] The Posavina Croats of the north were therefore in trouble. So were the Croats of Sarajevo, as by early May 1992, Serb forces had put the Bosnian capital and some of its environs (Ilidža, Hadžići, and Trnovo) under complete siege. The asymmetry of losses among BiH's Croat communities, which left the Herzegovina Croats in the west solidly entrenched while the Croats in the north and center were under siege, propelled a takeover on the part of the Herzegovina Croats; the strongest subgroup left intact responded to asymmetrically borne losses by taking over the group leadership.

In line with the theoretical framework, the regional differences among Bosnia's Croat subgroups were broadly known and had predated the war. The subgroup divisions, though largely geographic, also mapped a distinct urban-rural cleavage. Thirty percent of Bosnia's Croats lived in western Herzegovina in almost exclusively mono-ethnic rural areas, the exception being the city of Mostar that was largely multiethnic, albeit still with a Croat plurality. The rest of Bosnia's Croats lived in multiethnic urban centers in Central and Northern Bosnia.[120] These geographic divisions also reflected divergent political views. The Herzegovina Croats had a history of collaboration with the Nazis during World War II, and were largely nationalistic, with an intensely Croat identity.[121] Croats who lived in multiethnic Central and Northern Bosnia were considerably more cosmopolitan and their loyalties rested with a Bosnian state. The Herzegovina Croats in turn considered the Central Bosnia and Sarajevo Croats as "lesser Croats."[122] As recounted by Zoran Perić, a Croat in Mostar:

As far as Croats are concerned, once WWII ended there was a big change in Herzegovina and Ustashe came under communist control overnight. Churches closed, people were tortured, disappeared, or got deported. It was [more than] twenty years after the end of WWII, in the mid-1970s, that someone from western Herzegovina could become mayor or police officer in this place. Someone else would always lead them, be it a Serb or Muslim. That is why there is a huge aversion in western Herzegovina to anything that is not Croatian.... They think of their fight for survival that was fought for 20 or 30 years during communism. And that is why that part of western Herzegovina has always been practically Croatia and nothing else, while in other areas where Croats lived and it was ethnically mixed it was different.[123]

[119] Judah (1999), pp. 209–224.
[120] Silber and Little (1997), p. 292.
[121] Several of them had also participated in the Croatian civil war in 1991. Silber and Little (1997), p. 292.
[122] Burg and Shoup (1999), p. 66.
[123] Interview with Zoran Perić.

These geographic divisions were also mirrored in Bosnia's political arena. The two Croat members of the prewar Bosnian presidency represented the two divergent camps: Franjo Boras was from Herzegovina and was inclined to Croat-centric views, whereas Stjepan Kljujić, a sportswriter and urban Croat from Sarajevo, was of a more Bosnia-centric orientation.[124] The leading Croatian political party, the Croatian Democratic Union (Hrvatska Demokratska Zajednica – HDZ), was originally under the control of the latter, namely the Croat intellectual pro-Bosnia faction. That faction supported the territorial integrity of Bosnia and vehemently protested a plan for Bosnia's partition that Croatian President Tuđman had supported in late 1991.[125] The relationship between the two factions appears to have been tense even in the prewar context. Stjepan Kljujić, the Croat member of the presidency on the pro-Bosnia faction, described the other member, Franjo Boras, as provincial, inferior, and pro-Serb:

Boras' election to the presidency [in 1991] was a big surprise because there was disagreement in Herzegovina as to who would be their candidate. We Croats had two spots – one was for me, since I am from Bosnia, and another for a Croat representative from Herzegovina. A lawyer, Josip Veselinović, was planned, but he abstained and then Boras came up. People claimed that Boras was working for Yugoslav intelligence because he had committed a crime when he was a juvenile and had been imprisoned.... But he started cooperating with the police and was given amnesty.... Boras was inferior to me and though our relations were civil, our ideas had long parted ways.... After all, he was a provincial figure [who] later cooperated with the Serbs... Boras had married his daughter to a prominent Chetnik family, the Avdalović from Nevesinje [in Eastern Herzegovina]. He therefore had a pro-Serb orientation.[126]

Though HDZ's pro-Bosnia faction had supported the Bosnian government's proposal for a referendum centered on citizens rather than constituent nations, HDZ's Herzegovina faction preferred the constituent nations approach, declaring the sovereignty of the three main ethnic groups and opting for wording that allowed for future secession.[127] In what was seen as a victory for the HDZ's pro-Bosnia faction, the Bosnian Catholic church urged its overwhelmingly Croat constituents to vote in support of the referendum for independence in its original wording.[128] This victory, however, was short-lived. Soon after the declaration of independence, fighting broke out in Bosnia's northern area of Posavina, which had a sizable Croat population, with the Croats and the Muslims fighting against the advancing Serbs. There were, however, notable regional, subgroup differences. As related by the prewar Croat mayor of Mostar:

Croats in Central Bosnia and Posavina [northern Bosnia], unlike Croats in Western Herzegovina, supported cohabitation since they saw it as the only way for Croats to

---

[124] Silber and Little (1997), p. 293.
[125] Burg and Shoup (1999), p. 104.
[126] Interview with Stjepan Kljujić.
[127] Burg and Shoup (1999), p. 106.
[128] Ibid, p. 107.

have a chance to stay in the area. That is why in Posavina Muslims and Croats stayed till the late days in united formations and fought against Serbs. . . . But due to the progress of war the Croat political terrain changed.[129]

Indeed, the asymmetric losses among the two Croat subgroups prompted a leadership change among the Croats that amounted to a takeover. The elected Croat members of the presidency were soon sidelined by wartime Croat leaders.[130] Mate Boban, a former low-level manager, became the leader of the HDZ-Herzegovina faction in July 1992, upon the declaration of the Croat Community of Herceg Bosna (Hrvatska Zajednica Herzeg Bosna-HZHB). Stjepan Kljujić, the Croat prewar member of the presidency, gave the following assessment of his wartime rival:

Boban was a collaborator for the secret services who during the war was connected through Yugoslav intelligence services with Karadžić [the Bosnian Serb leader]. In the early days, he was a small provincial politician . . . and had been one of my 44 delegates in Parliament. At the HDZ convention in Mostar on 23 March 1991 there was a proposal that he becomes candidate for president. However, he did not get support, and then he came openly to me, gave up his candidacy in my support and congratulated me. But this was Judas's kiss . . . and war interests brought him to the fore and sidelined me.[131]

The Croat Community of Herceg Bosna adopted "Croatian" as the official language and took up the Croat currency, school curriculum, and system of local government.[132] The Croats also formed their own Croatian Defense Council, basing their claim on socialist Yugoslavia's legal provisions that provided for citizens' local self-defense organizations if the government failed to provide protection. They argued that this body was only provisional until the ABiH government developed adequate forces that could protect all its citizens.[133]

The positions emanating from the HDZ-Herzegovina faction gradually spread, slowly entrenching themselves in the more tolerant and pro-Bosnia Croat community in Central Bosnia. The Central and Northern Bosnia Croats, the more multiethnically inclined Croat constituency, found themselves between a rock and a hard place: dedicated to a united Bosnia but increasingly powerless as they were losing ground in the battle against the Serbs.[134] As a result, Dario Kordić, a Boban ally, rose as the leading HDZ politician in Central Bosnia. His ideologies were clearly anti-Bosnian. He argued that there was no distinct Muslim nation, but rather that Muslims were Croats of the Muslim faith.[135]

---

129 Interview with Milivoj Gagro.
130 Silber and Little (1997), p. 293; Burg and Shoup (1999), pp. 65–66.
131 Interview with Stjepan Kljujić.
132 Silber and Little (1997), p. 294.
133 Shrader (2003), p. 25.
134 Burg and Shoup (1999), p. 66.
135 Silber and Little (1997), p. 294; Burg and Shoup (1999), p. 66.

Indeed, it was a difficult time for Northern and Central Bosnia's Croats – the Sarajevo Croats and those in Posavina were besieged by the Bosnian Serbs, and their allies, the Muslims, were facing serious setbacks on the eastern front. Indeed, by the end of 1992, they had been pushed from territory north of the Posavina corridor, including Derventa, Modriča, Odžak, and Bosanski Šamac, and were confined to an enclave around Orašje.[136] Further, as noted earlier, the Croats accused the Muslims of not supporting them in the fight for their neighborhoods, impugning the efficacy of a Muslim-Croat alliance for a united Bosnia.

In contrast, the rise of the Herzegovina faction within the HDZ party was a direct result of the marginalization of Central and Northern Bosnia Croats on the battlefield. In Herzegovina, HVO forces with support from Croatia moved well into Bosnia, even securing high ground above the Serb town of Trebinje.[137] The major fight for control of the Croat-majority area of Herzegovina was fought in Herzegovina's capital of Mostar. The Serbs had controlled the eastern side of the city, as defined by the banks of the river Neretva, while the Croats were on the west. By mid-June 1992, the Croats entrenched their position by driving out the Serbs within three months of their attack through a set of coordinated and complex maneuvers.[138] Meanwhile, having driven the Serbs out of the Herzegovina territory, the Croat takeover of Mostar signaled serious internal tensions and prompted Stjepan Kljujić's resignation. According to Milivoj Gagro, prewar Croat mayor of the city of Mostar and Kljujić ally:

The secessionist policy [union with Croatia] was consistently supported by the Herzegovina side, not by Sarajevo, Posavina [Northern Bosnia], or Central Bosnia Croats.... Croats from Central Bosnia and Posavina, as well as those from urban centers who lived with Muslims and Serbs, thought differently. But when the war picked up, Posavina Croats were attacked, Sarajevo was surrounded... Kljujić was sidelined and Boban came in to forward this idea [the Croat separatist idea] in this area.... When they [Croats in Sarajevo as well as Northern and Central Bosnia] felt they could not survive any more they lifted their hands and accepted their fate. And the Herzegovina Croats promised them the stars and the sky and told them "come here and we will give you a place." And what happened? It resulted in an exodus. And all these miserable Croat refugee communities that look absolutely ugly.[139]

In a May 9, 1992 proclamation, Blaž Kraljević, a Croat favoring a united Bosnia who led the Croatian Defense Forces (HOS), called for a joint force of Croats and Muslims and asked the Croatian and Muslim people to ignore Mate Boban and fight for a united BiH: "Mate Boban cannot and does not have the right to lead Croats and Muslims into destruction."[140] But Kraljević

---

[136] Central Intelligence Agency (2002), vol. 1, p. 181.
[137] Burg and Shoup (1999), p. 134.
[138] Central Intelligence Agency (2002), vol. 1, pp. 156–157; Silber and Little (1997), p. 292.
[139] Interview with Milivoj Gagro.
[140] Proclamation of Commander of Croatian Defense Forces, against the division of BiH, Proglas, Hrvatske Obrambene Snage (HOS), Ljubuški, March 9, 1992.

appeared keenly aware of the internal divisions in the Croat camp. He closed his proclamation by saying: "We will get rid of the people with a dark past and suspicious present. . . . We will send them home but need to keep an eye on them as our destiny is at stake. We have a chance, but just this one."[141] As described previously with regard to the Serb-Croat alliances in much of Central Bosnia, this shift was further illustrated by the HDZ's strong-arming of local HVO units in Fojnica and Vareš into abandoning alliances with Muslim forces in tandem with support from Serb forces in 1993.[142]

Stjepan Kljujić's testimony indeed confirms this change in the state of affairs and Mate Boban's rise over him. The takeover of Herzegovina Croats over Northern and Central Bosnia Croats had taken place.

I was president and I had a political program that won the elections and the convention. And while there was peace they [HDZ Herzegovina faction] did not have the power to oppose this. Later, however, when the war started the aggression of 1992 that compromised us Croats in Sarajevo and Posavina in the north, they all ran down to Herzegovina and left me here. Then Boban said that in Sarajevo there are no Croats left, even though in Sarajevo there were 45,000 Croats before the war. . . . I was the leader of the Bosnian option among the Croats. . . . And there were many people in the field who supported me. I had the majority. . . . But once the fighting turned bad for us, many changed sides.[143]

The HDZ Herzegovina faction in turn accused Kljujić of naiveté and unrealistic politics. As related by Petar Zelenika, a Mate Boban ally and leading HDZ Herzegovina political and military figure in wartime Mostar:

Kljujić did not understand the game. He thought we still lived in Yugoslavia and they [Muslims and Serbs] were playing games. And look at what happened to him. He was besieged; he couldn't even walk out on the street in Sarajevo in 1993. . . . I don't want it to seem like I have anything against Stjepan . . . [but] there was a different mentality between Croats in Mostar and Croats in Sarajevo. He was a Croat who was assimilated as a minority and did not have a national consciousness. He was left on his own, prayed to God and that was it. . . . When he understood what was going on it was already too late.[144]

Indeed, the importance of subgroup relations was a constant theme in my interviews with local Croat elites of both camps. More specifically, as related by the prewar Croat mayor of Mostar, an advocate for a multiethnic Bosnia and a Kljujić ally:

[T]he saddest relationship is between those who are not of the same opinion within the same ethnic group. If you oppose the strongest in your group, then you may lose your head before the guy on the other side [the enemy] would. In the first phase of the war most of us Croats saw Bosnia as a multiethnic community and thought we could survive

---

[141] Ibid.
[142] Hoare (2004), p. 96.
[143] Interview with Stjepan Kljujić.
[144] Interview with Petar Zelenika.

only if we were united . . . but then the separatists with their increasing force subverted us.[145]

Along the same lines, Stjepan Kljujić stated:

For the misfortunes of Croats in Bosnia, Herzegovina Croats are the main culprits. There were Croats who wanted BiH to be a state and wanted to fight jointly with the Muslims against the Chetniks [Serbs] . . . but during the war they could not say anything because Boban had the power and guns. People stayed quiet. . . . For the evil that Serbs and Muslims did to us, we Croats are to blame.[146]

Taken together, the interviews with wartime personalities and the historical evidence provide strong support for the theoretical framework. Faced with asymmetric battlefield losses, the strongest subgroup faction left intact (in this case, the Herzegovina Croats) staged a takeover of the embattled subgroup, just as the theory would predict. Moreover, these subgroups predated the war itself – they were not endogenous to the conflict. As shown in the next section, the Muslim split in Bosnia also follows a logic consistent with the book's theory.

The Muslim (ABiH) Split[147]

The Muslim split was arguably the result of asymmetric losses suffered by the Muslims in Eastern Bosnia and Sarajevo, as opposed to their solidly entrenched ethnic kin in Western Bosnia. At a time when the Muslims in Eastern Bosnia were facing severe ethnic cleansing, were besieged in Sarajevo, and were engaged in fights with the Croats in Central Bosnia, a certain group of Muslims in Northwestern Bosnia – who had largely held their own against the Serbs – decided to deviate from their group. Supporting the theoretical predictions, asymmetric losses across subgroups made a subgroup (in this case, the Muslims of Cazinska Krajina) worry that its survival was at stake if it did not set off on its own. The split manifested itself in the declaration of the Autonomous Province of Western Bosnia in September 1993 and the resulting intra-Muslim civil war.

Western Bosnia, also known as Cazinska Krajina – 1,500 square kilometers in size, with a prewar population of 180,000 – was at the war's onset an overwhelmingly Muslim enclave bordering areas in Croatia in the west and north, and geographically cut off from Sarajevo by dense Serb populations to its east and south. There were attempts to prevent ethnic polarization in the area in April 1992 during the first few weeks of the war, but fighting still broke out by the end of May 1992.[148] Serb efforts to take over Bihać were, however,

---

[145] Interview with Milivoj Gagro.

[146] Interview with Stjepan Kljujić.

[147] This timeline draws from primary sources and interviews with the participants in the recounted events and appeared in Christia (2008). It is confirmed in descriptions of events in Silber and Little (1997), Burg and Shoup (1999), and Judah (1999).

[148] Glenny (1993), pp. 152–153; Silber and Little (1997), pp. 129–130.

unsuccessful, and even though the area was constantly under some sort of siege by the Serbs, fighting subsided during the early months of 1993, especially after the declaration of Bihać as a UN safe area in April 1993. In the meantime, Muslims were facing severe territorial losses and ethnic cleansing in eastern Bosnia and were under siege in the city of Sarajevo. As described previously, these losses were extensive, giving the Serb forces around 70 percent of the country, in a mostly contiguous territory. Illustratively, perhaps the most publicized fighting of 1992 was the drawn-out Serb siege of Sarajevo, in which Serb forces shelled the city and Bosnian forces were unable to liberate the capital of the Bosnian state.[149] Similarly, the Vance-Owen plan, developed at the end of 1992, called for an equal division of Sarajevo province, meaning that it would not serve as a Muslim-majority center of a unitary Bosnian state.[150] These losses were further emphasized by the surrender of cities in Eastern Bosnia, such as Jajce, and in Northern Bosnia, such as Bosanski Brod, without a major fight.[151]

In light of the asymmetry in losses faced by the different Muslim subgroups, Fikret Abdić, already a national political and military figure as well as the local Muslim leader of Western Bosnia, questioned the commitment and efficacy of forces in the eastern part of the country. In particular, in June 1993, he accused Izetbegović of seeking "genocidal" peace plans that would codify the ethnic partition of Bosnia and formalize Serb military gains.[152] He went on to declare the Autonomous Province of Western Bosnia (APWB) on September 27, 1993. The APWB had all the likings of a mini-state: "There is a Prime Minister, a government and a parliament, complete with all the usual trappings of the mini-state mania that has swept the former Yugoslavia. But the area remains very much a personal fief."[153] The declaration of autonomy was highly controversial. Abdić had secured 50,000 signatures in support of the initiative for the creation of the APWB and 75 percent of the delegates of local municipal councils had voted for autonomy, but his opponents – Muslims from the Bihać area who opposed autonomy and sided with the ethnic line dictated by Sarajevo – suggested that signatures were collected in a coercive manner and with the assistance of the local police that was under Abdić's control.[154] He also proceeded to sign pacts of cooperation and friendship with the Bosnian Serb Republic in October 1993 and an agreement on the development of political and economic cooperation with the Bosnian Serbs and Bosnian Croats in November of the same year. This signaled the era of what Abdić's supporters called the first autonomy. Abdić's control of the area was strong and locals would joke that after the end of the war all that would be left from former Yugoslavia would be

---

[149] Hoare (2004), pp. 73–74.
[150] Burg and Shoup (1999), p. 225.
[151] Ibid, p. 134.
[152] Central Intelligence Agency (2002), vol. 1, p. 187.
[153] Cohen (1994).
[154] Kličić (2002), pp. 91, 168.

"Velika Srbija, Velika Hrvatska, i Velika Kladuša" – Greater Serbia, Greater Croatia, and Greater Kladuša.[155] In Abdić's own words, during an interview in Karlovac jail in Croatia, from where he was recently released after serving a sentence for war crimes, his actions were humanitarian in nature and fully justified:

I could either protect this area through arms or through agreements. It would not pay off to do it militarily because we would be endangering the biggest capital of that area, the people, as well as jeopardizing the area's vast industrial potential. The agreements, except for agreements on cessation of hostilities, were also economic. The essence is that we Autonomists opened a corridor from Karlovac [in Croatia] to Velika Kladuša for goods and people, for trade and travelers. In order to get food we either had to fight and use violence or come to an agreement with the Serbs and Croats.[156]

The Fifth Corps of the Republic of BiH Army (ABiH), led by General Atif Dudaković, was the body representing the Sarajevo and Eastern Bosnia Muslims as reflected in the policies of Bosnian-Muslim President Alija Izetbegović. Dudaković argued that Abdić was the one who started the war by declaring the APWB.[157] Abdić in turn claimed that Dudaković declared war when ordering an attack that led to indiscriminate civilian deaths.[158] By January 1994, most of the Cazinska Krajina area was under the control of the Fifth Corps, whose leadership signed a ceasefire with Muslim forces loyal to Abdić.[159] The ceasefire agreement was short-lived and Abdić launched a new offensive on February 18, 1994. The fighting continued until the summer of 1994 and by late August Abdić's forces, along with 30,000 of his civilian supporters, were in full flight from Cazinska Krajina into neighboring Croatia.[160] While the Fifth Corps attained some victories, by mid-December 1994 Velika Kladuša was back in Abdić's hands. This signaled the start of what Abdić's supporters call the second period of autonomy, lasting until May 1995.

In May 1995, the Fifth Corps broke through Serb lines around Bihać and, strengthened by newly brokered agreements on Croat-Muslim cooperation, swiftly scored decisive victories against Abdić's Serbian-backed army. The Fifth Corps marched into Velika Kladuša and Abdić's people had to flee again, for the second time in less than a year.[161] In August 1995, Muslim and Croat leaders agreed to end the war and allow the return of Abdić's constituents to

---

[155] Judah (1999), p. 245.
[156] Interview with Fikret Abdić.
[157] Interview with Atif Dudaković.
[158] "The Fifth Corps chose the military way because they did not have the support of the people. They [the Fifth Corps] knew there was going to be a war. They planned it.... There was no vote on who was for me and who was for Alija [Izetbegović] in Cazin and Velika Kladuša. The Fifth Corps decided that." Interview with Fikret Abdić.
[159] *SPORAZUM o Prekidu Dejstava i Neprijateljstva* [Agreement on Ceasefire and Cessation of Hostilities between APWB and the Fifth Corps], January 18, 1994.
[160] Interview with Fikret Abdić; interview with Atif Dudaković.
[161] Judah (1999), p. 247.

Velika Kladuša.[162] The overall war came to an end soon after, with the Dayton agreement signed in December of that same year.

Although the two Muslim subgroups that surfaced after the split had distinct geographic constituents and power bases, there were no clear sub-ethnic differences between their supporters. Narratives were thus devised to create a sense of distance that could justify the split. Indeed, Izetbegović's Muslims attempted to create a religious rift and implied that the Muslims fighting for Abdić were not real Muslims but rather traitors who should be excommunicated. In September 1993, the Board of the Islamic Association of Bihać came up with a set of nine conclusions against imams and muftis who "had deviated from the right path."[163] Among others, they demanded the removal from the Islamic Association of a high-ranking imam and Abdić supporter Salih ef. Čolaković.[164] They also demanded the prohibition of celebration or any religious gatherings outside of mosques without the approval of the Islamic Association Board of Bihać, and declared themselves the only legitimate representative of Muslim believers in the area, claiming the support of more than 90 percent of the imams.[165]

Moreover, the newly elected Mufti of Bihać, Prof. Hasan ef. Makić, proceeded to issue a fatwa on November 24, 1993.[166] The fatwa declared that those who voluntarily chose to bear arms against fellow Muslims (referring to Abdić's men) were *murtedi* – outlaws of the Muslim faith. "Anyone in a leading role in the outlaw army or administration of the autonomous government," the fatwa declared, "cannot be buried by Islamic regulation and should be considered a pagan."[167] Regular Islamic laws would only apply to those who had been forcibly mobilized by Abdić's government. Additionally, "[a]ll those who got killed by a rebel defending Allah and the fatherland of the Muslim people would hold the title of *šehid* [martyr] and would be entitled to all religious honors."[168]

While there were attempts to ethnicize the cleavage within the Muslim warring groups, there were also attempts to construct a narrative to sustain the newly established alliances between Abdić's Muslims and Serb and Croat forces. That latter narrative was one of pacifism, arguing that they were mere proponents of interethnic cooperation rather than ethnic war. Muhamed Skrgić, an Abdić supporter, suggested that the fight was over different ideas within the Muslim camp: the pacifist-ethnic coexistence ideal versus the

---

162 *SPORAZUM* [Agreement between the ABiH Army, Croatia and APWB], Vojnić, Karlovac County, Croatia, August 8, 1995.
163 *Fetva* [Fatwa], Islamic Association of BiH, Bihać Mufti's Office, No 35/93, November 24, 1993.
164 Ibid.
165 Ibid.
166 Ibid.
167 Ibid.
168 Ibid.

intolerant ethnic ideational camp.[169] For them, the opposing Muslim side was fundamentalist, intolerant, and aggressive because they did not allow their ethnic kin to act on their own rationalist and ideational grounds. Interestingly enough, they would portray their ethnic brethren in the same terms employed by the Serbs and the Croats, calling them Islamic fundamentalists, aspiring to the creation of a solely Islamic Bosnia. As suggested by Admil Mulalić, a former mayor of Velika Kladuša and Fikret Abdić supporter:

Abdić and his group who called themselves Young Muslims all their lives have wanted Bosnia to be a Muslim state.... His whole life he worked to connect Bosnia with Islam.... The reason for the war was Alija Izetbegović and his circles, including mujahedin from Arab countries who came ready to fight for a radical version of Islam and die for their cause.[170]

In making the argument for why this northwestern province of Bosnia should be allowed to have autonomy, Abdić would often evoke a multiethnic ideology: "The being of BiH has been maintained over here and it can, objectively, initiate similar processes in other parts of the country. That is the big advantage of this area, and it has to be preserved."[171] Also, Muslims in that area insisted on calling themselves Muslims rather than Bosniaks, the ethnic identifier that was adopted by the Bosnian Muslims during the war. This was a way for the Abdić camp to claim that it espoused an ethnically ecumenical and tolerant ideology, by preserving the term that was used when Muslims, Serbs, and Croats were living more or less harmoniously together among other ethnic groups in Yugoslavia.

WHAT IS THE MINIMUM EFFECTIVE ACTOR? MUNICIPAL-LEVEL EVIDENCE FROM BIH

This book's theoretical framework, presented in Chapter 2, suggests that there are three levels of analysis pertaining to the question of civil war alliance formation – the alliance, the group, and the subgroup – with the degree of relevant aggregation varying with the conflict's trajectory. Like Chapter 5, which tested the validity of the argument on the level of the Afghan district commander, this section uses the municipality – a more fine-grained unit of inquiry than that captured by warring groups or subgroups in BiH to illustrate that the group is the relevant level of analysis for the outbreak of civil war. Specifically, the analysis shows that outcomes related to conflict onset on the level of the municipality – the most disaggregated administrative unit for which prewar systematic data exist – fully converge with those determined by the group.

---

[169] Interview with Muhamed Skrgić.
[170] Interview with Admil Mulalić.
[171] A founding document on the Autonomous Province of Western Bosnia, *Polazne Osnove za Formiranje Provincije Broj 1* [Starting Basis for the Foundation of Province Number One], p. 2.

If the relevant unit of analysis at the time of civil war outbreak is the group, then we would expect elite control over group constituents, manifested in coordinated outbreaks of violence across the country's localities, to conform to the main wartime cleavages. That is to say, we would expect to see local and national elites act in more or less fully coordinated attacks against the group's common enemy. (By focusing on "coordinated outbreaks of violence," I am not considering low-level illicit cooperation between smuggling networks of different ethnicities in spite of group-level alliance patterns to the contrary. Such cooperation was common in such cities as Sarajevo and Srebrenica,[172] but in my view constitutes a different phenomenon than cooperation in the domain of organized violence.)

The case of BiH can serve as a good empirical test for this claim, because territorial defense (Teritorijalna Odbrana, TO) was organized locally, linking the center to each of Bosnia's 109 municipalities. More specifically, TO in former Yugoslavia was organized on the level of Republics and the entire administration, as well as command and control, was under the Republics' jurisdiction.[173] BiH was the most armed Yugoslav republic in TO terms (even though the JNA had dramatically reduced the Bosnian TO's strength in the late 1980s).[174] This was a result of Yugoslavia's WWII experience, which had suggested that any attempt to occupy the country would be unsuccessful in the Bosnian mountains. In 1991 and before the onset of hostilities in BiH, the TO of the Socialist Republic of Bosnia and Herzegovina (SABiH) had approximately 90,000 members. It consisted of twenty-eight brigades with three infantry battalions, support units (with rocket launchers up to 120 mm), and units of antiaircraft defense. Each brigade had an average of 1,550 people, armed with semiautomatic rifles, M48 rifles, or automatic assault rifles (Kalashnikovs).[175] The amount of weaponry on the municipal level varied with the number of units in each municipality – in other words, it depended on demographic size. Weaponry and military equipment were stored in 632 different territorial defense facilities around BiH. These facilities contained 270,000 rifles, 19,000 rocket launchers, 320 antitank rockets, 84.7 million bullets, 580 tons of explosive devices, and 2,000 pieces of different communications equipment.[176]

Every municipality had its own TO headquarters that, depending on demographic size, belonged to one of three types. Type III municipalities were the smallest municipalities and had a unit on the level of a company, an

---

[172] Andreas (2008), pp. 64–67, 141.

[173] This military decentralization was also legally codified: If the central government failed to provide protection, socialist Yugoslavia's legal provisions allowed for citizens to resort to their local territorial defense units for protection. Shrader (2003), p. 25.

[174] Thomas and Mikulan (2006), p. 4.

[175] Interviews with Serb General Manojlo Milovanović and Muslim General Atif Dudaković.

[176] JNA archive data provided by JNA territorial defense sources (see References). The data were also confirmed in interviews with retired JNA air force officer, Gostimir Popović, Serb General Manojlo Milovanović, and Muslim General Atif Dudaković.

anti-sabotage unit, a rear unit, and a communications unit. In addition to all the assets of a type III municipality, each of the type I and type II municipalities had four and two light-armed infantry brigades, respectively. The commanders of type I and type II municipalities were colonels, whereas type III munici-palities were headed by majors. The ethnic background of the colonels and majors in control of the municipal arms caches was mostly dictated by the demographic consistency of the respective municipality.[177] Given the devolu-tion of territorial defense to the municipal level (i.e., it was not a state with a centralized defense system), BiH constitutes a prime example of a case where in the absence of centralized control, the availability of arms on the local level could have allowed for the outbreak of local fighting. After all, each of Bosnia's 109 prewar municipalities had the weapons to fight its local war of choice.

As discussed in the chronology of events earlier in the chapter, fighting broke out in Bosnia in April 1992. The main fighting parties were the Serbs fighting against the Croat-Muslim alliance. If the argument that the group is the relevant unit of analysis at the outbreak of civil war were to hold, we would expect the Serbs to be fighting against the Muslims and the Croats in all contested areas of the country, while the Croat and Muslim allies would remain peaceful and united. Indeed, in 70 out of a total of 109 of Bosnia's municipalities, fighting broke out within a month (between mid-April and mid-May 1992) of the original hostilities. All seventy of these municipalities had Serb and Muslim, Serb and Croat, or Serb, Muslim, and Croat populations – in other words, populations from the two competing camps. The thirty-nine remaining municipalities were either largely mono-ethnic – that is, there was no area of contestation or fighting to be done – or were largely populated by Croats and Muslims, who were allies when the war broke out. In most of the ethnically dominated municipalities, no fighting ever broke out, because the dominance of one of the ethnic groups in these municipalities was clear from early on, prompting the flight of civilians from other ethnic groups without any full-scale fighting ever taking place.

This simple test, indicating that in the vast majority of multiethnic munici-palities fighting broke out in a coordinated fashion, already suggests a degree of centralization at the time of civil war onset. In turn, the availability of 1991 municipal-level census data by ethnicity from prewar Bosnia allows us to test this assertion in a more rigorous fashion. Specifically, rather than coding munic-ipalities by strict ethnic majorities – a binary measure that does not capture the nuanced ethnic fractionalization that characterized prewar BiH – I assume that the probability of conflict between non-allied groups is proportional to the product of their relative population proportions.[178] That means that

---

[177] Ibid.

[178] I only code the three relevant groups – Muslims, Serbs, and Croats – and exclude Yugoslavs or Others without loss of generality, as the latter two groups together constituted less than 10% of Bosnia's population.

if groups A and B are enemies, the probability of conflict in a given municipality can be captured by:

$$prod_{AB} = \left(\frac{pop\,A}{pop\,A + pop\,B} \right) \left(\frac{pop\,B}{pop\,A + pop\,B} \right)$$

This probability is maximized at 0.25 when groups A and B have equal shares of
the population, and is minimized at 0 when one group dominates the population
of a given district. Thus, this model reflects the expectation that if one group is
strongly dominant, there need not be violence because it has control already,
but if the groups are nearly equal in size, fighting will be most likely to result.
The same logic can be extended to alliances. For example, if the Serbs are
on one side and the Muslims are allied with the Croats against them, as was
the case at the time of the war's onset, the probability of conflict would be
predicted by:

$$prod_{S-CM} = \left(\frac{S}{S + C + M} \right) \left(\frac{C + M}{S + C + M} \right)$$

Using a linear probability model (as the effect of $prod_{S-CM}$ on the probability
of fighting proves very nearly linear), I find that the relationship between this
measure of Serb-by-(Croat+Muslim) cohabitation is remarkably predictive of
the outbreak of violence ($p = 0.000$, R^2 of 0.24). Indeed, a graphic representation of the data (Figure 6.3) shows the probability of fighting to be highest
where the difference between the Serb proportion of the population and the
Croat or Muslim proportion is nearest to zero, with the probability falling
away as this difference gets greater in either a positive or a negative direction.

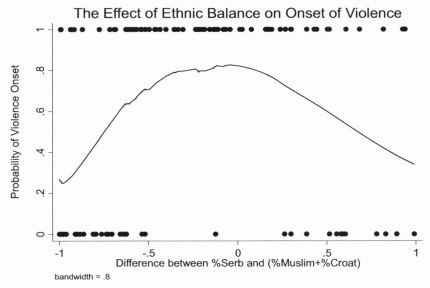

FIGURE 6.3. Municipal-Level Civil War Outbreak in BiH

TABLE 6.3 *BiH Municipal-Level Conflict Outbreak*

	Dependent Variable: Onset of Conflict in Municipality					
Prod_SvCM	2.878**	3.247**	3.018**		2.986**	3.286**
	(0.481)	(0.454)	(0.689)		(0.491)	(0.720)
Prod_MC		1.113	1.190			1.384
		(0.677)	(0.734)			(0.767)
Prod_MS			0.306			0.118
			(0.720)			(0.777)
Arms				0.098	− 0.055	0.062
				(0.092)	(0.084)	(0.134)
Population (log)						− 0.155
						(0.093)
Wage (log)						0.187
						(0.249)
Muslim Head of TO						0.195
						(0.115)
Serb Head of TO						0.114
						(0.110)
Constant	0.200	0.079	0.074	0.593	0.211	− 0.095
	(0.094)	(0.102)	(0.104)	(0.067)	(0.097)	(1.970)
Observations	109	109	109	109	109	109
R-squared	0.24	0.26	0.26	0.011	0.24	0.31

Notes: OLS estimates. Robust standard errors are in parentheses.
** Significant at 0.01 level; * Significant at 0.05 level.

Meanwhile, the presence of similar versus different numbers of Croats and Muslims should not be predictive of conflict, because these two groups should be allied. Indeed, both a bivariate and multivariate look at the relationship between Croat-Muslim tensions are suggestive of the lack of fighting between the two. As seen in Table 6.3, only the proportion of Serbs times the proportion of Croats+Muslims is predictive.

These regression results confirm the group as the relevant unit of analysis at the civil war's outbreak, by indicating an outbreak of violence on the local level in full accordance with group alliance dictates. They also show that even small municipalities that are more lightly armed and often cut off and farther away from the centers of decision making have more or less the same probability of facing an outbreak of violence, confirming the hypothesis of the center's control over the periphery at the time of war onset. Little else matters, including the presence of a larger armament cache or population size.

Although the data at onset are compelling in showing a convergence between the warring group choices and municipal-level ones, that convergence is not surprising at the beginning of the war. It is interesting to see if it lasts during the war. Unfortunately – and unsurprisingly – the requisite data that would allow a robust test are not available. Given the data that are available, there are only rough ways to generally assess whether the alliance behavior on the

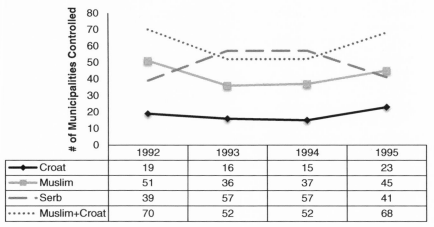

	1992	1993	1994	1995
◆ Croat	19	16	15	23
▦ Muslim	51	36	37	45
▬ Serb	39	57	57	41
⋯⋯ Muslim+Croat	70	52	52	68

FIGURE 6.4. Number of Municipalities Controlled by Warring Group and Alliance in BiH

municipal level was actually a balancing one during the conflict. Looking at the number of municipalities controlled by each of the warring groups (and insofar as the Muslim-Croat versus Serb is the general alliance arrangement) we see in Figure 6.4 that the dashed lines, which represent the two wartime alliances, are fairly well balanced.

Also, looking at how territory transferred from one warring group to another, all exchanges are consistent with the general alliances. For instance, all twenty municipalities that changed hands between April 1992 and December 1992 are consistent with the alliance of the Muslims and the Croats against the Serbs (fifteen majority Muslim municipalities and four majority Croat municipalities are taken over by the Serbs; one majority Serb municipality is taken over by the Croats). Similarly, in 1993–1994, there were municipalities that the Muslims lost to the Croats and the Croats to the Muslims (two and three municipalities, respectively) as part of the Muslim-Croat fight in Herzegovina and Central Bosnia. Finally, in the last period that led to the negotiated settlement of the war, the Serbs lost ten municipalities to the Muslims and seven to the Croats.

One can also look at municipal-level trends to see if the instances of group fractionalization, attributed to asymmetric losses among constituent subgroups, actually hold. Looking first at Fikret Abdić's territory, which attempted to secede in the infamous Muslim split, we see that these areas had by early 1993 suffered considerably lighter losses relative to their Muslim populations. Specifically, looking at the four western municipalities under Abdić's control – out of the total fifty-one Muslim municipalities in BiH – and using the number of Muslim fatalities at the end of 1992 out of the total (prewar) Muslim population of each municipality as the dependent variable, I find that the four western municipalities lost, on average, 0.5 percent of their Muslim population. (The one with the greatest proportion loss was at 1.1 percent). Meanwhile, the other Muslim districts lost an average of 1.7 percent, and one municipality, Višegrad, lost more than 10 percent. The proportion of Muslims killed in the non-western Muslim municipalities was, on average, more than three times the proportion killed in these four western municipalities. In other words, battlefield losses for Muslims appear to have been asymmetric. A simple t-test does not reach significance because of the small number of western Muslim municipalities ($t = 1.03$, $p = 0.308$). However, a more efficient test, which accounts for the different variances that result from differently sized municipalities (the municipalities with larger Muslim populations allow for a lower-variance estimate of the underlying proportion killed), produces very similar point estimates: Non-western Muslim municipalities lost a weighted average of 1.7 percent of their Muslim populations, whereas the western Muslim municipalities lost a weighted average of 0.46 percent. This is a statistically significant result ($t = 3.01$, $p < 0.01$).[179]

Using a similar approach to evaluate the Croat takeover,[180] I see that eastern Croat-dominated municipalities, those in Mate Boban's Herzegovina, had suffered far lower rates of loss in 1992. The difference is stunning: Eastern Croat municipalities lost 0.14 percent of their Croat populations, whereas non-eastern forces lost four times that at 0.64 percent. This difference is highly statistically significant ($t = 3.69$, $p < 0.001$). Again, a more appropriate test would weight municipalities inversely to their variance by using their Croat population sizes as weights. Doing so yields similar point estimates and a highly significant difference ($t = 3.34$, $p = 0.002$).

CONCLUSION

This chapter set out to illustrate the theory of this book in a non-Afghan context, using the alliance and group fractionalization dynamics in the 1992–1995 Bosnian civil war. As in the Afghan cases, alliance changes proved motivated by shifts in relative power that changed warring groups' optimal partners in potential minimum winning coalitions. These considerations resulted in the breakdown of the Muslim-Croat alliance, instances of Serb-Croat and Serb-Muslim collaboration, and in turn the re-formation of the Muslim-Croat alliance. Identity narratives justifying these alliances were rich, but ultimately changed as soon as relative power dictated new alliance configurations. Meanwhile, instances of within-group fractionalization – the Muslim split and the Croat takeover – can also be explained by this book's theory. These fractionalization events occurred within the context of asymmetrically borne relative power losses by the Croats and Muslims in 1993. Ultimately, group

---

[179] This is efficiently done by weighted least squares (WLS), weighting each municipality by the initial size of their Muslim populations.

[180] Croat municipalities are defined as those in which Croats made up 30% or more of the population, using the 1991 census data.

fractionalization and alliance reconfiguration came to an end only after NATO decisively intervened on the weaker side – that of the newly merged Muslim-Croat alliance – and got the relatively stronger Serbs to agree to a negotiated settlement. Municipal-level data, used to probe whether the theory holds on a lower level of analysis, yield consistent results.

In this chapter, the theory has made an important leap – a geographic one. In the next chapter, I make a second "character of war" leap instead, while holding geography constant. I discuss the ideological civil war in Bosnia between 1941 and 1945 and test the consistency of the warring group and subgroup behavior in that conflict against this book's theoretical predictions.

7

The Bosnian Civil War, 1941–1945

This book has so far emphasized the power motivations behind civil war alliance choices. These instrumental decisions, however, were always accompanied by evocative narratives. In the 1992–1995 Bosnian civil war discussed in Chapter 6, those narratives – of Serbs as royalist Chetniks and Croats as fascist Ustashe – directly referenced symbols and events from a past war that had traumatized the psyche of the different constituent nations residing in Bosnia. This chapter presents the warring group interactions and alliance and group fractionalization dynamics of that war of half a century earlier – Bosnia's 1941–1945 civil war – using primary archival documents from all warring sides. Specifically, this chapter references the Main Laws and Orders of the Independent State of Croatia (*Zakoni Nezavisne Države Hrvatske*); documents from the archive of the Communist Party of Bosnia and Herzegovina (*Arhiv Komunističke Partije Bosne i Hercegovine*); documents and a chronology on the National Liberation War of the Peoples of Yugoslavia (*Zbornik Dokumenata i Podataka o Narodno-Oslobodilačkom Ratu Jugoslovenskih Naroda* and *Hronologija Oslobodilačke Borbe Naroda Jugoslavije 1941–1945*); as well as documents from the Military Archive in Belgrade (*Vojni Arhiv*) along with its two sub-archives – the Chetnik fund and the National Liberation Army fund – as they relate to the intergroup and intragroup fighting in World War II Bosnia.

Before presenting the events that transpired in that civil war, I need to note the historical disagreement as to whether the war in Bosnia, in the broader context of World War II Yugoslavia, should be seen as a civil war in the first place. After all, in post–World War II Yugoslavia, it was largely portrayed as a war of liberation against foreign occupiers (Germany and Italy) rather than as an ideological civil war among different Yugoslav factions. Josip Broz Tito, the leader of the victorious Partisans who became renowned as the Yugoslav nation-builder, would not have had it any other way. However, whereas primary documents from the time clearly indicate that Tito and his Partisans cast the war as largely one of national liberation, Edmund Glaise-Horstenau, a Nazi military officer, talks of the war in Bosnia as a civil war.[1] So did Serb Chetnik leader Dobroslav Jevđević, who underlined the flexibility of population loyalties for Bosnia by concluding that "as in every other *civil war*, the masses are fluid and are joining the stronger party."[2]

My work does not intend to resolve the disagreement of whether this should be seen as a civil war or a war of liberation. That is a task for historians to settle. It does, however, regard the claim that this was a civil war as a largely plausible one, given the violence that transpired among the warring domestic factions, which actually constituted the bulk of the fighting in that war. The conflict took place in the different yet interconnected theaters of Bosnia and Herzegovina (BiH), Croatia, Serbia, and Montenegro, but my work focuses on alliance politics in the wartime area of BiH, a distinct theater where all relevant warring actors, as presented later in the chapter, were at play.

Much as in all the empirical chapters that preceded this one (Chapters 3–6), my analysis addresses the role of the Germans, Italians, Soviets, and British, all relevant actors in the broader context of World War II, only insofar as their involvement is reflected as an extension of the power of their local proxies – the royalist Chetniks, the fascist Ustashe, the Muslim nationalists, or the communist Partisans. And, as in the previous chapters, the intent of the discussion that follows is to show that relative power drove alliance and fractionalization choices among warring groups and subgroups, and that identity considerations placed few constraints on their decisions of whom to fight in the context of a civil war.

WARRING ACTORS

The ideological civil war in Bosnia, which ended in communist victory in May 1945, was fought within the broader context of World War II and was triggered by the Axis invasion of Yugoslavia in April 1941. The civil war involved four domestic groups: the communists (Partisans), the royalists (Chetniks), the fascists (Ustashe), and the Muslims. The last group, arguably not the same type as the aforementioned ideologically driven groups, largely served as an integral part of the fascists, and was mostly involved in their Home Guard (Domobrani), but toward the end of the conflict joined the Partisans' ranks.[3] From an ideological perspective, one could place these groups on a left-to-right spectrum starting with the communist Partisans, then the royalist-nationalist Chetniks, and then the fascist-nationalist Ustashe and the Muslim Home Guard.[4]

---

[1] *Zbornik Dokumenata i Podataka o Narodno-Oslobodilačkom Ratu Jugoslovenskih Naroda* (henceforth ZNOR), 2, 7, pp. 112–119; ZNOR, 12, 2, pp. 162–176.

[2] ZNOR, 14, 1, p. 468.

[3] The collaborationists, known as the Nedicites after the collaborationist Prime Minster Milan Nedić, were only active in Serbia proper and not in BiH. My discussion therefore focuses on the four groups that were active within BiH: the Partisans, the Chetniks, the Ustashe, and the Muslim nationalists.

[4] A similar categorization is also provided by Wilcox (1999), pp. 128–129.

The defining attributes of the groups were distinctly ideological, but they also featured a set of clear ethnic constituents. The Ustashe and their Home Guard were overwhelmingly Croat and Muslim, whereas the Chetniks were almost exclusively Serbs. The ethnic composition of the Partisans was the most diverse – claiming Serbs, Croats, and Muslims in their ranks – and as such the most disputed, and it appears to have increased in diversity over time. The Partisan leader, Tito, in an article dating from December 1941, claimed that Serbs formed the vast majority of the Partisans, although other ethnic groups were part of the cause, such as the First Muslim Partisan Company led by Mujo Hodžić, which was formed in Romanija in October 1941.[5] In a German report from a few months later, dating from February 1942, the Partisan rebels were identified as "mostly Orthodox [Serbian] with some Muslims and Croats also joining them."[6] An Ustashe report from April 1942 offered exact statistics: "Partisans in Central Bosnia consist of 70% Serb, 20% Muslim, 5% Jewish and 5% Catholic; political officers are 'Orthodox' and some Muslim."[7] Partisan membership became increasingly mixed – as discussed later – as their power increased.

The Partisans, led by Josip Broz Tito, espoused a communist ideology, prominently wore the Red Star, and were locally led by political commissars and People's Liberation Committees. Their official name changed from the National Liberation Movement to the National Liberation Army of Yugoslavia on November 1, 1942 and to the Yugoslav Army on March 1, 1945, when their victory was a mere two weeks away. Given that they were socialist rather than nationalist, it was easier for a various range of ethnic groups to join their ranks. Partisans themselves were actively trying to recruit Croats and Muslims since the early days of the war, calling civilians to join the struggle and for those who were part of opposing military units to defect.[8] They emphasized unity of different ethnic groups under a common ideological banner. For instance, in December 1941, the local Partisan Council announced in Rudo, in Eastern Herzegovina, that inciting ethnic hatred was punishable by death.[9] In the same vein, early in the war, whenever the Partisans took control of certain areas that had seen intense conflict, they did not allow for any form of retributive justice other than death.[10]

Although the Partisans' foot soldiers were mostly Serbs, the higher Partisan echelons were comprised of members of all Yugoslav nationalities. Specifically, primary sources are replete with references from all warring factions, suggesting that the Partisans' inclusion of ethnic groups other than the Serbs was extensively used by their enemies (such as the Serb royalist Chetniks) to point

---

[5] ZNOR, 2, 7, pp. 112–119.
[6] ZNOR, 12, 2, pp. 162–176.
[7] ZNOR, 4, 4, pp. 328–330.
[8] *Arhiv Komunističke Partije Bosne i Hercegovine* (henceforth KP BiH) 3, 1, pp. 30–37; KP BiH 3, 1, pp. 82–84; ZNOR, 2, 3, pp. 343–344; ZNOR, 2, 7, pp. 361–362; ZNOR 4, 2, pp. 90–95.
[9] KP BiH 3, 1, pp. 146–149.
[10] ZNOR 2, 5, pp. 307–310.

to what they argue was the Partisans' anti-Serb nature. For instance, a 1941 letter by the Chetnik supreme leader Dragoljub Mihailović stated that the Partisans were led by the Croatian Ustashe.[11] In a May 1942 communiqué from Herzegovina, Chetniks were running negative anti-Serb campaigns against the Partisans, calling them "traders of Serbian white slaves."[12] In a report by Chetnik leader Dragoslav Jevđević dating from June 1942, there were claims that the Partisan brigades consisted mainly of Muslims, Croats, and women and that they were getting ammunition from Croats.[13]

As indicated by their motto, "Belief in God, the King and the Fatherland," the Chetniks were a largely Serbian force that swore allegiance to the Serbian royal family. Unlike the Partisans, who aspired to a socialist republic, the Chetniks wished for a Yugoslav state under the scepter of Serbian royalty. The political platform of the Chetniks was set forth in several documents throughout the war. For instance, on June 30, 1941, Dr. Stevan Moljević, a member of Mihailović's General Staff, wrote a program, "On our State and its Borders," for which he envisioned three federal units for Yugoslavia: Serb, Croat, and Slovenian. Even though the program was unofficial, it was widely accepted in the party, and its primary goal – to create a Serbia inside the Yugoslav state that would include all territories inhabited by the Serbs and other important territories by means of population transfers – enjoyed great appeal.[14]

Six months later, on December 20, 1941, in instructions to his constituents, Chetnik supreme leader Dragoljub Mihailović outlined the goals of the movement in ten points, including the reestablishment of the Yugoslav monarchy with Greater Serbia within it, and the cleansing of minorities from the territory.[15] A year later, on December 2, 1942, the Chetnik (Youth) Conference of Šahovići reinforced the aforementioned program – a unitary Yugoslav monarchy, with Serbs, Croats, Slovenes, and no minorities.[16] Although almost exclusively Serb, they did feature some non-Serbs in their ranks later in the war, when the changes in the balance of power mandated some strange bedfellows – namely the political movement of pro-Chetnik Muslims known as the Muslim People's Military Organization, which was formed in late 1942 in Herzegovina under Ismet Popovac and Muhamed Pašić of Mostar. Fehim Musakadić from Sarajevo was assigned by Mihailović as a commander of the Muslim Chetnik Militia.[17]

Much like the Chetniks, the Ustashe were also nationalist. However, they had a largely fascist ideology and aimed at the establishment and preservation of an Aryan Croatian state, proclaiming the Independent State of Croatia (*Nezavisna Država Hrvatska*, henceforth NDH) on April 10, 1941, with legal provisions on citizenship, racial affiliation, and on protection of Aryan blood

[11] ZNOR, 14, 1, pp. 72–75.
[12] ZNOR, 4, 5, p. 369.
[13] ZNOR, 14, 1, pp. 397–405.
[14] Ibid, pp. 10, 101–103.
[15] Ibid, pp. 93–100.
[16] Ibid, pp. 736–739.
[17] Ibid, pp. 456–458; ZNOR, 14, 2, p. 139.

and honor of the Croat people.[18] Though anti-Semitic and anti-Serb, they were largely open to Muslim membership and recruited them both in their political and in their military divisions. Specifically, in 1941 and 1942 NDH reports from Bosnia, Muslims are presented as an integral part of the Croat people.[19] Their leader was Ante Pavelić, a fascist dictator, who had a Muslim vice president, Osman Kulenović. [20]

The Muslims, who at the time were not recognized as a separate ethnic group, appear to have had a primarily nationalistic objective, aiming to increase the power of their nation in the future postwar state. Their party, the Muslim People's Organization (*Muslimanska Narodna Organizacija* or MNO) – which in the interwar period was renamed the Yugoslav Muslim Organization (*Jugoslovenska Muslimanska Organizacija* or JMO) – was split on how best to acquire that power. One faction felt the best way would be through affiliation with the newly formed Croat state under the Ustashe. (Muslims had become an integral part of the NDH Home Guard known as Domobrani.) The competing camp felt Muslims should be seen as a distinct group rather than as Croats of the Muslim faith, using that objective as their guiding principle. This split among the Muslims further underlined the cross-cutting cleavages in terms of political affiliation within the different ethnic groups in World War II Bosnia, as discussed later.[21]

TIMELINE, WARTIME ALLIANCES, GROUP FRACTIONALIZATION, AND NARRATIVES

Civil war broke out in BiH soon after the Axis invasion of April 1941. The first round of hostilities occurred in Gacko in Herzegovina, where the local Serb population under a Chetnik banner revolted against violent abuses of Ustashe authorities on June 6, 1941.[22] The mass uprising started in Lukavac, in the area of Nevesinje, on June 24 of that year.[23] Early NDH reports from June 26 blamed the Serbs for the uprising and the NDH started arming the Ustashe.[24] Indeed, in their attempt to solidify their power in their newly instituted state, which had incorporated the whole of BiH along with the non-Croat populations residing in that territory,[25] the Ustashe had gone as far

---

[18] All of these provisions are from April 30, 1941. Provided in the original in Colić (1973), pp. 411, 418–420.

[19] ZNOR, 4, 2, pp. 538–544.

[20] Karchmar (1987), Vol. I, p. 35. Additional Muslim members of the Pavelić government included Džafer-beg Kulenović, vice-president of the government, and Himlija Bešlagić, minister of transport and public works. ZNOR, 4, 2, p. 430.

[21] Friedman (1996), pp. 122–123; Wilcox (1999), p. 96.

[22] *Vojni Arhiv, Narodnooslobodilačke Vojska Jugoslavije* (henceforth VA NOV) 6; VA NOV 8; VA NOV 9.

[23] ZNOR, 4, 1, pp. 513–514; see NDH report in ZNOR, 4, 1, pp. 524–526.

[24] Ibid, pp. 511–513.

[25] An early August 1941 German report on the NDH asserted that its main mistake was not recognizing that the new state consisted of only 50% Croats, which made the NDH a potentially nonviable entity. ZNOR, 12, 1, pp. 328–330.

as to declare the Muslims as the "purest of Croats" and call them "flowers of the Croatian people."[26] On April 6, 1941, the day of the Axis attack on Yugoslavia, a speech delivered by Ustashe leader Ante Pavelić referred to "Croatian soldiers, Catholic and Muslim."[27] Two weeks later, on April 19, 1941, minister of the Croatian Armed Forces Slavko Kvaternik said that the "most vital and noblest part of the Croatian people" were the Dalmatian Croats and the Muslims in BiH.[28]

Furthermore, the Ustashe made historic claims to the territory of BiH. NDH leader Ante Pavelić, in an article entitled "The Notion of Bosnia through the Centuries," argued that the first Croatian King Tomislav was crowned in 925 in Duvanjsko polje, in Bosnia, suggesting the Croat historic claim to Bosnian territory.[29] The NDH also wanted to phase out the term "BiH" and instead opted for the use of municipal and provincial names for the different territories.[30] The territorial and power underpinnings of the shared-identity narrative were thus clear. To further solidify their presence in BiH, Pavelić situated part of his cabinet, led by Muslim Deputy Prime Minister Kulenović, in the western Bosnian city of Banja Luka.[31] The political leadership move was also accompanied by a military consolidation in BiH: Four out of a total of six NDH Home Guard army divisions were situated in BiH (in the cities of Sarajevo, Doboj, Bihać, and Mostar), and only two in Croatia proper.[32]

Apart from the Croat-Muslim unifying narrative, the Ustashe also used overtly anti-Serb propaganda. They banned the Cyrillic alphabet, which is the Serb national alphabet, on April 25, 1941, and on May 3, 1941 passed legislation that viewed religious conversion for the Orthodox as the only way to grant them equal rights before the law.[33] An NDH report from July 12, 1941 also speaks of large deportations of Serbs.[34] An Ustashe prefect, Victor Gutić, was quite graphic about his plans for the Serb population: "These Serbian Gypsies will be sent to Serbia, part by trains, part through the river Sava, without boats. These unwanted elements will be rooted out by erasing their traces and the only thing that will remain will be the evil memory of them.

---

[26] KP BiH 3, 1, pp. 131–135.

[27] Colić (1973), pp. 97–98.

[28] Ibid, p. 93.

[29] Article published in *Spremnost* on March 1, 1942 from his earlier memorandum dating July 1940.

[30] NDH local divisions, Velike Župe, did not follow the borders of BiH. See map in Colić (1973), p. 158.

[31] Redžic (2005), p. 75.

[32] Ibid, p. 70; Colić (1973), pp. 202, 236–239.

[33] NDH anti-Serb legislation included: law on loyalty to the state (April 10); legal provision on protection of people and state (April 17); legal provision on so-called volunteer's immobility (mostly Serb land gained after World War I, April 18); legal provision on prohibition of Cyrillic (April 25); and legal provision on religious conversion (May 3). Colić (1973), pp. 414–422.

[34] ZNOR, 4, 1, pp. 523–524.

All Serbian pests older than 15 will be killed and their children will be put to monasteries and turned into good Catholics."[35]

According to NDH reports, the Herzegovina uprising was followed by joint Communist-Chetnik action in western Bosnia, particularly in the districts of Drvar and Grahovo, on July 27, 1941.[36] In clear defiance of their ideological distance, but in clear accordance with the theory of this book, the Partisan communists formed an alliance with the Chetnik royalists in an effort to balance against the increasing power of the Ustashe.[37] According to Redžić, a historian who is considered an authority on the 1941–1945 Bosnian civil war, "their survival [Chetniks and Partisans] demanded unification of their forces in the name of more efficient operations."[38] Hoare, another historian, agrees, noting the striking difference between the contentious Chetnik-Partisan relations in Serbia and their alliance in Bosnia:

The factors governing Partisan-Chetnik relations in Bosnia-Herzegovina were not equivalent to those in Serbia [where the two parties were fighting their own civil war].... Interests of survival, pure and simple, dictated different strategies for the... Bosnian Serbs.... In the summer and autumn of 1941, as the rebellion against the Ustashas increasingly assumed the form of a Serb chauvinistic backlash against the Muslim and Croat population... so the Communists were forced to seek accommodation with [the] embryonic Chetnik movement in the interests of rebel unity against the Ustashas.[39]

During the insurrection against the NDH in Doboj in August 1941, the rebels were shouting both "Long live Soviet Russia" and "Long live King Peter."[40] The first formal Partisan-Chetnik cooperation body for eastern Bosnia was established on September 1, 1941.[41] A Chetnik-Partisan accord was signed by three Chetnik and three Partisan representatives on October 1, 1941 in Drinjača, Bosnia, stipulating the creation of a temporary command staff of Bosnian military and Partisan units that would be comprised of three members from the Chetnik side and three from the Partisan side, and that would establish joint authority in any newly conquered territories.[42] Indeed, a Chetnik-Partisan collaboration led to the establishment of control over Rogatica on October 24, 1941.[43] They set up a joint command, with a Partisan commander and a Chetnik deputy commander, with narratives arising on both sides in justification of their respective alliance choices. In that regard, the accord's signatories called for "'honest and patriotic people of Bosnia'... to

---

[35] Redžić (2005), p. 13.
[36] ZNOR, 4, 1, pp. 527–528, 655–658, 735–745; KP BiH 3, 1, pp. 16–17.
[37] Redžić (2005), p. 82.
[38] Ibid, p. 12.
[39] Hoare (2006), pp. 95, 108.
[40] KP BiH 3, 1, pp. 85–86.
[41] Ibid, pp. 52–53.
[42] ZNOR, 14, 1, pp. 29–31.
[43] ZNOR, 1, 1, pp. 224–225.

unite in their fight against the Fascist occupying forces and the Ustasha."[44] As reflected in Partisan reports from the time, they also drew on their mostly Serb membership and highlighted the need for unity among the Serbs.[45] For instance, the Chetniks and the Partisans issued a joint proclamation explaining their alliance in terms of resistance to anti-Serb NDH policies.[46]

In their joint fighting arrangement, the Chetniks and the Partisans gained control of the mountain ranges of Romanija and Jahorina, as well as some major towns along the Drina River. They had coordinated operations in eastern Bosnia, and at the end of 1941, their joint administration still existed in the cities of Rogatica, Olovo, and Han-Pijesak.[47]

However, the alliance was short-lived – as historian Jozo Tomasevich states, "Since both sides... had entered into this agreement with ulterior motives, it could hardly have proved workable."[48] Consistent with the theory's predictions, as the relative power of the Partisan-Chetnik alliance increased, disputes emerged among the erstwhile allies about the division of political power. Fighting between the Partisans and the Chetniks broke out in early November 1941. A report from the Partisan Supreme Headquarters from the time blamed the conflicts with the Chetniks on a "power struggle" between them and the Partisans over control of the liberated territories.[49] Specifically, after a failed conference with the Partisans, scheduled for November 16 in Vlasenica, the Chetniks held their own conference on November 17 and formed a separate Chetnik authority for eastern Bosnia, based in Vlasenica.[50] Despite the tensions and increasing fallout, the Chetniks and the Partisans continued to negotiate during December of that year in Bosnia.[51] Tito's last call for negotiations with the Chetniks was sent as late as February 6, 1942.[52] What is also interesting to note is the gradual breakdown of the alliance based on the balance of power in the terrain. For instance, the last joint Partisan-Chetnik actions in western Bosnia were still ongoing in February 1942 in Mrkonjić Grad, months after the start of the alliance breakdown. In this period, the Partisans acknowledged the need to differentiate more from the Chetniks to avoid defections from their ranks.[53] They formalized this by stopping the use of the term "Guerilla" or "*Cheta*" and only using the term "Partisan."[54]

---

[44] Redžić (2005), p. 129.
[45] ZNOR, 4, 1, pp. 412–413.
[46] ZNOR, 4, 2, pp. 7–9.
[47] ZNOR, 14, 1, pp. 114–117.
[48] Tomasevich (1975), p. 157.
[49] ZNOR, 1, 1, pp. 242–247.
[50] ZNOR, 14, 1, pp. 79–82; on the Partisan perspective, see KP BiH 3, 1, pp. 122–126.
[51] ZNOR, 14, 1, pp. 83–84, ZNOR 4, 2, pp. 204–207.
[52] ZNOR, 4, 3, pp. 40–41.
[53] Ibid, pp. 240–242, 265–269.
[54] KP BiH 3, 1, p. 82.

By early 1942, the decline of German power had in turn confirmed the declining power of the Ustashe.[55] In their effort to maintain control, the fascists tried to gain wider support by ordering the cessation of violence against persons or property (but still allowing the burning of insurgent villages and the sending of hostages to concentration camps).[56] These measures could not avert the Ustashe power decline, which turned out to be asymmetrically borne by different subgroups within their fighting force.

Specifically, according to a November 1941 report, the Muslims complained about not being given enough support from the Ustashe against the royalist Chetniks. The Muslims also felt that they were contributing more than their fair share. As an example, they used the case of the Bosnian region of Tuzla, where 98 percent of the Ustashe volunteers in the area were Croat-Muslims, while the Croat-Catholics were barely volunteering.[57] After the Ustashe consistently failed to support the Muslims in that area, Major Muhamed Hadžiefendić, who commanded a unit of 5,000–6,000 Muslim men in the Usore i Soli region, split from the Ustashe army in late April 1942 to form the autonomous "Volunteer Legion of Popular Uprising" that challenged NDH authority.[58] Meanwhile, the Chetniks and the Partisans had grown more or less equally powerful.[59] Thus, in line with the hypotheses on fractionalization, asymmetric losses across subgroups led one faction (the Muslims of Usore i Soli) to break off on its own as it feared its own survival was at stake.

After the power-induced collapse of the Chetnik-Partisan alliance discussed earlier, the narrative changed from an ethnic (Serb) unifying one to a divisive ideological one. Chetnik rhetoric argued that the Partisans did not care for the future of the Serbian people and therefore were the worst type of Serbs and an enemy that had to be dealt with.[60] More specifically, after the break with the Partisans, Mihailović claimed there could be no cooperation with communists

---

[55] See the report of the Germans leaving Bosnia after the second offensive, ZNOR, 4, 3, pp. 209–211 and the February 1942 report on the Germans leaving Bosnia, ZNOR, 4, 3, pp. 181–184.

[56] ZNOR 4, 2, pp. 443–447.

[57] Redžić (2005), p. 172; Muslim grievances against the NDH are represented in other documents from that period, such as the November 22, 1941 Resolution-Letter of Bosnian Muslims of Banja Luka to the Muslim members of the NDH government. ZNOR, 4, 2, pp. 430–433.

[58] Redžić (2005), p. 91.

[59] The power balance in mid-1942 was diverse across the BiH theaters. The Chetniks dominated Herzegovina and were far stronger than either the Ustashe or the Partisans in that area. In western Bosnia, the Partisans were of equal strength with the Chetniks, who felt compelled to enter into an agreement with the NDH so as not to be left as the weakest party in the theater after the Partisan troops reorganized. In eastern Bosnia at the time, the Partisans had been defeated and the Chetniks were in control of Zvornik, Višegrad, Rogatica, Olovo, and the upper Drina region, ZNOR 14, 1, pp. 114–117. All other areas of Bosnia – north, central, and southwest – were controlled by the NDH.

[60] Redžić (2005), p. 139.

because they fought against the monarchy and wanted social revolution.[61] In Herzegovina, Chetnik leader Jevđević deliberately sought to make the ideological differences of the parties distinct in order to attract more people with existing anticommunist sentiments.[62] In a November 15, 1941 proclamation, the "Mountain Staff of the Bosnian Chetnik Detachments" deftly spun this new narrative:

[We started rebelling for] the holy Cross and golden freedom, for the King and fatherland, for the Serb nation and the Serb Orthodox faith.... [But] imposed on [us] is the anti-national fisted salute in place of our military salute, and on their hats they have put the five-pointed star to separate openly the true Chetniks from the followers of the Communist Party. Among all ignorant peasants, good and honorable, a ruthless propaganda is spread, no longer for the Serb nation and its sacred things and ideals but for the Communist Party.... We are fighting for a better future for the Serb nation... and we do not recognize any separate nations such as the Montenegrins, Bosnians, and Macedonians, like the Communists call us; we recognize only the Serb nation.[63]

Meanwhile, the Partisans constructed an ideological narrative against the Chetniks, who drew much of their support from the Serb peasantry. Speaking to their Serb audience, the Partisans emphasized a nonethnic, class-based narrative, accusing the Chetniks of being a fifth column, nothing other than rich peasants connected to the Soviet kulaks. For the Muslim Partisans, an ethnic narrative with an ideological dimension appeared. Specifically, in a January 25, 1942 address to Muslim civilians, the Muslim Partisans equated the Chetniks with the Ustashe, calling them "Serb Fascists."[64]

Because Ustashe propaganda had rested to a great extent on anti-Serb sentiment, and given their aggressive politics of conversion, forced migration, and ethnic cleansing, it was striking to see the Ustashe-Chetnik alliance come to life. In accordance with theoretical expectations, a prominent historian covering that period states that the Chetnik-Ustashe alliance – through an agreement signed on April 27, 1942 in western Bosnia's Mrkonjić Grad by representatives of the NDH and Chetnik leader Uroš Drenović – was created in an effort to balance against the Partisans' growing power. The agreement had eight points, including the termination of hostilities, an obligation of Ustashe and Chetnik forces to protect the Serb population from the Partisans, and a provision for joint Ustashe-Chetnik fighting against the Partisans.[65] Redžić, the renowned historian of the period, also confirms that it was military and political expediency that led to this alliance:

The Ustasha-Chetnik accords were driven neither by a confluence of Serbian and Croatian national interests nor by mutual desire for acceptance and respect, but rather

---

[61] ZNOR, 14, 1, pp. 93–100.
[62] Ibid, p. 468.
[63] Hoare (2006), p. 123.
[64] ZNOR, 4, 3, pp. 94–95; KP BiH 3, 2, pp. 36–40.
[65] Original agreement in ZNOR, 14, 1, pp. 215–218; also see Partisan report ZNOR, 4, 4, pp. 270–272; and Italian report ZNOR, 13, 2, pp. 381–383.

because each side needed to obstruct Partisan advances. The Ustasha and Chetniks, the two long-time foes, sought help from one another at a time when the Ustasha were facing national political disgrace among the Croats and the Chetniks were losing the support of the Serbs.[66]

An NDH report of July 1942 on the delineation of the NDH and the Chetniks, with whom they had agreements, explicitly mentions every pro-NDH Chetnik unit in western, northern, and central Bosnia.[67] The Chetniks of eastern and western Bosnia, in turn, held a July 1, 1942 conference in Grabska, in which they formed the Supreme Chetnik Headquarters for BiH and recognized all individual agreements with the NDH.[68] On May 28, 1942, it was decided that Chetnik units and the population they controlled had to recognize the authority of the Ustashe and pledge allegiance to the state, along with a promise of future Chetnik disarmament. In turn, the Ustashe offered equal rights to people living in Chetnik-controlled areas, also offering them state employment and positions in government projects. They also gave weapons and armaments to Chetnik units, who were to work under the orders and command of the Ustashe to target "Communist-Bolshevik bands."[69]

Both the Ustashe and the Chetniks rationalized this agreement to their constituents by claiming that they were both organizations of similar orientation – that is, both groups were national, anticommunist parties opposing the rise of the Partisans. Moreover, the Ustashe promised equal rights to the Orthodox Serbs comprising the Chetnik ranks. They agreed to "guarantee the Orthodox population equality before the law and provide material support to rebuild destroyed places of worship."[70] Given the intense conversion strategy that had been undertaken against the Orthodox, this was an unprecedented change. They also proceeded to set up the Croatian Orthodox Church that had its own Patriarchate, different from the one in Belgrade.[71] The rhetoric was clearly changing to accommodate the power changes in the field.

The alliance between the Ustashe and the Chetniks led to a strong and successful anti-Partisan campaign in spring 1942, with the Partisans facing mass desertion in their ranks.[72] The Partisans suffered serious losses but were not defeated – instead they moved west of the Bosna River. On June 22, 1942 Tito ordered the withdrawal of Proletarian brigades from eastern BiH to western Bosnia, where the focus of operations was anticipated to be during the following year.[73] It was at that time that Tito also appeared to want to put the whole social revolution component of the Partisan struggle to the side

---

[66] Redžić (2005), p. 88.
[67] ZNOR, 4, 6, pp. 413–415; see also typical Chetnik demands on pp. 377–380; the dates and places of the signing of all ten agreements are listed in ZNOR, 14, 1, p. 216.
[68] ZNOR, 14, 1, pp. 405–409.
[69] Ibid, pp. 276–280; Redžić (2005), p. 89.
[70] Redžic (2005), p. 87; ZNOR, 14, 1, pp. 215–218.
[71] ZNOR, 4, 1, pp. 545–548; ZNOR, 12, 2, pp. 139–142, 162–176.
[72] June 1942 in ZNOR, 4, 5, pp. 190–191; May 1942 in ZNOR, 4, 5, pp. 356–357, 372.
[73] ZNOR, 2, 4, pp. 395–399.

and focus on not alienating any potential recruits. In that spirit, he allowed for religious referents (Christian or Muslim) in the Proletarian brigades, at a time when the Partisans were most vulnerable, transitioning through enemy Muslim territory in Central Bosnia.[74]

The Partisans reached Bihać in late 1942, where they regrouped and formed what documents of the time call a mini-socialist republic. A Chetnik report of July 1942 estimated the strength of the "Soviet Republic" in the Bihać area of Western Bosnia at 12,000 well-armed soldiers who came from all over Yugoslavia.[75] A mere half a year later, a December 1942 report on an uprising in western Bosnia described Bihać as a "Communist state" that had 63,000 highly disciplined soldiers. On the other side, the Chetniks, led by Jevđević, were estimated at 24,000 strong.[76] In the first months of 1943, with the Ustashe state facing collapse as a result of the loss of large swaths of territory to the Partisans,[77] the Partisans recovered from their mid-1942 power deterioration and emerged again as a force to be reckoned with. After arriving in western Bosnia in July and August 1942, Tito suggested that the movement needed to pursue the liberation of major cities in western Bosnia and fight for the creation of a contiguous liberated territory.[78]

It was not until after the Battle of Sutjeska in June 1943 that the Partisans had made the requisite political progress. A German report from the time notes that the Chetniks were surrendering to the Partisans and that the Partisans had become a force to be reckoned with.[79] Coupled with the lack of basic supplies for their recruits, several Chetnik units decided to switch sides and go with the Partisans.[80] As the theory would expect, poor battlefield performance led to splits within the Chetnik ranks. The decline in Chetnik power also led them to soften their anticommunist narrative. A February 1943 German report noted that Chetnik anticommunism was becoming weaker than before, but that the Partisans had declined any possibility for talks.[81]

Croat and Muslim forces also defected from the Ustashe alliance. For instance, the Muslims of central Bosnia refused NDH mobilization during July 1943 and joined the Partisans in order to protect themselves from the Chetniks.[82] Sulejman Filipović, a well-known Home Guard colonel, led some 1,500 Muslims and 600 Croats to join the Partisans in September and

[74] ZNOR, 2, 4, pp. 403–406.
[75] ZNOR, 14, 1, pp. 417–427.
[76] ZNOR, 12, 2, pp. 952–957.
[77] Beside losing control of territory, an NDH report dating from late 1943 stated that Croat morale had reached an all-time low. ZNOR, 4, 20, pp. 725–734.
[78] ZNOR, 2, 5, pp. 317–322.
[79] ZNOR, 2, 9, pp. 467–477.
[80] After the Partisan military success against stronger forces in eastern BiH, the Chetniks reported very low morale and bad conditions of the units (ZNOR, 14, 2, p. 729). Chetnik units were defecting in large numbers to the Partisans near Tuzla during October 1943 (ZNOR, 4, 18, pp. 199–208).
[81] ZNOR, 12, 3, pp. 79–84.
[82] ZNOR, 4, 15, pp. 169–172.

October 1943, during battles for control over Tuzla.[83] That time period also saw an increase in cases of Home Guard defections in eastern Bosnia and in Herzegovina.[84] And the pattern continued: Muslim formations led by Muhamed-aga Hadžiefendić joined the Partisans in the fall of 1943.[85] They were considered to have 5,000 to 6,000 soldiers, and another 4,000 Muslim troops joined the Partisans in the winter of 1944.[86]

Moreover, the Croatian Peasant Party – originally one of the main support bases for the Ustasha regime – made an agreement with the Partisans in August 1943.[87] The Ustashe called them traitors for abandoning their party and "servants of Moscow imperialism."[88] In winter 1944, the Chetniks had also lost an insurmountable amount of territory to the advancing Partisans. A stark acknowledgment of their defeat came a few months later, when King Petar II himself called on Serbs, Croats, and Slovenes to follow the Partisans. A September 1944 letter from Chetnik leader Ostojić to Mihailović's headquarters revealed how the King's order for the Chetniks to go under Tito's command led to total disarray and ultimately to the complete disintegration of Chetnik units.[89]

With their power on the rise, given the assistance from the Soviets[90] and the British, as well as the defectors from all parties rushing to their side, Partisans rose – according to German estimates from the time – to a manpower of 120,000 by mid-1944.[91] On October 20, 1944, Partisan forces backed by Soviet troops entered Belgrade, signaling the end of the war.[92] The war in the Bosnian theater dragged on for more than half a year longer, until the liberation of Sarajevo on April 6, 1945 and the Ustashe capitulation on May 15, 1945. Thereafter, the Supreme Headquarters of the victorious Partisans ordered the army to hunt down the remaining Chetniks around Sarajevo and eastern Bosnia.[93]

CONCLUSION

This chapter has shown yet again that alliances and group fractionalization in the Bosnian conflict appeared to be tactical in nature, driven by the desire to be

---

[83] ZNOR, 4, 4, pp. 254–256; ZNOR, 4, 18, pp. 208–214; see also NDH report ZNOR, 4, 17, pp. 460–463.
[84] ZNOR, 2, 10, p. 278; ZNOR, 4, 18, pp. 64–69.
[85] ZNOR, 4, 14, pp. 223–227.
[86] Imamović (1997), p. 540; Wilcox (1999), p. 95.
[87] ZNOR, 2, 10, p. 205.
[88] Redžić (2005), p. 104.
[89] VA NOV, Četnički fond.
[90] Tito and the Soviets signed the Moscow Agreement on September 21, 1944, allowing the Red Army to cross the Danube and enter Yugoslavia. *Hronologija Oslobodilačke Borbe Naroda Jugoslavije 1941–1945* (1964), p. 881.
[91] According to ZNOR, 12, 4, p. 548, the total number of Partisan forces during Allied Operation Ratweek, in September 1944, was 120,000.
[92] Redžić (2005), p. 154.
[93] ZNOR, 2, 15, p. 375.

on the winning side while also possessing the largest share of the anticipated postwar political spoils. As illustrated throughout this chapter's narrative, the warring groups in World War II Bosnia formed partnerships that would be immensely puzzling if we relied on bonds of identity to explain such behavior. Instead, my interpretation of primary documents of this period – which appears to be shared by expert historians – is that groups allied, and factions within groups split off, when relative power considerations led them to calculate that their instrumental interests would be better served on another side of the fight. All the while, the elites of these groups constructed elaborate yet transient identity narratives to justify the instrumental choices they had made.

So far, the theory of this book has been illustrated across the Afghan and Bosnian ethnic civil wars and tested against their earlier civil wars that had strong ideological undertones. The consistency of the theory with this diverse array of empirical cases begs the question of how much further the external validity of the theory extends. Now that we have seen a number of case studies, both building and testing my theory of warring group alliances and fractionalization, the logic and the plausibility of the theory are hopefully evident. What remains to be seen is how well the theory applies to *all* cases of multiparty civil wars – all fifty-three that I have identified since 1816. Such a comprehensive test of the theory is more challenging methodologically, and is presented (to the degree data allow) in the next chapter.

PART IV

FURTHER EXTENSIONS

8

Quantitative Testing on the Universe of Cases of Multiparty Civil Wars

Thus far I have attempted to illuminate the dynamics of multiparty civil wars by focusing on how warring groups interacted with each other and with their constituents in some notoriously bloody and protracted conflicts. The main body of empirical evidence in this book (Chapters 3–7) draws on the bloody civil wars in Afghanistan and Bosnia. The warring groups in these conflicts exhibited considerable variation in their alliance choices, shares of power, and identities. These variations allowed for controlled comparisons within and across cases, highlighting the dynamics and mechanisms behind both alliance choices and warring group fractionalization, irrespective of whether the civil war was fought across ethnic or nonethnic lines. The results, identified on the level of alliances, warring groups, and subgroups, were then further probed – where data were available – on the municipality and local commander level.

Overall, what I have found is both simple and, on its face, generalizable. Put succinctly, relative power assessments drive both alliance behavior and warring group fractionalization during conflicts. Groups want to be on the side that is victorious, while also ensuring that they get maximum possible returns from their deal as alliance partners. As warring actors become relatively more powerful on the battlefield, they run the risk of alienating their partners, who are afraid that their rising ally cannot credibly commit to sharing power – but they also become less susceptible to within-group splits and takeovers. Variation in groups' ethnic, religious, or other identities helps explain the building blocks that form warring groups in the first place, and influences the narratives that group elites construct about their allies and adversaries – but shared identity as a variable does not sufficiently explain the variation in alliance choices and fractionalization outcomes. Relative power, instead, explains that variation, in a fashion notably consistent with the neorealist view of alliance behavior in the international system.

Given this argument's simplicity and apparent generality, it would be valuable to see how well it applies beyond the multiparty civil wars in Afghanistan and Bosnia. Indeed, as discussed in the introductory chapter of this book, there are numerous other multiparty civil wars to which the theory's predictions might – or might not – apply. This chapter will aim at probing the external validity of the theory by engaging with this broader universe of cases. To that end, I turn to the data on fifty-three multiparty civil wars, including the cases discussed at length earlier in the book, and measure the extent to which the observable implications of the relative power-based theory of alliances and warring group fractionalization holds. I find that although data are scarce, what we do know about these conflicts is consistent with the book's framework.

I first explain my approach to the broader external validity testing performed and introduce the relevant scope conditions for the test, as well as the dataset used. I then describe what would be needed to test the predictions of the theory with respect to alliance dynamics and group fractionalization, the limitations of the data, and how I have tried to overcome these limitations. Next, I perform a set of tests and discuss what the extended data can tell us about alliances and group fractionalization. I close with conclusions and implications for further research.

APPROACH TO EXTERNAL VALIDITY TESTING

Can the generality of the proposed alliance and fractionalization argument be tested and verified on a more systematic level, beyond the notorious civil wars of Afghanistan and Bosnia? Such systematic testing is challenging, because no civil war alliance dataset exists to date. The dynamic, endogenous relationship between relative power and alliance formation may help explain why such a dataset has not been constructed. Apart from the interconnected nature of the relationship over time, the theory is also hard to test because of the lack of requisite micro-level data. Creating a micro-level dataset, which can be a challenge even for times of peace, is extremely difficult for times of war. Moreover, even if one were to collect the requisite micro-level data for a specific case – which can be a highly involved and time-consuming process, as illustrated in the preceding empirical chapters of this book – the number of meaningful within-case observations remains limited. The internally consistent and systematic gathering of such micro-level data on a cross-conflict basis that would allow for cross-sectional and longitudinal analysis would by all accounts be a Herculean task.

A more expedient way to provide a test of the theory's generality would be at the level of the conflict rather than the alliance. That, however, would amount to a medium-N test given the limited number of observations of multiparty civil wars. Similar to a large-N test, a medium-N test identifies the cases from the universe of conflicts that meet the requisite scope conditions (multiparty civil wars), examines the alliances within those cases to produce summary statistics at the conflict level, and then evaluates these measures of alliance behavior based on a set of conflict-level factors that would verify different components of the theoretical framework. Specifically, it would test falsifiable hypotheses derived from the theory pertaining to the relative power of the warring actors, group fractionalization, and the role of the character of conflict. Unlike the large-N test, however, the medium-N test would only seek to make broad statements about alliance behavior across entire conflicts, rather than analyze the details of each individual alliance. Moreover, it would not have a time-variant dimension and would primarily test the subset of hypotheses pertaining to the overall conflict, with some tests also possible for one of the hypotheses on subgroup behavior. This greater level of abstraction and aggregation has costs in terms of detail and sample size, but benefits in terms of feasibility.

To clarify which hypotheses this chapter tests, I restate the full set of theoretical hypotheses introduced in Chapter 2. Those hypotheses that require time-variant information, granular detail, or narrative analysis were tested qualitatively in the preceding chapters on Afghanistan and Bosnia, namely Group Behavior Hypotheses 1, 2, and 3 and Subgroup Behavior Hypotheses 1, 2, and 3. This chapter focuses instead on testing the three hypotheses on overall outcomes, as well as Subgroup Behavior Hypothesis 4.

GROUP BEHAVIOR HYPOTHESES

1) As a given alliance increases in perceived relative power, past the point of being a minimum winning coalition, groups will defect from the alliance and try to form a smaller winning coalition (in the hopes of maximizing their share of the postwar political power).
2) When alliance composition changes over the course of a war, the identity-based justifications for alliances put forth at one point in time will often be contradicted by alliance composition at another point in time. Shared identity will thus not determine alliances among warring groups. Warring groups will rather form shared identity narratives to correspond to their power-determined alliance choices.
3) If the war either appears likely to end in a negotiated settlement or to continue on without foreseeable victory by either side, the balancing alliance tendencies will persist. If outright military victory appears to be the likely outcome, groups will bandwagon with whichever group appears most powerful.

SUBGROUP BEHAVIOR HYPOTHESES

1) As a given group's perceived relative power decreases, it will have an increased risk for fractionalization, either as a result of disagreements about strategy or an asymmetric distribution of the perceived relative power loss among its constituent subgroups, which threatens the group's survival and which leads to divergent opinions among subgroups as to which side is likely to win.
2) Group leaders who lose perceived relative power, but who still retain enough power to control the group, will suffer a group split. The splinter faction may join up with an opposing group, or it may strike out on its own.

3) Group leaders who lose enough relative power to lose control over the group will suffer an internal takeover by a stronger subgroup.
4) Groups that split are likely to fracture along regional lines or leadership disputes that predate the conflict.

OVERALL OUTCOME HYPOTHESES

1) Multiparty civil wars in which the intergroup distribution of power is more uneven will see fewer alliance changes than wars in which the distribution of power is more balanced. In power-balanced conflicts, small changes in relative power will substantively alter what constitutes a minimum winning coalition, incentivizing warring groups to change alliances frequently. In power-skewed conflicts (referred to as "hegemonic" conflicts here), only large – and therefore less common – changes in relative power will alter the optimal alliance configurations. (Generally, conflicts are hegemonic because the government is significantly stronger than the various rebel groups.)
2) Multiparty civil wars will last longer than binary civil wars.
3) Conflicts with more fractionalization will have more alliance changes.

The remainder of this chapter proceeds with such a medium-N external validity test. I use the dataset I coded based on the scope of multiparty civil wars, as described in the Introduction, and then examine the relationship between relative power distribution and "alliance portfolio volatility" (defined later) at the conflict level of analysis. I then describe the empirical landscape of group fractionalization and present some tests to see how well the proposed fractionalization argument corresponds to the broader empirical reality.

DESCRIPTION OF DATASET AND SCOPE CONDITIONS

To gauge the validity of the alliance and fractionalization arguments beyond the cases discussed so far, I extend the scope of the analysis to all multiparty civil wars, using the universe of cases briefly discussed in the introduction and presented in Table 8.2. My definition of multiparty civil war includes armed conflicts within a sovereign state in which there were three or more major *domestic* combatant groups, and in which there were at least 1,000 cumulative battle-related deaths. As the discussion in the introduction of this book indicated, the multiparty vs. two-party distinction is indeed analytically meaningful – multiparty civil wars comprise a third of all civil conflicts, account for a full half of conflict years, and strongly differ on a number of covariates of both theoretical and intrinsic interest. As referenced in the introduction, multiparty wars are significantly longer and more deadly than their binary counterparts, confirming Overall Outcome Hypothesis 2.[1] Multiparty wars

[1] Cunningham (2006, 2011) has a similar finding, although in his study external actors are counted as warring parties.

are also becoming increasingly common. They remain a greatly understudied subset of civil wars despite having been lengthier and bloodier than the average civil war.

Before delving into the analysis, I seek to empirically address a possible counterargument: that there is a selection effect at play whereby some omitted variable determines both (1) whether a conflict is multiparty (and thus enters the universe of cases) and (2) influences subsequent alliance and fractionalization dynamics. For example, it could be that especially weak states are more likely to suffer multiparty as opposed to binary wars, and that state weakness is the real determinant of alliance volatility and group fractionalization, whereas relative power shifts are epiphenomenal. Alternatively, it could be that multiparty wars are more likely to occur in countries with fewer ethnic divisions, and that this explains the apparent irrelevance of identity to explaining alliance choices. To address these critiques, Table 8.1 displays the results of two linear probability models. The first model explores the determinants of multiparty civil wars within Fearon and Laitin's full sample of 111 civil wars, and the second model explores the predictors of whether a war that starts out binary *transforms* into multiparty at some point during the conflict. Both models use the full set of explanatory variables employed by Fearon and Laitin (2003).

The only variable significant at the 95 percent level or higher in both regressions is ethnic fractionalization; the positive sign suggests that ethnic fractionalization is significantly higher in multiparty as opposed to binary civil wars. If anything, this should bias the results *against* finding support for relative power

TABLE 8.1. *Regression Analysis of Causes of Multiparty versus Non-Multiparty Civil Wars*

Independent Variable	(1) DV: Onset of Multiparty Civil War (among All Civil Wars)	(2) DV: Transformation of Binary Civil War into Multiparty Civil War
Prior war	0.283 (0.077)	0.006 (0.974)
Per capita income	−0.024 (.306)	−0.007 (0.605)
Log (population)	−0.051 (0.058)	−0.023 (0.239)
Log (% mountainous)	0.045 (0.249)	0.017 (0.486)
Noncontiguous state	−0.005 (0.964)	0.143 (0.115)
Oil exporter	−0.133 (0.232)	−0.145 (0.039)
New state	0.085 (0.570)	−0.093 (0.267)
Instability	0.056 (0.615)	−0.030 (0.681)
Anocracy	0.014 (0.906)	−0.050 (0.558)
Democracy	−0.007 (0.954)	0.039 (0.697)
Ethnic fractionalization	0.512 (0.002)	0.312 (0.042)
Religious fractionalization	−0.004 (0.985)	0.027 (0.866)
Constant	0.456 (0.135)	0.150 (0.444)
N	105	78

Note: Standard errors clustered by country. *P*-values in parentheses.

because it suggests multiparty wars are precisely where we would expect identity variables to operate most strongly. State strength (as proxied by GDP per
capita, political instability, and anocracy) is not significantly different between
multiparty and binary conflicts, suggesting that alliance volatility and group
fractionalization in multiparty conflicts are not simply the result of compar-
atively weak state capacity. Although population size (logged) is marginally
significant in the first regression ($p = 0.058$), its sign is negative, indicating
multiparty as opposed to binary wars occur in smaller countries on average.
This difference cannot plausibly explain alliance volatility and fractionalization
in multiparty conflicts; after all, one would intuitively expect more volatility
and fractionalization in countries with *larger* populations. Finally, oil exporter
and prior war are significant in one regression each; neither, however, provides
a satisfying alternative explanation for alliance and fractionalization dynamics, especially given the small-N associated with each dummy variable (five oil
exporters and eight prior wars out of fifty-three total multiparty wars).

Now that the selection effect critique has been discussed, I turn to the fifty-
three multiparty wars themselves. These cases became the basis of a larger
coding project in which extensive data were collected regarding the evolution
of the number and identity of warring groups, their alliance choices, the splits
and takeovers they experienced, and information on groups newly formed
by splits. Specifically, for each of these conflicts, I consulted detailed conflict
histories (listed in the references) to determine the number of major warring
groups,[2] and, for each of those groups, (1) with what other groups that group
allied and how the group's portfolio of intergroup alliances changed over the
course of the conflict, and (2) whether that group ever experienced a split or an
internal takeover during the conflict. Basic information on conflicts by country,
conflict years, and number of groups for all cases is shown in Table 8.2.

Fifty-three cases is a fairly awkward number for typical political science
research. It is too many on which to undertake detailed case studies of complex
conflict dynamics such as alliance behavior and group fractionalization, but too
few on which to run robust regression analyses. The number of cases drives
the choice of medium-N quantitative analysis, which I perform next as a way
to examine the direction of the effect of relative power distribution on alliance
behavior.

EXPLAINING ALLIANCE DYNAMICS ACROSS MULTIPARTY
CIVIL WARS

In this section I attempt to determine whether relative power appears to play
the same explanatory role in alliance dynamics across all multiparty civil wars
within the scope conditions, not just in the cases discussed so far. To conduct
this analysis, I need measures that capture group alliance behavior as well as

---

[2] It is decidedly up for interpretation what qualifies as a "major warring group." Some conflicts,
such as the civil war in Somalia, have had as many as forty separate internal combatants. I tried
to limit my focus to those groups that existed for a substantial interval during the war or that
played a major role in the war's overall trajectory.

TABLE 8.2. *List of Multiparty Civil Wars, the Years Those Conflicts Had Three or More Domestic Actors, and the Maximum Number of Warring Groups in Each Conflict*

War Number	Country	Onset (of multiparty component)	Termination (of multiparty component)	Maximum Number of Warring Groups
1	Afghanistan	1978	1992[a]	13
2	Afghanistan	1992	2001	6
3	Afghanistan	2002	Present	4
4	Algeria	1954	1962	4
5	Algeria	1992	2004	6
6	Angola	1961	1975	5
7	Angola	1975	2002	5
8	Austria	1848	1849	8
9	Bosnia	1992	1995	4
10	Burundi	1991	2003	6
11	Cambodia	1978	1991	4
12	Chad	1969	1997	11
13	Chad	1998	Present	6
14	China	1850	1878	8
15	China	1911	1931	14
16	Colombia	1965	Present	6
17	Congo-Kinshasa	1960	1965	6
18	Congo-Kinshasa	1996	1997	6
19	Congo-Kinshasa	1998	Present	8
20	Congo-Brazzaville	1993	1998	3
21	Côte D'Ivoire	2002	2005	4
22	Ethiopia	1974	1991	13
23	Georgia	1991	1994	5
24	Greece	1941	1944	7
25	Guatemala	1965	1995	7
26	India (Kashmir)	1988	1996	5
27	India (Northeast)	1977	Present	11
28	Indonesia	1958	1961	4
29	Israel	1974	Present	8
30	Iraq	1975	1996	4
31	Iraq	2004	Present	10
32	Lebanon	1975	1976	7
33	Lebanon	1982	1990	10
34	Liberia	1990	1996	9
35	Liberia	2000	2003	4
36	Mexico	1911	1915	6
37	Myanmar	1948	Present	10
38	Ottoman Empire	1876	1878	5

(*continued*)

TABLE 8.2 (*continued*)

War Number	Country	Onset (of multiparty component)	Termination (of multiparty component)	Maximum Number of Warring Groups
39	Greece	1821	1833	11
40	Pakistan	2007	Present	5
41	Peru	1989	1997	3
42	Philippines	1986	Present	8
43	Russia	1917	1922	26
44	Sierra Leone	1991	2001	5
45	Somalia	1981	Present	17
46	Sri Lanka	1983	1990	8
47	Sri Lanka	2004	2009	3
48	Sudan	2003	Present	13
49	Tajikistan	1992	1997	6
50	Uganda	1980	2002	11
51	Western Sahara	1975	1979	3
52	Yugoslavia/Bosnia	1941	1945	5
53	Zimbabwe	1972	1979	3

[a] The qualitative chapter on the Jihad (Chapter 4) examines the 1978–1989 period. There was a lull in fighting between 1989 and 1992, which is thus treated as a transition between the Jihad and Intra-Mujahedin War. However, in the statistical tests in this chapter, the Afghan Jihad is dated as 1978–1992 to be consistent with quantitative datasets on civil war (in particular, Fearon and Laitin (2003)).

the relative power distribution between groups at an aggregate, conflict level of analysis. One of the dependent variables for this external validity test is the absolute number of times in a given conflict that alliances changed. This metric gives a sense of how frequently groups make new alliances or switch sides during their conflicts. I define an "alliance portfolio change" as occurring when, at a given time, one warring group in a given conflict adds an alliance partner and/or removes an alliance partner.

However, the raw number of alliance portfolio changes arguably only takes us so far. In a conflict that has lasted more than sixty-two years and has had ten major warring groups (Myanmar), we should be unsurprised to see a high number of alliance portfolio changes (twelve). This is arguably a less striking finding than the fact that the recent Bosnian conflict, which lasted only four years and involved only three major warring groups and a splinter group, experienced three alliance portfolio changes. To really gauge how "volatile" the alliance configurations in a given conflict were, I thus normalize the raw number of changes to account for the amount of time a conflict goes on and the number of warring actors. Specifically, I am interested in the number of alliance change events per group per year. For each conflict, I thus sum for all warring groups the number of years each group has been fighting. I refer to this sum as the "group-years" for a given conflict (this quantity appears again later for purposes of weighting). Dividing the raw number of alliance portfolio changes by that conflict's number of group-years produces the "Alliance Port-folio Volatility" (APV) metric, which can thus be interpreted as a conflict's number of alliance changes per group per year. For conflict i, this is:

$$APV_i = \frac{\text{Number of alliance portfolio changes in conflict } i}{\sum_{\text{all } j} \text{years in conflict for group } j \text{ in conflict } i}$$

Thus Myanmar's APV is 0.040 and Bosnia's (1992–1995) APV is 0.214 – the latter reflecting a much higher volatility per group and per year.[3] Because this measure accounts for time and number of groups, it will be the principal dependent variable used here to measure alliance-shifting activity.

The chief explanatory variable of alliance portfolio changes, according to the theory of this book, is the distribution of relative power among the conflict's warring groups. Specifically, conflicts in which relative power is consistently skewed toward a single actor should see relatively stable alliances, and hence low APV. Groups have no tactical incentive to constantly add and drop alliance partners if one group holds a preponderance of relative power – the weaker groups should simply align to oppose the dominant actor and this alliance configuration should stay fairly static throughout the conflict. In contrast, the theory leads us to expect that conflicts in which warring groups are more or less at parity will see numerous alliance portfolio changes, as small changes in the relative power distribution substantively alter the ideal balancing coalitions and incentivize warring groups to back out of existing alliances or create new ones (Overall Outcome Hypothesis 1).

To test this theoretical prediction, ideally we would need estimates of each warring group's relative power at frequent intervals throughout each conflict. Not surprisingly, data this rich are unavailable. Even if we consider the number of combatants to be a reasonable proxy for a group's relative power – an oversimplification to be sure, given that sheer numerical superiority can lead to dominance over other groups in some cases (i.e., Guatemala) but not others (i.e., Iraq) – estimates on combatant numbers are sparse in many conflicts, in many others they range widely, and in almost none are they available at some regular interval (i.e., annually). Moreover, the endogeneity of war dynamics adds even more insurmountable difficulties. Suppose we had (a) a meaningful measure of relative power at all time points and (b) a clear record of all alliance change and fractionalization events. This would lead to substantially better tests of the theory's plausibility, but given that changes in power are not randomly distributed, it would remain difficult to know if relative power shifts caused those changes, or if some unmeasured confounder caused both. Ideally, some source of plausibly exogenous shocks to the power of a group – an "instrument" in the econometric sense – could be used to determine if the theorized shifts actually do result from changes in relative power. However, such events are extremely rare and their exogenous nature almost always difficult to defend.

As an alternative implementable approach, the extensive secondary sources I consulted for each of the conflicts allowed me to arrive at approximate estimates

---

[3] Each conflict's alliance portfolio changes are listed in the Appendix.

of most groups' sizes, or at least their sizes relative to other groups in the conflict. Based on these estimates, I was able to identify which civil wars had actors that throughout most of the conflict appeared to have had on their own at least 50-percent-plus-one of manpower. This does not mean, of course, that these groups had a minimum winning coalition of *actual* relative power, as manpower is only one proxy for power among many. (In the previous empirical chapters of this work I use over-time territorial control changes for each warring group as a proxy, but this is too difficult to code across all multiparty civil war cases.) The theory predicts that wars end when one group has a minimum winning coalition of actual power on its own, so evidently most of these actors with superior manpower were not able to also achieve minimum winning coalitions of actual power. I identified such conflicts, of which there are twenty-seven, as "hegemonic." The remaining twenty-six conflicts were classified as "balanced" – in these conflicts, the major warring groups appeared fairly equal in relative power.[4]

We would also like to know how identity affects alliance portfolio changes or APV, if at all. Using data from Fearon and Laitin and the secondary sources describing the histories of all multiparty civil wars of interest, I classified each war according to whether its primary intergroup cleavage was "ascriptive" or "ideological." By "primary cleavage" I mean the primary individual or group characteristic on which mobilization of the populace was grounded. In other words, a conflict with an ethnic intergroup cleavage (such as revolutionary Russia) is not necessarily an "ascriptive" civil war if that cleavage was not the primary grievance and/or mark of distinction between the warring groups. Most of the multiparty civil wars are in fact ascriptive – the primary cleavage is predominantly ethnic, and in a few more cases the primary cleavage is sectarian (i.e., the recent Iraq conflict). However, the following eleven wars appear to have had primarily ideological cleavages: Afghanistan (1978–1992), Afghanistan (2002–present), Bosnia (1941–1945), Cambodia (1978–1991), Colombia (1965–present), Greece (1941–1944), Guatemala (1965–1995), Indonesia (1958–1961), Peru (1989–1997), Russia (1917–1922), and Tajikistan (1992–1997).

If the nature of identity cleavages is important to intergroup alliance behavior, then presumably the conflicts with ascriptive primary cleavages would experience different alliance behavior from the conflicts with ideological primary cleavages. Specifically, we would expect ascriptive conflicts to see less alliance volatility than ideological conflicts, because ascriptive cleavages are considered fairly stable whereas ideological cleavages are somewhat more malleable. In ascriptive conflicts, groups would pick their allies based on shared ascriptive identities and then keep those allies throughout the conflict; in ideological conflicts, groups would undertake the same in-group construction initially but might abandon alliance partners as their ideological platforms evolve. Thus an ascriptive primary cleavage, if it were to affect alliance volatility per

---

[4] Each conflict's classification appears in the Appendix.

TABLE 8.3. *Comparison of Alliance Portfolio Volatility by Conflict Type (two-tailed test)*

	Hegemonic	Balanced
Average Number of Alliance Portfolio Changes per Conflict ($N = 53$; OLS: $t = 1.80$; $p = 0.079$)	2.63	4.23
Average Alliance Portfolio Volatility ($N = 53$; OLS: $t = 2.21$; $p = 0.033$)	0.049	0.084
Group-year Weighted Alliance Portfolio Volatility ($N = 53$; WLS: $t = 2.67$; $p = 0.011$)	0.038	0.067

the existing view of identities during conflict, should have a statistically signifi-cant negative impact on the dependent variable. However, the central claim of my argument is that alliance formation is determined by relative power calcu-lations, not by the nature of a conflict's cleavages, and thus my theory predicts that cleavage type will not be related to APV.

Table 8.3 shows a simple difference-of-means test, for both APV and the absolute number of alliance portfolio changes, according to whether the con-flict has been classified as hegemonic or balanced. Overall Outcome Hypothesis 1 appears to be borne out in this first-cut external validity test. Hegemonic conflicts have a lower absolute number of alliance portfolio changes than bal-anced conflicts, a difference that is statistically significant at the 0.10 level. More importantly, they also have a lower APV than balanced conflicts, a result that is significant at the 0.033 level using ordinary least squares (OLS), and significant at the 0.011 level under arguably the most appropriate specifica-tion of Weighted Least Squares (WLS).[5] In all models, standard errors are clustered on country as multiple conflicts sometimes occur in a given coun-try, and we would expect lower within-country than across-country conflict variance.

Although multivariate regression is a difficult tool to use at the conflict level of analysis because of the modest number of observations, preliminary

---

[5] Here and in the following analyses, I employ WLS, weighting each observation in each conflict by the number of years of fighting summed across all the groups in a conflict (*group-years*). There are two reasons for this. First is the intuitive reason – that we suppose there is some "true mean APV" for a conflict of a given type, which governs the expected number of alliance events per group per year of fighting. But we have only a conflict-wise average for APV. Thus averaging across conflicts, we must weight each observation by the number of group-years that conflict represents. The second reason is more technical but fundamentally related to this logic: OLS presumes homoskedastic errors, and achieves maximum efficiency under the Gauss-Markov theorem only when this is upheld. The measure of APV taken for each conflict will be more stable and precisely measured (lower variance) for conflicts with many group-years and more volatile (high variance) for conflicts with fewer group-years. Weighting by this measure has the equivalent effect to transforming the data such that it achieves homoskedasticity and is thus efficient under the Gauss-Markov theorem. Note that because the WLS transformation is used to achieve homoskedasticity, it is not appropriate or necessary to use robust standard errors (although the earlier finding holds at $p = 0.011$ with robust standard errors as well).

TABLE 8.4. *Regression Models of Alliance Portfolio Volatility (APV) on Hegemonic Power Distribution and Ascriptive Primary Cleavage*

Variable APV	Model I OLS, Robust	Model II OLS, Robust	Model III WLS	Model IV WLS
Hegemonic Power Distribution (1 if hegemonic, 0 if balanced)	−0.0346 (0.016, $p = 0.033$)	−0.0338 (0.015, $p = 0.025$)	−0.0289 (0.011, $p = 0.011$)	−0.0278 (0.011, $p = 0.013$)
Ascriptive Primary Cleavage (1 if ascriptive, 0 if ideological)		0.00474 (0.0198, $p = 0.812$)		0.00353 (0.0114, $p = 0.759$)
N	53	53	53	53
R^2	0.10	0.10	0.12	0.12

Note: Robust standard errors, clustered by country, are in parentheses.

regression results corroborate these bivariate findings. As shown in Table 8.4, when controlling for the presence or absence of an ascriptive primary cleavage, hegemonic conflicts consistently have substantially lower alliance portfolio volatility than balanced conflicts. In particular, using an analysis that gives each group-year an equal weight (WLS, used in models III and IV), hegemonic conflicts had APV levels of 0.038 while non-hegemonic conflicts had APV levels of 0.067 (almost a doubling, or an absolute difference of 0.029, $p = 0.011$). Controlling for primary cleavage type (*ascriptive*), hegemonic conflicts were still associated with a reduction of APV by almost the identical amount, 0.028 ($p = 0.013$). Meanwhile, the coefficient on the ascriptive primary cleavage variable is never statistically significantly different from zero.

The sample here is clearly too small for conclusive inference, but the results suggest that hegemonic conflicts do appear to have substantially fewer alliance shifts per group per year (on the order of 40 percent). While ideological intergroup cleavages do not appear to give rise to more stable alliance patterns in multiparty conflicts than ascriptive cleavages (as one might predict if one subscribed to an identity-based hypothesis about warring group alliance behavior), this "non-result" cannot be reliably interpreted, particularly in light of the very small number of multiparty conflicts coded as identity-based in my sample (eleven out of fifty-three).

These results, though quite basic, suggest that the inferences made about the relative importance of power and identity vis-à-vis alliance behavior, as captured in the theoretical framework and the in-depth empirical discussion of Afghanistan and Bosnia, appear to hold in general across all fifty-three multiparty civil wars. The multiparty civil war data have allowed me to test and verify that when the intergroup distribution of power is more uneven (i.e., hegemonic), conflicts will see fewer alliance changes than wars in which the distribution of power is more balanced. In other words, the theory appears to travel – if a new multiparty civil war sprang up tomorrow, we could reasonably assume that it would be best to look to the warring groups' relative power distribution, rather than to the nature of the conflict's primary identity cleavage, to try to predict alliance behavior.

GROUP FRACTIONALIZATION

For the proposed framework of group fractionalization to be conclusively tested against the universe of fifty-three multiparty civil wars, one would need to determine whether group splits and takeovers in those wars were caused by relative power losses that threatened the group's survival or that were borne in an asymmetric fashion across different subgroups. That would require gathering information on all warring groups participating in each of the fifty-three civil war cases that meet the definition and scope conditions of multiparty civil wars. That in turn would involve coding over an appropriate time interval – which would arguably have to be at least annual to be meaningful – whether each of these groups fractionalized or not and whether the fractionalization amounted to a split or a takeover. In terms of explanatory variables, one would need to collect data on pre-conflict subgroups comprising each group and prewar cleavages, be they geographic/regional or based on leadership disputes, as well as data at annual time intervals that capture warring group and subgroup size, group alliances, and relative group and subgroup power. Given the lack of reliable micro-level data during civil wars that would enable the adequate operationalization of the requisite variables on a conflict-year level, the task would be a massive undertaking, before even considering the coding of a set of necessary controls on the requisite level of analysis.

Even if the data were available, inference would be limited because of identification concerns inherent in the question of group fractionalization during civil wars – much along the lines for those of alliances – for which it would be difficult to instrument. For example, to test the hypothesis that heavy asymmetric losses trigger fractionalization, even if we have all the data on such losses, the event in which a group suffers heavy asymmetric losses is likely to be endogenous to other conflict processes. These losses could be caused by factors such as a recent reduction in military capability of the group for other reasons, changes in the state's capability, the defeat of other groups, recent defectors from the lead group or its coalition partners, and so on. Such causes of asymmetric losses can themselves influence fractionalization through channels other than the loss itself. Unobserved confounders of this sort would result in a biased estimate of the causal effect of asymmetric losses on the likelihood of fractionalization. In theory, some event that is plausibly exogenous and correlates with heavy asymmetric costs in an exogenous fashion, and which would arguably lead to fractionalization only through its relationship to such losses and not through any other channel, could serve as a valid instrument. Unsurprisingly, such instruments are difficult to find, and while "lucky airstrikes" or the unanticipated death of an important leader may be essentially exogenous events and suitable instruments in some cases, so far I have not found an instrument that applies to a suitably broad set of cases and for which data collection would be feasible.

However, coding the requisite dependent variable, *fractionalization*, was a more manageable task. Using a variety of secondary sources, I was able to review detailed conflict histories for all multiparty civil wars to determine the number of major warring groups – all 397 of them – across all conflicts. For each of those groups I in turn collected information on whether that group ever experienced a split or an internal takeover during the conflict.[6] Looking at the instances of group fractionalization, the empirical reality is that they happen, and do so with notable frequency: 36 percent of all warring groups in the sample fractionalized at some point during the conflict. This average rate of fractionalization is somewhat deceptive, however, because it counts equally groups that were present at the start of a conflict and groups that formed later in the conflict's course – often as the result of a group split. For example, both Akbari's Hizb-i-Wahdat party and Mazari's/Khalili's Hizb-i-Wahdat party are counted equally as warring groups in the 1992–1998 Afghan civil war, even though Akbari's Hizb-i-Wahdat party became a full-fledged warring group when it split from Mazari's faction in 1994. A better metric for assessing the frequency of group fractionalization is "percent fractionalized," which calculates, per conflict, the percentage of groups that were present at the *onset* of the multiparty civil war that split or were taken over at some point during the subsequent war. For this statistic, the mean is 46 percent and the median is 50 percent, considerably higher than the rate of fractionalization reported earlier; overall, twenty-eight of the fifty-three multiparty civil wars saw 50 percent or more of the "original" warring groups fractionalize, as shown in Figure 8.1.

If we label each conflict as one with or without any splits, and with or without any takeovers (among the warring groups at conflict onset), we see that each conflict had an 85 percent chance of witnessing a split and a 42 percent chance of witnessing a takeover.

Although group fractionalization is certainly a prevalent phenomenon, it is less frequent than alliance change, which is consistent with the prediction derived from the theoretical argument (as the changes of relative power that lead to alliance changes are arguably more frequent than sizable losses among a group's constituent subgroups). The difference in means of per-conflict alliance changes (3.42) and per-conflict fractionalization events (2.07) is statistically significant ($p = 0.0091$).[7] In addition, conflicts with more fractionalization tend to have more alliance shifts, with a correlation coefficient of

---

[6] Full lists of the codings, which were vetted by subject-matter experts to the extent possible, can be found in the Appendix.

[7] This metric counts *any* split or takeover as a fractionalization event, even if the group in question experienced both.

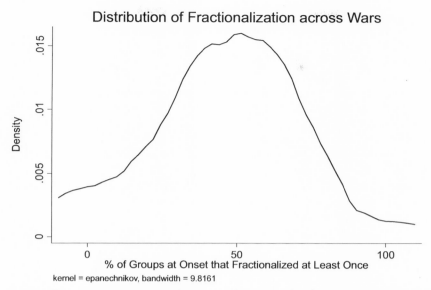

FIGURE 8.1. Density Estimate of Percent of Fractionalized Warring Groups in Multiparty Civil Wars

0.28 ($p = 0.11$, with robust standard errors for the null hypothesis that the regression coefficient, and thus the correlation, is zero). One may worry that this relationship is an artifact of the finding that both the increased number of fractionalization events and increased number of alliance changes are driven by longer conflicts. However, comparing fractionalization events per year to alliance change events per year to address this, the relationship holds even more strongly ($r = 0.49$, $p = 0.001$, robust standard errors from a regression analysis). Even though this relationship cannot be interpreted as a causal one without making implausibly strong assumptions about the absence of other potential confounders, it provides preliminary support for Overall Outcome Hypothesis 3.

When looking at the causes of splits across the conflicts, they appear consistent with the theoretical predictions and Subgroup Hypothesis 4. I returned to the historical sources and, for each of the 121 warring group splits coded in the dataset, attempted to determine whether (1) the leader of the faction that split off was an influential political or military figure before the onset of the multiparty war (coded as a dummy variable, *prior leader*); or (2) the faction that split off had a regional identity distinct from that of the main group (coded as a dummy variable, *regional subgroup*). The intent was to determine how frequently one or both of these factors were present during splits and their relative prevalence. As shown in Figure 8.2, of the 121 splits, *prior leader* could be coded in 75 percent of cases and *regional subgroup* could be coded in 78 percent of cases. In 108 cases, at least one of these two

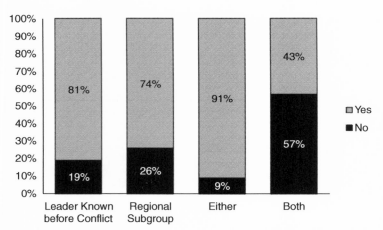

FIGURE 8.2. Subgroup Cleavages Associated with Group Splits in Multiparty Civil Wars

factors was known to be either present or not present, and out of these, 98 (91 percent) had one or both of these two traits. These findings should be interpreted with some caution because they are selected on the dependent variable – only those cases in which splits occurred were analyzed. These results simply demonstrate that conditional on a split occurring, a large majority of them (91 percent) occur along at least one of the cleavages, whereas almost half (43 percent) occur along both – supporting but not proving Subgroup Hypothesis 4's prediction that fractionalization occurs along prewar fault lines between subgroups.

In short, the initial summary statistics across the 53-case universe of multiparty civil wars and their 397 warring parties are entirely consistent with the proposed group fractionalization framework.

EVALUATION OF EXTENSIONS

In this chapter I have tried to extend the theoretical argument made in the previous chapters to a broader set of empirical cases. Specifically, I tried to determine whether, in a universe of fifty-three multiparty civil wars, alliance patterns are more stable when a conflict has a single dominant actor. I indeed found that hegemonic conflicts showed less "alliance portfolio volatility" than conflicts in which relative group strength was more evenly balanced, while identity appears not to explain variation in alliance behavior adequately. Meanwhile, although the specific hypotheses pertaining to group fractionalization cannot be tested at this time, initial summary statistics were encouraging.

All of this is good news for the theory, as it suggests that when the present Afghanistan conflict ends, when the Bosnian conflict of the 1990s fades into distant memory, and when a new multiparty civil war arises, this theory seems likely to apply to it. As should be apparent by now, however, these external validity tests are only suggestive. Because of data limitations inherent in the questions at hand, intergroup and intragroup dynamics in civil wars remain ripe for future research. There are several natural extensions to the project presented here. First, the theory's external validity would be strengthened by direct and time-variant measures of warring groups' and subgroups' power. Scattered estimates of group population sizes do exist, and could be supplemented by geospatial analyses of groups' territorial control.[8]

Another important type of data missing at present is time-varying information about splits and takeovers. Not all splits and takeovers are the same. Splits in particular vary widely in severity, with some groups splitting into two roughly equal factions (i.e., the Hazara split discussed in Chapter 3) and other groups "splintering" into numerous factions (i.e., the NPFL and ULIMO in Liberia). Understanding the causes of the most fractious warring group splits, and fitting those cases more explicitly into the theory, would advance our knowledge of these conflict dynamics considerably.

One should keep in mind that it was this paucity of data that led to an inquiry focused on building a theory about alliance and fractionalization processes, leaving several possible additional research avenues to undertake in order to test the predictions of this theory. Some of these additional research directions are discussed in the concluding chapter of this book.

---

[8] Conflicts such as eastern Burma have very well-mapped-out areas of control (by organizations such as the Thai-Burma Border Consortium), and with conflict mapping taking off in not only academic but also international organization circles, recent conflicts such as Darfur are also being mapped intensively.

Conclusion

As late as September 10, 2001, anyone asking an average American to locate Afghanistan on a map most likely would have gotten a blank stare in response. Afghanistan was a far-flung, long-forgotten place, as irrelevant and passé as the Cold War. It had made some headlines in the late 1990s for its Islamist Taliban leadership and their repressive and regressive human rights policies, but all that mostly resonated with area experts and was lost on the broader public. Osama bin Laden and the 9/11 attacks changed all that. They brought Afghanistan to every American home and, over the next decade, more than 100,000 American troops to Afghan soil.

True to the theme of this book, this recent Afghan war started with a defection. In its three years of uninterrupted reign over 90 percent of Afghanistan since the end of the 1998 intra-mujahedin war, the Taliban had consolidated their hold on state power by wooing into their ranks commanders, technocrats, and even some of the old mujahedin leadership against whom they had fought brutally in the not-so-distant past. But their hold proved precarious and was under threat as soon as it became clear that they could not avert the U.S.-led invasion in support of the Northern Alliance, prompted by the 9/11 attacks. In light of that invasion, the Taliban had issued a fatwa, calling their people to arms against the infidels:

Afghanistan's religious scholars express their condolences for the losses in America and they are hopeful that America will not attack Afghanistan and will instead work with patience and carry out an extensive and thorough investigation. . . . If America refuses to accept the content of this fatwa and tries to invade Afghanistan, then according to Shari'a law, the scholars will issue the below order [for jihad against the U.S.] . . . . According to all Islamic jurisprudence, when non-Muslims prepare to invade an Islamic country then Jihad will be proclaimed on them. [Detailed reference to list of relevant verses in Qur'an and Hadith] . . . When non-Muslims are about to occupy an Islamic country and that country does not have the capacity to defend itself, then Jihad becomes compulsory to all Muslims in the world. They all have to come and fight in order to rescue that Islamic state.... During the American invasion, Muslims who cooperate and spy for Americans, no matter if they are Afghan or not, they will be labeled as foreign invaders and their execution will be certain.[1]

The U.S.-led invasion of Afghanistan went ahead despite the fatwa, and the minority groups of the Northern Alliance (Tajiks, Uzbeks, and Hazaras) reunited once again to drive out the Pashtun-dominant Taliban. The justification they used for resistance against the Taliban was broadcast via radio and on leaflets to their respective constituents:[2]

It is not you, the honorable people of Afghanistan, who are targeted, but those who would oppress you, seek to bend you to their own will, and make you their slaves ... the battle against these fanatics that feed off the blood of the Afghan people cannot be won without your help...[3]

You have lived together for hundreds of years before the Taliban. What do the Taliban give you? Do they listen to you? Do they supply you with food and medicine or do they hoard it for themselves? The Taliban tells you that dying for their fanatical form of Islam is a proud and noble thing to do. They encourage you to be martyrs, but in reality, they are cowards hiding behind farmers, and families. If dying for this form of Islam is noble, why doesn't Mullah Omar go to the fronts? He is enjoying his luxurious quarters and his wives while you are asked to die. ... Resist, and encourage your friends and neighbors to resist! The Taliban have gone too far! The Taliban can only rule if you choose to let them...[4]

Afghanistan's economy is nearly non-existent, and because of the Taliban's support for terrorists... Afghanistan has been shunned by the international community. Even now the Taliban undermines the lives and rights of the people of Afghanistan, treating women as little more than slaves, and treating the rest of the population little better. The so-called leaders of the Taliban are disrespectful of Afghan cultural and Islamic tradition and its proud past. Now they have brought the anger of the United States and the international community upon themselves through their terrorist actions.[5]

Once the forcefulness of the U.S.-supported Northern Alliance offensive became clear, the Taliban lost their ability to assert a monopoly of leadership within

---

[1] "Religious scholars' resolution and fatwa regarding invasion of our country," Kabul, September 21, 2001. Copy in possession of the author.

[2] These are messages that were crafted in cooperation with the U.S. military and broadly disseminated via radio transmissions and colorful flyers with pictures, thrown from planes. A detailed list of such scripts and images can be found at http://www.psywarrior.com/radioscripts.html and at http://www.psywarrior.com/Afghanleaflinks.html, accessed May 24, 2006.

[3] The Partnership of Nations is here to help (1): http://archives.cnn.com/2001/US/10/18/ret.flyers, accessed March 1, 2008.

[4] Taliban actions are Non-Islamic (5), http://archives.cnn.com/2001/US/10/18/ret.flyers, accessed March 1, 2008.

[5] The Partnership of Nations is here to help (2), http://archives.cnn.com/2001/US/10/18/ret.flyers, accessed March 1, 2008.

their group. Rather, commanders who had joined them but retained links to their old mujahedin networks invoked these links to ally themselves with the rapidly advancing anti-Taliban opposition. The split in Taliban ranks is evident in a Mullah Omar decree addressed to officials of the Islamic Emirate of Afghanistan and to the Taliban:

There has been lethal activity in our midst which may result in our destruction. Taliban accuse each other behind each other's backs, ... resorting to false and unfounded accusations.... There is no doubt that this backstabbing is happening. I once again appeal to you to stop this or else whoever is involved will be cursed in this world and in the afterlife, over which I have no control. These acts are damaging Islam. For God's sake, stop doing this![6]

Within less than two months, the Northern Alliance had driven the Taliban leadership out of the country. They were, however, to return by late 2005 in the form of a forceful insurgency, which is presently ongoing despite a "surge" of 30,000 U.S. troops into Afghanistan in 2010. This book has refrained from talking about the current war in Afghanistan, as the situation is still in flux. Although scholars are often advised never to speculate on events that are ongoing, I would offer a prediction, consistent with the book's broader argument: Given what we have learned about the susceptibility of intergroup alliances and intragroup cohesion to the stark logic of power balances – and given the relative unimportance of identity (race, language, religion, etc.) to the stability of these coalitions, we should expect to see rationalist behaviors consistent with the theory's expectation of how the conflict will end. This book predicts that the warring parties will start bandwagoning with the winner if they see one party heading toward a decisive victory, and that they will maintain their balancing posture until the end of the civil war as a way to get the highest negotiating leverage if the outcome is expected to be a negotiated settlement.

Given the announced 2014 coalition troops' withdrawal and the Taliban office set up in Qatar to allow for possible negotiations, neither party appears to expect an outright military victory, but rather seems to be trying to find common ground for negotiations. Indeed, there are two likely scenarios given that no side will achieve outright victory before the end of NATO deployment in 2014: The resulting stalemate could either open the way for a political agreement between the Taliban and other Afghan factions to end the war, or it could set the scene for a new round of civil war. NATO forces thus still have a valuable role to play between now and 2014. They should (1) support a settlement and ceasefire if those prove attainable through the political process or (2) step up the wooing of Taliban defectors if their leadership fails to deliver a ceasefire and expand the support of self-defense mechanisms for the Kabul government and its allies, so as to strengthen the impression that the political system cannot be forcibly overthrown.

---

[6] Taliban decree in author's possession.

IRAQ: THE CASE OF ANBAR

Apart from tribal Afghanistan and multi-confessional Bosnia, this book's theory also sheds light on the developments in Anbar Province during the recent Iraqi civil war, which has secured its own claim to infamy in the civil war pantheon because of its bloody and protracted fighting across and within Iraq's sectarian groups. Given the complexity of the Anbar case and the confines of space and parsimony, the intent of this section is modest and prescribed: to verify whether this book's theoretical framework proves largely consistent with warring group alliance behavior as manifested during that conflict. I argue that the empirical reality of this case lends further support to the generality of the proposed theory.

Anbar Province, located in western Iraq, is the country's largest province and one of its most desolate, where the well-known alliance shift of Sunni tribesmen away from the insurgency took place between 2004 and 2007. The events in Anbar provide a useful additional test for my theory, while also having considerable policy relevance. Anbar is seen by U.S. policy makers as a tremendous, if surprising, success, and the province has become an emblem of what now needs to be accomplished by U.S. forces in Afghanistan. Determining what actually happened in Anbar, then, is of substantial policy as well as theoretical importance. First, however, it is important to identify and describe the warring actors involved.

Iraq's sizable population and heterogeneity lent themselves to a proliferation of major and minor warring actors once the conflict began. In western Iraq, broadly speaking, there appear to have been three major actors. The first warring actor was the Iraqi government in Baghdad, represented by the Iraqi Security Forces (ISF) and supported externally by the United States and its allies. (I operationalize this actor as a domestic group, supported by an external power that, under the scope conditions of my theory, is not a warring group of its own.) Although by far the preponderant actor in the Iraqi conflict overall, ISF forces were weakly concentrated in the vast expanse of western Iraq.

The second warring actor was the insurgency, consisting of both foreign and domestic fighters. Foreign fighters were largely gathered under Al Qaeda in Mesopotamia (also known as Al Qaeda in Iraq, or AQI), a group that had a relatively small number of combatants – between 1,000 and 12,000 in all of Iraq in 2007 – but disproportionate control over the local economy and security situation in Anbar Province.[7] In addition to these foreign insurgents, there was a population of domestic, "nationalist" insurgents, mainly former Baathists who had been aligned with Saddam Hussein until his ouster in 2003. However, when referring to the "insurgents" in this discussion, I will primarily be referencing AQI and related Islamist groups. By 2006, the Baathist elements of the Iraqi insurgency were marginalized and considered only a minor threat

---

[7] Tilghman (2007) cites the U.S. State Department Bureau of Intelligence and Research estimate of "more than 1,000"; Bruno (2008a) reports a figure of 12,000 in 2007.

by the U.S. government.[8] Baathists were still suspected of playing a role in financing the insurgency, but seemingly not in defining strategy or carrying out attacks. Some Baathists have joined the Anbar Awakening (discussed later in this section), while others continue to resist the sitting Iraqi government to this day,[9] but the latter component has become so obscure and fractionalized that "U.S. officials say they have frequently suspected that [the Baathist leader] is dead."[10]

The third warring actor, and the one of the most interest in this case study, were the Sunni tribesmen of Anbar Province. Although they are treated as one warring group in the analysis that follows, the tribesmen have no central leadership, instead being divided into roughly twenty major tribes and numerous subtribes.[11] Each tribe is led by a sheikh, making these sheikhs the local elites who proved critical to the turnaround in Anbar Province. Now that the key actors have been described, we turn to the conflict itself.

After coalition forces invaded Iraq in 2003 and displaced the Baathist regime of Saddam Hussein, the U.S. government dismantled the major institutions of Iraqi government and society, namely the army and the infrastructure of the Baath Party.[12] In the ensuing vacuum, civil war, both within and between Sunni and Shiite factions, broke out throughout Iraq. Anbar Province was no exception to these national-level developments. In fact, it became the heart of the insurgency as the vast expanses of western Iraq proved the hardest for ISF forces to secure. Until 2007, Anbar was the most violent region in the country.[13] This was arguably linked to the fact that Anbar was almost exclusively Sunni Arab, and many of Saddam's high-ranking party and military officers hailed from that province. The insurgents themselves were fairly small in number, as noted earlier. Hence the key rank and file of the anti-ISF movement proved to be the numerous Sunni tribesmen who aligned with AQI early in the conflict. (Because these Sunni tribes generally did not have the same political-religious motivations as the foreign fighters, they are treated here as a distinct warring group that was allied with the actual insurgents.)

For most of the war, Anbar Province lagged behind the progress of the other Iraqi provinces in terms of both pacification and integration with the central government in Baghdad. In fact, some of the war's worst fighting took place in Anbar's cities of Fallujah and Ramadi between 2004 and 2006. According to McCary, "[b]y 2006, al Qaeda had become nearly unstoppable as both a political and tactical force in the region, and the U.S. military unofficially declared al Anbar politically and militarily 'lost.'"[14] But starting in early 2004

---

[8] Cordesman (2008), p. 283.
[9] Ibid, pp. 290, 573.
[10] Spiegel and Parker (2007).
[11] Todd (2006).
[12] McCary (2009), p. 45; Lindsay and Long (2009), p. 29.
[13] McCary (2009), p. 43.
[14] Ibid, p. 44.

and continuing through 2007, the situation in Anbar slowly shifted from "lost" to the most heralded U.S. strategic victory in the Iraq war.

What prompted that change? The conventional U.S. military, Special Forces advocates, and scholars tell different stories, but they all involve one crucial element: the realignment of Sunni tribesmen away from AQI and toward ISF forces.[15] The realignment began in early 2004 when the Albu Nimr Sunni tribe "[stood] up tribesmen as local police and civil defense forces" aligned against AQI.[16] The Albu Nimr were ultimately crushed, but other tribal leaders quietly built alliances with ISF forces, against AQI, throughout 2005 and 2006. This activity culminated in September 2006, when "an Iraqi-led coalition of Sunni tribal sheikhs...publicly announced their split with al Qaeda and began working with [ISF and] U.S. military forces to oust the foreign-led terrorist group."[17] The Sunni tribal coalition called itself the "Awakening Council." The public announcement of the Awakening Council's creation constituted what several military analysts have since referred to as a "tipping point."[18] A cascade of public tribal defections from Al Qaeda alignment to ISF alignment began, and by April 2008, more than 90,000 western Iraqis (80 percent of them Sunni)[19] had joined the so-called Anbar Awakening.

The alliance shift of the Sunni tribesmen from AQI to ISF forces demonstrated just how pivotal the tribesmen had been to the prior intensity of the insurgency. The top U.S. commander in Ramadi, Anbar's largest city, said in 2007, "Once a tribal leader flips [from AQI to our side], attacks on American forces in that area stop almost overnight."[20] The U.S. count of "violent events" in Anbar Province declined from a peak of about 2,000 in September 2006 to 155 in January 2008.[21] The alliance shift of the Sunni tribal sheikhs may not have ended the insurgency in western Iraq, but it certainly placed a significant damper on it and brought its intensity back in line with the more central, pacified parts of the country.

In addition to being relevant to the theory of this book, the reasons behind the alliance shift in Anbar Province have been debated extensively by U.S. policy makers and scholars. Arguments that the "surge" of U.S. troops in early 2007 caused the shift do not match up temporally, because tribal defections began in early 2004 and culminated in September 2006,[22] although it may be that the "surge" was necessary for the Awakening movement to survive and thrive.[23]

---

[15] A partial exception is Berman, Shapiro, and Felter (2011), who argue that increased public goods provision combined with improved security during the "surge" to reduce violence in Iraq.

[16] Biddle, Friedman, and Shapiro (2011), p. 10.

[17] McCary (2009), pp. 43–44.

[18] Smith and MacFarland (2008), pp. 48–49.

[19] Bruno (2008a).

[20] McCary (2009), pp. 51–52.

[21] Lindsay and Long (2009), p. 1.

[22] Ibid, p. 3.

[23] Biddle et al. (2011).

Likewise, arguments that it was the level of brutality inflicted on the Sunni population by AQI that catalyzed the shift do not appear to hold empirically, because "Anbar [has] a long history of using violence for political ends."[24] Rigorous analyses of the Anbar Awakening seem to agree that the brutal violence employed by AQI against Sunni defectors was the *product* of the alliance shift, not the cause.[25] These two insufficient explanations aside, there appear to be two plausible explanations for the Sunni shift away from AQI – one of which, I argue, is more plausible than the other.

The first plausible explanation for the Anbar Awakening emphasizes U.S. activism and a decline in AQI's relative power, suggesting that the Sunni sheikhs bandwagoned with power-ascendant ISF forces. By this logic, the stage for the alliance shift was set by the U.S. attack on Fallujah in late 2004 and the Iraqi elections in early 2005, both of which demonstrated the rising power of the ISF counterinsurgency and led Sunni sheikhs "to conclude that the political process might hold more benefit than continued fighting."[26] In addition, this explanation argues, the Sunni sheikhs "flipped" because the United States began "sending money through [the] sheikhs instead of contract bids or the central government" and "authorized, funded, and armed Sunni militias" to restore order.[27] In particular, the U.S. military went to great lengths to ensure the personal security of the sheikhs themselves. Marine Brigadier General John Allen once "escort[ed] a sheikh personally from Jordan to Fallujah, and walk[ed] him to his door."[28] Two principal American officers involved in this co-optation strategy, Major Niel Smith and Colonel Sean MacFarland, described some of their other tactics as follows:

We . . . took some extraordinary measures to ensure the survival of tribal leaders who "flipped" to our side. We established neighborhood watches that involved deputizing screened members of internal tribal militias as "Provincial Auxiliary Iraqi Police." . . . In a few cases, we also planned to provide direct security to key leaders' residences, [such as] armored vehicles at checkpoints along the major access roads to their neighborhoods.[29]

As this first explanation would have it, the increased support and protection provided by U.S. forces to tribal sheikhs – constituting an increase in ISF relative power in the province – gave sheikhs the motivation and the cover to switch sides.

The most plausible explanation, however, is that the Sunni sheikhs were balancing against a rising power – AQI – rather than bandwagoning with one. The successes in late 2004 and early 2005 notwithstanding, the general picture of Anbar from the ISF perspective was bleak in the 2005–2006 time frame. Furthermore, many of the U.S. efforts to enrich and protect the Sunni

---

[24] McCary (2009), p. 44.
[25] See, for instance, Long (2008), pp. 77–78.
[26] Ibid, p. 77.
[27] McCary (2009), p. 45.
[28] Ibid, p. 50.
[29] Smith and MacFarland (2008), p. 43.

sheikhs seem to have come *after* the sheikhs started flipping (as attested to by the preceding quote), meaning that these actions, while certainly sound policy, did not cause the initial decision on the part of the sheikhs to switch sides.

As noted earlier, the ISF forces had severely limited control over western Iraq by 2006, and AQI had risen to a level of control far disproportionate to the actual number of foreign fighters in-country. This proto-hegemony of the jihadists included their "competing for control of revenue sources – such as banditry and smuggling – that had long been the province of the tribes."[30] Hence AQI, which at the beginning of the insurgency had been a key ally of the tribesmen against the growing and unwanted influence of Baghdad, was itself becoming more influential than the sheikhs. The sheikhs feared for their revenue streams and their own personal well-being if AQI dominance was allowed to persist. Furthermore, because the United States explicitly planned to withdraw from Iraq at some point in the not-so-distant future, "jihadists . . . loom[ed] as more dangerous long-term threats to the local tribes than the inevitably temporary Americans."[31] According to this explanation, an increase in AQI's relative power, coupled with the threats to the sheikhs' interests that this increase posed, prompted the sheikhs to abandon the jihadists and align with their former enemies in Baghdad (and Washington).[32] This view of what happened in Anbar appears most consistent with the tactical realities in the province during this time period, and is also consistent with the theory of this book – that groups seek to form optimally sized coalitions against allies that have grown too strong.

As in Afghanistan and Bosnia, narratives used to justify the tribal alignment with AQI and the subsequent realignment with ISF forces appear to have been purely tactical and fleeting. McCary notes the use of jihadist rhetoric against "the occupation of a Muslim land by a largely Christian force, a deep affront to traditional Muslim values harkening back to the Crusades," but characterizes the tribal-AQI alliance as foremost "a marriage of convenience."[33] Bing West agrees: "A few [insurgents] were charismatic zealots, but the rank and file was filled with criminals and opportunists motivated by money, power, and adventure."[34] Furthermore, although the Sunni tribes had realigned with ISF forces, the turnaround "did not resolve the deep rift between the Sunni province and the Shi'a-dominated central government,"[35] which means that no stable narrative exists to hold that alliance together. If relative power considerations dictate, we should fully expect another alliance shift in Iraq, and another instrumental narrative to justify it.

---

[30] Long (2008), p. 77.
[31] Lindsay and Long (2009), p. 40.
[32] McCary (2009), pp. 44, 48.
[33] Ibid, p. 43.
[34] West (2008), p. 186.
[35] Lindsay and Long (2009), pp. 1–2.

Indeed, such a dynamic appears to be currently unraveling on the ground. Several members of the Awakening councils have allegedly defected to the insurgency in light of the uncertainty in their standing given the U.S. withdrawal from Iraq.[36] Instances of reduced or delayed pay, along with the confiscation of their arms by the government, have signaled a lack of commitment to integrating Awakening Council members into the army or police. Indeed, only a tenth or so of the 94,000 Awakening members have been hired into the Iraqi national security forces.[37] According to a former Awakening Council leader, Nathum al-Jubouri: "The Awakening doesn't know what the future holds because it is not clear what the government intends for them.... At this point, Awakening members have two options: Stay with the government, which would be a threat to their lives, or help Al Qaeda."[38]

A member of the Sons of Iraq, Mohammed Hussein al-Jumaili from Dora, described how he was approached by Al Qaeda:

Ten days ago, I was in a cafe with another person from my neighbourhood. ... Two people came to me. I knew them. They were from my area. They said: "You know the Sons of Iraq experiment has failed and they will be slaughtered one after the other. If you work with us, we will support you. We will give you a good salary and you can do whatever operation you want to do. You will get extra money for anything that you do that hits the Americans, or the Iraqi forces."[39]

His stated reasons for entertaining the idea of switching sides are consistent with the instrumentality that this book's theory predicts.

Overall, the alliance shifts in Iraq's Anbar Province – both in favor of the Iraqi government and now increasingly against it – seem to coincide well with this book's predictions. Relative power considerations were certainly the key motivator behind the Anbar Awakening and its potential demise, and my reading of the movement is that it grew out of a desire to balance against AQI's rising power at first and then against the increasingly powerful (and nonresponsive) Iraqi government. Meanwhile, identity considerations and alliance narratives, to the extent they were invoked at all, appear to have been entirely instrumental and fleeting. This story should look familiar – it is evocative of the stories of Afghanistan and Bosnia recounted so far.

THE ARGUMENT AND ITS CONTRIBUTION

Apart from taking a close look at the different Afghan warring factions, as well as their interactions and trajectories in their civil wars since the Jihad, this book tried to walk through the machinations among allies and adversaries in some of

---

[36] Al Touarji (2010).
[37] Williams and Adnan (2010).
[38] Ibid.
[39] Chulov (2010).

the most horrific conflicts of the last century. It attempted to explain why ene-mies in bloody civil wars will become friends and then foes again, and when schisms, instead of unity, will arise among brethren and kin. The intent has been in part to show that if there is any group of internal armed conflicts that academics and policy practitioners need to understand better, multiparty civil wars are that group. Such understanding has been hindered by the rela-tive underemphasis within the civil war literature on conflict processes – the focus instead being primarily on conflict onset and termination. However, even the more recent work that has investigated civil war processes tends to treat civil war as a contest between two coherent, unitary actors – an empirically problematic stance that this book seeks to address. The understanding of mul-tiparty conflicts has also been hindered by the sheer complexity of conflicts such as those in Afghanistan, Bosnia, and Iraq. Indeed the number of warring actors and their interactions complicate the dynamics behind recruitment, vio-lence, and conflict duration, and amplify the analytical quandaries behind such processes.

This work has attempted to explain one crucial element of that complexity: the tendency for intergroup alliances in multiparty conflicts to shift constantly, and for groups themselves to be perpetually at risk for internal splits and takeovers. By making at least these within-conflict dynamics better understood and to a certain degree predictable, this book will hopefully contribute to containing such multiparty civil wars and seeing them to a quicker end.

My approach to this question spans political science subfields and involves a range of methodologies. Theoretically, I have engaged the neorealist literature within international relations, as well as the identity, ethnicity, and coalition literatures within comparative politics and political economy. By examining local elites in detail, I have attempted to bridge the divide between micro- and macro-level studies that has long characterized the literature on civil war. Empirically, I have closely engaged with four comprehensive comparative case studies of multiparty civil wars (the Afghan civil wars of 1978–1989 and 1992–1998 and the Bosnian civil wars of 1941–1945 and 1992–1995), which involved both qualitative and quantitative analysis of primary data collected in the field. I also modestly examined the applicability and extensions of my theoretical framework to the recent wars in Iraq and Afghanistan, and to the broader universe of fifty-three multiparty civil wars. The main motivation behind my theoretical and empirical eclecticism has been the need to triangulate findings and approaches. It is so difficult to know anything with certainty about these conflicts that all relevant literature and all relevant methods must be marshaled to the task.

Ultimately, I found support for a theory based on, essentially, a neorealist conception of civil war alliance politics and group fractionalization. (In fact, as discussed in Chapter 2, in some ways neorealism seems to fit my subject matter better than it does international politics.) Warring groups in multiparty civil wars are motivated first and foremost by relative power considerations. These groups dwell in an anarchic environment where they seek not only to survive, but also to profit. As a result, each group seeks to form wartime intergroup alliances that constitute minimum winning coalitions: alliances with enough aggregate power to win the conflict, but with as few partners as possible so that the group can maximize its share of postwar political control. A minimum winning coalition thus suggests that warring groups will ally in ways that even out the power distribution because they realize that the more powerful group cannot credibly commit to dividing power fairly if they choose to side with it. Therefore, alliances form and change when the intergroup relative power distribution in a conflict changes or when groups fractionalize, breaking the overall power in the conflict into smaller units that can be combined in different ways.

Group fractionalization itself is also largely a function of relative power considerations. In this context of uncertainty over which alliances will lead to victory, fractionalization is expected to be triggered if a warring group experiences a serious decline in its power. When groups suffer power losses in conflicts, those losses are generally borne asymmetrically across the group's constituent subgroups. A power loss that undermines the group's standing in the conflict, threatening its survival, can lead either to a split, if the group's leadership holds onto enough power to maintain its position across a subset of its constituents, or a takeover, if the leadership is defunct.

As noted throughout the book, identity is largely missing from this story. Group and subgroup elites spend plenty of time talking about the reasons they are allied with this group and not that one, or why they are loyal to this group and not the other, and these purported reasons are generally based on shared identity of one form or another. Hopefully, the theory and empirics of this book have shown this talk for what it is: talk. In reality, there appears to be no alliance that is impossible because of identity differences. If relative power considerations dictate that two groups unite in an alliance, then the elites involved will always find some characteristic that they share and construct a justifying narrative around that attribute. Therefore, despite the rhetoric we see coming from elites about the importance of identity to their decision making vis-à-vis alliances and intergroup loyalty, identity generally does not explain these decisions.

In terms of policy contributions, this book has shown that despite intuitive arguments to the contrary, policy makers should not be looking to race, language, or religion to predict or preclude civil war allies. As the case of Bosnia indicates, Christians can align with Muslims at one point in the conflict and be their enemies at another. Similarly, in Afghanistan, Sunnis can befriend Shiites now and fight against them later. Shared identity attributes, much like ancient hatreds or historical friendships, are constants that fail to capture the variable nature of civil war alliances. Rather, such processes obtain a life of their own as the conflict unravels. And while the reasons that may have prompted the onset of conflict could remain important, they may just as easily get reshaped and recast, with their saliency ebbing and flowing throughout the civil war's trajectory. Depending on the victories and losses on the war's multiple fronts, local cleavages may also rise in prominence at one stage in the conflict and get trumped by other power imperatives at another. And it is these changes in the relative power distribution among warring parties that will determine the actors' decisions on whether to stay with their existing allies or to change sides. Policy makers who want to follow civil war alliance choices therefore need to monitor closely the developments among the warring actors in the civil war's theater of operations.

Changes in the distribution of relative power are not just good predictors of alliance shifts; they also indicate which of the warring actors may be susceptible to fractionalization. Indeed, the number and type of warring actors in civil wars should not be considered fixed, but rather liable to change depending on each actor's wartime performance. More specifically, if a warring party is faced with survival-threatening losses, or losses that are asymmetrically borne among its constituents, that group is a candidate for fractionalization. Tribal and geographic in-group divisions, as well as preexisting leadership disputes, can serve as good indicators of the lines along which group fractionalization is likely to happen. These divisions predate the conflict and tend to be manifested at the level of local elites. Awareness of the geographic and tribal subdivisions of the warring groups, as well as the idiosyncrasies of the groups' local leaders, can enhance policy makers' understanding of how groups will fractionalize and what could be done to avert fragmentation.

Wartime rhetoric, though inflammatory, is only marginally informative on alliance and fractionalization choices, as discussed at length throughout the book. In practical terms, and in the context of the current Afghan and Iraqi civil wars, this suggests that the present pro- and anti-Taliban coalitions in Afghanistan or the pro- and anti-Baghdad coalitions in Iraq are not capable of being sustained by existing narratives of cooperation – and could easily collapse based on the relative power dictates of the conflict.

Through the discussion of civil war alliance formation and group fractionalization, this work also touches on issues of external intervention. I have suggested that in the absence of a warring actor that can win the war on its own, the vicious cycle of alliance shifts and fractionalization is likely to go on until the intervention of a powerful and determined external arbiter that can enforce peace. This book is by no means a work on external intervention or civil war termination – subjects that span rich literatures in their own right – but it does put forth the claim that for a civil war deadlock to come to an end, it may often require a credible external intervener willing to commit massive resources. This should not be interpreted as a case for imperialism or encouragement of third-party actors to meddle in the internal affairs of sovereign states. I simply recognize that external interference is almost ubiquitous in civil wars, and that the resultant deadlocks and quagmires are unlikely to come to an end without the involvement of a credible external guarantor.

The present-day context of Bosnia and Afghanistan further confirms the need for committed and sustained external assistance after the guns are silenced. In Bosnia, which received the highest amount of humanitarian aid in the world in the six years following the cessation of conflict, lasting peace has been largely effected.[40] Conversely, in the Afghan conflict, hostilities rose as the United States diverted resources and aid to Iraq.[41] These examples suggest that intervention in terms of developmental aid needs to be lasting and committed for years after the cessation of hostilities. And that may be a more viable policy prescription in Europe, where regional institutions such as the EU can continue to work as external credible guarantors, than it is in Central Asia, the Middle East, or Africa, where there is a regional institutional void.

ON FUTURE RESEARCH

This work has attempted to theorize upon the difficult dynamics of multiparty civil wars. In the process of addressing some long-standing questions on conflict, it has also identified an additional set of research directions that would result from a broadening of this work's scope or its theoretical or empirical framework.

Specifically, this book has focused only on multiparty conflicts, because that is the analytically meaningful subgroup of civil wars in which to examine alliances. While intergroup alliances can *only* take place in multiparty conflicts, group fractionalization can also occur in two-sided conflicts. (Here I am referring to fractionalization that does *not* result in the formation of a third warring group, because that would change the nature of the conflict to multiparty cases that are already accounted for in this analysis. So this scope includes internal takeovers and splits in which the faction that breaks off joins the opposing group.) Fractionalization in two-sided conflicts could well be the result of relative power considerations, or it could be more a function of identity, or of some other variable. The theory of this book does not seek to explain that phenomenon, so that would be a natural direction for future research.

In the same vein, it would be a grave misinterpretation to view this work as dismissive of the importance of identity to civil war more generally, as identity considerations could doubtlessly affect other within-conflict processes beyond alliances, such as recruitment and violence. Indeed, I find identity to be more binding in relationships among a group's constituent subgroups. Specifically, although groups and subgroups mostly behave similarly in my theory, in one key area they differ: While a warring group that is increasing in relative power is likely to attract enmity from other groups, it will maintain the loyalty of all its constituent subgroups. As we clearly see in the instances of group fractionalization, shared identity among subgroups works in ways that assuage commitment problems: Subgroups only break off in contexts of asymmetric

---

[40] The total humanitarian aid Bosnia and Herzegovina received between 1995 and 2001 amounted to $1.644 billion. "Trends in Humanitarian Assistance," p. 19, available at http://www.globalhumanitarianassistance.org/GHA2003/WeblinkPDFs/2p4-6W.pdf, accessed February 29, 2008.
[41] On the withdrawal of aid from Afghanistan to Iraq, see Rohde and Sanger (2003, 2007). On the increase of hostilities in Afghanistan, see Rubin (2008).

losses or when the group's survival is at stake, and not when the group is winning. As discussed in Chapter 2, the reason for this difference has to do with the lessened importance that subgroups attach to the maximization of postwar political control compared to the groups themselves, and this in turn seems to be related to the identity bonds between various subgroups. Identity also proves to be important in explaining the lines along which groups fracture into constituent subgroups. Thus identity, while still not as important as relative power in explaining behavior in this context, seems to matter at the subgroup level considerably more than at the group level. Future research on the differing salience of identity across and within groups and different levels of analysis would certainly make a valuable theoretical contribution.

Relatedly, although this work only examines the use of alliance narratives in the context of civil war, it would be interesting to consider the relevance of such narratives – if any – in the postconflict context. Policy makers may stand to benefit from this flexible notion of shared identity, which could open up the possibility of a broad range of reconciliation narratives that can in turn enhance peacebuilding in the context of a newly instituted state. In other research, my collaborator and I find that for such narratives to work effectively, they have to be used alongside economic and political incentives for all the actors involved.[42] That said, much more work remains to be done on why these narratives are effective and how the most successful among them are constructed.

Two additional avenues of research are the potential utility of foreign intervention in bringing multiparty civil wars to an end and the relative efficacy of foreign intervention in binary versus multiparty conflicts. Whereas much has been written on civil war intervention and termination, and several works explore whether the number of factions influences the success of postconflict peacebuilding,[43] little attention has been paid to whether the number of warring actors influences the probability of success for interventions designed to bring ongoing conflicts to an end. From a policy perspective, it would be useful to know whether successful foreign intervention is easier in multiparty or two-party contexts, and whether the act of foreign intervention itself causes alliance shifts or group fractionalization.

Beyond broadening the scope, future research can also broaden this work's empirical and theoretical approach. The clearest future research direction arising from this book is arguably empirical and revolves around the need to test the theory more comprehensively on the full universe of cases. The reader should be thoroughly unsurprised by this book's chief empirical limitation: paucity of data. As noted earlier, deep expertise on a multiparty civil war takes time to develop: To complete the comprehensive case studies on Afghanistan and Bosnia, I spent more than two years in the field, interviewing key players and experts in the local languages. To achieve the same level of depth on all fifty-three multiparty civil wars identified in this book would probably be beyond

---

[42] Alexander and Christia (2011).
[43] Fortna (2004); Doyle and Sambanis (2006).

the capability of any one researcher unless it became a sole career project. Instead, I have relied on secondary sources and subject-matter experts to flesh out my knowledge of the other cases.

Meanwhile, I hope that researchers who are already interested and knowledgeable about the other multiparty conflicts not studied in depth in this book will take it upon themselves to explore whether the proposed theoretical framework of alliance behavior and group fractionalization applies to the cases they know. In that regard, a call for coordinated data collection on the subnational level is warranted to allow for effective comparison of findings. The Correlates of War data project has long been such a resource (albeit an imperfect one) for scholars of international conflict, and more recent coordinated data collection on internal armed conflicts by the Center for the Study of War at the Peace Research Institute, Oslo (PRIO), is off to an encouraging start. The data collection I am proposing could complement these larger projects by providing more granular information on the conflict processes that underlie the wars cataloged, and could potentially be linked to the geocoded data that some PRIO researchers are beginning to assemble.

Finally, there is more work to be done on the connection between the theory of this book and the international relations literature on neorealism. First, neorealism in this book has taken a rather stylized and simplistic form that does not fully capture the richness of international relations theory over the past three decades. In particular, there has been considerable debate over whether "offensive realism" – states are power-maximizing[44] – or "defensive realism" – states are security-seeking[45] – better fits the empirical landscape of international politics. For the purposes of my project, I have sidestepped this debate by arguing that the actors of interest in the multiparty civil war context – warring groups – fit both paradigms equally well. They are both security-seeking *and* power-maximizing (or, to be more precise, they are postwar political control-maximizing when seeking minimum winning coalitions). Although I do believe both goals matter to these actors, it is probably not completely accurate to state that the goals are truly balanced in each actor's decision making. Therefore, further research could explore whether there is a consistent hierarchy of security-seeking and power-maximizing goals among warring actors in multiparty conflicts and how that hierarchy, if it exists, affects their decision making.

On a related note, as much as this book's research agenda could be better adapted to international relations theory, there is also a great deal that international relations theorists could learn from this book's research agenda. The idea that actors can be simultaneously security-seeking and power-maximizing is a relatively new one in international relations, although scholars have suggested for some time that states can have multiple, simultaneous, and sometimes conflicting goals and strategies.[46] In light of the findings of this book, this idea

---

[44] Mearsheimer (2001).
[45] Waltz (1979).
[46] See, for example, Lake (1993), pp. 470–472; Edelstein (2002), pp. 5–6; Fearon (2011).

should be taken more seriously. And, more importantly, multiparty civil wars could well be the extended "laboratory" of empirics that the international relations discipline has been in need of for some time. As a mine of empirical material for theory-building and theory-testing, the international system of states from 1816 to the present has more or less been exhausted – consider the number of works written on the causes of WWI alone. International relations scholars have tried to remedy the overuse of a relatively small amount of historical material by going further back in time – for example, Wohlforth and colleagues have looked at whether actors balance against power in historical settings as diverse as Warring States China and the pre-Columbian Americas.[47] A different, and possibly more feasible, solution is to look beyond international politics altogether and to consider what actor behaviors in multiparty civil wars tell us about international relations paradigms such as neorealism.

A considerable amount of work has been done to relate international relations theory to the civil war domain,[48] but the goal of such work has generally been to apply international relations theory, unmodified, to civil wars rather than to *adapt* international relations theory itself on the basis of what we observe in the civil war context. This book makes a strong argument for the value of the latter approach; for example, we have learned that under truer conditions of anarchy like those experienced in multiparty civil wars, actors balance against rising powers without much apparent regard for intentions. International relations scholars might gain similar theoretical insights from the further study of multiparty or other civil conflicts.

Little of this research will be easy – the easy work, by and large, has been done. But the questions this work raises are crucial nevertheless. They bear not only on the conduct of civil wars, but also on the role that identity plays throughout the trajectory of a dispute, and on the nature of the international relations theories on which much scholarly understanding of the world is constructed. The more of this research that gets undertaken, and the more collaborative and cumulative that research is, the more scholars of conflict will contribute to the endless policy debates that invoke these questions.

---

[47] Wohlforth et al. (2007).
[48] See, for example, Posen (1993).

Note on Sources

This work is motivated by social scientific questions of when groups cooperate and when they break apart in times of conflict. The proposed theory is meant to be one that is generally applicable to multiparty civil wars, irrespective of the type of warring group or the part of the globe where they are fighting, but it has its inductive underpinnings in the conflicts of Afghanistan and Bosnia. In my more than half a dozen extended trips to each of these countries from 2002 to 2010 (amounting to more than two full years spent in the field), I interviewed numerous individuals who were involved in these civil wars and gathered rich and diverse types of data. Each of my sources is cited in references at the end of this book. In this note, I want to give some basic context on the sources at hand as a supplement to the general research design of this work (presented in detail in Chapter 1 of this book).

Starting with Afghanistan, the ethnographic component of my work involved interviews with seventy-one individuals who were either participants in or experts on the country's civil wars, be they warlords, mujahedin, or international experts. These included leading figures in the Jamiat-i-Islami party, including the intra-mujahedin war acting president Burhanuddin Rabbani and his known commanders, Ismael Khan in Herat and Nur Mohammad Atta in Mazar-i-Sharif; as well as Jamiat-i-Islami Panjshiris close to the assassinated commander Ahmad Shah Massoud, such as Abdullah Abdullah and Yunis Qanooni; leading figures in the Hizb-i-Islami party of Gulbuddin Hekmatyar, such as Wahidullah Sabawoon and Hussain Mangal; established Hazara figures in the Hizb-i-Wahdat party and its splinter group, such as Haji Mohammad Mohaqeq and Mohammad Akbari; and the Uzbek defector Abdul Malik Pahlawan, among others.

Individuals Interviewed on Afghan Civil Wars	
Pashtun	22
Tajik	9
Uzbek	3
Hazara	12
Other Minorities (Pashai, Seyed, Aimaq, etc.)	10
International Experts	15
Total	71

Apart from the extensive field interviews, the ethnographic material also included a collection of Taliban decrees and fatwas, as well as publications from the Taliban government and party publications from the leading Pashtun, Tajik, Uzbek, and Hazara parties – Hizb-i-Islami, Jamiat-i-Islami, Junbish-i-Milli, and Hizb-i-Wahdat. Other primary documents, this time on the U.S. side, included 8,080 pages of Guantanamo Bay detainee-related documents, including detainee testimony and Administrative Review Board summaries of detention or release factors; as well as a collection of 32 declassified documents on the Taliban from the U.S. State Department and the Defense Intelligence Agency. Relevant articles in the leading press publications were also consulted, along with an extended set of the secondary literature on the country.

The holding of interviews and the gathering of primary documents (Taliban or otherwise) in Afghanistan posed their own considerable challenges, but the most ambitious analytical enterprise involved the coding of a dataset on influential district-level commanders (presented in Chapter 5 of this book) for the three politically most important Afghan provinces (other than Kabul, which is examined in detail in the book's other empirical chapters) of Balkh, Kandahar, and Nangarhar. The enterprise involved close consultation with Michael Semple and Mervyn Patterson, two leading area experts on Afghanistan broadly recognized for their training, language credentials, and more than two decades of on-the-ground experience. They both appreciated and were directly involved in my efforts to systematize and codify information on these influential personalities while key informants who can provide and verify the requisite data are still alive and accessible. Because of their complementary expertise, Michael Semple vetted the codings for Kandahar and Nangarhar and Mervyn Patterson vetted the codings for Balkh.

I compiled the original list of commanders through close consultation of Ludwig Adamec's *Biographical Encyclopedia of Afghanistan*; Fida Yunas's two-volume work entitled *Afghanistan, Political Parties, Groups, Movements, and Mujahideen Alliances and Governments (1879–1997)*; and through the review of two internal documents on the *Disbandment of Illegal Armed Groups* (DIAG) and an internal document on the *Afghanistan New Beginnings Program (ANBP)* on commander demobilization.

In a largely oral culture such as that of Afghanistan, the most reliable information comes from key informants who have come from the same geographical area but were fighting on competing sides. The informants involved in this enterprise were of mixed political affiliation. Some were already part of Michael Semple's *Oral History* project. Others were contacted and interviewed specifically to provide input and verification for this coding exercise. The final list of 141 commanders across the three provinces of Balkh, Kandahar, and Nangarhar includes individuals on whom there was consensus or near-consensus that they merited inclusion on a list of the most influential commanders in the province during at least one warring period. This purposely excluded commanders who only exerted influence at the pleasure of an appointing authority rather than their personal political standing.

For each individual commander, the dataset includes information on ethnicity, tribe, language, sect, education, and party affiliation. The relative power of each commander is assessed using information about the number of fighters they controlled, their battlefield performance, and their source of influence. To capture within-war variation – these wars were lengthy affairs, with the Jihad lasting eleven years and the intra-mujahedin war six – I coded commander behavior for historically analytically relevant periods for each war. The resulting five periods constituted the only realistic and analytically tractable way to try to get at within-conflict variation of commander behavior. As with any data collection exercise that reduces humans and their complicated interactions into a spreadsheet, there are of course limitations to what these data can tell us. But the fact that what they do tell us, as per the results by province and on the aggregate, is consistent with people's qualitative and historical sense of what transpired, offers an additional degree of validation to the measures at hand.

In Bosnia and Herzegovina, I also conducted an array of interviews with individuals who participated in or were experts on the recent conflict (1992–1995). The table that follows shows the breakdown of the sixty-four interviews that I conducted in-country with Bosniacs/Muslims, Serbs, Croats, or international experts. Among the interviewees were convicted war criminals such as Fikret Abdić, the Muslim secessionist leader from western Bosnia, and Simo Zarić and Milojica Kos, Serbs from Bosanksi Šamac who were convicted by the International Criminal Tribunal for Yugoslavia for crimes they perpetrated against civilians in their area; leading political leaders such as Haris Silajdžić, who was minister of foreign affairs (1990–1993) and then prime minister of the Bosnian government (1993–1995), and Stjepan Kljujić, the Croat prewar member of the Bosnia and Herzegovina rotating presidency; as well as leading military figures such as Atif Dudaković and Rasim Delić, generals in the Bosnian army; Manojlo Milovanović, general in the Bosnian Serb army; and leading figures in the Mostar conflict such as Petar Zelenika on the Croat side and Esad Humo on the Muslim side.

Individuals Interviewed on Bosnian Civil War	
Bosniac/Muslim	22
Croat	9
Serb	23
International Experts	10
Total	64

For the prewar demographic information that gauges municipal-level alliance behavior at the onset of conflict, I relied on 1991 Yugoslav census data on Bosnia and Herzegovina that offer – among other information – ethnic breakdown of the prewar population as well as average income and educational levels. For military assets on the municipal level at the onset of war, I used data from the Yugoslav National Army. Those data also offer the ethnic affiliation of the individual in charge of the arms depot in each municipality (termed the "arms keeper"). For casualties during the war (military and civilian), I referred to *The Bosnian Book of Dead* for municipal-level data by ethnic group by year. For territorial changes as well as changes in the alliance narratives among the different warring groups, I relied on the local press and mostly on *Oslobođenje* (Freedom), the leading Bosnian newspaper from 1992 to 1995. For the discussions of the factional disputes among Croats and Muslims, apart from interviews with the protagonists, I looked to regional newspapers as well as relevant archival material provided to me by the warring subgroups.

For WWII Bosnia I used archival data from all warring sides. Specifically, I referenced an appendix on the Main Laws and Orders of the Independent State of Croatia (*Zakoni Nezavisne Države Hrvatske*); documents from the archive of the Communist Party of Bosnia andHerzegovina (*Arhiv Komunističke Partije Bosne i Hercegovine*); documents from the National Liberation War of the Peoples of Yugoslavia (*Zbornik Dokumenata i Podataka o Narodno-Oslobodilačkom Ratu Jugoslovenskih Naroda*); as well as documents from the Military Archive in Belgrade (*Vojni Arhiv*) along with its two sub-archives – the Chetnik fund and the National Liberation Army fund. The referenced documents are hosted in Belgrade's Military Archive. The information on documents in the Archive is ordered on index cards by funds, organizational or military units that produced them, and by chronology. Since it was not possible to browse through the whole archive, two main edited collections were used and cross-referenced: the *Zbornik* referenced earlier and *Hronologija*, a 1,265-page volume with the daily events of the war in each former Yugoslav republic.

What is obvious in the *Zbornik* is the large imbalance in the number of sources of documents. Out of fourteen volumes, only three are dedicated to "enemy" Archives: German (four books), Italian (three books), and Chetnik (four books). The documents of the Independent State of Croatia, its civil or military units, are published in books of documents related to Croatia (Volume 3) or Bosnia and Herzegovina (Volume 4). These were arranged at the end of the books, usually comprising one-fourth to one-third of the documents. Although they were included and referenced with the intent to portray "enemy propaganda," they were an excellent counterpoint to the preponderant Partisan sources. The commentaries on the "enemy documents" portray the events and actors of the war in obvious ideological terms, presenting the "other side" as traitors or villains, but the actual content of the documents from the enemy side is presented intact and not modified in any way. Also, to the degree that the different sources allow for triangulation, the alliances and breaches thereof are similarly described in the Croat, Partisan, and Chetnik sources. For instance, both Croatian and Serb-Chetnik sources justify the Western Bosnia alliances of 1942 in purely tactical terms, as they do the Partisan-Chetnik alliance in Herzegovina that preceded them.

In sum, WWII Yugoslavia was a complicated affair that has spun a large historiography both in the local languages and in English. My account on civil war alliances does not attempt to resolve any of the large historical debates over whether the war was just a war of national liberation rather than a civil war (even though the targeting and violence would suggest otherwise), or the extent of crimes perpetrated by the various warring sides, be they royalist Chetniks, communist partisans, or fascist Ustashe. The intent here has been to ensure a nonpartisan interpretation of the facts. And the instrumental nature of the alliances on all warring sides, as manifested in their agreements and fighting behaviors, was conducive to that.

Unlike the extended primary research on Afghanistan and Bosnia, references to the alliance choices in present-day Afghanistan and Iraq's Anbar Province are based on secondary sources only. These are, however, short, bare-bones shadow treatments that undoubtedly leave plenty of fleshing-out potential for researchers who care to investigate alliances in those time periods or areas of the world. Similarly, the only realistic way to code the dataset of all fifty-three multiparty civil wars with three or more domestic actors in terms of their alliances, number and size of warring groups, and their fractionalization – as presented in detail in the introduction and in Chapter 8 of this book and extensively cited in the references – was through consulting authoritative works in the secondary literature and through verifying the codings with area experts. The results are robust to the exclusion of two cases, whose inclusion was questioned by some (Israel and Côte D'Ivoire), as well as the exclusion of the four nineteenth-century cases (Hapsburg Austrian Empire, Chinese Rebellion, Ottoman Empire-Balkans, and Ottoman Empire-Greece).

Appendix

Table A.1 shows that the subset of multiparty civil wars in the Fearon and Laitin (FL) (2003) dataset (by my definition of three or more internal warring groups) is relatively representative of my full set of fifty-three multiparty wars (which spanned a greater time period than the FL dataset and had slightly different rules for the number of fatalities). Specifically, I compared all available covariates present in both datasets for these two sets of wars. Despite scope and definitional differences, the fifty-three cases I identified did not differ significantly from the subset of thirty-six multiparty wars matching those in the FL dataset on any of the covariates tested, including duration, mortality rates (and log transformations of these two measures), or year of onset (Table A.1, compare column 1 to 2).

Comparing multiparty conflicts to non-multiparty conflicts within the FL dataset (Table A.1, compare column 2 to 3), we see that the subtypes of war seem to differ systematically on a number of covariates. In bivariate tests, multiparty conflicts were associated with significantly longer mean durations by a stunning eight years ($p = 0.001$). Similarly, when fitting a survival model using a Weibull distribution, multiparty wars were found to be 2.2 times longer ($p < 0.000$). Multiparty conflicts also had higher fatality rates when measured in natural logs ($p = 0.0005$), later years of onset ($p = 0.024$, reflecting the increasing rate of multiparty wars over the decades), higher ethnic fractionalization ($p = 0.0009$), a greater share of the population belonging to the largest ethnic group ($p = 0.0003$), and what may be a greater likelihood of employing symmetrical nonconventional war (SNC) (20% for multiparty vs. 6% for biparty, $p = 0.10$) as coded by Kalyvas and Balcells (2010b).

This relationship between *multiparty* and *SNC* is only significant at the 90 percent level. However, further evidence that there is a meaningful effect of "multiparty-ness" on the likelihood of SNC emerges in the finding that the number of warring parties in a conflict (assumed to be two for non-multiparty

253

TABLE A.1. *Comparison of Means for Available Covariates on Multiparty versus Biparty Civil Wars (t-tests with unequal variance, two-tailed p-values, standard errors in parentheses)*

	(1) Christia set (Multiparty)	(2) F&L set (Multiparty)	(3) F&L set (Biparty)	(1) vs. (2) (|t|, 2-sided p)	(2) vs. (3) (|t|, 2-sided p)
Duration (years)	13.57	14.6	6.59	0.38	3.47
	(1.68)	(2.15)	(0.83)	($p = 0.70$)	($p = 0.001$)
Log (duration)	2.26	2.31	1.34	0.25	5.03
	(0.12)	(0.15)	(0.12)	($p = 0.80$)	($p < 0.0000$)
Deaths	57,066	58,346	67,268	0.062	0.248
	(13,595)	(15,681)	(32,450)	($p = 0.95$)	($p = 0.81$)
Log (deaths)	10.12	10.05	8.78	0.22	3.61
	(0.21)	(0.26)	(0.24)	($p = 0.83$)	($p = 0.0005$)
Year of onset	1983	1980	1973	0.95	2.31
(if onset $\geq$1945)	(2.23)	(2.24)	(1.90)	($p = 0.34$)	($p = 0.024$)
1989 or later	0.45	0.42	0.27	0.54	1.53
(if onset $\geq$1945)	(0.076)	(0.083)	(0.051)	($p = 0.59$)	($p = 0.13$)
Log (population)		9.55	9.61		0.20
		(0.21)	(0.20)		($p = 0.84$)
Ethnic		0.65	0.48		3.46
fractionalization		(0.039)	(0.031)		($p = 0.0009$)
Percent mountainous		26.2	23.0		0.65
terrain		(4.26)	(2.54)		($p = 0.52$)
Polity2		−0.44	−1.81		1.21
		(0.90)	(0.69)		($p = 0.23$)
Log (gdp pc), year		6.86	7.07		1.21
before conflict		(0.13)	(0.12)		($p = 0.23$)
Plural		0.47	0.66		3.84
		(0.040)	(0.028)		($p = 0.0003$)
Religious		0.41	0.37		1.00
fractionalization		(0.039)	(0.023)		($p = 0.32$)
Kalyvas-Balcells		0.52	0.48		0.29
technology:		(0.091)	(0.063)		($p = 0.78$)
irregular					
Kalyvas-Balcells		0.29	0.45		1.57
technology:		(0.083)	(0.063)		($p = 0.12$)
conventional					
Kalyvas-Balcells		0.17	0.053		1.66
technology: SNC		(0.063)	(0.026)		($p = 0.10$)

wars) is strongly predictive of *SNC* ($p = 0.004$ for a logit model with robust standard errors clustered on country).

Table A.2 captures the results of an OLS regression for *multiparty* civil wars simultaneously on all the variables that had statistically different means for multiparty versus two-party conflicts in the bivariate analyses. This allows me to determine whether or not each of these covariates would remain correlated with *multiparty* conditional on all the other variables included in the model (insofar as OLS is a reasonable method for implementing this conditioning).

TABLE A.2. *Relevance of Factors for Multiparty Civil Wars*

Dependent Variable: Multiparty Civil Wars	
Duration (log)	0.115
	(3.08)***
Deaths (log)	0.075
	(3.68)***
Ethnic Fractionalization	−0.187
	(−0.25)
Onset Year	0.006
	(2.60)**
Plural Group	−0.612
	(−0.75)
SNC	0.191
	(1.37)
Constant	−12.597
	(−2.57)**
Observations	106
R-squared	0.35

Notes: OLS Estimates. T-statistics (calculated with robust standard errors) in parentheses.
*** Significant at 0.01 level; ** Significant at 0.05 level.

The results indicate that log *duration*, log *deaths*, and *year* of onset remain significantly different between multiparty and two-party conflicts, conditional on all the other variables in the model. *Ethnic fractionalization*, a greater share of the population belonging to the largest ethnic group, and a greater likelihood of employing symmetrical nonconventional war (*SNC* as coded per Kalyvas and Balcells [2010b]) appear to drop out, indicating that we cannot reject the null hypothesis of nonzero coefficients, and thus cannot reject the hypothesis that they are independent of *multiparty* once we have conditioned on the other variables.

APPENDIX MATERIAL FOR CHAPTER 2

The alliance model outlined in Chapter 2 assumes complete and symmetric information across groups. In actuality, however, groups only have incomplete information on each other's relative power, and every group is working off its own reference model. Groups thus often make mistakes in their relative power assessment, pursuing alliance switches they would not have made otherwise. Figure A.1 considers an illustration of this misperception.

Assume that a group is in a winning coalition that temporarily starts to lose. Because the group has incomplete information, it may think that the relative power of the coalition has fallen below $p = 0.5$ and as a result may switch alliances. This switch would be suboptimal, as the group is on the winning side but, because of incomplete information, thinks it is not. These miscalculations are even more likely when alliances are of largely comparable power – for

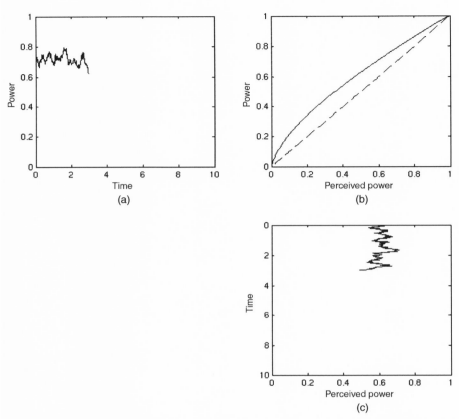

FIGURE A.1. Simulation Graphs of Actual and Perceived Power. (a) Actual relative power change, starting with initial power level $p = 0.7$ and assuming $\delta(p) = 0.25(p - 0.5)$ and $\sigma(p) = 1$. (b) Relationship between actual and perceived levels of relative power for alliance A, where perceived power $p_p = p^{1.5}$. (c) Perceived relative power change, where $p_p = p^{1.5}$.

example, when they find themselves in the $p = 0.5$ range. If groups hover around that stalemate range, they are more likely to make mistaken assessments of the relative power of their alliance. Figure A.1 provides simulation graphs on actual versus perceived power as a way to illustrate the possibility of unwarranted alliance switches among groups. These graphs are intended to be read clockwise: Starting from the left, the first graph denotes the evolution of the actual power over time, showing that A's power remains above 0.5 (the switching point) throughout the depicted interval – suggesting that in expectation, coalition A wins. However, because of incomplete information, groups act based on perceived rather than actual power. The second graph, in turn, shows the translation between actual power and perceived power, illustrating in this case the extent to which perceived power is lower than actual power. Lastly, the bottom graph is a translation of the actual power (as depicted in the graph on the left) in perceived power terms. The graph stops at $p = 0.5$, when the group switches alliances, mistakenly thinking that it is on the losing side.

APPENDIX MATERIAL FOR CHAPTER 3

The two tables presented here capture the power distribution of the alliances at two distinct moments. Table A.3 displays the distribution of political, economic, and military assets at the beginning of the civil war (1992). Table A.4 presents the power distribution as the Taliban entered the stage in 1996, drastically altering the alliance structure.

TABLE A.3. *Military Balance in Afghanistan in 1992*

	Alliance One	Alliance Two
Military capacity[1] (Troops/ Equipment)	Hizb-i-Islami (Hekmatyar): 8,000+ troops[2] and 4 divisions, and 2 brigades[3] from the Afghan Army including air, air defense, and mechanized assets. Ittihad-i-Islami (Sayyaf): 8,000 troops[4] and 1 corps and 2 divisions.[5]	Tajiks (Jamiat-i-Islami): 12,000 troops,[6] 3 divisions and 1 brigade from the Afghan Army, including air, air defense, mechanized, and rocket assets.[7] Uzbeks (Junbish-i-Milli): 45,000 troops on paper, although some estimates put them closer to 25,000,[8] including 6 divisions from the Afghan Army as well as substantial air, air defense, and mechanized resources.[9] Hazaras: 8,000 troops[10] as well as 2 Afghan Army divisions.[11]

(continued)

[1] Note that given the attrition of the Afghan army during the late 1980s and severe desertion following the communist collapse, the size of divisions and brigades varied widely. However, there was generally the same distribution everywhere in the country, except in the south where desertion was the highest.

[2] O'Ballance (2002), p. 235.

[3] Davis (1993), p. 134; interview with Wahidullah Sabawoon, leadership figure in Hizb-i-Islami at the time. This included the 5th Division, Sarandoi 7th Brigade, 11th Division Jalalabad, 70th Mechanized Brigade (Farah), 8th Sarandoi, and 21st Division (Shindand).

[4] Matinuddin (1999), p. 55.

[5] This included the 6th Corps and 54th Division (Kunduz), and part of the 10th Division (Baghi-Daoud). Davis (1993), p. 135.

[6] Sinno (2008), p. 178; O'Ballance (2002), p. 235.

[7] These included the 1st division, 99th Rocket Brigade, 2nd Division (Jabal Saraj), and 40th Division (Bagram Air Base). Davis (1993), pp. 134–135.

[8] Giustozzi (2004), p. 57; Rubin (1995b), p. 133; Davis (1993), p. 136.

[9] These included the 53rd Division (Shiberghan), the 70th Division (Heratan), the 18th Division (Balkh Garrison), the 511th Division (Maimana), the 80th Division (Pul-i-Khumri), and the 54th Division (Samangan). Davis (1993), pp. 137–138.

[10] Matinuddin (1999), p. 55.

[11] These included the 96th Tribal Division (Maidanshar) and the 95th Tribal Division (Kabul). Davis (1993), p. 135.

TABLE A.3 *(continued)*

	Alliance One	Alliance Two
Political capacity	Hizb-i-Islami (Hekmatyar): Close links with Khalq communists and hard-line Pashtun officers. Thought to be main political actor in a "Pashtun" solution for the transition from Najibullah.	Tajiks (Jamiat-i-Islami): Connections with Parcham members of the communist regime including Foreign Minister Abdul Wakil and party leader Farid Mazdak.[12] Major legitimacy bestowed from the strong performance during the Soviet Jihad.
		Uzbeks (Junbish-i-Milli): Dostum led a pro-government militia under the control of the PDPA,[13] which provided connections with Tajik and Uzbek officers, in particular Abdul Mumin. However, with the withdrawal from the communist government, Dostum was left with little political capital.[14]
		Hazaras (Hizb-i-Wahdat): Strong political position because Hizb had nearly universal Hazara support, an autonomous presence in Hazarajat, and control of much of western Kabul.[15]
Economic capacity	Hizb-i-Islami (Hekmatyar): Main client of Pakistan with support from narcotics trade. Additional support from Iraq, Libya,[16] and Saudi Arabia[17] in the form of military supplies, cash, and fighters.	Tajiks (Jamiat-i-Islami): Low foreign support, but some U.S. and Indian support.
		Uzbeks (Junbish-i-Milli): Medium financial support, though substantial arms and logistics support from Uzbekistan and Russia.[18] Excessive printing of Junbish Afghanis, which were rapidly devalued vis-à-vis the Afghani.
		Hazaras (Hizb-i-Wahdat): Strong financial, logistics, and weapons support from Iran.[19]

[12] Maley (2009), p. 157.
[13] Rasanayagam (2003), p. 130.
[14] Dorronsoro (2005), p. 243.
[15] Harpviken (1997), p. 280.
[16] Rubin (1995a), p. 272.
[17] Coll (2004), p. 226.
[18] Giustozzi (2004), p. 4.
[19] Ahady (1998), pp. 123–124.

TABLE A.4. *Military Balance in Afghanistan in Late 1996*

	Alliance One	Alliance Two
Military capacity (Troops /Equipment)	Taliban: 20,000–25,000 troops with 200 tanks and armored vehicles, 12 MiG 23s and more than 12 helicopters (though a number of the helicopters and MiGs were not functional),[20] as well as 12 aircraft and a "very large amount" of heavy ammunition.[21] Uzbeks (Junbish-i-Milli): 35,000 troops, 11 fighter planes, 9 helicopters, and 3 air transporters.[22] Hazaras (Khalili): 5,000 troops.[23]	Tajiks (Jamiat-i-Islami): 20,000–30,000 troops including Massoud's Central Corps (Kabul), the 6th Corps (Kunduz), and the 5th Corps (Herat). The Central Corps probably represented the most complete and best organized force in the country. At least 6 operational (possibly 10)[24] Su-22s, "several" Mi-24 Hind helicopters, 10 air transporters,[25] and a "considerable" number of tanks and armored vehicles.[26] Hizb-i-Islami (Hekmatyar): 5,000 troops and significantly reduced arms, air resources, and logistical elements as the Taliban absorbed much of this resource base in its march northward.[27] Hazaras (Akbari): 3,000 troops.[28]
Political capacity	Taliban: Growing legitimacy throughout southern Afghanistan and control of government functions in more than 50% of the country.[29] Uzbeks (Junbish-i-Milli): Continued autonomy in northern Afghanistan but with decreasing control of northern areas.	Tajiks (Jamiat-i-Islami): Increasing political control over the center as the actors in their coalition were weakened. However, control beyond the center and northern Afghanistan was faltering quickly.[30] Hizb-i-Islami (Hekmatyar): Drastically weakened with little to no support in southern Afghanistan. However, during this period, Hekmatyar finally assumed the prime minister position.

(continued)

[20] Davis (1995), p. 316.
[21] National Security Archive, Freedom of Information Act, Taliban File, Document 6, p. 7.
[22] Matinuddin (1999), p. 55.
[23] Ibid, p. 55.
[24] Ibid.
[25] Ibid.
[26] Davis (1995), p. 317.
[27] Magnus (1997), p. 152.
[28] Matinuddin (1999), p. 55.
[29] Goodson (2001), p. 77.
[30] Ibid.

TABLE A.4 *(continued)*

	Alliance One	Alliance Two
	Hazaras (Khalili): Increased political autonomy in Hazarajat and a bolstered movement.[31]	Hazaras (Akbari): Politically strengthened by the alliance with Massoud, giving them access to some levers of government.
Economic capacity	Taliban: Substantial support from Pakistan covering financial, logistical, armaments, and potentially direct military support.[32] (Further information in "Pakistan Intervention" in Chapter 3). Uzbeks (Junbish-i-Milli): Continued support from Uzbekistan, although in declining amounts as Uzbekistan was opposed to the Taliban.[33]	Tajiks (Jamiat-i-Islami): Major support from Russia, Tajikistan, Iran, India, and Ukraine.[34] Additionally, the United States began providing money to the Northern Alliance.[35] Hizb-i-Islami (Hekmatyar): Drastically reduced support from both Saudi Arabia and Pakistan.

[31] Sinno (2008), p. 228.
[32] Rashid (2000), pp. 44–45; Rasanayagam (2003), pp. 142–143; Davis (1998).
[33] Giustozzi (2004), p. 4.
[34] Rashid (2000), p. 44.
[35] Coll (2004), p. 345.

APPENDIX MATERIAL FOR CHAPTER 5

TABLE A.5. *Commander Tribe (Kandahar and Nangarhar Only)*

Tribe	Jihad			Intra-Mujahedin War		
	All $(K + N)$ $N = 83$	Kandahar $N = 42$	Nangarhar $N = 41$	All $(K + N)$, $N = 62$	Kandahar $N = 24$	Nangarhar $N = 38$
Popolzai	5%	10%	0	2%	4%	0
Barakzai	2%	5%	0	0	0	0
Alokozai	5%	10%	0	8%	21%	0
Alizai	1%	2%	0	2%	4%	0
Esakzai	1%	2%	0	2%	4%	0
Mohmand	11%	0	22%	15%	0	24%
Khogyani	10%	2%	17%	15%	4%	21%
Tareen	2%	5%	0	3%	8%	0
Kakar	0	0	0	2%	4%	0

	Jihad			Intra-Mujahedin War		
Tribe	All ($K + N$) $N = 83$	Kandahar $N = 42$	Nangarhar $N = 41$	All ($K + N$), $N = 62$	Kandahar $N = 24$	Nangarhar $N = 38$
Achakzai	4%	7%	0	2%	4%	0
Ludin	2%	2%	2%	3%	4%	3%
Hotak	4%	7%	0	5%	13%	0
Kharoti	1%	2%	0	0	0	0
Tokhi	1%	2%	0	0	0	0
Noorzai	14%	29%	0	5%	13%	0
Seyed	5%	10%	0	3%	8%	0
Other	8%	5%	12%	6%	8%	5%
Kuchi	5%	0	10%	5%	0	8%
J. Kheil	6%	0	12%	8%	0	13%
Shinwari	5%	0	10%	6%	0	11%

APPENDIX MATERIAL FOR CHAPTER 8

TABLE A.6. *Rates of Fractionalization versus Rates of Alliance Change*

	(1) Number of Groups at Onset × Percent Fractionalized	(2) Number of Alliance Changes
Total number in dataset	110	181
Mean number per conflict	2.07	3.42
Median number per conflict	2	3

TABLE A.7. *Coding of Alliance Portfolio Changes by Conflict*

Conflict	Number of Alliance Portfolio Changes	List of Changes	Alliance Portfolio Volatility[36]
Afghanistan (1978–1992)	5	• 1983: Jamiat adds PDPA • 1983: Jamiat removes PDPA • 1984: Massoud removes Hekmatyar (or vice versa) • 1985: Massoud adds Hekmatyar (or vice versa) • 1992: Northern Militias add mujahedin, remove PDPA	0.028

(continued)

TABLE A.7 *(continued)*

Conflict	Number of Alliance Portfolio Changes	List of Changes	Alliance Portfolio Volatility
Afghanistan (1992–2001)	7	• 1993: Wahdat adds Hizb; removes Jamiat, Jinbush • 1994: Jinbush adds Wahdat, Hizb, removes Jamiat • 1995: Hizb adds Jamiat, Wahdat splinter; removes Wahdat, Jinbush • 1996: Wahdat adds Jamiat, removes Taliban • 1996: Jinbush adds Jamiat, removes Taliban • 1997: Jinbush adds Taliban; removes Jamiat, Wahdat • 1997: Jinbush adds Jamiat, Wahdat; removes Taliban	0.156
Afghanistan (2002–present)	0	N/A	0
Algeria (1954–1962)	0	N/A	0
Algeria (1992–2004)	2	• 1993: AIS adds MIA • 2000: AIS adds Algerian Armed Forces	0.0476
Angola (1961–1975)	3	• 1968: MPLA removes UNITA, FNLA • 1969: FNLA removes UNITA • 1972: MPLA adds FNLA	0.0441
Angola (1975–2002)	1	• No date: FNLA removes UNITA (or vice versa)	0.0114
Austria (1848–1849)	1	• 1848: Austrians add Croats; remove Hungary, Viennese Radicals	0.0625
Bosnia and Herzegovina (1992–1995)	3	• 1993: Croats add Serbs, Abdić; remove Muslims • 1993: Muslims add Serbs, Croats (Herzegovina only) • 1994: Croats add Muslims; remove Serbs, Abdić	0.214
Burundi (1991–2003)	1	• 2003: CNDD-FDD adds Burundi Armed Forces, removes Palipehutu-FNL	0.0278

Conflict	Number of Alliance Portfolio Changes	List of Changes	Alliance Portfolio Volatility
Cambodia (1978–1991)	3	• 1982: Khmer Rouge adds KPNLF and Sihanouk • ca. 1991: Sihanouk adds Cambodian state, removes Khmer Rouge • ca. 1991: KPNLF adds Cambodian state, removes Khmer Rouge	0.0577
Chad (1969–1997)	4	• 1979: FAP removes FAN, First Liberation Army • 1979: Kamogue adds FAP • 1986: FAP adds FAN • 1990s: MDD adds MPS/Government of Chad	0.0417
Chad (1998–present)	2	• ca. 2007: UFDD adds RFC • 2008: UFDD adds UFDD-Fondamentale	0.0645
China (1850–1878)	0	N/A	0
China (1911–1931)	23	• 1911: Republicans add Military Faction of Yuan Shih-Kai • 1913: Military Faction of Yuan Shih-Kai removes Republicans • 1920: Republicans remove Military Faction of Ch'en Chiung-Ming • 1920: Forces of Wu Peifu add Forces of General Feng and Forces of Chang Tso-Lin to oust Anfu Clique • 1920: Forces of General Feng add Forces of Wu Peifu and Forces of Chang Tso-Lin to oust Anfu Clique • 1922: Republicans add Kwangsi Provincial Army and Yunnan Provincial Army to balance against Military Faction of Ch'en Chiung-Ming • 1923: Republicans remove Kwangsi Provincial Army and Yunnan Provincial Army by creating their own Nationalist Army; Kwangsi and Yunnan later cooperate against the Republicans • 1923: Republicans add CCP, who are interested in balancing against Forces of Wu Peifu	0.137

(continued)

TABLE A.7 *(continued)*

Conflict	Number of Alliance Portfolio Changes	List of Changes	Alliance Portfolio Volatility
		• 1924: Forces of General Feng remove Forces of Wu Peifu and Forces of Chang Tso-Lin	
		• 1924: Forces of Chang Tso-Lin remove Forces of Wu Peifu and Forces of General Feng	
		• 1926: CCP removes Republicans (or vice versa)	
		• 1926: Republicans add Kwangsi Provincial Army	
		• 1926: Forces of General Feng add Forces of Chang Tso-Lin and Forces of Sun Chuan-Feng – the "Committee of Public Safety"	
		• 1926: Forces of Chang Tso-Lin add Forces of General Feng and Forces of Sun Chuan-Feng – the "Committee of Public Safety"	
		• 1927: Forces of General Feng add Republicans, remove Forces of Chang Tso-Lin and Forces of Sun Chuan-Feng	
		• 1927: Forces of Yen Hsi-Shan remove Forces of Chang Tso-Lin, add Republicans	
		• 1927: Forces of General Feng add Western Muslims	
		• 1929: Kwangsi Provincial Army removes Republicans	
		• 1929: Forces of General Feng remove Republicans, seemingly add Forces of Yen Hsi-Shan	
		• 1929: Forces of Yen Hsi-Shan remove Republicans, seemingly add Forces of General Feng	
		• 1930: Forces of Chang Tso-Lin add Forces of General Feng and Forces of Yen Hsi-Shan	
		• 1930: Forces of Chang Tso-Lin add Republicans, remove Forces of General Feng	
		• 1930: Forces of Yen Hsi-Shan add Republicans, remove Forces of General Feng	

Conflict	Number of Alliance Portfolio Changes	List of Changes	Alliance Portfolio Volatility
Colombia (1965–present)	5	• 1985: M-19 adds ELN • 1985: EPL adds ELN • Late 1980s: FARC adds M-19, ELN, EPL • Early 1990s: M-19 adds Armed Forces of Colombia; removes FARC, ELN • Early 1990s: EPL adds Armed Forces of Colombia; removes FARC, ELN	0.0260
Congo-Kinshasa (1960–1965)	3	• 1961: Congolese National Army adds Tshombe, Kalonji • 1962: Lumumbist Forces add Baluba Tribal Forces • 1965: Congolese National Army removes Tshombe	0.1875
Congo-Kinshasa (1996–1997)	1	• No date: Mayi-Mayi group adds AFDL, removes FAZ	0.0833
Congo-Kinshasa (1998–present)	5	• 1998: Kabila adds FGOR, removes Tutsis • 1998: RCD adds Tutsis, removes Kabila • No date: Mayi-Mayi group adds Kabila, removes RCD • 2002: RCD adds Kabila • 2004: National Congress for the Defense of the People removes Kabila	0.192
Congo-Brazzaville (1993–1998)	1	• 1994: Ninjas add Cacayos	0.0556
Côte D'Ivoire (2002–2005)	2	• 2003: MPCI adds MPIGO • 2003: MJP adds MPIGO	0.125
Ethiopia (1974–1991)	6	• 1976: ELF adds EPLF • Late 1970s: EPLF removes ELF • 1980s: TPLF removes EPLF • 1986: TPLF adds EPDM • 1988: TPLF adds EPLF • Late 1980s: TPLF removes OLF (creating OPDO to compete with it)	0.0343

(continued)

TABLE A.7 *(continued)*

Conflict	Number of Alliance Portfolio Changes	List of Changes	Alliance Portfolio Volatility
Georgia (1991–1994)	0	• N/A	0
Greece (1941–1944)	3	• 1943: PAO removes ELAS (or vice versa) • 1943: ELAS adds EOK • No date: ELAS adds SNOF	0.0811
Guatemala (1965–1995)	2	• 1982: FAR adds EGP, ORPA • 1982: PGT adds EGP, ORPA	0.0142
Northeast India (1977–present)	5	• 1990: NSCN-K adds UNLF • Early 1990s: PLA adds PREPAK and KCP • Early 1990s: PREPAK adds PLA and KCP • 1997: NSCN-K adds Government of India (state government of Nagaland, to balance against NSCN-IM); removes UNLF • 2004: MCC and PWG merge	0.0164
India Kashmir Conflict (1988–1996)	4	• 1990–1993: Hizbul Mujahideen removes JKLF • 1990–1993: Ikhwan-ul Muslimeen removes JKLF • 1990–1993: Muslim Janbaz Force removes JKLF • 1993–1996: Hizbul Mujahideen removes Ikhwan-ul Mislimeen, Muslim Janbaz Force	0.0889
Indonesia (1958–1961)	3	• 1959: PRRI adds Darul Islam • 1961: Permesta removes PRRI, adds Government of Indonesia • 1961: PRRI removes Darul Islam, adds Government of Indonesia	0.1875
Iraq (1975–1996)	4	• 1983: PUK adds Government of Iraq • 1985: PUK adds KDP, removes Government of Iraq • 1994: KDP adds Government of Iraq, removes PUK • 1996: KDP removes Jash, accusing them of collaboration with PUK (unclear if this was true)	0.0556

Conflict	Number of Alliance Portfolio Changes	List of Changes	Alliance Portfolio Volatility
Iraq (2004–present)	3	• 2004: Mahdi Army adds ISF • 2005: Sons of Iraq add ISF, remove AQI • 2007: Mahdi Army removes ISF	0.0508
Israel (1974–present)	5	• 1974: PFLP adds PFLP-GC • 1993: Fatah/PLO adds Government of Israel • 2000: Fatah/PLO removes Government of Israel • 2004: Fatah/PLO adds AMB • 2005: AMB removes Fatah/PLO	0.0248
Lebanon (1975–1976)	2	• 1976: PLO adds LNM • 1976: NLP removes Phalange (or vice versa)	0.143
Lebanon (1982–1990)	6	• 1985: Amal removes PSP • 1985: PLO adds PSP and Mourabitoun, removes Amal/LNM • 1986: LF-Gaega adds Phalange (or vice versa) • No date: Hezbollah adds SLA (Israeli proxy) • 1988: Lebanese Army Faction (Aoun) removes LF-Gaega • ca. 1990: LF-Gaega adds LF-Hobeika	0.0896
Liberia (1990–1996)	2	• 1994: CRC-NPFL adds LPC, ULIMO-K, removes NPFL, LDF • 1996: ULIMO-K adds NPFL, LDF; removes ULIMO-J, AFL, LPC	0.0625
Liberia (2000–2003)	1	• 2002: LDF adds LURD, removes Liberian Government Forces	0.0769
Mexico (1911–1915)	2	• 1914: Villa removes Obregon, Carranza • 1914: Zapatistas remove Obregon, Carranza	0.125
Myanmar (1948–present)	12	• 1948: KNU adds MNDO • 1949: KNU adds CPB, PVO; removes Burmese state • 1952: KNU adds KMT • Post-1952: nine opposition alliance changes (1959, 1960, 1965, 1967, 1975, 1976, 1988, 1990, shortly thereafter) listed in UCDP conflict summary on Karen conflict	0.0396

(continued)

TABLE A.7 *(continued)*

Conflict	Number of Alliance Portfolio Changes	List of Changes	Alliance Portfolio Volatility
Ottoman Greek Revolt (1821–1833)	8	• 1821: Forces of Theodore Vladimirescu remove Philiki Eteria, add Ottoman Empire • 1821: Forces of Theodhoros Kolokotronis add Philiki Eteria • 1823: Forces of Theodhoros Kolokotronis remove Forces of Georgios Koundouriotis, Forces of Andreas Londos, Forces of Alexander Mavrokordhatos, and Forces of East Roumeli – this is the split in the resistance government between the Executive (led by Kolokotronis) and the Senate (led by Koundouriotis/Kolettis) • 1824: Forces of Andreas Londos add Forces of Theodhoros Kolokotronis, remove Forces of Georgios Koundouriotis, Forces of Alexander Mavrokordhatos, and Forces of East Roumeli • 1825: Forces of Theodhoros Kolokotronis add Forces of Georgios Koundouriotis, Forces of Alexander Mavrokordhatos, and Forces of East Roumeli (another split in government is narrowly avoided in 1827, but low-level civil strife remains) • 1831: Forces of Alexander Mavrokordhatos remove Government of Iannis Kapodhistrias and Forces of Theodhoros Kolokotronis, add Maniots • 1831: Forces of Georgios Koundouriotis remove Government of Iannis Kapodhistrias and Forces of Theodhoros Kolokotronis, add Maniots • 1832: Forces of East Roumeli remove Forces of Theodhoros Kolokotronis; add Forces of Alexander Mavrokordhatos, Forces of Georgios Koundouriotis, and Maniots	0.0860

Conflict	Number of Alliance Portfolio Changes	List of Changes	Alliance Portfolio Volatility
Ottoman Balkan Revolt (1876–1878)	0	N/A	0
Pakistan (2007–present)	0	N/A	0
Peru (1989–1997)	0	N/A	0
Philippines (1986–present)	7	• 1996: MNLF adds Government of the Philippines • 2001: MNLF-NM adds ASG, removes Government of the Philippines • Mid-2000s: MILF adds Government of the Philippines: "joint action arrangements with the [Filipino government] for the interdiction of criminal elements, and its actual cooperation with the [Filipino armed forces] in striking against such elements as the Pentagon gang" (Santos 2005, p. 21) • 2007: ASG adds MILF, MNLF, MNLF-HM • 2007: MILF adds ASG, seemingly removes Government of the Philippines • 2007: MNLF adds ASG, seemingly removes Government of the Philippines • 2008: CPP adds Mindanao rebels	0.0574
Russia (1917–1922)	7	• 1918: Komuch adds Provisional Government of Autonomous Siberia, creating the Directorate • 1918: Czech Legion removes Komuch/Directorate • 1918: Ex-Tsarists in Siberia add Kolchak (formerly Komuch) • 1919: Red Army removes Ukrainian Anarchists under Nestor Makhno • 1920: Volunteer Army adds Kuban Cossacks	0.125

(continued)

TABLE A.7 *(continued)*

Conflict	Number of Alliance Portfolio Changes	List of Changes	Alliance Portfolio Volatility
		• 1920: Red Army adds Ukrainian Anarchists under Nestor Makhno • 1920 (later): Ukrainian Anarchists under Nestor Makhno remove Red Army	
Sierra Leone (1991–2001)	1	• 1996: SLA removes CDF	0.0244
Somalia (1981–present)	7	• 1991: SNM removes USC • 1991: SPM removes USC • No date: SNF adds SSA, removes Barre • Late 1997: SNA adds SSA (or vice versa) • 2001: SNA adds RRA to form SRRC • 2001: SPM adds SRRC • ca. 2001: TNG adds Juba Valley Alliance	0.0707
Sri Lanka (1983–1990)	4	• 1986: LTTE removes TELO, EPRLF • No date: LTTE adds Sri Lankan state • No date: Sri Lankan state removes LTTE (or vice versa) • No date: EPDP removes EPRLF, PLOTE, and TELO	0.0851
Sri Lanka (2004–2009)	1	• 2007: TMVP adds Government of Sri Lanka	0.0556
Sudan (2003–present)	5	• No date: JEM-SLM/A form alliance against government • After 2005: SLM/A and JEM occasionally remove each other • 2006: Government adds SLM-Minawi • No date: JEM and some SLM splinters ally into National Redemption Front (NRF) • 2009: SLM-Unity adds JEM	0.0877
Tajikistan (1992–1997)	0	N/A	0
Uganda (1980–2002)	5	• 1985: FEDEMU adds Ugandan state • 1985: FUNA adds Ugandan state • 1985: UFM adds Ugandan state • 1985: UNRF adds Ugandan state • 1988: UPDA adds NRM/A (Ugandan state)	0.0588

Conflict	Number of Alliance Portfolio Changes	List of Changes	Alliance Portfolio Volatility
Western Sahara (1975–1979)	1	• 1979: Government of Mauritania removes Morocco, adds POLISARIO (subsequently signing a peace agreement and exiting the conflict, making it two-sided)	0.0667
Yugoslavia/ Bosnia (1941–1945)	2	• 1942: Chetniks add Ustashe, remove Partisans • 1943: Muslim Forces add Partisans; remove Ustashe, Chetniks	0.0833
Zimbabwe (1972–1979)	1	• 1976: ZAPU adds ZANU	0.0417

[36] Some cases such as Russia are missing a significant amount of data on group-years, because we cannot be sure how long some groups fought in their conflicts. These missing observations – 50 out of 397 group-level observations total – are currently coded as blanks, potentially biasing estimates of APV upward for those conflicts since the sum of group-years is in the denominator of this metric. However, if we code these 50 missing observations as lasting 1 group-year each (assuming that any significant warring group coded in this dataset probably stayed active in the conflict for at least a year), the substantive statistical results shown in Chapter 8 are the same.

TABLE A.8. *Classification of Intergroup Manpower by Conflict*

Conflict	Power Distribution Hegemonic or Balanced?	Rationale
Afghanistan (1978–1992)	Hegemonic	Only all mujahedin groups together were close to a match for the PDPA; even in the two-sided context, PDPA appears to have had the advantage.
Afghanistan (1992–2001)	Balanced	Until 1996, no minimum winning coalitions of manpower existed.
Afghanistan (2002–present)	Hegemonic	The combination of Afghan Security Forces and the Northern Alliance has always had a minimum winning coalition of manpower, even in 2006–2007.
Algeria (1954–1962)	Hegemonic	French Armed Forces were much larger than the insurgent groups.

(continued)

TABLE A.8 *(continued)*

Conflict	Power Distribution Hegemonic or Balanced?	Rationale
Algeria (1992–2004)	Hegemonic	Algerian Armed Forces appear to have always had a minimum winning coalition of manpower.
Angola (1961–1975)	Hegemonic	The Army of Portugal dwarfed the insurgent groups.
Angola (1975–2002)	Hegemonic	MPLA appears to have had a minimum winning coalition of manpower for most of the conflict, especially when foreign forces (Cuba, Soviet Union, South Africa) are taken into account.
Austria (1848–1849)	Balanced	Austrians and Hungarians were roughly equal in terms of territorial control, and while the Austrian army was large (up to 80,000 on a front), the Hungarians also had a substantial mobilization capacity (up to 200,000 mobilized against the Balkan counterinsurgency)
Bosnia and Herzegovina (1992–1995)	Balanced	Throughout the war, no minimum winning coalitions of manpower.
Burundi (1991–2003)	Hegemonic	Although data are limited, the Army of Burundi appears to have had a minimum winning coalition of manpower from at least 1998 onward.
Cambodia (1978–1991)	Hegemonic	People's Republic of Kampuchea army appears much larger than insurgent groups, except in mid-1980s when it did not have a minimum winning coalition of manpower (but with Vietnamese troops, it probably did).
Chad (1969–1997)	Balanced	Aside from brief periods in the late 1980s and early 1990s when FAN had more than 28,000 men under arms, no one group appears dominant.
Chad (1998–present)	Balanced	Poor data, but no evidence of a minimum winning coalition of manpower.
China (1850–1878)	Balanced	The Taiping Rebels were dominant in the 1850s, but by the 1860s (when the alliance activity takes place), multiple groups were able to mobilize six-figure armies.
China (1911–1931)	Balanced	At least four warring groups had the ability to raise six-figure armies.
Colombia (1965–present)	Hegemonic	The Colombian Army appears to have had a minimum winning coalition of manpower throughout the conflict.
Congo-Kinshasa (1960–1965)	Balanced	After 1960 coup, no clearly dominant group.

Congo-Kinshasa (1996–1997)	Balanced	Zairean forces appear evenly matched with Rwandan-national rebel forces; other groups small.
Congo-Kinshasa (1998–present)	Balanced	No minimum winning coalitions of manpower apparent.
Congo-Brazzaville (1993–1998)	Hegemonic	With Angolan support, Cobras appear dominant.
Côte D'Ivoire (2002–2005)	Hegemonic	National Army of Côte D'Ivoire appears to have had a strong minimum winning coalition of manpower.
Ethiopia (1974–1991)	Balanced	Army of Ethiopia may have had a slight advantage in the 1970s; in the 1980s, the Army appears roughly matched with EPLF and TPLF combined.
Georgia (1991–1994)	Balanced	Including Mkhedroni (missing data), there is probably no minimum winning coalition of manpower.
Greece (1941–1944)	Balanced	Seemingly no strong minimum winning coalition of manpower; however, Nazi Germany would obviously be a hegemon if it were included as a group.
Guatemala (1965–1995)	Hegemonic	Guatemalan Army is much larger than the insurgent groups, even combined.
Northeast India (1977–present)	Hegemonic	Indian Army is much larger than the insurgent groups in the northeast, even combined.
India Kashmir Conflict (1988–1996)	Hegemonic	Salehyan dataset estimates roughly 5,000 for Kashmiri rebel strength, much smaller than Indian security forces.
Indonesia (1958–1961)	Hegemonic	Insurgent groups were sizable but not as large as Indonesian Army, even combined.
Iraq (1975–1996)	Hegemonic	Iraqi forces were larger than Kurdish forces until 1991, when Jash defection to Kurdish side led to relative parity.
Iraq (2004–present)	Hegemonic	Iraqi Army has minimum winning coalition of manpower, especially when foreign forces are included.
Israel (1974–present)	Hegemonic	Although Fatah/PLO is a large insurgent group, the Israeli Defense Forces are much larger; the other insurgent groups are fairly small.
Lebanon (1975–1976)	Balanced	No minimum winning coalition of manpower.
Lebanon (1982–1990)	Balanced	Only candidate for a minimum winning coalition of manpower is Amal in the early 1980s, which, given splits, seems unlikely.
Liberia (1990–1996)	Balanced	Major warring groups basically at parity.

(continued)

TABLE A.8 *(continued)*

Conflict	Power Distribution Hegemonic or Balanced?	Rationale
Liberia (2000–2003)	Balanced	No clear minimum winning coalitions of manpower.
Mexico (1911–1915)	Balanced	Federal Army of Mexico was large but faced major challenges from the Villa/Zapatista coalition, which in 1914 controlled "most of Mexico" (Tutino 1986, 338)
Myanmar (1948–present)	Balanced	PVO appears dominant in late 1940s, although uncertain if the number of combatants (100,000) can be trusted; later, no minimum winning coalition of manpower.
Ottoman Greek Revolt (1821–1833)	Hegemonic	Ottoman Imperial Forces appear to dwarf insurgent groups.
Ottoman Balkan Revolt (1876–1878)	Hegemonic	Ottoman Imperial Forces appear to dwarf insurgent groups.
Pakistan (2007–present)	Hegemonic	Most trustworthy estimate of Pakistani counterinsurgency forces (Lalwani 2009) puts state far ahead of insurgent groups.
Peru (1989–1997)	Hegemonic	Peruvian Army dwarfs both insurgent groups.
Philippines (1986–present)	Balanced	CPP, MNLF, and MILF are all substantially sized, and together outnumber government forces.
Russia (1917–1922)	Hegemonic	Red Army, with upward of 5 million combatants, dwarfs insurgent groups.
Sierra Leone (1991–2001)	Balanced	Three major groups, including state army, appear to be at rough parity.
Somalia (1981–present)	Balanced	No clearly dominant actor in 2000s; possible that Somali Armed Forces were dominant in 1980s, but force size is likely overestimated.
Sri Lanka (1983–1990)	Hegemonic	Armed Forces of Sri Lanka clearly dominant for all but the very beginning of conflict.
Sri Lanka (2004–2009)	Hegemonic	Armed Forces of Sri Lanka clearly dominant.
Sudan (2003–present)	Balanced	Janjawiid at peak size (20,000 in 2003–2004) would have minimum winning coalition of manpower of 5,000, but peak size may be inflated and was likely not maintained for long.
Tajikistan (1992–1997)	Balanced	Two major groups (state army and UTO) appear to have been more or less at parity.

Conflict	Power Distribution Hegemonic or Balanced?	Rationale
Uganda (1980–2002)	Balanced	Possible Ugandan Army dominance in early 1980s; otherwise, no minimum winning coalition of manpower.
Western Sahara (1975–1979)	Hegemonic	Mauritanian Army was quite small (smaller than POLISARIO), but Moroccan Army was substantially larger than the other two forces combined.
Yugoslavia/ Bosnia (1941–1945)	Balanced	Until Partisans swell to 120,000 in 1944, actors appear to be roughly at parity.
Zimbabwe (1972–1979)	Hegemonic	Armed Forces of Rhodesia appear dominant.

TABLE A.9. *Coding of Warring Groups that Split during Their Conflict*

Conflict	Group Name	Notes
Afghanistan (1978–1992)	Hizb-i Islami	Split in 1979.
Afghanistan (1978–1992)	PDPA	Northern militias split off in 1992.
Afghanistan (1992–2001)	Wahdat	1994 split of Wahdat between the Mazara and Akbari factions.
Afghanistan (1992–2001)	Taliban	Split in 2001.
Afghanistan (2002– present)	Taliban	Numerous Taliban defections noted in Christia and Semple (2009).
Afghanistan (2002– present)	Hizb-i-Islami	Split in 2003.
Algeria (1954–1962)	French Armed Forces	OAS essentially split from the French military in 1961.
Algeria (1992–2004)	GIA	GIA split in the 1990s, leading to the formation of the GSPC.
Angola (1961–1975)	FNLA	Savimbi split from FLNA (where he was the Foreign Minister) in 1964.
Angola (1975–2002)	MPLA	Failed intra-MPLA coup attempt of Alves against Neto in 1977, put down with Cuban help.
Angola (1975–2002)	UNITA	Split.

(continued)

TABLE A.9 *(continued)*

Conflict	Group Name	Notes
Angola (1975–2002)	FLEC	FLEC split and remerged repeatedly.
Austria (1848–1849)	Viennese Radicals	Viennese radicals became factionalized between bourgeoisie/proletariat and German/Hungarian/Slavic camps.
Austria (1848–1849)	Hungarian forces	Croats, Serbs, Romanians, and Slovaks split off from Hungarian revolution because of "Magyarization."
Bosnia-Herzegovina (1992–1995)	Army of Bosnia-Herzegovina	Abdić declared autonomy from Izetbegovic in 1993.
Burundi (1991–2003)	Palipehutu	Frolina broke from Palipehutu in 1990 before the start of the conflict, and the FNL (its armed wing) broke in late 1991 after a disastrous offensive.
Burundi (1991–2003)	Palipehutu-FNL	Split in 2001.
Burundi (1991–2003)	CNDD	1998 split of CNDD-FDD from CNDD.
Burundi (1991–2003)	CNDD-FDD	Split in 2001.
Chad (1969–1997)	Second Liberation Army	Split into Habre and Gukuni factions.
Chad (1969–1997)	FAN	Deby, a subordinate of Habre in the FAN, launched a failed coup.
Chad (1969–1997)	MPS	MPS split around 1992, when CNR (a splinter) broke off.
Chad (1998–present)	MDJT	In 2002, after the death of its leader, a faction of MDJT broke away and joined the government.
Chad (1998–present)	UFDD	Around 2006, the UFDD split.
China (1850–1878)	Taiping Rebels	Takeover attempt and major internal power struggle among the Taiping rebels in 1856.
China (1911–1931)	Military Faction of Yuan Shih-Kai	1913: Governor of Kwangtung Province split off from Military Faction of Yuan Shih-Kai over KMT expulsion, sided with KMT.
China (1911–1931)	Military Faction of Ch'en Chiung-Ming	1913: "Several of Ch'en's military colleagues who did not agree with his liberal views seized control of various parts of the territory" (Botjer 1979, p. 19).

Conflict	Group Name	Notes
China (1911–1931)	CCP	1923: CCP faction ("Paris Group"), including Chou En-Lai, split from main party in early 1920s.
China (1911–1931)	Republicans/KMT	1925: Leftist factions start to split off from the KMT; also, there was a Hankow/Shanghai split in 1927.
China (1911–1931)	Forces of Wu Peifu	1926: General T'ang Sheng-Chih defected from Forces of Wu Peifu, joined up with KMT.
China (1911–1931)	Forces of Chang Tso-Lin	1926: Students split off from Forces of Chang Tso-Lin to join Forces of General Feng; also an attempted coup in 1929.
China (1911–1931)	Forces of General Sun Chuan-Feng	1927: Defectors left Forces of General Sun Chuan-Feng for KMT.
Colombia (1965–present)	FARC	FARC split led to the formation of M-19.
Colombia (1965–present)	ELN	Serious factionalization within both ELN and EPL in the late 1960s and 1970s.
Colombia (1965–present)	EPL	Serious factionalization within both ELN and EPL in the late 1960s and 1970s.
Colombia (1965–present)	Autodefensas	In 2002, the Autodefensas "dissolved" and then "reconstituted" the organization, trying to rid it of factions involved in the drug trade (globalsecurity.org).
Congo (Kinshasa) (1960–1965)	Congolese National Army	Failed coup by Kasavubu against his premier, Lumumba.
Congo (Kinshasa) (1960–1965)	Katangan Armed Forces	Katanga itself experienced a secessionist movement led by Jason Sendwe.
Congo (Kinshasa) (1998–present)	Congolese Armed Forces	Kabila assassinated in 2001, likely by a bodyguard during a failed coup attempt.
Congo (Kinshasa) (1998–present)	RCD	RCD split when its two main state sponsors, Uganda and Rwanda, split.
Congo (Kinshasa) (1998–present)	RCD-ML	Split in 2000 (also taken over).

(continued)

TABLE A.9 *(continued)*

Conflict	Group Name	Notes
Congo (Brazzaville) (1993–1998)	Ninjas	Some Ninjas were drawn off by Ntsiloulous, a religious movement led by a self-proclaimed prophet.
Côte D'Ivoire (2002–2005)	National Army of Côte D'Ivoire	Apparent attempted coup within Ivoirian army.
Côte D'Ivoire (2002–2005)	MPCI	Substantial infighting within MPCI during 2003.
Ethiopia (1974–1991)	Army of Ethiopia	Officers' faction split off from Army of Ethiopia in 1989 (Ethiopian Democratic Officers' Revolutionary Movement), joined EPDRF.
Ethiopia (1974–1991)	ELF	The EPLF formed from splinters of the ELF, an early predecessor, in the 1970s.
Ethiopia (1974–1991)	OLF	IFLO was an OLF splinter.
Ethiopia (1974–1991)	EPRP	In 1980, EPDM split from EPRP and largely joined up with TPLF.
Greece (1941–1944)	ELAS	ELAS eventually had defection problems with EDES and the British.
Greece (1941–1944)	EDES	EDES was factionalized, and its Athens branch became "tainted with collaboration" in 1943 (Hondros (1983), pp. 106–107)
Greece (1941–1944)	EKKA	Factionalization problems among EKKA – specifically, generals deserting or joining up with ELAS.
Greece (1941–1944)	PAO	PAO also had a problem with desertion to ELAS.
Guatemala (1965–1995)	Guatemalan Army	M-13 was the product of a failed coup in 1960 by army officers.
Guatemala (1965–1995)	PGT	FAR was formed by elements of earlier guerrilla groups such as M-13 and from the PGT, from which it split in 1968.
Northeast India (1977– present)	PWG	1980s: PWG suffered an "internal crisis," likely a split (Kujur 2008, p. 13).
Northeast India (1977– present)	ATTF	1992: ATTF split, and a faction was renamed "All Tripura Tiger Force" – the other faction surrendered.
Northeast India (1977– present)	NLFT	2001: NLFT split "along ethnic lines" (UCDP conflict summary).
India Kashmir Conflict (1988–1996)	Ikhwan-ul Muslimeen	Split.

Conflict	Group Name	Notes
India Kashmir Conflict (1988–1996)	Muslim Janbaz Force	Split.
Indonesia (1958–1961)	PRRI	1961: PRRI split into amnesty seekers and fighters as military victory drew near.
Iraq (1975–1996)	Iraqi Army	1991: "Jash" (Kurdish tribal forces organized by Saddam in 1980s) deserted from Iraqi Army and reconciled with KDP.
Iraq (1975–1996)	PUK	1979: KSM (Socialist Movement of Kurdistan) faction split from PUK and joined up with a minor party.
Iraq (1975–1996)	KDP	1981: Kurdistan Popular Democratic Party split off from KDP (known as KDP-PL at the time).
Iraq (2004–present)	Iraqi Security Forces	"Facilities Protection Service" has reportedly split off from Iraqi Security Forces, collaborating with the Mahdi Army. Split again into ISF and Basra.
Iraq (2004–present)	Mahdi Army	Al-Sadr (Mahdi Army) claimed his group had "rogue elements" that were continuing attacks (UCDP conflict summary).
Iraq (2004–present)	Badr Brigades	"Shaybani network" split off from Badr Brigade some time before 2007.
Iraq (2004–present)	Dawa Militia	Dawa Party split in 2007.
Iraq (2004–present)	Al Qaeda in Iraq	By 2008, AQI was "experiencing the defection of members" (State Department Country Reports on Terrorism 2008).
Iraq (2004–present)	Ansar-al-Islam	JAAS (Ansar-al-Islam) split in 2007.
Iraq (2004–present)	1920 Revolutionary Brigade	Split.
Israel (1974–present)	Fatah/PLO	UCDP conflict summary: "The security situation within the territories under control of the Palestinian Authority deteriorated throughout 2005 and the end of 2006 as violent criminality became increasingly common as the [Palestinian National Authority], which had been shattered by Israeli attacks, could not control the activities of militant factions and armed gangs."
Lebanon (1975–1976)	PLO	Arafat began to lose control over the PLO in late 1976.

(continued)

TABLE A.9 *(continued)*

Conflict	Group Name	Notes
Lebanon (1975–1976)	Lebanese Army	Lebanese Army began to split apart in January 1976.
Lebanon (1982–1990)	Amal	Hezbollah split from Amal, possibly in 1982; Hashem split from Amal in 1987 but was put down by Berri.
Lebanon (1982–1990)	LF-Gaega	Split in 1984 (6th Army Brigade defected).
Liberia (1990–1996)	NPFL	INPFL split from NPFL as NPFL seemed to approach victory. 1994: CRC-NPFL split from NPFL.
Liberia (1990–1996)	INPFL	After killing Doe, Johnson went into exile and the INPFL disintegrated.
Liberia (1990–1996)	ULIMO	1993: LPC split from ULIMO. ULIMO split ethnically into Krahn (ULIMO-J) and Mandingo (ULIMO-K) factions.
Liberia (2000–2003)	LURD	2003 split of MODEL from LURD.
Myanmar (1948– present)	CPB	Split in 1989.
Myanmar (1948– present)	KNU	Splits in 1964, 1995, and 1997.
Ottoman Greek Revolt (1821–1833)	Forces of the Ottoman Empire	1821: Ottoman Empire faced attempted coup by Greeks in Turkish Navy; also defection of Theodhoros Negris.
Ottoman Greek Revolt (1821–1833)	Philiki Eteria	1821: Various factions split off from Philiki Eteria after its devastating defeat and restarted the revolution in the Peloponnese.
Ottoman Greek Revolt (1821–1833)	Forces of Alexander Mavrokord-hatos	1822: Split in Forces of Alexander Mavrokordhatos as Captain Gogos Bakolas defected to the Turks.
Ottoman Greek Revolt (1821–1833)	Forces of East Roumeli	1825: Forces of East Roumeli split when Odysseus Andhroutsos joined the Turks.
Ottoman Greek Revolt (1821–1833)	Forces of Theodhoros Kolokotronis	1830: Maniots split from Forces of Theodhoros Kolokotronis and formed opposition to Government of Iannis Kapodhistrias.
Pakistan (2007– present)	TNSM	Split in 2007, with one faction allying with TTP and the other joining with the government.

Conflict	Group Name	Notes
Pakistan (2007–present)	TTP	MTT split from TTP.
Peru (1989–1997)	Government of Peru	1992: Army faction within Government of Peru plotted a coup against Fujimori, which was abandoned only when Guzman was captured in September.
Peru (1989–1997)	Sendero Luminoso	1993: Sendero Luminoso split following the 1992 capture of its leader, Abimael Guzman. The factions were "pacifists" (pro-Guzman) and "hardliners" (under Oscar Ramirez Durand).
Philippines (1986–present)	Government of the Philippines	1989: Attempted coup attempt against Government of the Philippines. Successful 2001 coup appeared unrelated to these conflicts.
Philippines (1986–present)	CPP	Late 1980s: Factions split off the CPP in the wake of an "ideological purge" (UCDP conflict summary); one such faction was the Alex Boncayao Brigade.
Philippines (1986–present)	MNLF	Several factions split off MNLF, including ASG (1991), MNLF-NM (2001), and MNLF-HM (2007).
Russia (1917–1922)	Red Army	Splitting factions included the Left SRs, the Armenians in Azerbaijan, parts of the Third Red Army, and the Kronstadt Reds.
Russia (1917–1922)	Volunteer Army	Kuban Regionalists split off in 1919; more revolts later that year.
Russia (1917–1922)	Provisional Government of Autonomous Siberia	Komuch split off in 1918.
Russia (1917–1922)	Komuch	Massive defections from Kolchak (who took over Komuch) in November 1919.
Russia (1917–1922)	Ukrainian Government	Numerous splinter groups emerged in early 1919.
Russia (1917–1922)	Supreme Administration of the North	Mutiny by First Archangelsk Infantry Regiment in early 1919.
Russia (1917–1922)	Northwestern White Army	Renegade generals split off in late 1919.
Sierra Leone (1991–2001)	Sierra Leone Army	AFRC split from SLA.

(continued)

TABLE A.9 *(continued)*

Conflict	Group Name	Notes
Sierra Leone (1991–2001)	RUF	West Side Boys formed from elements of SLA, RUF, and AFRC.
Sierra Leone (1991–2001)	AFRC	West Side Boys formed from elements of SLA, RUF, and AFRC.
Somalia (1981–present)	SNM	Intra-SNM, early 1990s "full-fledged war between coalitions of Isaaq clans" (Compagnon 1998, p. 82)
Somalia (1981–present)	USC	The USC disintegrated after it seized Mogadishu.
Somalia (1981–present)	ICU	The Ethiopian defeat of the ICU caused it to fracture, with hard-line al Shabaab continuing the fight.
Sri Lanka (1983–1990)	EROS	Split twice in the 1980s.
Sri Lanka (1983–1990)	TELO	Split into three factions around 1986.
Sri Lanka (1983–1990)	PLOTE	Numerous splits and attempted takeovers, 1984–1986.
Sri Lanka (1983–1990)	EPRLF	1986 or 1987 split.
Sri Lanka (2004–2009)	LTTE	LTTE split in 2004, generating the Karuna group (TMVP)
Sudan (2003–present)	Janjawiid	In 2007, the Janjawiid split. "By early 2007, Mujeeb [SLA deputy] had arranged three non-aggression treaties with Janjawiid groups and more than 500 Janjawiid (including a cousin of Musa Hilal) had left their camps and been integrated into the SLA's in Jebel Marra" (Flint and De Waal 2008, p. 259).
Sudan (2003–present)	SLM/SLA	By 2005, both JEM and SLM/SLA began fracturing and producing splinter groups.
Sudan (2003–present)	JEM	By 2005, both JEM and SLM/SLA began fracturing and producing splinter groups.
Uganda (1980–2002)	Ugandan Army	Ugandan Army split in 1980, leading to the eventual formation of NRM/A.
Uganda (1980–2002)	UPA	UPA split in 1988.
Uganda (1980–2002)	FUNA	FUNA split in 1981, leading to the formation of UNRF.
Western Sahara (1975–1979)	POLISARIO	1976: Some minor defectors from POLISARIO joined up with Morocco and/or Mauritania.

Conflict	Group Name	Notes
Yugoslavia/ Bosnia (1941–1945)	Ustashe	1942: Split of Hadziefendic's Muslim forces from the Ustashe. Split again in October 1943, with Colonel Filipovic defecting to Partisans.
Yugoslavia/ Bosnia (1941–1945)	Chetniks	Defections to Partisans in mid-1943.
Yugoslavia/ Bosnia (1941–1945)	Muslims	Political movement of pro-Chetnik Muslims in late 1942 in Herzegovina (Muslim People's Military Organization, Izmet Popovac, Mohamed Pasic).

TABLE A.10. *Coding of Warring Groups that Experienced Internal Takeovers during Their Conflict*

Conflict	Group Name	Notes
Afghanistan (1978–1992)	Armed Forces of Afghanistan	PDPA takeover by the Parcham faction over the Khalq faction.
Afghanistan (1978–1992)	Shura-I-Inqilab-I Ittegaq-I Islami Afghanistan	Islamist takeover among the Shi'a/Hazara groups.
Afghanistan (1978–1992)	Harakat-I-Islami	Islamist takeover among the Shi'a/Hazara groups.
Afghanistan (1978–1992)	Sazman-I Nasr-I Islam-yi Afghanistan	Islamist takeover among the Shi'a/Hazara groups.
Afghanistan (1978–1992)	Pazdaran-I Jihad-I Islami	Islamist takeover among the Shi'a/Hazara groups.
Afghanistan (1992–2001)	Jinbush	1997: Takeover of Jinbush by Malik Pahlawan from Dostum.
Afghanistan (1992–2001)	Hizb-i-Islami	1995–1995: Takeover by Taliban.
Algeria (1992–2004)	GSPC	Leader deposed in 2003.
Angola (1961–1975)	MPLA	1972–1974: Factional conflicts in the MPLA. Three factions: Neto, Chipenda, and de Andrade. Neto prevailed.
Austria (1848–1849)	Army of Austria	Military coup against the Hapsburg government in late 1848.

(continued)

TABLE A.10 *(continued)*

Conflict	Group Name	Notes
Bosnia-Herzegovina (1992–1995)	Croat Defense Council	Croat takeover of Mate Boban over Stjepan Kljujić in 1993.
Burundi (1991–2003)	Army of Burundi	President deposed in a 1996 coup.
Chad (1969–1997)	Chadian Armed Forces (FAT)	1975: Coup killed Tombalbaye; Malloun took office.
Chad (1969–1997)	FAN	After his failed coup, Deby formed MPS, and then returned to take over.
China (1911–1931)	Republicans/KMT	1926: Chiang staged a takeover of the KMT.
China (1911–1931)	CCP	1927: Takeover in CCP as Ch'en Tu-Hsiu was ousted, succeeded by Mao.
Congo (Kinshasa) (1960–1965)	Congolese Armed Forces	A few days after the failed coup, Mobutu ousted Lumumba in a successful coup.
Congo (Kinshasa) (1998–present)	RCD-ML	Taken over in 2000 (also split).
Congo (Brazzaville) (1993–1998)	Cocoyes	Lissouba lost real control of the Cocoyes after he fled the country in October 1997.
Côte D'Ivoire (2002–2005)	MPIGO	MPIGO's leader, Felix Doh, was "executed by his own forces on 24 August 2003 upon asking them to respect the peace accords" (Kohler 2003, p. 6).
Georgia (1991–1994)	Government of Georgia	December 1991 coup ousted Gamsakhurdia.
Guatemala (1965–1995)	Guatemalan Army	Successful coup in 1982 (other attempted coups coded as splits).
India (1977–present)	PLA	Apparent takeover of Indian PLA. "Bisheshwar Singh ultimately came to a violent end, probably at the hands of his former comrades in August 1994" (Chadha 2005, p. 316).

Conflict	Group Name	Notes
Lebanon (1982–1990)	PLO	Syrian backing helped anti-Arafat PLO faction gain dominant position in Lebanon refugee camps in intra-Palestinian battles.
Liberia (1990–1996)	ULIMO-J	1996: Violent takeover of ULIMO-J by William Kayree.
Mexico (1911–1915)	Federal Army of Mexico	1913: Takeover when General Huerta overthrew Madero.
Myanmar (1948–present)	Burmese Armed Forces	1958 and 1962: Takeovers of the Burmese government.
Ottoman Greek Revolt (1821–1833)	Forces of East Roumeli	1822: Forces of East Roumeli taken over by Odysseus Andhroutsos.
Philippines (1986–present)	Communist Party of the Philippines	1992: Takeover of CPP as Jose Maria Sison returns from the Netherlands.
Russia (1917–1922)	Volunteer Army	In 1920, Denikin was ousted from command of the Volunteer Army and replaced by General Wrangel.
Russia (1917–1922)	Komuch	Komuch/Directorate taken over in 1918 by Admiral Kolchak.
Russia (1917–1922)	Ukrainian Government	Pro-German Ukrainian Government overthrown in 1919 by Simon Petliura.
Russia (1917–1922)	Crimean Government	Pro-German Crimean Government overthrown in 1919 by a Kadet coalition.
Sierra Leone (1991–2001)	Sierra Leone Army	NPRC takeover of SL government from APC in a coup in 1992.
Uganda (1980–2002)	Ugandan Army	General Okello overthrew Obote in 1985 and took over.
Uganda (1980–2002)	Lord's Resistance Army	HSM (LRA precursor) taken over in 1988 by Kony.
Western Sahara (1975–1979)	Government of Mauritania	Government of Mauritania taken over in a 1978 coup related to the conflict. New president is ousted less than a year later, in April 1979.

TABLE A.11. *Characteristics of Warring Groups that Split*

Conflict	Warring Group	Leader of Split-Off Subgroup Influential Prior to War Onset?	Split-Off Subgroup Regionally Based (Distinct from Main Group)?
Afghanistan (1978–1992)	Armed Forces of Afghanistan	Yes	No
Afghanistan (1978–1992)	Hizb-i-Islami (Hizb)	Yes	Yes
Afghanistan (1992–2001)	Hizb-i-Wahdat-I Islami-yi Afghanistan (Wahdat)	Yes	Yes
Afghanistan (1992–2001)	Taliban	No	Yes
Afghanistan (2002–present)	Taliban	Yes	Yes
Afghanistan (2002–present)	Hizb-i-Islami (Hizb)	Yes	Cannot Determine
Algeria (1954–1962)	French Armed Forces	Yes	No
Algeria (1992–2004)	Armed Islamic Group (GIA)	No	No
Angola (1961–1975)	National Front for the Liberation of Angola (FNLA)	Yes	Yes
Angola (1975–2002)	Popular Movement for the Liberation of Angola (MPLA)	Yes	No
Angola (1975–2002)	UNITA	Cannot Determine	Yes
Angola (1975–2002)	Front for the Liberation of the Enclave of Cabinda (FLEC)	Yes	Cannot Determine
Austria (1848–1849)	Viennese Radicals	Cannot Determine	Yes
Austria (1848–1849)	Hungarian Forces	Yes	Yes
Bosnia (1992–1995)	Army of Bosnia-Herzegovina	Yes	Yes
Burundi (1991–2003)	Party for the Liberation of the Hutu People (Palipehutu)	Cannot Determine	No
Burundi (1991–2003)	Party for the Liberation of the Hutu People – Forces for National Liberation (Palipehutu-FNL)	Yes	No

Conflict	Warring Group	Leader of Split-Off Subgroup Influential Prior to War Onset?	Split-Off Subgroup Regionally Based (Distinct from Main Group)?
Burundi (1991–2003)	National Council for the Defense of Democracy (CNDD)	Yes	Yes
Burundi (1991–2003)	National Council for the Defense of Democracy – Forces for the Defense of Democracy (CNDD-FDD)	Yes	Yes
Chad (1969–1997)	Second Liberation Army	Yes	Yes
Chad (1969–1997)	Forces Armées du Nord (FAN)	No	Yes
Chad (1969–1997)	MPS	Cannot Determine	Yes
Chad (1998–present)	MDJT	Yes	Yes
Chad (1998–present)	UFDD	Yes	Yes
China (1850–1878)	Taiping Rebels	Yes	No
China (1911–1931)	Military Faction of Yuan Shih-Kai	Yes	Yes
China (1911–1931)	Military Faction of Ch'en Chiung-Ming	Yes	Yes
China (1911–1931)	CCP	No	No
China (1911–1931)	Republicans/KMT	Cannot Determine	Yes
China (1911–1931)	Forces of Wu Peifu	Yes	Yes
China (1911–1931)	Forces of Chang Tso-Lin	Yes	Yes
China (1911–1931)	Forces of General Sun Chuan-Feng	Cannot Determine	Cannot Determine
Colombia (1965–present)	Revolutionary Armed Forces of Colombia (FARC)	Yes	Yes
Colombia (1965–present)	National Liberation Army (ELN)	Cannot Determine	Yes
Colombia (1965–present)	People's Liberation Army (EPL)	Cannot Determine	Yes
Colombia (1965–present)	Autodefensas	Cannot Determine	Yes
Congo (Kinshasa) (1960–1965)	Congolese National Army	Yes	No
Congo (Kinshasa) (1960–1965)	Katangan Armed Forces	Yes	Yes

(continued)

TABLE A.11 *(continued)*

Conflict	Warring Group	Leader of Split-Off Subgroup Influential Prior to War Onset?	Split-Off Subgroup Regionally Based (Distinct from Main Group)?
Congo (Kinshasa) (1998–present)	Congolese Armed Forces	Yes	No
Congo (Kinshasa) (1998–present)	Congolese Rally for Democracy (RCD)	Yes	Yes
Congo (Kinshasa) (1998–present)	RCD-ML	Yes	Yes
Congo (Brazzaville) (1993–1998)	Ninjas	Yes	Yes
Côte D'Ivoire (2002–2005)	National Army of Côte D'Ivoire	Yes	Yes
Côte D'Ivoire (2002–2005)	Patriotic Movement of Côte D'Ivoire (MPCI)	Yes	Yes
Ethiopia (1974–1991)	Army of Ethiopia	No	No
Ethiopia (1974–1991)	Eritrean Liberation Front (ELF)	Yes	Yes
Ethiopia (1974–1991)	Oromo Liberation Front (OLF)	No	Yes
Ethiopia (1974–1991)	EPRP	Cannot Determine	Yes
Greece (1941–1944)	National People's Liberation Army (ELAS)	Cannot Determine	Yes
Greece (1941–1944)	National Republican Greek League (EDES)	Cannot Determine	Yes
Greece (1941–1944)	National and Social Liberation (EKKA)	Yes	No
Greece (1941–1944)	Panhellenic Liberation Organization (PAO)	No	No
Guatemala (1965–1995)	Guatemalan Army	No	No
Guatemala (1965–1995)	Guatemalan Party of Labor (PGT)	Cannot Determine	Yes
Northeast India (1977–present)	PWG	Cannot Determine	Cannot Determine
Northeast India (1977–present)	ATTF	Cannot Determine	Cannot Determine
Northeast India (1977–present)	NLFT	Cannot Determine	Cannot Determine

Conflict	Warring Group	Leader of Split-Off Subgroup Influential Prior to War Onset?	Split-Off Subgroup Regionally Based (Distinct from Main Group)?
India Kashmir Conflict (1988–1996)	Ikhwan-ul Muslimeen	Cannot Determine	Cannot Determine
India Kashmir Conflict (1988–1996)	Muslim Janbaz Force	Cannot Determine	Cannot Determine
Indonesia (1958–1961)	PRRI	Yes	Cannot Determine
Iraq (1975–1996)	PUK	Cannot Determine	Cannot Determine
Iraq (1975–1996)	KDP	Yes	Yes
Iraq (1975–1996)	Iraqi Army	Cannot Determine	Yes
Iraq (2004–present)	Iraqi Security Forces (ISF)	Yes	Yes
Iraq (2004–present)	Mahdi Army	No	No
Iraq (2004–present)	Badr Brigades	Yes	Cannot Determine
Iraq (2004–present)	Dawa militia	Yes	Yes
Iraq (2004–present)	Al Qaeda in Iraq (AQI)	Cannot Determine	Yes
Iraq (2004–present)	Ansar-al-Islam	Yes	Cannot Determine
Iraq (2004–present)	1920 Revolutionary Brigade	No	No
Israel (1974–present)	Fatah/PLO	Cannot Determine	Cannot Determine
Lebanon (1975–1976)	Palestine Liberation Organization (PLO)	Cannot Determine	Cannot Determine
Lebanon (1975–1976)	Lebanese Army	Yes	No
Lebanon (1982–1990)	Amal	Yes	Cannot Determine
Lebanon (1982–1990)	LF-Geaga	Yes	Cannot Determine
Liberia (1990–1996)	National Patriotic Front of Liberia (NPFL)	Yes	Cannot Determine
Liberia (1990–1996)	Independent National Patriotic Front of Liberia (INPFL)	Cannot Determine	Cannot Determine
Liberia (1990–1996)	United Liberian Movement for Democracy (ULIMO)	Yes	Cannot Determine

(continued)

TABLE A.11 *(continued)*

Conflict	Warring Group	Leader of Split-Off Subgroup Influential Prior to War Onset?	Split-Off Subgroup Regionally Based (Distinct from Main Group)?
Liberia (2000–2003)	Liberians United for Reconciliation and Democracy (LURD)	Cannot Determine	Yes
Myanmar (1948–present)	Karen National Union (KNU)	Yes	Yes
Myanmar (1948–present)	Communist Party of Burma (CPB)	No	Yes
Ottoman Greek Revolt (1821–1833)	Forces of the Ottoman Empire	Yes	Yes
Ottoman Greek Revolt (1821–1833)	Forces of Alexander Mavrokordhatos	Yes	Yes
Ottoman Greek Revolt (1821–1833)	Philiki Eteria	Cannot Determine	Cannot Determine
Ottoman Greek Revolt (1821–1833)	Forces of East Roumeli	Yes	No
Ottoman Greek Revolt (1821–1833)	Forces of Theodhoros Kolokotronis	Yes	Yes
Pakistan (2007–present)	TNSM	Yes	Cannot Determine
Pakistan (2007–present)	TTP	Yes	Yes
Peru (1989–1997)	Government of Peru	Yes	No
Peru (1989–1997)	Sendero Luminoso	Yes	Cannot Determine
Philippines (1986–present)	Government of the Philippines	Yes	No
Philippines (1986–present)	CPP	Yes	Yes
Philippines (1986–present)	MNLF	Yes	Yes
Russia (1917–1922)	Red Army	Yes	Yes
Russia (1917–1922)	Volunteer Army	Cannot Determine	Yes
Russia (1917–1922)	Provisional Government of Autonomous Siberia	Yes	Yes

Conflict	Warring Group	Leader of Split-Off Subgroup Influential Prior to War Onset?	Split-Off Subgroup Regionally Based (Distinct from Main Group)?
Russia (1917–1922)	Komuch	Yes	Yes
Russia (1917–1922)	Ukrainian Government	Yes	Yes
Russia (1917–1922)	Supreme Administration of the North	Cannot Determine	Cannot Determine
Russia (1917–1922)	Northwestern White Army	Yes	Cannot Determine
Sierra Leone (1991–2001)	Sierra Leone Army (SLA)	Yes	Yes
Sierra Leone (1991–2001)	Revolutionary United Front (RUF)	No	Yes
Sierra Leone (1991–2001)	Armed Forced Revolutionary Council (AFRC)	No	Yes
Somalia (1981–present)	Somali National Movement (SNM)	Yes	Yes
Somalia (1981–present)	United Somali Congress (USC)	Yes	Yes
Somalia (1981–present)	Islamic Courts Union (ICU)	No	Yes
Sri Lanka (1983–1990)	Eelam Revolutionary Organization of Students (EROS)	No	Yes
Sri Lanka (1983–1990)	Tamil Eelam Liberation Organization (TELO)	No	No
Sri Lanka (1983–1990)	People's Liberation Organization of Tamil Eelam (PLOTE)	No	No
Sri Lanka (1983–1990)	Eelam People's Revolutionary Liberation Front (EPRLF)	Yes	No
Sri Lanka (2004–2009)	LTTE	Cannot Determine	Cannot Determine
Sudan (2003–present)	Janjawiid	Yes	Yes

(continued)

TABLE A.11 *(continued)*

Conflict	Warring Group	Leader of Split-Off Subgroup Influential Prior to War Onset?	Split-Off Subgroup Regionally Based (Distinct from Main Group)?
Sudan (2003–present)	Sudan Liberation Movement/Army (SLM/A)	Yes	Yes
Sudan (2003–present)	Justice and Equality Movement (JEM)	Yes	No
Uganda (1980–2002)	Ugandan Army	Yes	Cannot Determine
Uganda (1980–2002)	UPA	Yes	Cannot Determine
Uganda (1980–2002)	FUNA	Cannot Determine	Yes
Western Sahara (1975–1979)	POLISARIO	Yes	Yes
Yugoslavia/Bosnia (1941–1945)	Ustashe	Yes	Yes
Yugoslavia/Bosnia (1941–1945)	Chetniks	Yes	Yes
Yugoslavia/Bosnia (1941–1945)	Muslims	Yes	Yes

References

Historical Sources for Alliance, Fractionalization, Cleavage, and Relative Power Coding (Afghanistan 1978–1992, 1992–1998; Bosnia 1941–1945, 1992–1995; and Iraq/Anbar 2004–present presented above).

Afghanistan (2002–present).

Christia, Fotini and Michael Semple. (2009). "Flipping the Taliban: How to Win in Afghanistan," *Foreign Affairs* 4 (88): 1–13.

Crowley, Michael. (2010). "Our Man in Kabul? The Sadistic Afghan Warlord Who Wants to Be Our Friend," *The New Republic*, March 9.

DiManno, Rosie. (2009). "Taliban Turncoat's Got a New Mission," *Toronto Star*, August 13.

Human Rights Watch. (2007). *The Human Cost: The Consequences of Insurgent Attacks in Afghanistan*, April 15.

International Institute for Strategic Studies. Various years. *The Military Balance*. London: IISS.

Perlez, Jane. (2009). "Rebuffing U.S., Pakistan Balks at a Crackdown," *New York Times*, December 14.

Rohde, David and David E. Sanger. (2003). "A Job Half-Done in Afghanistan," *The New York Times*, May 15.

Rohde, David and David E. Sanger. (2007). "How a 'Good War' in Afghanistan Went Bad," *The New York Times*, August 12.

Rubin, Elizabeth. (2008). "Battle Company Is Out There," *The New York Times Magazine*, February 24.
U.S. State Department. (2005). *Country Reports on Terrorism* (p. 241, on Hizb-i-Islami), http://www.state.gov/j/ct/rls/crt/2005/index.htm, accessed April 20, 2011.

Algeria (1954–1962 and 1992–2004)

Ciment, James. (1997). *Algeria: The Fundamentalist Challenge*. New York: Facts on File.
Crenshaw, Martha. (2010). Personal communication, July 14.
Henissart, Paul. (1970). *Wolves in the City: The Death of French Algeria*. New York: Simon and Schuster.
Hutchinson, Martha Crenshaw. (1978). *Revolutionary Terrorism: The FLN in Algeria, 1954–1962*. Stanford, CA: Hoover Institution Press.
FIS, GIA, and GSPC articles at http://www.globalsecurity.org
International Crisis Group. (2004). *Islamism, Violence, and Reform in Algeria: Turning the Page*, http://www.crisisgroup.org/~/media/Files/Middle%20East%20North%20Africa/North%20Africa/Algeria/Islamism%20Violence%20and%20Reform%20in%20Algeria%20Turning%20the%20Page.pdf, accessed April 20, 2012.
Kohlmann, Evan F. (2007). "Two Decades of Jihad in Algeria: the GIA, the GSPC, and Al Qaeda." NEFA Foundation, http://www.nefafoundation.org/miscellaneous/nefagspc0507.pdf, accessed April 20, 2012.
Martinez, Luis. (2000). *The Algerian Civil War, 1990–1998*. New York: Columbia University Press.
Rubin, Barry. (2009). *Conflict and Insurgency in the Contemporary Middle East*. London: Taylor and Francis (p. 243, on AIS).

Angola (Portugal) (1961–1975 and 1975–2002)

Ciment, James. (1997). *Angola and Mozambique: Postcolonial Wars in Southern Africa*. New York: Facts on File.
James, W. Martin III. (1992). *A Political History of the Civil War in Angola, 1974–1990*. New Brunswick, NJ: Transaction Publishers.
Malaquias, Assis. (2007). *Rebels and Robbers: Violence in Post-Colonial Angola*. Uppsala: Nordiska Afrikainstitutet.

Austria (1848–1849)

Hahn, Hans Joachim. (2001). *The 1848 Revolutions in German-Speaking Europe*. Harlow: Longman.
Hahn, Hans Joachim. (2010). Personal communication, July 3.
Kann, Robert A. (1970). *The Multinational Empire: Nationalism and National Reform in the Hapsburg Monarchy, 1848–1918*. Vol. I. New York: Octagon Books.
Palmer, Alan. (1994). *Twilight of the Hapsburgs: The Life and Times of Emperor Francis Joseph*. New York: Grove Press.
Taylor, A. J. P. (1948). *The Hapsburg Monarchy, 1809–1918*. London: Hamish Hamilton.

Burundi (1991–2003)

Associated Press. (2006). "Burundi Rebel Group to Disarm," September 12.

BBC News. (2001). "Burundi Army 'Kills 500 Rebels'," December 25.

Center for International Development and Conflict Management, University of Maryland. "Chronology for Hutus in Burundi," http://www.cidcm.umd.edu/mar/chronology.asp?groupId=51601, accessed April 20, 2011.

Maundi, Mohammed O. et al. (2006). "Burundi, 1993–1998." In *Getting In: Mediators' Entry into the Settlement of African Conflicts*. Washington, DC: United States Institute of Peace Press, pp. 57–84.

Samii, Cyrus. (2010). Personal communication, November 12.

UNHCR Refworld entry on Palipehutu, http://www.unhcr.org/refworld/topic,463af2212,469f2d0c2,3ae6ad4c74,0.html, accessed April 20, 2011.

United States Institute of Peace. (2002). *International Commission of Inquiry for Burundi: Final Report*, http://www.usip.org/files/file/resources/collections/commissions/Burundi-Report.pdf, accessed April 20, 2011.

Cambodia (1978–1991)

Brown, MacAlister and Joseph J. Zasloff. (1998). *Cambodia Confounds the Peacemakers 1979–1998*. Ithaca, NY: Cornell University Press.

Chandler, David. (2008). *A History of Cambodia*. 4th ed. Boulder, CO: Westview Press.

Chandler, David. (2010). Personal communication, July 2.

International Institute for Strategic Studies. Various years. *The Military Balance*. London: IISS.

Khmer Rouge Trial Portal entry on Ieng Sary, http://www.krtrial.info/showarticle.php?language=english&action=showarticle&art_id=7&needback=1, accessed November 10, 2009.

Chad (1969–1997 and 1998–present)

Associated Press. (2009). "Chad Claims Victory in Rebel Fight," May 11.

Atlas, Pierre and Roy Licklider. (1999). "Conflict among Former Allies after Civil War Settlement: Sudan, Zimbabwe, Chad, and Lebanon," *Journal of Peace Research* 36 (1): 35–54.

Azevedo, Mario J. (1998). *Roots of Violence: A History of War in Chad*. Ajanta Offset: Gordon and Breach Publishers.

Azevedo, Mario J. and Emmanuel U. Nnadozie. (1998). *Chad: A Nation in Search of Its Future*. Boulder, CO: Westview Press.

BBC News. (2008a). "Q&A: Chad Rebellion," February 4.

BBC News. (2008b). "France Watches Chad-Sudan Border," February 6.

BBC News. (2009a). "Country Profile: Chad," April 15.

BBC News. (2009b). "Chad Says Rebel Attack Defeated," May 7.

Collelo, Thomas, ed. (1988). *Chad: A Country Study*. Washington, DC: GPO for the Library of Congress.

Eriksson, Hans and Bjorn Hagstromer. (2005). *Chad: Towards Democratization or Petro-Dictatorship?* Uppsala: Nordiska Afrikainstitutet.

McGregor, Andrew. (2008). "Oil Industry at the Heart of the Zaghawa Power Struggle in Chad," *Terrorism Monitor* 6 (5), http://www.jamestown.org/single/? no_cache=1&tx_ttnews%5Btt_news%5D=4776, accessed April 20, 2012.

Project Ploughshares. (2006). "Conflict Descriptions: Chad," http://www.ploughshares. ca/content/chad-1965-first-combat-deaths, accessed April 20, 2011.

STRATFOR. (2008). "Chad: The Rebel Advance Continues," February 1, http: //ufdd-ftchad.org (no longer in operation).

China (1850–1878 and 1911–1931)

Bonavia, David. (1995). *China's Warlords*. Hong Kong: Oxford University Press.

Botjer, George F. (1979). *A Short History of Nationalist China, 1919–1949*. New York: G.P. Putnam's Sons.

Hsu, Immanuel C. Y. (2000). *The Rise of Modern China*. Oxford: Oxford University Press.

McCord, Edward. (2010). Personal communication, July 2.

Colombia (1965–present)

Hylton, Forrest. (2006). *Evil Hour in Colombia*. London: Verso.

Kline, Harvey F. (1995). *Colombia: Democracy under Assault*. Boulder, CO: Westview Press.

National Consortium for the Study of Terrorism and Responses to Terrorism (START). *Terrorist Organization Profile: Simon Bolivar Guerilla Coordinating Board (CGSB)*. Available online: http://www.start.umd.edu/start/data/tops/terrorist_ organization_profile.asp?id=4393, accessed April 20, 2012.

Pearce, Jenny. (1990). *Colombia: Inside the Labyrinth*. London: Latin America Bureau.

Proyect, Louis. *Revolution in Colombia, Part 2: Guerilla Origins*, http://www.columbia. edu/~lnp3/mydocs/state_and_revolution/revolution_in_colombia.htm, accessed April 20, 2012.

Safford, Frank. (2010). Personal communication, July 5 and 26.

Safford, Frank and Marco Palacios. (2002). *Colombia: Fragmented Land, Divided Society*. Oxford: Oxford University Press.

Simons, Geoff. (2004). *Colombia: A Brutal History*. London: SAQI.

START Terrorist Organization Profile of the Pedro Leon Arboleda Movement, http: //www.start.umd.edu/start/data/tops/terrorist_organization_profile.asp?id=4193, accessed April 20, 2012.

U.S. State Department. (2008). *Country Reports on Terrorism*, http://www.state.gov/j/ ct/rls/crt/2008/index.htm, accessed April 20, 2011.

Zukerman, Sarah. (2010). Personal communication, January 25.

Congo (Kinshasa) (1960–1965, 1996–1997, and 1998–present)

Afoaku, Osita. (2002). "Congo's Rebels: Their Origins, Motivations, and Strategies," in Clark, John F., ed., *The African Stakes of the Congo War*. New York: Palgrave Macmillan, pp. 109–128.

Agence France Press. (2009). "DR Congo Government, CNDP Rebels 'Sign Peace Deal,'" March 23.

BBC News. (2009). "Amnesty Law for DR Congo Militias," May 7.

Epstein, Howard M., ed. (1965). *Revolt in the Congo, 1960–64*. New York: Facts on File.

Haskin, Jeanne M. (2005). *The Tragic State of the Congo: From Decolonization to Dictatorship*. New York: Algora Publishing.

International Crisis Group. (2006). "Congo's Elections: Making or Breaking the Peace," April 27, http://www.crisisgroup.org/~/media/Files/africa/central-africa/dr-congo/Congos%20Elections%20Making%20or%20Breaking%20the%20Peace.pdf, accessed April 20, 2011.

IRIN Humanitarian News and Analysis. (n.d.). "In-Depth: Ituri in Eastern DRC," http://www.irinnews.org/InDepthMain.aspx?InDepthId=33&ReportId=70835, accessed April 20, 2011.

Kanza, Thomas. (1978). *The Rise and Fall of Patrice Lumumba: Conflict in the Congo*. London: Rex Collings.

McCrummen, Stephanie. (2007). "For Tutsis of Eastern Congo, Protector, Exploiter, or Both?" *Washington Post*, August 6.

O'Ballance, Edgar. (2000). *The Congo-Zaire Experience, 1960–1998*. New York: St. Martin's Press.

Prunier, Gerard. (2009). *Africa's World War: Congo, the Rwandan Genocide, and the Making of a Continental Catastrophe*. Oxford: Oxford University Press.

Prunier, Gerard. (2010). Personal communication, July 3.

Reed, Wm. Cyrus. (1998). "Guerrillas in the Midst: The Former Government of Rwanda (FGOR) and the Alliance of Democratic Forces for the Liberation of Congo-Zaire (ADFL) in Eastern Zaire," in Claphman, Christopher, ed. *African Guerrillas*. Bloomington: Indiana University Press, pp. 134–154.

Turner, Thomas. (2002). "Angola's Role in the Congo War," in Clark, John F., ed. *The African Stakes of the Congo War*. New York: Palgrave Macmillan, pp. 75–92.

Turner, Thomas. (2007). *The Congo Wars: Conflict, Myth, and Reality*. London: Zed Books.

U.S. State Department. (2002). *Country Reports on Human Rights Practices: Democratic Republic of the Congo, 2001*, http://www.state.gov/j/drl/rls/hrrpt/2001/af/8322.htm, accessed April 20, 2012.

Congo (Brazzaville) (1993–1998)

Bazenguissa-Ganga, Remy. (1999). "The Spread of Political Violence in Congo-Brazzaville," *African Affairs* 98 (390): 37–54.

Maundi, Mohammed O. et al. (2006). "Congo-Brazzaville, 1993–1999," in *Getting In: Mediators' Entry into the Settlement of African Conflicts*. Washington: United States Institute of Peace Press, pp. 85–101.

Côte D'Ivoire (2002–2005)

BBC News. (2004). "Ivoirian Rebel Minister Sacked," May 20.

Boher, Anne. (2003). "West Africa: Ivory Coast Coalition Government Raises Hopes," *Independent Online*, April 16.

Coalition to Stop the Use of Child Soldiers. (2004). *Child Soldiers Global Report*, http://www.child-soldiers.org/document/get?id=966, accessed April 20, 2011.

Coulibaly, Loucoumane. (2007). "Soro Is Ready to Be Premier of the Ivory Coast," *Independent Online*, March 27.

International Crisis Group. (2003). *Côte D'Ivoire: "The War Is Not Yet Over,"* http://www.crisisgroup.org/~/media/Files/africa/west-africa/cote-divoire/Cote% 20dIvoire%20The%20War%20Is%20Not%20Yet%20Over.pdf, accessed April 20, 2011.

Kohler, Jessica. (2003). *From Miraculous to Disastrous: The Crisis in Côte D'Ivoire.* Geneva: Center for Applied Studies in International Negotiations.

The New York Times. (2002). "With Rebels on Attack, Ivory Coast Leader Fires Defense Minister," October 13.

Zabadi, Istifanus. (2005). "Civil Militias: Threats to National and Human Security in West Africa," in Francis, David J., ed., *Civil Militias: Africa's Intractable Security Menace?* Burlington, VT: Ashgate, pp. 117–130.

Ethiopia (1974–1991)

Marchal, Roland. (1992). "L'après-Mengistu dans la Corne de l'Afrique: une stabilisation impossible?" *Cultures & Conflits* 8 (1): 32–47.

Tareke, Gebru. (2009). *The Ethiopian Revolution: War in the Horn of Africa.* New Haven, CT: Yale University Press.

Tareke, Gebru. (2010). Personal communication, July 2.

Young, John. (1998). "The Tigray People's Liberation Front," in Claphman, Christopher, ed., *African Guerrillas.* Bloomington: Indiana University Press, pp. 36–52.

Georgia (1991–1994)

Areshidze, Irakly. (2007). *Democracy and Autocracy in Eurasia: Georgia in* Transition. East Lansing: Michigan State University Press.

Aves, Jonathan. (1996). *Georgia: From Chaos to Stability?* London: The Royal Institute for International Affairs.

Zürcher, Christopher. (2010). Personal communication, July 4.

Greece (1941–1944)

Fleischer, Hagen. (1981). "Contacts between German Occupation Authorities and the Major Greek Resistance Organizations: Sound Tactics or Collaboration?" in Iatrides, John O., ed., *Greece in the 1940s: A Nation in Crisis.* Hanover: University Press of New England, pp. 48–60.

Fleischer, Hagen. (1995). "The National Liberation Front (EAM), 1941–1947: A Reassessment," in Iatrides, John O. and Linda Wrigley, eds., *Greece at the Crossroads: The Civil War and Its Legacy.* University Park: Pennsylvania State University Press, pp. 48–89.

Hondros, John. (1981). "The Greek Resistance, 1941–1944: A Reevaluation," in Iatrides, John O., ed., *Greece in the 1940s: A Nation in Crisis.* Hanover: University Press of New England, pp. 37–47.

Hondros, John. (1983). *Occupation and Resistance: The Greek Agony, 1941–1944.* New York: Pella.

Iatrides, John O. (1981). "Introduction," in Iatrides, John O., ed., *Greece in the 1940s: A Nation in Crisis.* Hanover: University Press of New England, pp. 17–26.

Iatrides, John O. (1995). "Greece at the Crossroads," in Iatrides, John O. and Linda Wrigley, eds., *Greece at the Crossroads: The Civil War and Its Legacy.* University

Park: Pennsylvania State University Press, pp. 1–30. (Also see his chronology, p. 320 of this volume.)

Liaras, Evangellos. (2010). Personal communication, November 3.

Svoronos, Nicolas. (1981). "Greek History, 1940–1950: The Main Problems," in Iatrides, John O., ed., *Greece in the 1940s: A Nation in Crisis*. Hanover: University Press of New England, pp. 1–14.

Woodhouse, C. M. (1981). "The National Liberation Front and the British Connection," in Iatrides, John O., ed., *Greece in the 1940s: A Nation in Crisis*. Hanover: University Press of New England, pp. 81–101.

Guatemala (1965–1995)

Barry, Tom. (1992). *Inside Guatemala: The Essential Guide to its Politics, Economy, Society, and Environment*. Albuquerque, NM: The Inter-Hemispheric Education Resource Center.

Benjamin, Roger and John Kautsky. (1968). "Communism and Economic Development," *American Political Science Review* 62 (1): 110–123.

Bibler, Jared S. (2007). *The Ideological Underpinnings of the Revolutionary Organization of the People in Arms*. MA Thesis, Ohio State University.

Doyle, Kate and Michael Evans. (2000). "Colonel Byron Disrael Lima Estrada: Alleged Mastermind behind the Murder of Bishop Juan Jose Gerardi of Guatemala," *National Security Archive Electronic Briefing Book No. 25, George Washington University*, http://www.gwu.edu/~nsarchiv/NSAEBB/NSAEBB25/index.htm, accessed April 20, 2011.

Jonas, Susanne. (2000). *Of Centaurs and Doves: Guatemala's Peace Process*. Boulder, CO: Westview Press.

Jonas, Susanne and David Tobis, eds. (1974). *Guatemala*. Berkeley, CA: North American Congress on Latin America.

Segesvary, Louis S. (1984). "Guatemala: A Complex Scenario," *CSIS Significant Issues Series* 6 (3): 1–43.

Northeast India (1977–present)

Chadha, Vivek. (2005). *Low Intensity Conflicts in India: An Analysis*. New Delhi: Sage Publications.

Kujur, Rajat. (2008). *Naxal Movements in India: A Profile*. Research paper, Institute of Peace and Conflict Studies.

Staniland, Paul. (2010). Personal communication, October 25.

India Kashmir Conflict (1988–1996)

Uppsala Conflict Data Program Database. Available online: http://www.ucdp.uu.se/database, accessed April 20, 2011.

Indonesia (1958–1961)

Feith, Herbert and Daniel S. Lev. (1963). "The End of the Indonesian Rebellion," *Pacific Affairs* 36 (1): 32–46.

Jackson, Karl D. (1980). *Traditional Authority, Islam, and Rebellion: A Study of Indonesian Political Behavior*. Berkeley: University of California Press.

Tajima, Yuhki. (2010). Personal communication, October 24.

Iraq (1975–1996 and 2004–present, including non-Anbar parts of Iraq for the latter)

Al-Sadr entry at http://www.globalsecurity.org.

Beehner, Lionel. (2005). "Iraq: Militia Groups," *Council on Foreign Relations* (June 9), http://www.cfr.org/publication/8175, accessed April 20, 2011.

Bruno, Greg. (2008a). "The Preparedness of Iraqi Security Forces," *Council on Foreign Relations* (March 27), http://www.cfr.org/publication/14112, accessed April 20, 2012.

Bruno, Greg. (2008b). "The Role of the 'Sons of Iraq' in Improving Security," *Washington Post*, April 28.

Bruno, Greg. (2009). "Finding a Place for the 'Sons of Iraq'," *Council on Foreign Relations* (January 9), http://www.cfr.org/publication/16088, accessed April 20, 2012.

Dagher, Sam. (2007). "Iraq's Sadr Uses Lull to Rebuild Army," *Christian Science Monitor*, December 11.

Dehghanpisheh, Babak. (2007). "Baghdad Briefing," *Newsweek Web Exclusive* (February 11), http://www.newsweek.com/id/56824, accessed April 20, 2011.

Dreyfuss, Robert. (2008). "Is Iran Winning the Iraq War?" *The Nation*, February 21.

Government of Australia. (2012). "What Governments Are Doing: Ansar al-Islam," http://www.ema.gov.au/agd/WWW/NationalSecurity.nsf/Page/What_Governments_are_doing_Listing_of_Terrorism_Organisations_Ansar_Al-Islam, last modified March 15, accessed April 25, 2012.

International Institute for Strategic Studies. Various years. *The Military Balance*. London: IISS.

Jafarzadeh, Alireza. (n.d.). "Targeting Ayatollah's Terror Machine," *Fox News*, http://www.foxnews.com/story/0,2933,322628,00.html, accessed April 20, 2011.

Knickmeyer, Ellen. (2006). "Iraq Begins to Rein in Paramilitary Force," *Washington Post*, May 14.

Lindsay, John. (2010). Personal communication. October 24.

McDowall, David. (1996). *A Modern History of the Kurds*. London: I.B. Tauris.

Ramzi, Kholoud. (2008). "The Dawa Party's Bumpy Path," *Niqash: Briefings from Inside and Across Iraq* (June 16), http://www.niqash.org/content.php?contentTypeID=75&id=2225&lang=0, accessed April 20, 2011.

Roggio, Bill. (2008). "Al Qaeda in Iraq Under Pressure in Balad, Anbar," *Long War Journal* (February 10), http://www.longwarjournal.org/archives/2008/02/al_qaeda_in_iraq_und.php, accessed April 20, 2011.

Romano, David. (2010). Personal communication, July 11.

Schanzer, Jonathan. (2004). "Ansar al-Islam: Back in Iraq," *Middle East Quarterly* 11 (1): 41–50.

Tilghman, Andrew. (2007). "The Myth of AQI," *Washington Monthly* 39 (10): 34–42.

U.S. State Department. 2008. *Country Reports on Terrorism*, http://www.state.gov/j/ct/rls/crt/2008/index.htm, accessed April 20, 2011.

Israel (1974–present)

Uppsala Conflict Data Program Database. Available online: http://www.ucdp.uu.se/database, accessed April 20, 2011.

Lebanon (1975–1976 and 1982–1990)

Abraham, A. J. (1996). *The Lebanon War.* Westport, CT: Praeger.
Al-Jazeera. (2004). *The War of Lebanon* (documentary film series).
Evron, Yair. (1987). *War and Intervention in Lebanon: The Israeli-Syrian Deterrence Dialogue.* London: Croom Helm.
Fisk, Robert. (1990). *Pity the Nation: The Abduction of Lebanon.* New York: Atheneum.
Gilmour, David. (1983). *Lebanon: The Fractured Country.* New York: St. Martin's Press.
Haley, Edward and Lewis Snider, eds. (1979). *Lebanon in Crisis: Participants and Issues.* Syracuse, NY: Syracuse University Press.
Hanf, Theodor. (1993). *Coexistence in Wartime Lebanon: Decline of a State and Rise of a Nation.* John Richardson, trans. London: Center for Lebanese Studies.
Khazen, Farid el. (2000). *The Breakdown of the State in Lebanon, 1967–1976.* Cambridge, MA: Harvard University Press.
Makdisi, Ussama. (2000). *The Culture of Sectarianism: Community, History, and Violence in Nineteenth-Century Lebanon.* Berkeley: University of California Press.
O'Ballance, Edgar. (1998). *The Civil War in Lebanon, 1975–1992.* New York: St. Martin's Press.
Picard, Elizabeth. (1996). *Lebanon, A Shattered Country: Myths and Realities of the War in Lebanon.* Franklin Philip, trans. New York: Holmes & Meier.
Salibi, Kamal. (1976). *Crossroads to Civil War.* Delmar: Caravan Books.

Liberia (1990–1996 and 2000–2003)

Adebajo, Adekeye. (2002). *Liberia's Civil War.* Boulder, CO: Lynne Rienner.
Dennis, Peter. (2006). "A Brief History of Liberia," *The International Center for Transitional Justice,* http://www.ictj.org/static/Africa/Liberia/BriefHistory.pdf, accessed February 10, 2010.
Ellis, Stephen. (1998). "Liberia's Warlord Insurgency," in Claphman, Christopher, ed., *African Guerrillas.* Bloomington: Indiana University Press, pp. 155–171.
PBS Frontline. (2005). "Who's Who in Liberia's Fragile Peace and Former Conflict." Available online: http://www.pbs.org/frontlineworld/stories/liberia/relationshipsa. html, accessed April 20, 2012.
Pham, John-Peter. (2004). *Liberia: Portrait of a Failed State.* New York: Reed Press.
Zabadi, Istifanus. (2005). "Civil Militias: Threats to National and Human Security in West Africa," in Francis, David J., ed., *Civil Militias: Africa's Intractable Security Menace?* Burlington, VT: Ashgate, pp. 117–130.

Mexico (1911–1915)

Camin, Hector Aguilar and Lorenzo Meyer. (1993). *In the Shadow of the Mexican Revolution: Contemporary Mexican History, 1910–1989.* Luis Alberto Fierro, trans. Austin: University of Texas Press.
Raat, W. Dirk and William H. Beezley, eds. (1986). *Twentieth-Century Mexico.* Lincoln: University of Nebraska Press.
Tutino, John. (1986). *From Insurrection to Revolution in Mexico.* Princeton, NJ: Princeton University Press.

Myanmar (1948–present)

Callahan, Mary P. (2003). *Making Enemies: War and State-Building in Burma*. Ithaca, NY: Cornell University Press.
Charney, Michael W. (2009). *A Modern History of Burma*. Cambridge: Cambridge University Press.
Hazlett, Chad. (2010). Personal communication, November 12.
Smith, Martin. (1999). *Burma: Insurgency and the Politics of Ethnicity*. London: Zed Books.

Ottoman Greek Revolt (1821–1833)

Brewer, David. (2001). *The Flame of Freedom: The Greek War of Independence, 1821–1833*. London: John Murray.
Liaras, Evangellos. (2010). Personal communication, October 24.

Ottoman Balkan Revolt (1876–1878)

Davison, Roderic H. (1963). *Reform in the Ottoman Empire, 1856–1976*. Princeton, NJ: Princeton University Press.
McCarthy, Justin. (2001). *The Ottoman Peoples and the End of Empire*. London: Arnold Publishers.
McCarthy, Justin. (2010). Personal communication, July 2.
Shaw, Stanford J. and Ezel Kural Shaw. (1977). *History of the Ottoman Empire and Modern Turkey. Volume II: Reform, Revolution, and Republic: The Rise of Modern Turkey, 1808–1975*. Cambridge: Cambridge University Press.

Pakistan (2007–present)

ADN Kronos. (n.d.). "Pakistan: Top Taliban Militant Announces Split," http://www.adnkronos.com/AKI/English/Security/?id=3.0.2601642662, accessed April 20, 2011.
Khan, Riaz. (2007). "Inside Rebel Pakistan. Cleric's Domain," *Associated Press*, October 27.
Lalwani, Sameer. (2009). *Pakistani Capabilities for a Counterinsurgency Campaign: A Net Assessment*. Washington, DC: New America Foundation.
Lalwani, Sameer. (2010). Personal communication, July 28.
NEFA Foundation. (2008). "An Interview with Mangal Bagh, Commander of Lashkar-e-Islam (LI)," *Bara, Khyber Agency* (May 1), http://www.nefafoundation.org/miscellaneous/nefamangalbagh0608.pdf, accessed April 20, 2011.
Sheikh, Mona Kanwal. (2009). "Disaggregating the Pakistani Taliban," *DIIS Brief* (September), http://www.diis.dk/graphics/Publications/Briefs2009/Disaggregating_Pakistani_Taliban.pdf, accessed April 20, 2011.
Sulaiman, Sadia. (2009). "Hafiz Gul Bahadur: A Profile of the Leader of the North Waziristan Taliban," *Terrorism Monitor* 7 (9), April 10, http://www.jamestown.org/programs/gta/single/?tx_ttnews%5Btt_news%5D=34839&tx_ttnews%5BbackPid%5D=412&no_cache=1, accessed April 20, 2011.
"Tribal Tribulations: The Pakistani Taliban in Waziristan," (2009). *Jane's Intelligence Review* 21 (2): 8–13.

Peru (1989–1997)

Obando, Enrique. (1998). "Civil-Military Relations in Peru, 1980–1996: How to Control and Co-Opt the Military (and the Consequences of Doing So)," in Stern, Steve J., ed., *Shining and Other Paths: War and Society in Peru, 1980–1995*. Durham, NC: Duke University Press, pp. 385–410.
Sanchez, W. Alejandro. (2003). "The Rebirth of Insurgency in Peru," *Small Wars and Insurgencies* 14 (3): 185–198.
Sanchez, W. Alejandro. (2010). Personal communication, July 5.
Tarazona-Sevillano, Gabriela. (1992). "The Organization of Shining Path," in Palmer, David Scott, ed., *The Shining Path of Peru*. New York: St. Martin's Press, pp. 171–190.

Philippines (1986–present)

Abuza, Zachary. (2005). "The Moro Islamic Liberation Front at 20: State of the Revolution," *Studies in Conflict and Terrorism* 28 (6): 453–479.
Fernandez, Edwin S. (2006). "The Quest for Power: The Military in Philippine Politics, 1965–2002," *Asia Pacific: Perspectives* 6 (1): 38–47.
Marks, Thomas A. (1996). *Maoist Insurgency since Vietnam*. London: Frank Cass.
Santos, Soliman M., Jr. (2005). *Evolution of the Armed Conflict on the Moro Front.* Background Paper to Philippine Human Development Report, http://hdn.org.ph/wp-content/uploads/2005_PHDR/2005%20Evolution_Moro_Conflict.pdf, accessed April 20, 2011.
Walgren, Scott A. (2007). *Explaining Intervention in Southeast Asia: A Comparison of the Muslim Insurgencies in Thailand and the Philippines*. MA Thesis, Naval Postgraduate School.

Russia (1917–1922)

Lincoln, W. Bruce. (1991). *Red Victory: A History of the Russian Civil War*. New York: Touchstone.
Wade, Rex A. (2001). *The Bolshevik Revolution and Russian Civil War*. Westport, CT: Greenwood Press.
Wade, Rex A. (2010). Personal communication, July 2.

Sierra Leone (1991–2001)

Abdullah, Ibrahim and Patrick Muana. (1998). "The Revolutionary United Front of Sierra Leone: A Revolt of the Lumpenproletariat," in Claphman, Christopher, ed., *African Guerrillas*. Bloomington: Indiana University Press, pp. 172–193.
Alie, Joe. (2005). "The Kamajor Militia in Sierra Leone: Liberators or Nihilists?" in Francis, David J., ed., *Civil Militias: Africa's Intractable Security Menace?* Burlington, VT: Ashgate, pp. 51–70.
BBC News. (2000). "Captured Leader 'Regrets' Kidnap," September 11.
Gebrewold, Belachew. (2005). "Civil Militias and Militarisation of Society in the Horn of Africa," in Francis, David J., ed., *Civil Militias: Africa's Intractable Security Menace?* Burlington, VT: Ashgate, pp. 187–212.

Ginifer, Jeremy and Hooman Peimani. (2005). "Civil Defense Forces and Post-Conflict Security Challenges: International Experiences and Implications for Africa," in Francis, David J., ed., *Civil Militias: Africa's Intractable Security Menace?* Burlington, VT: Ashgate, pp. 251–280.

Humphreys, Macartan and Jeremy Weinstein. (2006). "Handling and Manhandling Civilians in Civil War," *American Political Science Review* 100 (3): 429–447.

Richards, Paul. (2010). Personal communication, July 2 and 4.

The Telegraph. (2000). "Caught with Their Guard Down," September 3.

Zabadi, Istifanus. (2005). "Civil Militias: Threats to National and Human Security in West Africa," in Francis, David J., ed., *Civil Militias: Africa's Intractable Security Menace?* Burlington, VT: Ashgate, pp. 117–130.

Somalia (1981–present)

Adam, Hussein M. (1999). "Somali Civil Wars," in Ali, Taisier M. and Robert O. Matthews, eds., *Civil Wars in Africa: Roots and Resolution*. Montreal: McGill-Queen's University Press, pp. 169–192.

Ali, Abdisaid. (2008). "The Al-Shabaab al-Mujahidin: A Profile of the First Somali Terrorist Organization," *Institut für Strategie- Politik- Sicherheits- und Wirtschaftsberatung*, http://www.isn.ethz.ch/isn/Digital-Library/Publications/Detail/?id=55851&lng=en, accessed April 20, 2011.

BBC News. (2006). "Somali Deaths in Fierce Clashes," March 24.

BBC News. (2009a). "Q&A: Somalia's Conflict," May 13.

BBC News. (2009b). "Ethiopia Rejects Somali Request," June 21.

Compagnon, Daniel. (1998). "Somali Armed Movements: The Interplay of Political Entrepreneurship & Clan-Based Factions," in Claphman, Christopher, ed., *African Guerrillas*. Bloomington: Indiana University Press, pp. 73–90.

Connell, Dan. (2002). "War Clouds over Somalia," *Middle East Report* (March 22), http://www.merip.org/mero/mero032202, accessed April 20, 2011.

"Former Members of Radical Somali Group Give Details of Their Group." (2007). *Voice of America News* (January 6), http://www1.voanews.com/english/news/a-13-2007-01-06-voa25-66764342.html, accessed February 20, 2010.

Gebrewold, Belachew. (2005). "Civil Militias and the Militarization of Society in the Horn of Africa," in Francis, David J., ed., *Civil Militias: Africa's Intractable Security Menace?* Burlington, VT: Ashgate, pp. 187–212.

Human Rights Watch. (2007). *Shell-Shocked: Civilians under Siege in Mogadishu*, http://www.hrw.org/reports/2007/08/12/shell-shocked, accessed April 20, 2011.

Lyons, Terrence and Ahmed I. Samatar. (1995). *Somalia: State Collapse, Military Intervention, and Strategies for Political Reconstruction*. Washington, DC: The Brookings Institution.

Mohamoud, Abdullah A. (2006). *State Collapse and Post-Conflict Development in Africa: The Case of Somalia (1960–2001)*. West Lafayette, IN: Purdue University Press.

"Simultaneous Heavy Fightings [sic] Erupt in Somalia." (2001). *People's Daily*, August 6, http://english.peopledaily.com.cn/english/200108/06/eng20010806_76593.html, accessed April 20, 2011.

Tareke, Gebru. (2009). *The Ethiopian Revolution: War in the Horn of Africa*. New Haven, CT: Yale University Press.
Various articles from http://www.britannica.com and http://www.internal-displacement.org.

Sri Lanka (1983–1990 and 2004–2009)

BBC News. (2009). "Tamils Look for Leadership after Tigers," June 17.
Gunaratna, Rohan. (1990). *Sri Lanka, a Lost Revolution? The Inside Story of the JVP*. Colombo: Institute of Fundamental Studies.
Gunaratna, Rohan. (1993). *Indian Intervention in Sri Lanka*. Colombo: South Asian Network on Conflict Research.
Hellman-Rajanayagam, Dagmar. (1994). *The Tamil Tigers: Armed Struggle for Identity*. Stuttgart: Farnz Steiner Verlag.
International Institute for Strategic Studies. Various years. *The Military Balance*. London: IISS.
Liaras, Evangelos. (2010). Personal communication, October 24.
Senaratne, Jagath P. (1997). *Political Violence in Sri Lanka, 1977–1990: Riots, Insurrections, Counterinsurgencies, Foreign Intervention*. Amsterdam: VU University Press.
Staniland, Paul. (2010). Personal communication, January 4 and 26 and July 2.

Sudan (2003–present)

De Waal, Alex. (2008). "In Memoriam: Prof. Abdel Rahman Musa Abakar," *Making Sense of Sudan Blog, Social Science Research Council*, http://blogs.ssrc.org/sudan/2008/08/11/in-memoriam-prof-abdel-rahman-musa-abakar/, accessed February 25, 2010.
Flint, Julie and Alex De Waal. (2008). *Darfur: A New History of a Long War*. London: Zed Books.
PBS Wide Angle. (2008). "Heart of Darfur: Guide to Factions and Forces." Available online: http://www.pbs.org/wnet/wideangle/episodes/heart-of-darfur/guide-to-factions-and-forces/299, accessed April 20, 2011.
Reuters. (2009). "Factbox: The Darfur Rebel Facing War Crimes Charges," October 19.
Uppsala Conflict Data Program Database. Available online: http://www.ucdp.uu.se/database, accessed April 20, 2011.

Tajikistan (1992–1997)

Akiner, Shirin. (2001). *Tajikistan: Disintegration or Reconciliations?* London: The Royal Institute of International Affairs.
Akiner, Shirin. (2010). Personal communication, July 4.
Jonson, Lena. (2006). *Tajikistan in the New Central Asia*. London: I.B. Tauris.
Various articles at http://www.globalsecurity.org.

Uganda (1980–2002)

Friedman, Jeffrey. (2010). Data for "Boots on the Ground: The Theoretical and Practical Significance of Manpower in Counterinsurgency." Working paper provided to author.

Kiyaga-Nsubuga, John. (1999). "Managing Political Change: Uganda under Museveni," in Ali, Taisier M. and Robert O. Matthews, eds., *Civil Wars in Africa: Roots and Resolution*. Montreal: McGill-Queen's University Press, pp. 13–34.

Ngoga, Pascal. (1998). "Uganda: The National Resistance Army," in Clapham, Christopher, ed., *African Guerrillas*. Bloomington: Indiana University Press, pp. 91–106.

Ofcansky, Thomas P. (1996). *Uganda: Tarnished Pearl of Africa*. Boulder, CO: Westview Press.

Reuters. (2007). "Uganda Army Says Troops Kill 38 Rebel Fighters," March 28.

Western Sahara (1975–1979)

Hodges, Tony. (1983). *Western Sahara: The Roots of a Desert War*. Westport, CT: Lawrence Hill & Company.

International Institute for Strategic Studies. Various years. *The Military Balance*. London: IISS.

Zimbabwe (1972–1979)

International Institute for Strategic Studies. Various years. *The Military Balance*. London: IISS.

Preston, Matthew. (2004). *Ending Civil War: Rhodesia and Lebanon in Perspective*. London: Tauris Academic Studies.

References

Sources on Afghanistan

Interviews[1]

Abdullah, Abdullah. Afghan Minister of Foreign Affairs. He joined Jamiat-i-Islami in the early 1980s as part of the anti-Soviet resistance, and was a close associate of the assassinated Tajik leader Ahmad Shah Massoud. Interview held at Ministry of Foreign Affairs, Kabul, Afghanistan, July 2005.

Ahmad, Khaleeq. Deputy Spokesman on International Affairs for President Karzai. Interviews held in Kabul, July and August 2005.

Ahmadzai, Ahmad Shah. Member of Afghan Parliament, engineer by training, leading figure in Rasul Sayyaf's Ittihad party during the Jihad and served as prime minister in the 1988 interim government and as deputy minister in Rabbani's mujahedin government. Interview held in Shar-i-Naw, Kabul, Afghanistan, July 2005.

Akbari, Mohammad. Head of Afghanistan National Islamic Unity Party. Wartime leader of the smaller of the two factions of the National Unity Party of Afghanistan (Hizb-i-Wahdat). Interview held in Karte-Se, Kabul, Afghanistan, July 2005.

Atta, Mohammad Nur. Governor of Balkh Province. He was a Jamiat-i-Islami commander close to Ahmad Shah Massoud during Afghanistan's ethnic civil war. Interview held in Mazar-i-Sharif, Afghanistan, July 2005.

Babbington, Peter. Director of Afghanistan's New Beginning Program, a partnership between the Afghan Ministry of Defence and the international community that offers a financial package to commanders and officers who fulfilled all the requirements of the Demobilization, Demilitarization, and Reintegration (DDR) process. Interview held at UN Compound, Kabul-Jalalabad Road, Afghanistan, July 2005.

Bhayani, Lubna. Program coordinator and grants manager, Ockenden International Afghanistan. Interview held in Kabul, Afghanistan, August 2005.

---

[1] All positions shown on the list are as of the time of the interview, unless otherwise noted. More information on the background of the Afghan personalities listed in this interview list can be found in Girardet and Walter (2004) and Afghanistan On-line, http://www.afghan-web.com/bios/.

Dadfar, Spanta. Advisor to President Karzai on International Affairs. Interview held at the Presidential Palace, Kabul, Afghanistan, July 2005.

Dimitroff, Peter. Country Director of National Democratic Institute (NDI) in Afghanistan. Interview held in Shar-i-Naw, Kabul, Afghanistan, July–August 2005.

Dupree, Nancy. Director of ACBAR Resource and Information Center and wife of late Afghan anthropologist Louis Dupree. Interview held in Shar-i-Naw, Kabul, Afghanistan, August 2005 and July 2010.

Faivre, Yves. Director of Amite Franco-Afghane (AFRANE), a French Humanitarian Aid NGO in Afghanistan, who had worked in Afghanistan throughout the Taliban years. Interview held in Silo, Kabul, Afghanistan, July 2005.

Filkins, Dexter. *The New York Times* reporter covering Afghanistan. Interview held in Cambridge, MA, September 2006.

Haji Mangal, Hussain. A high-ranking member of Hizb-i-Islami, a party he joined in the early days of the Jihad. During the Jihad and the intra-mujahedin war he served as Hizb-i-Islami's spokesperson. He had a falling-out with Hekmatyar after the victory of the Northern Alliance over the Taliban and has served as minister of irrigation in the Karzai interim government. Interview held in Shar-i-Naw, Kabul, Afghanistan, July 2005.

Hussaini, Amir. Political advisor and interpreter for Vice President Mohammed Karim Khalili. Interview held in Kabul, Afghanistan, June 2005.

Karzai, Majid. Advisor to the Afghan president. Interviews held in Kabul, July and August 2005 and July 2007.

Khan, Ismael. Minister of Power and Water. Known as "Amir of Herat," he remains one of the most powerful and influential figures in present-day Afghanistan. He made his name as a leading Jamiat-i-Islami commander during the anti-Soviet struggle and the intra-mujahedin war. Interview held at the Ministry of Power and Water, Kabul, Afghanistan, August 2005.

Kljuver, Robert. Head of a cultural NGO in Kabul. Interview held in Shar-i-Naw, Kabul, Afghanistan, July 2005.

Mahmudi, Musa Mohammad. Senior political analyst, National Democratic Institute (NDI). Interview held in Shar-i-Naw, Kabul, Afghanistan, June–August 2005.

Malik, Abdul Alhaj. Head of Party, Uzbek from Faryab province, and a general in Abdul Rashid Dostum's Junbish-i-Milli party, Malik mutinied against Dostum and chose to briefly collaborate with the Taliban in May 1997. Interview held in Macrorayon, Kabul, Afghanistan, June 2005.

Mangal, Hussein. Candidate for Afghan Parliament. He had served as cultural secretary for Gulbuddin Hekmatyar's party of Hizb-i-Islami. Interview conducted in Kabul, July 2005.

Mansur, Abdul Hamiz. Member of Jamiat-i-Islami and editor of the party's main periodical, *Payam-i-Mujahed*. After the fall of the Taliban regime, he served as the director of Afghan state radio and television. Interview held in Khayr Khane, Kabul, Afghanistan, July 2005.

Mawji, Aly. Resident representative in Afghanistan for the Aga Khan Development Network. Interview held in Shar-i-Naw, Kabul, Afghanistan, June 2005.

Mohaqeq, Haji Mohammad. High-ranking member of Afghan Parliament. The main commander of the Hazara party of Hizb-i-Wahdat in Balkh province. Interview held in Karte-Se, Kabul, Afghanistan, July 2005.

Mojaddidi, Sibghatullah. President of the Islamic Republic of Afghanistan, April to June 1992, and head of the Afghan National Reconciliation Commission. He led one of the small Sunni mujahedin groups based in Peshawar, the National Liberation Front of Afghanistan. Interview held in Afghanistan, July 2005.

Mutawakil, Wakil Ahmad. Had served as the Taliban's Foreign Minister. Interview held in Kabul, Afghanistan, August 2005.

North, Andrew. BBC News correspondent in Afghanistan. Interview held in Kabul and in Mazar-i-Sharif, July and August 2005.

Qanooni, Yunis. Member of Afghan Parliament. Qanooni joined the Jamiat forces of commander Ahmad Shah Massoud soon after the Soviet invasion. He served as a minister in Rabbani's mujahedin government during the intra-mujahedin civil war and was minister of education in President Karzai's Interim Administration before deciding to run against Karzai for the presidency. He came second in the presidential elections but won the bid for speaker in the Afghan parliament. Interview held in Khayr Khane, Kabul, Afghanistan, July 2005.

Quraishi, Hameed. UNDP regional office manager in charge of Demobilization, Demilitarization, and Reintegration (DDR), Interview held in Mazar-i-Sharif, Afghanistan, July 2005.

Rabbani, Burhanuddin. Member of Afghan Parliament. Rabbani served as President of the Islamic state of Afghanistan from 1992 until the Taliban takeover of Kabul in 1996. He was the founder of the anticommunist Islamist movement of Afghanistan in the 1960s and served as leader of Jamiat-i-Islami since the early 1970s. His party became one of the main Afghan resistance parties during the Jihad against the Soviets. Interview held in Shar-i-Naw, Kabul, Afghanistan, August 2005.

Rohde, David. *The New York Times* reporter covering Afghanistan. Interview held in Cambridge, MA, May 2005.

Ruttig, Thomas. Political adviser, German embassy. Interview held in Shar-i-Naw, Kabul, Afghanistan, June 2005.

Sabawoon, Wahidullah. Senior lieutenant in Hekmatyar's Hizb-i-Islami party during part of the Jihad and the intra-mujahedin war. Interview held in Kabul, Afghanistan, June 2005.

Samar, Sima. Chair of Afghan Independent Human Rights Commission (AIHR). Former minister of women's affairs. Interview held in Karte-Se, Kabul, Afghanistan, July 2005.

Sarwary, Bilal. Assistant producer, BBC Bureau. Interviews held in Shar-i-Naw, Kabul, Afghanistan, June–August 2005.

Sayyaf, Abdul Rasul. Member of Afghan Parliament. Sayyaf was the leader of the Ittihad party, the power base of which is concentrated in the Kabul suburb of Paghman. Interview held in Paghman, Afghanistan, July 2005.

Schiewek, Eckart. Political affairs officer, UN Assistance Mission to Afghanistan (UNAMA). Interview held in Shar-i-Naw, Kabul, Afghanistan, June 2005.

Semple, Michael. Deputy to the Special Representative of the European Union for Afghanistan (EUSR) and Harvard University Carr Center Fellow. Interviews held in Shar-i-Naw, Kabul, Afghanistan, July and August 2005, July 2007, and Cambridge, MA, 2009–2012.

Stewart, Rory. Founder of the Turquoise Mountain Foundation and Author of *The Places in Between*, an award-winning book on Afghanistan. Interviews held in Cambridge, MA, February 2005, and Kabul, Afghanistan, July 2007.

Tanai, Shahnawaz. Was at the time running for Afghan Parliament and got elected in September 2005. A known member of the Afghan Communist Party's Khalq (Masses) faction, Tanai served as minister of defense from 1988 to 1990 in the last

Afghan communist government led by Najibullah. With the assistance of Hekmat-yar, Tanai organized a coup against the Najibullah government in 1990. Tanai fled to Pakistan after the coup and has allegedly also cooperated with the Taliban movement. Interview held in Macrorayon, Kabul, Afghanistan, August 2005.

Van Bijlert, Martine. Political advisor, Office of the Special Representative of the European Union for Afghanistan. Interview held in Kabul, Afghanistan, June 2005.

Zadran, Amanullah. Minister of Tribal and Border Affairs after defecting from the Taliban. Interview held in Shar-i-Naw, Kabul, Afghanistan, July 2005.

Zaki, Faizullah. An Uzbek from Kabul, Zaki was a member of the Parcham faction of the Afghan Communist Party and fled to Uzbekistan during the intra-mujahedin war. After the victory of the Northern Alliance over the Taliban, Zaki served as the top political advisor to Uzbek General Dostum. Interview held in Mazar-i-Sharif, Afghanistan, August 2005.

Zekrya, Lema. Advisor to the Afghan minister of finance. Interview held in Kabul, Afghanistan, July 2005.

Interviews Conducted by Research Assistant Niamatullah Ibrahimi

Alizadah, Muhammad Ali. Member of Nasr party and a writer for *Emroz-i-Ma*, a weekly publication of Hizb-i-Wahdat of Mazari. He is originally from Jaghori district of Ghazni. Interview held in Kabul, Afghanistan, December 2005.

Jawadi, Sarwar. Member of the Cultural Committee of Hizb-i-Wahdat during the Kabul civil war. Originally from Bamyan, he was, at the time of the interview, a member of parliament. Interview held in Kabul, Afghanistan, December 2005.

Murtazawi, Rahmatullah. A member of *Bahar Weekly* in Kabul and previously a member of Sepah-i-Pasdaran. Interview held in Kabul, Afghanistan, December 2005.

Wahidi, Kazim. A writer for *Khabarnahmah Wahdat*, a publication of Hizb-i-Wahdat during the Kabul civil war. He has not been affiliated with any of the factions since. He is originally from Behsud in Wardak province. Interview held in Kabul, Afghanistan, November 2005.

Unpublished Interviews from Michael Semple's Oral Narratives Project

Baghlani, Najibullah. From Baghlan province, son of a fighter during the Jihad, Taliban ally in the intra-mujahedin war years.

Bashi Habib. From Ghazni Province, fighter during the Jihad who became a Taliban ally during the intra-mujahedin war.

Haji Malik. From Kabul province, fighter during the Jihad, who suffered in Taliban hands during the intra-mujahedin war.

Haji Mohammed. From Baghlan province, fighter during the Jihad, and later a Taliban ally.

Haji Safai. From Saripol province, fighter during the Jihad who rose to become a resistance commander.

Hashemi, Kareem. From Kunduz province, fighter during the Jihad who rose in the ranks to become a resistance official.

Kakar, Tajwar. Fighter during the Jihad, active in the north in Jowzjan and Kundujz provinces.

Karim, Fazl. Fighter during the Jihad, active in the north in Kunduz province.

Kochai, Sher Zaman. From Laghman province, during the Jihad he was affiliated with the communist government secret service (Khad) but also fought alongside the mujahedin and later on with the Taliban.

Mawlvi Jalil. From Baghlan province, a madrassah-student-turned-Taliban-commander.

Mohmand, Feridun. Tribal figure and leader of pro-communist militia in Nangarhar province during the Jihad.

Mullah Hassan. From Zabul province, Taliban commander

Mullah Izzat. Fighter during the Jihad, active in Kabul province.

Mullah Malang. From Badghis province, fighter during the Jihad.

Mullah Tawakul. From Faryab province, fighter during the Jihad and Taliban commander during the intra-mujahedin war.

Qadir, Abdul. Fighter during the Jihad, known as Imami Ghori for his religious education and for his origin from Ghor province.

Qahraman, Jabbar. From Helmand province, pro-government militia general during the Jihad who became a commander for the Uzbek party of Junbish-i-Milli during the intra-mujahedin war.

Qari Sadaat. From Baghlan province, madrassah student and political broker.

Qazi Sattar. Fighter during the Jihad, from Kabul province.

Saq, Juma. From Khost province, served as general for the communist government army during the Jihad.

Seyed Ikram. Fighter during the Jihad, from Wardak province.

Seyed Yaqeen. From Gardez province but active in Paktia, fighter during the Jihad and civil war intermediary.

Ustad Dawari. From Daikundi province, fighter during the Jihad.

Ustad Jaffar. From Wardak province but active in Takhar, fighter during the Jihad and civil war intermediary.

Taliban Primary Documents in Author's Possession

1) Taliban decree (*farman*) advising individuals how to conduct their prayers.
2) Taliban decree (*farman*) mandating conscription of young males to Taliban ranks.
3) Taliban decree (*farman*) condemning the fighting within Taliban ranks.
4) Taliban fatwa issued against the October 2001 U.S. invasion of Afghanistan.
5) Taliban decree (*farman*) regarding the dismantling of political parties and groups.
6) Taliban decree (*farman*) regarding the unauthorized beating of people.
7) Taliban decree (*farman*) regarding the timely processing of court cases.
8) Taliban decree (*farman*) regarding intelligence gathering.
9) Taliban decree (*farman*) regarding arrests.
10) Taliban decree (*farman*) regarding prisoners.
11) Taliban decree (*farman*) regarding nationalists.
12) Taliban decree (*farman*) regarding racists and nationalists in Taliban ranks.
13) Taliban decree (*farman*) regarding demobilization.
14) Taliban decree (*farman*) regarding conscription of former combatants to Taliban army.

15) Taliban decree (*farman*) regarding the exclusion of the underage from Taliban ranks.
16) Taliban decree (*farman*) regarding frontline radio communication.
17) Taliban decree (*farman*) regarding education of the youth.
18) Taliban decree (*farman*) against the killing of women and children.
19) Taliban decree (*farman*) regarding prayer.
20) Taliban decree (*farman*) regarding the targeting of intelligence agents.

Additional Party Documents

Wahdat News Bulletin, Issued by Hizb-i-Wahdat (all issues until December 1994), Kabul University Archive.
Afghan News, Issued by Jamiat-i-Islami (all issues until December 1995), Kabul University Archive.

Afghanistan Freedom of Information Act Declassified Documents

Guantanamo Bay Detainee-Related Documents (8,080 pages)
Combatant Status Review Tribunal (CSRT) and Administrative Review Board (ARB) Documents Released March 3, April 3, and April 19, 2006.

Testimony of Detainees before the Combatant Status Review Tribunal (3,849 pages)

Set_1_0001–0097;	Set_2_0098–0204;	Set_3_0205–0319;	Set_4_0320–0464;
Set_5_0465–0672;	Set_6_0673–0740;	Set_7_0741–0887;	Set_8_0887–1017;
Set_9_1018–1088B;	Set_10_1089–1144;	Set_11_1145–1178;	Set_12_1179–1239;
Set_13_1240–1291;	Set_14_1292–1317H;	Set_15_1318–1362;	Set_16_1363–1446;
Set_17_1447–1462;	Set_18_1463–1560;	Set_19_1561–1605;	Set_20_1606–16;
Set_21_1645–1688;	Set_22_1689–1741;	Set_23_1742–1789;	Set_24_1790–1831;
Set_25_1832–1847;	Set_26_1848–1900;	Set_27_1901–1948;	Set_28_1949–2000;
Set_29_2001–2047;	Set_30_2048–2144;	Set_31_2145–2265;	Set_32_2266–2301;
Set_33_2302–2425;	Set_34_2426–2457;	Set_35_2458–2492;	Set_36_2493–2577;
Set_37_2578–2607;	Set_38_2608–2628;	Set_39_2629–2646;	Set_40_2647–2664;
Set_41_2665–2727;	Set_42_2728–2810;	Set_43_2811–2921;	Set_44_2922–3064;
Set_45_3065–3095;	Set_46_3096–3129;	Set_47_3130–3248;	Set_48_3249–3297;
Set_49_3298–3380;	Set_50_3381–3489;	Set_51_3490–3642;	Set_52_3643–3869;
Set_53_3870–3959			

Testimony of Detainees and Documents Submitted on Their Behalf before the Administrative Review Boards (sets 1–4 released March 3, 2006, sets 5–15 released April 3, 2006, sets 16–19 released April 19, 2006) (3,940 pages)

ARB_Transcript_Set_1_395–584;	ARB_Transcript_Set_2_585–768;
ARB_Transcript_Set_3_769–943_FINAL;	ARB_Transcript_Set_4_1431–1455;
ARB_Transcript_Set_5_20000–20254;	ARB_Transcript_Set_6_20255–20496;
ARB_Transcript_Set_7_20497–20750;	ARB_Transcript_Set_8_20751–21016;
ARB_Transcript_Set_9_21017–21351;	ARB_Transcript_Set_10_21352–21661;
ARB_Transcript_Set_11_21662–22010;	ARB_Transcript_Set_12_22011–22244;
ARB_Transcript_Set_13_22245–22523;	ARB_Transcript_Set_14_22524–22682;
ARB_Transcript_Set_15_22683–22733;	ARB_Transcript_Set_16_22734–22821;

ARB_Transcript_Set_17_22822–23051;   ARB_Transcript_Set_18_23052–23263;
ARB_Transcript_Set_19_23264–23359

Administrative Review Board Summaries of Detention/Release Factors (291 pages)
ARB_Factors_Set_1_944–1045;   ARB_Factors_Set_2_1046–1160;
ARB_Factors_Set_3_1161–1234

The National Security Archive: The Taliban File
Source: Freedom of Information Act Release to the National Security Archive, http://www.gwu.edu/~nsarchiv/NSAEBB/NSAEBB97/index.htm, accessed February 20, 2006.

Document 1: U.S. Consulate (Peshawar) Cable, "New Fighting and New Forces in Kandahar," November 3, 1994, Confidential, 13 pp. Excised.

Document 2: U.S. Department of State, Cable, "Weekly South Asia Activity Report," November 4, 1994, Confidential, 13 pp.

Document 3: U.S. Embassy (Islamabad), Cable, "The Taliban – Who Knows What the Movement Means?" November 28, 1994, Confidential, 14 pp.

Document 4: U.S. Department of State, Memorandum, "Developments in Afghanistan," December 5, 1994, Classification Unknown, 1 p.

Document 5: U.S. Embassy (Islamabad), Cable, "[Excised] Believe Pakistan Is Backing Taliban," December 6, 1994, Secret, 3 pp.

Document 6: U.S. Embassy (Islamabad), Cable, "The Taliban: What We've Heard," January 26, 1995, Secret, 10 pp.

Document 7: U.S. Embassy (Islamabad), Cable, "Meeting with the Taliban in Kandahar: More Questions than Answers," February 15, 1995, Confidential, 7 pp.

Document 8: U.S. Embassy (Islamabad), Cable, "Finally, A Talkative Talib: Origins and Membership of the Religious Students' Movement," February 20, 1995, Confidential, 15 pp.

Document 9: U.S. Embassy (Dushanbe), Cable, "Rabbani Emissary States Rabbani Will Not Surrender Power to Interim Council until Taliban Join," February 21, 1995, Confidential, 9 pp.

Document 10: U.S. Embassy (Islamabad), Cable, "Afghanistan: Taliban Take Shindand Air Base; Herat Threatened – Will Iran Intervene?" September 4, 1995, Confidential, 6 pp.

Document 11: U.S. Embassy (Islamabad), Cable, "Afghanistan: Heavy Fighting Rages West of Kabul; Herat Calm after Taliban Take-Over," September 6, 1995, Confidential, 6 pp.

Document 12: U.S. Embassy (Islamabad), Cable, "Eyewitness to the Fall of Herat Says Taliban are Winning Hearts and Minds – For Now," February 18, 1995, Confidential, 11 pp.

Document 13: U.S. Department of State, Cable, "Pak Foreign Minister Asks U.S. Cooperation on Afghanistan," February 21, 1996, Confidential, 6 pp.

Document 14: U.S. Embassy (Islamabad), Cable, "Senator Brown and Congressman Wilson Discuss Afghanistan with Pakistani Officials," April 14, 1996, Confidential, 4 pp.

Document 15: U.S. Embassy (Islamabad), Cable, "A/S Raphel Discusses Afghanistan," April 22, 1996, Confidential, 7 pp.

Document 16: U.S. Embassy (Moscow), Cable, "A/S Raphel Consultations with Deputy FM Chernyshev," May 13, 1996, Confidential, 6 pp.

Document 17: U.S. Department of State, Cable, "Dealing with the Taliban in Kabul," September 28, 1996, Confidential, 6 pp.

Document 18: U.S. Embassy (Islamabad), Cable, "Afghanistan: Taliban Official Says that Relations with Russia and Iran 'Tense,'" September 29, 1997, Confidential, 10 pp.

Document 19: U.S. Embassy (Islamabad), Cable, "Ambassador Meets Taliban: We Are the People," November 12, 1996, Confidential, 17 pp.

Document 20: U.S. Department of State, Cable, "Afghanistan: Taliban Rep Won't Seek UN Seat for Now," December 13, 1996, Confidential, 6 pp.

Document 21: U.S. Embassy (Islamabad), Cable, "Scenesetter for Your Visit to Islamabad: Afghan Angle," January 16, 1997, Confidential, 6 pp.

Document 22: U.S. Embassy (Islamabad), Cable, "Afghanistan: GOP Denies Pakistani Involvement in Fighting; Taliban Reportedly Enlisting Supporters in Frontier Areas," June 4, 1997, Confidential, 4 pp.

Document 23: U.S. Embassy (Islamabad), Cable, "Afghanistan: Observers Report Uptick in Support for Anti-Taliban Factions by Iran," July 7, 1997, Confidential, 10 pp.

Document 24: Department of State, Cable, "Afghanistan: Meeting with the Taliban," December 11, 1997, Confidential, 13 pp.

Document 25: U.S. Consulate (Peshawar), Cable, "Afghanistan: A Report of Pakistani Military Assistance to the Taliban," March 24, 1998, Confidential, 3 pp.

Document 26: Department of State (Washington), Cable, "Afghanistan: Taliban Convene Ulema, Iran and Bin Ladin on the Agenda," September 25, 1998, Confidential, 5 pp.

Document 27: Defense Intelligence Agency, Defense Intelligence Assessment, "Usama Bin Ladin / Al-Qaida Information Operations," September 1999, Top Secret, 15 pp.

Document 28: Defense Intelligence Agency, Cable, "IIR [Excised]/Veteran Afghanistan Traveler's Analysis of Al Qaeda and Taliban Exploitable Weaknesses," October 2, 2001, Secret, 10 pp.

Document 29: Defense Intelligence Agency, Cable, "IIR [Excised]/Veteran Afghanistan Traveler's Analysis of Al Qaeda and Taliban Military, Political and Cultural Landscape and its Weaknesses," October 2, 2001, Secret, 7 pp.

Document 30: Department of Defense, Cable, [Title Excised,] October 4, 2001, Confidential, 5 pp.

Document 31: Defense Intelligence Agency, Cable, "IIR [Excised]/The Assassination of Massoud Related to 11 September 2001 Attack," November 21, 2001, Secret, 5 pp.

Document 32: Defense Intelligence Agency, Cable, "IIR [Excised] Pakistani Political, Military Situation, and Terrorism Issues," January 9, 2002, Secret, 5 pp.

English Language Press, Essays and Reports on Afghanistan

"Afghan Ex-Warlord Living in London," *The Tribune of India*, On-Line Edition, http://www.tribuneindia.com/2000/20000728/world.htm, accessed February 2, 2005.

Christia, Fotini and Michael Semple. (2009). "Flipping the Taliban: How to Win in Afghanistan," *Foreign Affairs* 4 (88): 1–13.

Cooper, Kenneth J. (1997a). "Islamic Militia's Advance Threatens Afghan Oasis of Peace," *The Washington Post*, February 27.

Cooper, Kenneth J. (1997b). "For Afghan Rivals, Warrior Traditions Complicate Unity: Clashes, Defections Deal Swift Blows to Taliban's Goal of 'One Government,'" *The Washington Post*, June 4, p. A25.

Davis, Anthony. (1993). "The Afghan Army," *Jane's Intelligence Review* 5 (3): 134–139.

Davis, Anthony. (1994). "The Battleground of Northern Afghanistan," *Jane's Intelligence Review* 6 (7): 323–327.

Davis, Anthony. (1995). "Afghanistan's Taliban," *Jane's Intelligence Review* 7 (7): 315–321.

Davis, Anthony. (1996). "Afghanistan – Past, Present, and Future," *Jane's Intelligence Review* 8 (4): 181–185.

Davis, Anthony. (1997). "Taliban Found Lacking When Nation-Building Beckoned," *Jane's Intelligence Review* 9 (8): 359–364.

Davis, Anthony. (1998). "Taliban Continue the Killing but Fail to Finish the Crusade," *Jane's Intelligence Review* 10 (11): 17–22.

"Defecting General Says Afghanistan Won't Threaten Russia, Central Asia," (1997). *BBC Monitoring Service: Asia-Pacific*, May 27 (Source: ITAR-TASS news agency [World Service], Moscow, in English May 25).

Gannon, Kathy. (1997). "Reports: Warlord Tossed out of Province in Northwestern Afghanistan," Associated Press Newswires, May 19.

"The Great 'Ustad' Mazari," http://millatehazara.tripod.com/mazari.html, accessed May 25, 2006.

"Hezb-e Wahdat Official Blames Mazari for West Kabul Fighting," (1994). *BBC Monitoring Service, Asia-Pacific*, September 22.

Human Rights Watch. (2005). *Blood-Stained Hands: Past Atrocities in Kabul and Afghanistan's Legacy of Impunity*, http://www.hrw.org/sites/default/files/reports/afghanistan0605.pdf, accessed July 15, 2005.

Isby, David C. (1992). "Afghanistan – Civil War Next?" *Jane's Intelligence Review* 4 (10): 463–467.

"Key Defection Hastens Ultimate Taliban Triumph," *The Australian*, May 27, 1997.

Johnston, Tim. (1997a). "Afghan Mutineer Has Differences with Opposition Leader," *Reuters News*, May 20.

Johnston, Tim. (1997b). "Afghan Rivals Fight for Northern City," *Reuters News*, September 10.

Johnston, Tim. (1997c). "Opposition Leader Dostum Returns to Afghanistan," *Reuters News*, September 12.

Lyon, Alistair. (1997). "Street Battles Rage in Conquered Afghan Town," *Reuters News*, May 28.

Mazari, Abdul Ali. Wartime speech. Text available at http://www.hazarapress.com/best_choice_of_politics/mazari.htm, accessed May 1, 2008.

McGirk, Tim. (1997). "Into the Massacre Rode the Taliban: The Fierce Islamists Thought They Had Conquered All Afghanistan – Until a Surprise Counterattack," *Time International* 149 (23).

Pratt, David. (1998). "Warlord Rivalry and Ethnic Hatred behind Atrocities," *The Scotsman*, January 1.

Rashid, Ahmed. (1997). "Highly Explosive: Renewed Fighting Alarms Central Asian Neighbors," *Far Eastern Economic Review* 160 (24): 24–26.

Rupert, James and Steve Coll. (1990). "U.S. Declines to Probe Afghan Drug Trade; Rebels, Pakistani Officers Implicated," *The Washington Post*, May 13.

Salahuddin, Sayed. (1997). "Dostum Replaces Mutinous General in Afghan North," *Reuters News*, May 21.

Siddiqi, Kamal. (1997). "Taliban Plays Its Trump Defection Card," *Asia Times*, May 21.

"Situation Tense in North Afghanistan amid Reports of Revolt," (1997). *Agence France-Presse*, May 19.

Smith, Stefan. (1997). "Pro-Taliban Commanders Maintain Northern Afghan Battle," Agence France-Press, September 15.

"The Battle for Afghanistan," (1997). *The Economist* 343 (8019): 37–38.

Thomas, Christopher. (1997a). "Seizure of Key Pass Puts Defiant North at Taleban's Mercy," *The Times*, February 26.

Thomas, Christopher. (1997b). "Defecting General Boosts Taleban's Chances of Victory," *The Times*, May 20.

Thomas, Christopher. (1997c). "Foreigners Flee Afghan Dance of Death," *The Times*, May 31, p. 12.

Wyllie, James. (1994). "Afghanistan – Spiraling Decline,"*Jane's Intelligence Review* 6 (6): 273–274.

Secondary Literature on Afghanistan

Adamec, Ludwig W. (1996). *Dictionary of Afghan Wars, Revolutions and Insurgencies*. Lanham, MD: Scarecrow Press.

Adamec, Ludwig W. (2008). *Biographical Encyclopedia of Afghanistan*. New Delhi: Pentagon Press.

Ahady, Anwar-ul-Haq. (1995). "The Decline of the Pashtuns in Afghanistan," *Asian Survey* 35 (7): 621–634.

Ahady, Anwar-ul-Haq. (1998). "Saudi Arabia, Iran, and the Conflict in Afghanistan," in William Maley, ed., *Fundamentalism Reborn? Afghanistan and the Taliban*. New York: New York University Press, pp. 117–134.

Anderson, Jon Lee. (2002). *The Lion's Grave: Dispatches from Afghanistan*. New York: Grove Press.

Arnold, Anthony. (1983). *Afghanistan's Two-Party Communism: Parcham and Khalq*. Stanford, CA: Hoover Institutions, Stanford University.

Azoy, G. Whitney. (2003). *Buzkashi: Game and Power in Afghanistan*. Long Grove, IL: Waveland Press.

Bradsher, Henry S. (1999). *Afghan Communism and Soviet Intervention*. Oxford: Oxford University Press.

Canfield, Robert L. (1989). "Afghanistan: The Trajectory of Internal Alignments," *Middle East Journal* 43 (4): 635–648.

Coll, Steve. (2004). *Ghost Wars: The Secret History of the CIA, Afghanistan and Bin Laden, from the Soviet Invasion to September 10, 2001*. New York: Penguin Press.

Davis, Anthony. (1998). "How the Taliban Became a Military Force," in William Maley, ed., *Fundamentalism Reborn? Afghanistan and the Taliban*. New York: New York University Press, pp. 43–71.

Dorronsoro, Gilles. (2005). *Revolution Unending: Afghanistan, 1979 to the Present*. John King, trans. London: C. Hurst.

Dorronsoro, Gilles and Lobato, Chantal. (1989). "The Militia in Afghanistan," *Central Asian Survey* 8 (4): 95–108.

Dupree, Louis. (1980). *Afghanistan*. Princeton, NJ: Princeton University Press.

Edwards, David B. (2002). *Before Taliban: Genealogies of the Afghan Jihad*. Berkeley and Los Angeles: University of California Press.

Emadi, Hafizullah. (1995). "Exporting the Revolution: Radicalization of Shiite Movement in Afghanistan," *Middle Eastern Studies* 31 (1): 1–12.

Emadi, Hafizullah (2006). "The Hazaras and Their Role in the Process of Political Transformation in Afghanistan," http://boozers.fortunecity.com/jerusalem/47/Political_Role/political_role.html#8, accessed May 25, 2006.

Ewans, Martin. (2002). *Afghanistan: A Short History of Its People and Politics*. New York: Harper Collins.

Fänge, Anders. (1995). "Afghanistan after April 1992: A Struggle for State and Ethnicity," *Central Asian Survey* 14 (1):17–24.

Filkins, Dexter. (2008). *The Forever War*. New York: Knopf.

Gall, Sandy. (1993). "Masoud Builds Afghan Power Base with National Army," *Jane's Defence Weekly* 20 (14): 17–19.

Gearing, Julian. (1993). "Intriguing Changes of Fortune (The Possible Return to Power of Former Communists in Afghanistan)," *The Middle East* (224): 22.

Girardet, Edward and Walter, Jonathan. (2004). *Afghanistan: CROSSLINES Essential Field Guides to Humanitarian and Conflict Zones*. Geneva: Media Action International.

Giustozzi, Antonio. (2000). *War, Politics and Society in Afghanistan, 1978–1992*. London: C. Hurst Publishing.

Giustozzi, Antonio. (2004). "The Demodernization of an Army: Northern Afghanistan, 1992–2001," *Small Wars and Insurgencies* 15 (1): 1–18.

Giustozzi, Antonio. (2009). *Empires of Mud: War and Warlords in Afghanistan*. London: Hurst and Company.

Glatzer, Bernt. (1998). "Is Afghanistan on the Brink of Ethnic and Tribal Disintegration?" in William Maley, ed., *Fundamentalism Reborn? Afghanistan and the Taliban*. New York: New York University Press, pp. 167–178.

Goodson, Larry P. (2001). *Afghanistan's Endless War*. Seattle, WA: University of Seattle Press.

Goodson, Larry and Thomas Johnson. (2011). "Parallels with Past: How Soviets Lost in Afghanistan, How US Is Losing," *Eurasia Review* (April 26), http://www.eurasiareview.com/parallels-with-past-how-soviets-lost-in-afghanistan-how-us-is-losing-analysis-26042011/, accessed 30 April 2011.

Grau, L. W. (1996). *The Bear Went Over the Mountain*. Washington, DC: National Defense University Press.

Griffin, Michael. (2001). *Reaping the Whirlwind: The Taliban Movement in Afghanistan*. Sterling, VA: Pluto Press.

Gvosdev, Nikolas. (2009). "The Soviet Victory That Never Was," *Foreign Affairs* (December 10), http://www.foreignaffairs.com/articles/65713/nikolas-k-gvosdev/the-soviet-victory-that-never-was, accessed April 30, 2011.

Harpviken, Kristian Berg. (1996). *Political Mobilization among the Hazara of Afghanistan: 1978–1992*. Oslo: Institutt for sosiologi og samfunnsgeografi.

Harpviken, Kristian Berg. (1997). "Transcending Traditionalism: The Emergence of Non-State Military Formation in Afghanistan," *Journal of Peace Research* 34 (3): 271–287.

Ishtiaq Ahmad. (2004). *Gulbuddin Hekmatyar: An Afghan Train from Jihad to Terrorism*. Islamabad: PanGraphics.

Kaplan, Robert D. (2001). *Soldiers of God: With Islamic Warriors in Afghanistan and Pakistan*. New York: Vintage Departures.

Khalizad, Zalmay. (1995). "Afghanistan in 1994: Civil War and Disintegration," *Asian Survey* 35 (2): 147–152.

Khalilzad, Zalmay and Daniel Byman. (2000). "Afghanistan: The Consolidation of a Rogue State," *The Washington Quarterly* 23 (1): 65–78.

Magnus, Ralph. (1997). "Afghanistan in 1996: Year of the Taliban," *Asian Survey* 37 (2): 111–117.

Maley, William. (1998). "Interpreting the Taliban," in William Maley, ed., *Fundamentalism Reborn? Afghanistan and the Taliban*. New York: New York University Press, pp.1–23.

Maley, William. (2009). *The Afghanistan Wars*. 2nd ed. New York: Palgrave McMillan.

Marshall, D. A. (2006). *Phased Withdrawal, Conflict Resolution and State Reconstruction*. London: Defence Academy of the United Kingdom, Conflict Studies Research Centre.

Matinuddin, Kamal. (1999). *The Taliban Phenomenon: Afghanistan 1994–1997*. Oxford: Oxford University Press.

Minkov, Anton and Gregory Smolynec. (2007). "Social Development and State Building in Afghanistan during the Soviet Period, 1979–1989," *Lessons Learned from the Soviet Experience in Afghanistan*," Technical Memorandum: 2009-033 Ottawa: Defense R & D Canada, Centre for Operational Research & Analysis, July 2009, p. 35.

Mousavi, Sayed Askar. (1997). *The Hazaras of Afghanistan: A Historical, Cultural, Economic and Political Study*. New York: St. Martin's Press.

O'Ballance, Edgar. (2002). *Afghan Wars*. London: Brassey's.

Poladi, Hassan. (1989). *The Hazaras*. Stockton, CA: Mughal Publishing Corporation.

Rasanayagam, Angelo. (2003). *Afghanistan: A Modern History*. London: I.B. Tauris.

Rashid, Ahmed. (2000). *Taliban: Militant Islam, Oil and Fundamentalism in Central Asia*. New Haven, CT: Yale University Press.

Rashid, Ahmed. (2001). *Taliban: The Story of the Afghan Warlords*. London: Pan.

Roy, Oliver. (1990). *Islam and Resistance in Afghanistan*. New York: Cambridge University Press.

Roy, Oliver. (1995). *Afghanistan: From Holy War to Civil War*. Princeton, NJ: Darwin Press.

Rubin, Barnett R. (1995a). *The Fragmentation of Afghanistan: State Formation and Collapse in the International System*. New Haven, CT: Yale University Press.

Rubin, Barnett R. (1995b). *The Search for Peace in Afghanistan: From Buffer State to Failed State*. New Haven, CT: Yale University Press.

Saikal, Amin. (1998). "The Rabbani Government 1992–1996," in William Maley, ed., *Fundamentalism Reborn? Afghanistan and the Taliban*. New York: New York University Press, pp. 29–42.

Semple, Michael. (2010). *Afghanistan Oral Narratives Project*. Unpublished Manuscript.

Shay, Shaul. (2002). *The Endless Jihad . . . The Mujahidin, the Taliban and Bin Laden*. Herzliya: The International Policy Institute for Counter-Terrorism at the Interdisciplinary Center.

Sinno, Abdulkader H. (2008). *Organizations at War in Afghanistan and Beyond*. Ithaca, NY: Cornell University Press.

Weitz, Richard. (1992). "Moscow's Endgame in Afghanistan," *Journal of Conflict Studies* 12 (1): 25–46.

Williams, Brian. (2006). "Dostumname: Living with a Warlord in Afghan Turkestan," paper prepared for presentation at 2006 Association for the Study of Nationalities (ASN) Conference, New York, March 23–25.

Yunas, Fida. (1997). *Afghanistan, Political Parties, Groups, Movements and Mujahideen Alliances and Governments (1879–1997)*. Peshawar: Peshawar Area Studies Center.

Sources on Bosnia and Herzegovina

Interviews[2]

Abdić, Fikret. Founder and CEO of Agrokomerc. President of the Autonomous Province of Western Bosnia (APWB) and leader of the secessionist Muslims in Cazinska Krajina. At the time of the interview he was incarcerated in Karlovac Jail, Karlovac, Croatia, July 2004.

Alen (alias). A fighter from Lubija, in Western Bosnia, who fought against the Serbs in Prijedor. Interview conducted in Sanski Most, June 2002.

Aurelija (alias). Supporter of Muslim secessionists in Velika Kladuša. Her father, in Bihać, was supporting the Muslims opposing the secession. Interview conducted in Velika Kladuša, June 2004.

Beloni, Roberto. Expert on Bosnia and Herzegovina. Lecturer in International Politics, Queens University, Belfast, Northern Ireland. Interview conducted in Sarajevo, July 2004.

Berthoud, Julien. Head of Political Section, Office of the High Representative (OHR). Interview conducted in Mostar, August 2004.

Bieber, Florian. Expert on Bosnia and Herzegovina. Lecturer in East European Politics, Kent University, United Kingdom. Interview conducted in New York, April 2005.

Blagojević, Branislav. Political Officer, Organization for Security and Cooperation in Europe; wartime fighter. Interview conducted in Banja Luka, June 2004.

Cohen, Roger. Award-winning *New York Times* reporter who covered the war in Bosnia and Herzegovina and the secessionist efforts in Western Bosnia. Interview conducted in New York, June 2007.

Delić, Rasim. Bosnian Muslim Chief of Staff of the ABiH army during the war. Accused of war crimes and crimes against humanity by the International Criminal Tribunal for Yugoslavia (ICTY). Sentenced to three years imprisonment. Died in 2010. Interview conducted in a building of the RBiH Presidency, Sarajevo, BiH, July 2004.

Dolić, Rifet. DNZ acting president at the time of the interview. Interview conducted in Velika Kladuša, August 2004.

Dragan (alias). Fighter in the western Bosnian theaters. Interview conducted in Prijedor, June 2004.

Drasko (alias). Fighter in the western Bosnian theaters. Interview conducted in Prijedor, June 2004.

---

[2] All positions shown on the list are as of the time of the interview, unless otherwise noted. Additional information on these personalities, who mostly served as local elites for their respective ethnic groups during the civil war's trajectory, can be found in *Who Is Who among Bosniacs* (2001).

Dudaković, Atif. Served as army division general, deputy headquarters commander of the Joint National Army Forces; commander to the National Army 502nd Brigade, as well as commander of the National Army 5th Corps. Interview conducted at the Rajlovac Army Base and Command Center, Sarajevo, BiH, July 2004.

Elvira (alias). Velika Kladuša resident and Abdić supporter during the war. Interview conducted in Bihać, BiH, July 2004.

Farid (alias). Fighter in the Posavina Corridor. Interview conducted in Bosanski Šamac, July 2004

Fehro (alias). Fighter in the Doboj area of Bosnia. Interview conducted in Sanski Most, July 2003 and August 2004.

Gagro, Milivoj. Prewar mayor of the city of Mostar. Interview conducted in Mostar, June 2005.

Hadžiomerović, Zijad. President of the Mostar city council and leading figure in the 1993–1994 Croat-Muslim war in Mostar. Interview conducted in East Mostar, June 2005.

Horvat, Ivana. Human Rights Officer, Organization for Security and Cooperation in Europe, Croatia. Interview conducted in Karlovac, Croatia, August 2004.

Humo, Esad. A major in the 441 Famous Mountain Brigade at the 4th Corps of the ABiH Army. Received a Golden Lily Award for Military Merits, dated June 10, 1994. Interview conducted in Mostar, June 2005.

Kapić, Muso. Mostar wartime fighter. Interview conducted in Mostar, July 2004.

Kasagić, Rajko. Wartime Prime Minister of the Serb Republic (Republika Srpska) under President Radovan Karadzic. Interview conducted in Banja Luka, June 2004.

Kljujić, Stjepan. Prewar member of the Bosnia-Herzegovina rotating presidency. Interview conducted at the Sarajevo Presidential Palace, June 2006.

Kos, Milojica. Fought in the Omarska area of western Bosnia during the war and was convicted by the ICTY for war crimes perpetrated against Muslim civilians. He served a reduced sentence. Interview conducted in Omarska, July 2004.

Kuznetsov, Vladimir. Political Advisor, Organization for Security and Cooperation in Europe. Interview conducted in Mostar, August 2004.

Marko (alias). Combatant in Bihać during the war. Interview conducted in Banja Luka, Republika Srpska, BiH, August 2004.

Martin, Jose Lewis. Human Rights Officer, Organization for Security and Cooperation in Europe, Prijedor Office. Interview conducted in Prijedor, July 2002.

Moratti, Massimo. Human Rights Officer, Organization for Security and Cooperation in Europe. Interview held in Sarajevo, July 2002.

Miho (alias). Combatant in Mostar during the war. Interviews conducted in Mostar, August 2004, June 2005, and May 2006.

Milovanović, Manojlo. General in the Bosnian Serb army. Interview conducted in Banja Luka, Republika Sprska, BiH, July 2004.

Mulalić, Admil. Commander in the AWPR's army during the war. At the time of the interview, he was serving as Mayor of Velika Kladuša under DNZ. Interview conducted in Velika Kladuša, BiH, July 2004.

Namir (alias). Fifth Corps combatant in Bihać. Interview conducted in Bihać, BiH, July 2004.

Nermin (alias). Fighter in the Zenica area. Interview conducted in Sanski Most, June 2003.

Nevena (alias). Civilian who witnessed the taking of Ključ by Bosniac forces in late 1995. Interview conducted in Prijedor, BiH.

Nino (alias). Combatant in Banja Luka during the war. Interview conducted in Banja Luka, BiH, August 2004.

Oručević, Safet. Wartime (and postwar) politician in the city of Mostar. Interview conducted in Mostar, June 2006.

Pejanović, Ratko. President of the Serb civic council in Mostar. Interview conducted in Mostar, June 2005.

Perić, Zoran. Mostar politician. Interview conducted in Mostar, June 2005.

Popić, Alexandra. Human Rights Assistant, Organization for Security and Cooperation in Europe, Prijedor/Banja Luka office. Interview conducted in Prijedor, July 2002, August 2004, and in Banja Luka, June 2006.

Popović, Gostimir. Wartime political analyst and writer, retired air force colonel from the Yugoslav People's Army (JNA). Interview conducted in Banja Luka, June 2004.

Radić, Marko. Mostar police chief who was ex-commander in the Bosnian Croat Armed forces in the city during the 1993–1994 Croat-Muslim conflict. Interview conducted in Mostar, June 2005.

Rohde, David. Reporter who covered the Bosnian war for the *The Christian Science Monitor* and had been abducted by the Bosnian Serb army. He was the first to report on the Srebrenica massacre. Interview held in Cambridge, MA, May 2005.

Sarandrea, Lucio Valerio. Human Rights Officer, Office for Security and Cooperation in Europe, Drvar. Interview conducted in Drvar, July 2004.

Sead (alias). Combatant in Prijedor during the war. Interview conducted in Banja Luka, BiH, August 2004.

Sekulić, Dušanka. Rule of Law Monitor, Office for Security and Cooperation in Europe. Interview conducted in Banja Luka, July 2004.

Silajdžić, Haris. Served as minister of foreign affairs of the Bosnian government from 1990 to 1993 and as Prime Minister of the Bosnian government from 1993 to 1996. He was also the Vice President of SDA from 1990 to 1995 and one of the chief negotiators on the BiH side at the Dayton Peace Accords. Interview conducted in Sarajevo, BiH, June 2004.

Simić, Milan. A wartime member of the Bosnian Serb Crisis Staff and President of the Municipal Assembly of Bosanski Šamac. He was convicted for war crimes by the ICTY and served a reduced sentence. Interview conducted in Bosanski Šamac, July 2004.

Skrgić, Mohamed. Manager of Agrokomerc before the war and staunch supporter of Muslim secessionist leader Fikret Abdić. At the time of the interview he was serving as Canton One Municipal Council Member with DNZ (Abdic's party). Interview conducted in Pecigrad, BiH, July 2004.

Solaja, Miloš. Director of the Center for International Relations in Banja Luka. Interview conducted in Banja Luka, June 2004.

Topić, Marin. Mostar resident and fighter during the 1993–1994 Croat-Muslim conflict. Interview conducted in Mostar, July 2004.

Topić, Tanja. Political consultant. Interview conducted in Banja Luka, July 2004.

Vesna (alias). Civilian who witnessed the fighting between the secessionist Muslims and the Fifth Corps.

Zana (alias). Civilian who witnessed the ethnic cleansing in Bosanski Šamac, in the Posavina corridor.

Zanni, Giulio. Head of the EC Delegation Office in Banja Luka. Interview conducted in Banja Luka, July 2004.

Zarić, Simo. Wartime Chief of National Security Service in Bosanski Šamac. He was convicted for war crimes by the ICTY and served a reduced sentence. Interview conducted in Bosanski Šamac, June 2004.

Zelenika, Petar. Wartime brigadier with the Bosnian Croat armed forces in Mostar. Interview conducted in Mostar, June 2005.

Živanović, Živadin. Professor of philosophy, University of Banja Luka. Interview conducted in Banja Luka, July 2004.

Focus Group: With six Serbian local elected officials who had remained in Mostar during the war, including the Orthodox priest. Focus group conducted in Mostar, in the courtyard of the makeshift Orthodox church, June 2005.

Interviews Conducted by Research Assistant Gostimir Popović

Bajčetić, Miloš. Commander of the BiH Territorial Defense in 1989. Interview conducted in Banja Luka, July 2006.

Bosnić, Rajko. High-ranking officer in the BiH Territorial Defense in 1991 in Drvar. Interview conducted over the phone, July 2006.

Crnovrsanin, Adem. Brigadier in the BiH Army. Interview conducted over the phone, July 2006.

Glamočanin, Ranko. High-ranking officer in the BiH Territorial Defense in 1991. Interview conducted in Banja Luka, July 2006.

Kafedžić, Mujo. High-ranking officer in the BiH Territorial Defense in 1991. Interview conducted in Banja Luka, July 2006.

Kandić, Zdravko. High-ranking officer in the BiH Territorial Defense in 1991 in Mostar. Interview conducted over the phone, July 2006.

Primary Documents

Documents from DNZ Party Archive in Velika Kladuša

(Accessed in July 2004 with the authorization of Admil Mulalić, a supporter of Fikret Abdić and then-mayor of the town of Velika Kladuša in western Bosnia)

Agreement on Ceasefire and Cessation of Hostilities [between APWB and the Fifth Corps] (*Sporazum o Prekidu Dejstava i Neprijateljstva*), January 18, 1994.

Agreement between the ABiH Army, Croatia and APWB (*Sporazum*), Vojnić, August 8, 1995.

Starting Basis for the Foundation of Province Number 1 (*Polazne Osnove za Formiranje Provincije Broj* 1), Velika Kladuša, May 1993.

Fatwa (*Fetva*), Islamic Association of BiH, Bihać Mufti's Office, No 35/93, November 24, 1993.

Report (*Izvestaj*), Assembly of the Bihać Islamic Association, September 14, 1993.

Primary documents favorable to the Fifth Corps were found in Smail Kličić's book referenced among the following.

Primary Sources for Coding Prewar Demographics and Military Assets, as Well as Wartime Territorial Changes and Casualties

1991 Yugoslav Census Data. Data include municipal-level information for all 109 of Bosnia's prewar municipalities on ethnic composition, educational levels, and average income.

The Bosnian Book of Dead, Research and Documentation Center, Sarajevo, June 21, 2007. Data include municipal-level information on casualties by ethnicity by year for the four years of the war (1992–1995).

"Strategy for Defense of Public Property" *(Strategija Opštenarodne Odbrane i Društvene Samozaštite)*, SSNO, Belgrade 1989.

"Collection of Documents on Yugoslav Security" *(Zbornik: Dokumenti o Bezbednosti Jugoslavije)*, Military Publishing Institute (*Vojnoizdavački Zavod*), Belgrade, 2002.

Hronologija Događaja 1990–1995 godina, Dokumentacioni Centar Vlade Republike Srpske, Banja Luka, 2002.

Oslobođenje, leading newspaper published in Sarajevo (all issues from 1992 to 1994).

Maglajske Novine, local newspaper published in Maglaj (all issues from 1993 to 1995).

Livanjski Vidici, local newspaper published in Livno (all issues from 1992 to 1993).

Herceg Bosna, newspaper published in Sarajevo (all issues from 1991 to 1993).

HVO Riječ, newsletter published in Sarajevo (all issues from 1993).

RIJEČ HVO, newsletter published in Mostar (all issues from 1992 to 1993).

English-Language Press on Bosnia and Herzegovina

"33 Soldiers Die in Bosnia City as Croats Battle the Muslims," *The New York Times*, August 18.

Bruce, James. (1995). "Arab Veterans of the Afghan War," *Jane's Intelligence Review* 7 (4): 175–179.

Burns, John. (1992a). "Serbs and Croats Now Join in Devouring Bosnia's Land," *The New York Times*, October 22.

Burns, John. (1992b). "Attacks by Croatian Force Put New Strains on Bosnian Government's Unity," *The New York Times*, October 27.

Burns, John. (1992c). "THE WORLD: Bosnians Run Short Of Time and Allies," *The New York Times*, November 1.

Burns, John. (1993). "Plight of Muslims Reported to Ease in Bosnia Area Set for U.S. Airdrops," February 28.

Cohen, Roger. (1994). "Breakaway Bosnian Fief Makes Deals, Not War," *The New York Times*, July 4.

Goldsmith, Charles. (1992). "EC, Hoping to End Fighting, Recognizes Bosnia-Herzegovina," *International Herald Tribune*, April 7.

Hedges, Chris. (1992). "Muslims from Afar Joining 'Holy War' in Bosnia," *The New York Times*, December 5.

Lewis, Paul. (1993). "New Croat-Muslim Fighting Erupts in Southern Bosnia," *The New York Times*, May 10.

"Muslims Accuse Croats of Massacring 80 Villagers," *The New York Times*, October 26, 1993.

Sudetic, Chuck. (1992a). "Serbs Attack Muslim Slavs and Croats in Bosnia," *The New York Times*, April 4.

Sudetic, Chuck. (1992b). "Forces in Bosnia Begin to Unravel," *The New York Times*, May 6.

Sudetic, Chuck. (1992c). "Better-Armed Muslims Warn Croats," *The New York Times*, November 6.

Sudetic, Chuck. (1992d). "Muslims from Abroad Join in War Against Serbs," *The New York Times*, November 14.

Sudetic, Chuck. (1992e). "Muslims Oust Some Serbian Forces from Sarajevo Siege, Bosnians Say," *The New York Times*, December 5.
Sudetic, Chuck. (1993a). "Muslim-Croatian Clashes," *The New York Times*, May 20.
Sudetic, Chuck. (1993b). "Bosnians Disband Sarajevo Croats," *The New York Times*, November 7.

Secondary Literature on Bosnia and Herzegovina (in local languages and in English)

Alagić, Mehmed. (1997). *Rat u Srednjoj Bosni*. Bemust: Zenica.
Andreas, Peter. (2008). *Blue Helmets and Black Markets: The Business of Survival in the Siege of Sarajevo*. Ithaca, NY: Cornell University Press.
Bax, Mart. (2000). "Warlords, Priests and the Politics of Ethnic Cleansing: A Case Study from Rural Bosnia Hercegovina," *Ethnic and Racial Studies* 23 (1): 16–36.
Bjelakovic, Nebojsa and Francesco Strazzari. (1999). "The Sack of Mostar, 1992–1994: The Politico-Military Connection," *European Security* 8 (2): 73–102.
Blažanović, Jovo. (2001). *Traganje za Istinom*. Banja Luka: Boračka Organizacija Republike Srpske.
Blažanović, Jovo. (2003). *Prećutani Zločini*. Banja Luka: Boračka Organizacija Republike Srpske.
Bose, Sumantra. (2002). *Bosnia after Dayton: Nationalist Partition and International Intervention*. Oxford: Oxford University Press.
Botev, Nikolai. (1994). "Where East Meets West: Ethnic Intermarriage in the Former Yugoslavia," *American Sociological Review* 59 (3): 461–480.
Burg, Steven and Paul S. Shoup. (1999). *The War in Bosnia-Herzegovina: Ethnic Conflict and International Intervention*. Armonk, NY: M.E. Sharpe.
Caspersen, Nina. (2010). *Contested Nationalism: Serb Elite Rivalry in Croatia and Bosnia in the 1990s*. New York: Berghahn Books.
Central Intelligence Agency. (2002). *Balkan Battlegrounds: A Military History of the Yugoslav Conflict, 1990–1995*. Washington: CIA Office of Russian and European Analysis.
Cohen, Roger. (1998). *Hearts Grown Brutal: Sagas of Sarajevo*. New York: Random House.
Collinson, Christopher. (1994). "Bosnian Army Tactics," *Jane's Intelligence Review* 6 (1): 11–13.
Delić, Rasim. (2004). *Rat u BiH*. Sarajevo: Vojna biblioteka.
Efendić, Hasan. (1998). *Who Defended Bosnia? Association of Citizens of Noble Origins (Ko je branio Bosnu? Udruženje građana plemičkog porijekla)*. Sarajevo: BiH.
Ekwall-Uebelhart, Barbara and Andrei Raevsky. (1996). *Managing Arms in Peace Processes: Croatia and Bosnia-Herzegovina*. New York: United Nations.
Glenny, Misha. (1993). *The Fall of Yugoslavia: The Third Balkan War* (New York: Penguin Books.
Gutman, Roy. (1993). *A Witness to Genocide: The 1993 Pulitzer Prize-Winning Dispatches on the 'Ethnic Cleansing' of Bosnia*. New York: Macmillan.
Halilović, Sefer. (1997). *Lukava Strategija*. Sarajevo: Marsal d.o.o.
Hoare, Marko Attila. (2004). *How Bosnia Armed*. London: Saqi Books.
Holbrooke, Richard. (1998). *To End a War*. New York: Random House.
Ignatieff, Michael. (1998). *The Warrior's Honor: Ethnic War and the Modern Conscience*. New York: Henry Holt and Company.
Indijić, Milan. (1991). "BiH Territorial Defense" *(Teritorijalna Odbrana BiH)*. Sarajevo.

International Institute for Strategic Studies. (1994). *The Military Balance, 1993–1994* 94 (1): 73–106.

Judah, Tim. (1999). *The Serbs: History, Myth and the Destruction of Yugoslavia.* 2nd ed. New Haven, CT: Yale University Press.

Kadrić, Jusuf. (2004). *Bosnjaci Žrtve i Svjedoči.* Sarajevo: Centar za Istraživanje i Dokumentaciju.

Kalyvas, Stathis and Nicholas Sambanis. (2005). "Bosnia's Civil War: Origins and Violence Dynamics," in Paul Collier and Nicholas Sambanis, eds., *Understanding Civil War: Europe, Central Asia, and Other Regions.* Washington DC: World Bank and Oxford University Press, Vol. 2, pp. 191–229.

Kličić, Smail. (2002). *Intra-Bosniac Conflict in Cazinska Krajina 1992–1995 (Međubosnjački Sukob u Cazinskoj Krajini 1992–1995).* Bihać: Bihać University.

Latić, Nedžad and Zehrudin Isaković. (1997). *Ratna Sjećanja Mehmeda Alagića: Rat u Srednoj Bosni.* Zenica: Bemust.

Law on National Defense (Zakon o Narodnoj Odbrani). (1985). Belgrade: SSNO, Belgrade.

Maass, Peter. (1996). *Love Thy Neighbor: A Story of War.* New York: Alfred A. Knopf.

MacKinnon, Catharine A. (1994). "Turning Rape into Pornography: Postmodern Genocide," in Alexandra Stiglmayer, ed., *Mass Rape: The War Against Women in Bosnia-Herzegovina.* Lincoln, NE: University of Nebraska Press, pp. 73–81.

O'Ballance, Edgar. (1995). *Civil War in Bosnia, 1992–1994.* New York: St. Martin's Press.

Radinović, Radovan. (2004). *Laži o Sarajevskom Ratistu.* Beograd: Svet knjige.

Rohde, David. (1997). *Endgame: The Betrayal and Fall of Srebrenica, Europe's Worst Massacre since World War II.* New York: Farrar, Straus and Giroux.

Shrader, Charles, R. (2003). *The Muslim-Croat Civil War in Central Bosnia: A Military History, 1992–1994.* College Station: Texas A&M University Press.

Silber, Laura and Alan Little. (1997). *Yugoslavia: Death of a Nation.* New York: Penguin Books.

Sudetic, Chuck. (1998). *Blood and Vengeance: One Family's Story of the War in Bosnia.* New York: Norton.

Tabeau, Ewa and Bijak Jakub. (2005). "War-Related Deaths in the 1992–1995 Armed Conflicts in Bosnia and Herzegovina: A Critique of Previous Estimates and Recent Results," *European Journal of Population* 21 (2–3): 187–215.

Thomas, Nigel and Krunoslav Mikulan. (2006). *The Yugoslav Wars (2): Bosnia, Kosovo, and Macedonia, 1992–2001.* New York: Osprey Publishing.

Tomasevich, Jozo. (2001). *War and Revolution in Yugoslavia, 1941–1945: Occupation and Collaboration.* Stanford: Stanford University Press.

West, Rebecca. (1982). *Black Lamb and Grey Falcon.* New York: Penguin Books.

Who Is Who among Bosniacs. (2001). Sarajevo: Council of the Congress of Bosniac Intellectuals.

Wilcox, Richard M. (1999). *The Politics of Transitional Anarchy: Coalitions in the Yugoslav Civil Wars, 1941–1945 and 1991–1995.* PhD dissertation, Massachusetts Institute of Technology.

Woodward, Susan L. (1995). *Balkan Tragedy: Chaos and Dissolution after the Cold War.* Washington, DC: The Brookings Institution.

Zbornik Radova. (1996). *Herceg Bosna ili . . . ?* Mostar: ZIRAL.

Zijad Rujanac. (2003). *Opkoljeno Sarajevo.* Sarajevo: Centar za Istraživanje i Dokumentaciju.

Zubac Aleksa. (1998). "Poseta Razorenim Srpskim Svetinjama Grada Mostara Dana 21 Jula 1994 Godine," in *Knjiga o Mostaru*. Beograd: Svet Knjige, pp. 205–209.

References for World War II Bosnia and Herzegovina

Published primary sources:

Collection of Documents and Data on the National-Liberation War of the Yugoslav People *(Zbornik Dokumenata i Podataka o Narodno-Oslobodilačkom Ratu Jugoslovenskih Naroda)*, a 14-volume set comprised of 173 books published in Belgrade from 1949 to 1985 by the War-History Institute *(Vojnoistoriski Institut)*.

Archive of the Communist Party of Bosnia-Herzegovina *(Arhiv Komunističke Partije Bosne i Hercegovine)* printed in a three-volume set comprised of six books and published in Sarajevo between 1950 and 1953 by the Historical Department of the Central Committee of the Communist Party of Bosnia and Herzegovina *(Istorisko Odjeljenje Centralnog Komiteta Komunističke Partije Bosne i Hercegovine)*.

Belgrade Military Archive *(Vojni Arhiv, Narodnooslobodilačke Vojska Jugoslavije)*, Belgrade, and its two subarchives: the Chetnik Fund and the National-Liberation Army Fund.

Colić, Mladen. (1973). *Takozvana Nezavisna Država Hrvatska 1941*. Beograd: Delta Press.

Laws and Orders of Independent State of Croatia, which were published as an annex in Mladen Colić, the author of *"Takozvana Nezavisna Država Hrvatska 1941"* ("The so-called Independent State of Croatia"), published in Belgrade, by DELTA-PRES in 1973.

Secondary sources:

Friedman, Francine. (1996). *The Bosnian Muslims: Denial of a Nation*. Boulder, CO: Westview Press.

Historical Atlas of the Liberation War of the Yugoslav People *(Istoriski Atlas Oslobodilačkog Rata Naroda Jugoslavije 1941–1945)*, published in Belgrade in 1952 by the War History Institute of the Yugoslav National Army *(Vojnoistoriski Institut Jugoslovenske Narodne Armije)*. (*Note*: Thirty-two detailed maps of liberated territories and main military offensives spanning through the war were consulted for this research.)

Hoare, Marko Attila. (2006). *Genocide and Resistance in Hitler's Bosnia: The Partisans and the Chetniks, 1941–1943*. Oxford: Oxford University Press.

Imamović, Mustafa. (1997). *Historija Bosnjaka* (The History of the Bosniaks). Sarajevo: Bosanska Knjiga.

Karchmar, Lucien. (1987). *Draza Mihailovic and the Rise of the Chetnik Movement, 1941–1942*, vols. I and II. New York and London: Garland Publishing.

Pavlowitch, Stevan K. (2008). *Hitler's New Disorder: The Second World War in Yugoslavia*. New York: Columbia University Press.

Redžić, Enver. (2005). *Bosnia and Herzegovina in the Second World War*. London: Frank Cass.

Tomasevich, Jozo. (1975). *The Chetniks*. Stanford, CA: Stanford University Press.

The Chronology of the National-Liberation Struggle of the Yugoslav People *(Hronologija Oslobodilačke Borbe Naroda Jugoslavije 1941–1945)*. (1964).

Belgrade: War-History Institute (*Vojnoistorijski Institute*). (*Note:* Hronologija contains 18,300 chronological units. Only those related to general events and Bosnia and Herzegovina were researched.)

References for Iraq Shadow Case

Al-Touajri, Ali. (2010). "Anti-Qaeda Militiamen Defecting in Iraqi Hotspots," *Middle East Online* (October 19), http://www.middle-east-online.com/english/?id=42023, accessed April 20, 2011.

Berman, Eli, Jacob N. Shapiro, and Joseph H. Felter. (2011). "Can Hearts and Minds Be Bought? The Economics of Counterinsurgency in Iraq," *Journal of Political Economy* 119 (4): 766–819.

Biddle, Stephen, Jeffrey Friedman, and Jacob N. Shapiro. (2011). *Testing the Surge: Why Did Violence Decline in Iraq in 2007?* Working Paper.

Bruno, Andrew. (2008a). "The Role of the 'Sons of Iraq' in Improving Security," *Washington Post*, April 28.

Bruno, Greg. (2008b). "The Preparedness of Iraqi Security Forces," *Council on Foreign Relations* (March 27), http://www.cfr.org/publication/14112, accessed April 20, 2011.

Chulov, Martin. (2010). "Fears of Al-Qaida Return in Iraq as US-Backed Fighters Defect," *The Guardian*, August 10.

Cleveland, William. (2004). *A History of the Modern Middle East*. Boulder, CO: Westview Press.

Cordesman, Anthony H. (2008). *Iraq's Insurgency and the Road to Civil Conflict*. Westport, CT: Praeger Security International.

Dagher, Sam. (2007). "Iraq's Sadr Uses Lull to Rebuild Army," *Christian Science Monitor*, December 11.

Dehghanpisheh, Babak. (2007). "Baghdad Briefing," *Newsweek Web Exclusive*, http://www.newsweek.com/id/56824, accessed April 20, 2011.

Dreyfuss, Robert. (2008). "Is Iran Winning the Iraq War?" *The Nation*, February 21.

Gordon, Michael R. (2007). "The Former-Insurgent Counterinsurgency," *The New York Times*, September 2.

Government of Australia. (2012). "What Governments Are Doing: Ansar al-Islam," http://www.ema.gov.au/agd/WWW/NationalSecurity.nsf/Page/What_Governments_are_doing_Listing_of_Terrorism_Organisations_Ansar_Al-Islam, last modified March 15, accessed April 20, 2011.

Jafarzadeh, Alireza. (2008.). "Targeting Ayatollah's Terror Machine," *Fox News*, http://www.foxnews.com/story/0,2933,322628,00.html, January 14, accessed April 20, 2011.

Knickmeyer, Ellen. (2006). "Iraq Begins to Rein in Paramilitary Force," *Washington Post*, May 14.

Lindsay, Jon and Austin Long. (2009). *Counterinsurgency Theory and the Stabilization of Iraq's Anbar Province*. Paper presented at Yale Program on Order, Conflict, and Violence.

Long, Austin. (2008). "The Anbar Awakening," *Survival* 50 (2): 67–94.

McCary, John A. (2009). "The Anbar Awakening: An Alliance of Incentives," *The Washington Quarterly* 32 (1): 43–59.

Ramzi, Kholoud. (2008). "The Dawa Party's Bumpy Path," *Niqash: Briefings from Inside and Across Iraq* (June 16), http://www.niqash.org/content.php?contentTypeID=75&id=2225&lang=0, accessed April 20, 2011.

Roggio, Bill. (2008). "Al Qaeda in Iraq under Pressure in Balad, Anbar," *Long War Journal* (February 10), http://www.longwarjournal.org/archives/2008/02/al_qaeda_ in_iraq_und.php, accessed April 20, 2011.

Smith, Niel and Sean MacFarland. (2008). "Anbar Awakens: The Tipping Point," *Military Review* 88 (2): 41–52.

Spiegel, Peter and Ned Parker. (2007). "Baath Party Leaders Divided," *Los Angeles Times*, April 25.

Tilghman, Andrew. (2007). "The Myth of AQI," *Washington Monthly* 39 (10): 34–42.

Todd, Lin. (2006). *Iraq Tribal Study, al-Anbar Governorate*. Arlington, VA: Global Resources Group.

Uppsala Conflict Data Program Database. Iraq entry. Available online: http://www.ucdp.uu.se/database, accessed April 20, 2011.

U.S. State Department. (2008). *Country Reports on Terrorism*, http://www.state.gov/j/ct/rls/crt/2008/index.htm, accessed April 20, 2011.

West, Bing. (2008). *The Strongest Tribe: War, Politics, and the Endgame in Iraq*. New York: Random House.

Williams, Timothy and Duraid Adnan. (2010). "Sunnis in Iraq Allied with U.S. Rejoin Rebels," *New York Times*, October 16.

Sources for Multiparty Civil War Dataset

Internal Armed Conflict Lists and Control Variable Data Sources

Collier, Paul and Anke Hoeffler. (2004). "Greed and Grievance in Civil Wars," *Oxford Economic Papers* 56: 563–595. Replication data.

Fearon, James D. (2003). "Ethnicity, Insurgency, and Civil War," *American Political Science Review* 97 (1): 75–90. Replication data.

Friedman, Jeffrey. (2010). Data for "Boots on the Ground: The Theoretical and Practical Significance of Manpower in Counterinsurgency." Working paper provided to author.

Gleditsch, Nils Petter, Peter Wallensteen, Mikael Eriksson, Margareta Sollenberg, and Håvard Strand. (2002). "Armed Conflict 1946–2001: A New Dataset," *Journal of Peace Research* 39(5): 615–637. Version 4–2009.

Lacina, Bethany and Nils Petter Gleditsch. 2005. "Monitoring Trends in Global Combat: A New Dataset of Battle Deaths." *European Journal of Population* 21 (2–3): 145–166. Version 3.0 used for battle deaths in multiparty civil wars; Version 2.0 used to calculate population average in Fearon and Laitin (2003) dataset.

Sambanis, Nicholas. Data on civil war. Available online: http://pantheon.yale.edu/~ns237/index/research.html#Data, accessed April 20, 2011.

Sarkees, Meredith Reid. (2000). "The Correlates of War Data on War: An Update to 1997," *Conflict Management and Peace Science* 18 (1): 123–144. Version 3.0.

Uppsala Conflict Data Program Database. Available online: http://www.ucdp.uu.se/database, accessed April 20, 2012.

World Development Indicators, The World Bank, 2009.

Relevant Literature References

Acharya, Amitav. (2001). *Constructing a Security Community in Southeast Asia: ASEAN and the Problem of Regional Order*. London: Taylor and Francis.

Adler, Emmanel and Michael Barnett. (1998). "A Framework for the Study of Security Communities," in Adler, Emmanel and Michael Barnett, eds., *Security Communities*. Cambridge: Cambridge University Press, pp. 29–65.

Alesina, Alberto and Spolaore Enrico. (1997). "On the Number and Size of Nations," *The Quarterly Journal of Economics* 112 (4): 1027–1056.

Alesina, Alberto et al. (2003). "Fractionalization," *Journal of Economic Growth* 8 (2): 155–194.

Alexander, Marcus and Fotini Christia. (2011). "Context Modularity of Human Altruism," *Science* 334 (6061): 1392–1394.

Anderson, Benedict. (1983). *Imagined Communities: Reflections on the Origin and Spread of Nationalism*. London: Verso.

Atlas, Pierre M. and Roy Licklider. (1999). "Conflict among Former Allies after Civil War Settlement: Sudan, Zimbabwe, Chad and Lebanon," *Journal of Peace Research* 36 (1): 35–54.

Axelrod, Robert. (1970). *Conflict of Interest: A Theory of Divergent Goals with Applications to Politics*. Chicago: Markham Publishing Co.

Axelrod, Robert. (1990). *The Evolution of Cooperation*. London, New York: Penguin Books.

Bakke, Kristin, Kathleen Cunningham, and L. J. M. Seymour. (2011). *A Plague of Initials: Fragmentation, Cohesion, and Infighting in Civil Wars*. Paper presented at the annual meeting of the American Political Science Association, Seattle, WA, September 1–4.

Balcells, Laia. (2010). "Rivalry and Revenge: Violence against Civilians in Conventional Civil Wars," *International Studies Quarterly* 54 (2): 291–313.

Balcells, Laia. (2011). "Continuation of Politics by Two Means: Direct and Indirect Violence in Civil War," *Journal of Conflict Resolution* 55 (3): 397–422.

Balch-Lindsay, Dylan and Andrew J. Enterline. (2000). "Killing Time: The World Politics of Civil War Duration 1820–1992," *International Studies Quarterly* 44 (4): 615–642.

Baldwin, Kate and John Huber. (2010). "Economic versus Cultural Differences: Forms of Ethnic Diversity and Public Goods Provision," *American Political Science Review* 104 (4): 644–662.

Barkow, Jerome et al., eds. (1992). *The Adapted Mind: Evolutionary Psychology and the Generation of Culture*. New York: Oxford University Press.

Barnett, Michael N. (1996). "Identity and Alliances in the Middle East," in Peter J. Katzenstein, ed., *The Culture of National Security: Norms and Identity in World Politics*. New York: Columbia University Press, pp. 400–447.

Bates, Robert H. (1974). *Patterns of Uneven Development in Zambia: Causes and Consequences*. Monograph, Graduate School of International Studies, University of Denver, Denver, CO.

Bates, Robert H. (1983). "Some Core Assumptions in Development Economics," in Ortiz, Sutti, ed., *Economic Anthropology: Topics and Theories: Monographs in Economic Anthropology*, no. 1. New York: University Press of America, pp. 361–398.

Bates, Robert H. (2006). "Ethnicity," in David Alexander, ed., *The Elgar Companion to Development Studies*. Cheltenham, U.K.: Edward Elgar Publishing, pp. 167–173.

Bates, Robert H. et al. (1998). "The Politics of Interpretation: Rationality, Culture and Transition," *Politics and Society* 26 (4): 603–642.

Berman, Eli and David Laitin. (2008). "Religion, Terrorism, and Public Goods," *Journal of Public Economics* 92 (10–11): 1942–1967.

Brass, Paul R. (1974). *Language, Religion, and Politics in North India*. Cambridge: Cambridge University Press.

Bredal, Mats and David M. Malone. (2000). "Introduction," in Bredal, Mats and David M. Malone, eds., *Greed & Grievance: Economic Agendas in Civil Wars*, Boulder, CO: Lynne Rienner Publishers, pp. 1–15.

Brubaker, Rogers. (2004). *Ethnicity without Groups*. Cambridge, MA: Harvard University Press.

Brubaker, Rogers and David D. Laitin. (1998). "Ethnic and Nationalist Violence," *Annual Review of Sociology* 24: 423–452.

Bueno de Mesquita, Ethan. (2005). "Conciliation, Counterterrorism, and Patterns of Terrorist Violence," *International Organization* 59 (1): 145–176.

Buhaug, Halvard, Lars-Erik Cederman, and Jan Ketil Rod. (2006). *Modeling Ethnic Conflict in Center-Periphery Dyads*. Paper presented at the Workshop on Polarization and Conflict, Nicosia, Cyprus, April 26–29.

Buhaug, Halvard and Scott Gates. (2002). "The Geography of Civil War," *Journal of Peace Research* 39 (4): 417–433.

Burch, Michael and Leslie Ochreiter. (2010). *Nothing Will Keep Us Together: Fractionalization in Intrastate Conflict*. Paper presented at the annual meeting of the Peace Science Society, Fort Worth, TX, October 23.

Carment, David and Patrick James. (1995). "Internal Constraints and Interstate Ethnic Conflict: Toward a Crisis-Based Assessment of Irredentism," *Journal of Conflict Resolution* 39 (1):82–109.

Caselli, Francesco and John Coleman. (2001). *On the Theory of Ethnic Conflict*. Unpublished Manuscript, Harvard University, Cambridge, MA.

Cederman, Lars-Erik and Luc Girardin. (2007). "Beyond Fractionalization: Mapping Ethnicity onto Nationalist Insurgencies," *American Political Science Review* 101 (1): 173–185.

Cederman, Lars-Erik, Luc Girardin, and Kristian Skrede Gleditsch. (2009). "Ethno-Nationalist Triads: Assessing the Influence of Kin Groups on Civil Wars," *World Politics* 61 (3): 403–437.

Cederman, Lars-Erik, Jan Ketil Rod, and Nils Weiderman. (2006). *Geo-Referencing of Ethnic Groups: Creating a New Database*. Paper presented at the GROW-Net Workshop, International Peace Research Institute (PRIO), Oslo, February 10–11.

Cederman, Lars-Erk, Andreas Wimmer, and Brian Min. (2010). "Why Do Ethnic Groups Rebel? New Data and Analysis," *World Politics* 62 (1): 87–119.

Chandra, Kanchan. (2001). "Cumulative Findings in the Study of Ethnic Politics," *APSA-CP* 12 (1): 7–11.

Chandra, Kanchan. (2004). *Why Ethnic Parties Succeed: Patronage and Ethnic Headcounts in India*. Cambridge: Cambridge University Press.

Chandra, Kanchan. (2006). "What Is Ethnic Identity and Does It Matter?" *Annual Review of Political Science* 9: 397–424.

Chandra, Kanchan and Cilanne Boulet. (2003). *A Model of Change in an Ethnic Demography*. Paper presented at the CAEG meeting, Philadelphia, August 25–27.

Chandra, Kanchan and David Laitin. (2003). *Ethnic Diversity and Democratic Stability*. Paper presented at the annual meeting of the American Political Science Association, Philadelphia, August 29.

Chandra, Kanchan and Steven Wilkinson. (2008). "Measuring the Effect of 'Ethnicity,'" *Comparative Political Studies* 41 (4–5): 515–563.

Christia, Fotini. (2008). "Following the Money: Muslim versus Muslim in Bosnia's Civil War," *Comparative Politics* 40 (4): 461–480.

Collier, Paul and Anke Hoeffler. (2000). *Greed and Grievance in Civil War.* World Bank Policy Research Paper 2355, World Bank, Washington, DC.

Collier, Paul and Nicholas Sambanis. (2002). "Understanding Civil War: A New Agenda," *Journal of Conflict Resolution* 46 (1): 3–12.

Cunningham, David. (2006). "Veto Players and Civil War Duration," *American Journal of Political Science* 50 (4): 875–892.

Cunningham, David. (2011). *Barriers to Peace in Civil Wars.* Cambridge: Cambridge University Press.

Cunningham, Kathleen, Kristin Bakke, and Lee Seymour. (2009). *Shirts Today, Skins Tomorrow: The Effects of Fragmentation on Conflict Processes in Self-Determination Disputes.* Paper presented at the annual meeting of the International Studies Association, New York, February 15–18.

Dertwinkel, Tim. (2006). *Strategy, Power and Alliances of Ethnic Groups in Conflict.* Unpublished Manuscript, Research Proposal for PhD Project at ETH Zurich, June.

De Swaan, Abram. (1973). *Coalition Theories and Cabinet Formation: A Study of Formal Theories of Coalition Formation Applied to Nine European Parliaments after 1918.* Amsterdam: Elsevier Scientific.

Downes, Alexander B. (2008). *Targeting Civilians in War.* Ithaca, NY: Cornell University Press.

Doyle, Michael. (1986). "Liberalism and World Politics," *American Political Science Review* 80 (4): 1151–1169.

Doyle, Michael and Nicholas Sambanis. (2000). "International Peacebuilding: A Theoretical and Quantitative Analysis," *American Political Science Review* 94 (4) : 779–801.

Doyle, Michael and Nicholas Sambanis. (2006). *Making War and Building Peace: United Nations Peace Operations.* Princeton, NJ: Princeton University Press.

Driscoll, Jesse. (2009). *Commitment Problems or Bidding Wars? Rebel Fragmentation as Peace-Building.* Paper presented at the annual meeting of the Association for the Study of Nationalities, New York, April 23–25.

Dunning, Thad and Lauren Harrison. (2010). "Cross-Cutting Cleavages and Ethnic Voting: An Experimental Study of Cousinage in Mali," *American Political Science Review* 104 (1): 21–39.

Edelstein, David. (2002). "Managing Uncertainty: Beliefs about Intentions and the Rise of Great Powers," *Security Studies* 12 (1): 1–40.

Eifert, Benn, Edward Miguel, and Daniel Posner. (2010). "Political Competition and Ethnic Identification in Africa," *American Journal of Political Science* 54 (2): 494–510.

Elbadawi, Ibrahim and Nicholas Sambanis. (2000). *How Much War Will We See? Estimating the Probability of Civil War in 161 Countries.* Manuscript, World Bank, July.

Elster, Jon. (1989). *Nuts and Bolts for the Social Sciences.* Cambridge: Cambridge University Press.

Fazal, Tanisha M. (2007). *State Death: The Politics and Geography of Conquest, Occupation, and Annexation.* Princeton, NJ: Princeton University Press.

Fearon, James. (1995). "Rationalist Explanations for War," *International Organization* 49 (3): 379–414.

Fearon, James D. (1998). "Commitment Problems and the Spread of Ethnic Conflict," in Lake, David and Donald Rothchild, eds., *The International Spread of Ethnic Conflict: Fear, Diffusion, and Escalation*. Princeton, NJ: Princeton University Press, pp. 107–126.

Fearon, James D. (2003). "Ethnic and Cultural Diversity by Country," *Journal of Economic Growth* 8 (2): 195–222.

Fearon, James D. (2004). "Why Do Some Civil Wars Last So Much Longer Than Others?" *Journal of Peace Research* 41 (3): 275–301.

Fearon, James D. (2011). "Two States, Two Types, Two Actions," *Security Studies* 20 (3): 431–440.

Fearon, James, Kimuli Kasara, and David Laitin. (2007). "Ethnic Minority Rule and Civil War Onset," *American Political Science Review* 101 (1): 187–193.

Fearon, James and David D. Laitin. (1996). "Explaining Interethnic Cooperation," *American Political Science Review* 90 (4): 715–735.

Fearon, James and David D. Laitin. (2000a). *Ordinary Language and External Validity: Specifying Concepts in the Study of Ethnicity*. Paper presented at the annual meeting of the American Political Science Association, Washington, DC, August 31–September 3.

Fearon, James and David D. Laitin. (2000b). "Violence and the Social Construction of Ethnic Identity," *International Organization* 54 (4): 845–877.

Fearon, James and David D. Laitin. (2003). "Ethnicity, Insurgency, and Civil War," *American Political Science Review* 97 (1): 75–90.

Fearon, James and David D. Laitin. (2007). *Civil War Termination*. Paper presented at the annual meeting of the American Political Science Association, Chicago, August 30–September 2.

de Figueiredo Jr., J. P. Rui, and Barry R. Weingast. (1999). "The Rationality of Fear: Political Opportunism and Ethnic Conflict," in Barbara F. Walter and Jack Snyder, eds., *Civil War, Insecurity and Intervention*. New York: Columbia University Press, pp. 261–302.

Findley, Michael, and Peter Rudloff. (2009). *Combatant Fragmentation and the Dynamics of Civil Wars*. Paper presented at the annual meeting of the American Political Science Association, Toronto, Canada, September 3–6.

Findley, Michael and Peter Rudloff. (2011). *The Downstream Effects of Combatant Fragmentation on Civil War Recurrence*. Paper presented at the annual meeting of the International Studies Association, Montreal, Canada, March 16–19.

Fjelde, Hanne and Desiree Nilsson. (2011). *Rebels Divided: Explaining Rebel Group Fragmentation in Civil War, 1975–2008*. Paper presented at the annual meeting of the International Studies Association, Montreal, Canada, March 16–19.

Fortna, Page. (2004). "Does Peacekeeping Keep Peace? International Intervention and the Duration of Peace after Civil War," *International Studies Quarterly* 48 (2): 269–292.

Gagnon, V. P., Jr. (2004). *The Myth of Ethnic War: Serbia and Croatia in the 1990s*. Ithaca, NY: Cornell University Press.

Goodwin, Jeff. (2001). *No Other Way Out: States and Revolutionary Movements, 1945–1991*. Cambridge: Cambridge University Press.

Grofman, Bernard. (1982). "A Dynamic Model of Protocoalition Formation in Ideological n-Space," *Behavioral Science* 27 (1): 77–90.

Gurr, Ted Robert. (1993). *Minorities at Risk: A Global View of Ethnopolitical Conflicts*. Washington, DC: United States Institute of Peace Press.

Gurr, Ted Robert. (2000). *Peoples versus States: Minorities at Risk in the New Century*. Washington, DC: United States Institute of Peace Press.

Gurr, Ted R., Marshall Monty et al. (2001). *Peace and Conflict 2001: A Global Survey of Armed Conflicts, Self-Determination Movements and Democracy*. College Park: Center for International Development and Conflict Management, University of Maryland.

Haas, Mark L. (2003). "Ideology and Alliances: British and French External Balancing Decisions in the 1930s," *Security Studies* 12 (4): 34–79.

Habyarimana, James, Macartan Humphreys, Daniel Posner, and Jeremy Weinstein. (2007). "Why Does Ethnic Diversity Undermine Public Goods Provision?" *American Political Science Review* 101 (4): 709–725.

Harff, Barbara, and Ted Robert Gurr. (1994). *Ethnic Conflict in World Politics*. Boulder, CO: Westview Press.

Hartzell, Caroline A. (1999). "Explaining the Stability of Negotiated Settlements to Intrastate Wars," *Journal of Conflict Resolution* 43 (1): 3–22.

Hegre, Havard, et al. (2001). "Toward a Democratic Civil Peace? Democracy, Political Change, and Civil War 1816–1992," *American Political Science Review* 95: 33–48.

Hirshleifer, Jack. (1995). "Anarchy and its Breakdown," *Journal of Political Economy* 103 (1): 26–52.

Hobsbawm, Eric. (1984). "Introduction: Inventing Traditions," in Hobsbawm, Eric and Terrence Ranger, eds., *The Invention of Tradition*. Cambridge: Cambridge University Press, pp. 1–14.

Horowitz, Donald. (1985). *Ethnic Groups in Conflict*. Berkeley: University of California Press.

Humphreys, Macartan and Jeremy Weinstein. (2006). "Handling and Manhandling Civilians in Civil War," *American Political Science Review* 100 (3): 429–447.

Humphreys, Macartan and Jeremy Weinstein. (2008). "Who Fights? The Determinants of Participation in Civil War," *American Journal of Political Science* 52 (2): 436–455.

Huntington, Samuel. (1968). *Political Order in Changing Societies*. New Haven, CT: Yale University Press.

Johnston, Patrick. (2008). "The Geography of Insurgent Organizations and its Consequences for Civil Wars: Evidence from Liberia and Sierra Leone," *Security Studies* 17 (1): 107–137.

Jones, Christopher P. (1999). *Kinship Diplomacy in the Ancient World*. Cambridge, MA: Harvard University Press.

Kalyvas, Stathis N. (2001). "'New' and 'Old' Civil Wars: A Valid Distinction?" *World Politics* 54 (1): 99–118.

Kalyvas, Stathis N. (2002). *Incorporating Constructivist Propositions into Theories of Civil War*. Paper presented at the CAEG meeting, Massachusetts Institute of Technology, December 6–8.

Kalyvas, Stathis N. (2003). "The Ontology of 'Political Violence': Action and Identity in Civil Wars," *Perspectives on Politics* 1 (3): 475–494.

Kalyvas, Stathis N. (2006). *The Logic of Violence in Civil War*. New York: Cambridge University Press.

Kalyvas, Stathis N. (2008). "Ethnic Defection in Civil Wars," *Comparative Political Studies* 41 (8): 1043–1068.

Kalyvas, Stathis and Laia Balcells. (2010a). *Did Marxism Make a Difference? Marxist Rebellions and National Liberation Movements*. Paper presented at the annual meeting of the American Political Science Association, Washington, DC, September 2–5.

Kalyvas, Stathis and Laia Balcells. (2010b). "International System and Technologies of Rebellion: How the End of the Cold War Shaped Internal Conflict," *American Political Science Review* 104 (3): 415–429.

Kalyvas, Stathis N. and Matthew Adam Kocher. (2007a). "Ethnic Cleavages and Irregular War: Iraq and Vietnam," *Politics and Society* 35 (2): 183–223.

Kalyvas, Stathis N. and Matthew Adam Kocher. (2007b). "How Free Is 'Free Riding' in Civil Wars? Violence, Insurgency, and the Collective Action Problem," *World Politics* 59 (2): 177–216.

Kasfir, Nelson. (1979). "Explaining Ethnic Political Participation," *World Politics* 31 (3): 365–388.

Kasfir, Nelson. (2003). "Domestic Anarchy, Security Dilemmas and Violent Predation: Causes of Failure," in Robert Rotberg, ed., *When States Fail: Causes and Consequences*. Princeton, NJ: Princeton University Press, pp. 53–76.

Kaufman, Stuart J. (2001). *Modern Hatreds: The Symbolic Politics of Ethnic War*. Ithaca, NY: Cornell University Press.

Kaufmann, Chaim. (1996a). "Intervention in Ethnic and Ideological Civil Wars: Why One Can Be Done and the Other Can't," *Security Studies* 6 (1): 62–100.

Kaufmann, Chaim. (1996b). "Possible and Impossible Solutions to Ethnic Civil Wars," *International Security* 20 (4): 136–175.

Kenny, Paul. (2010). "Structural Integrity and Cohesion in Insurgent Organizations: Evidence from Protracted Conflicts in Ireland and Burma," *International Studies Review* 12 (4): 533–555.

King, Gary Robert Keohane and Sidney Verba. (1994). *Designing Social Inquiry: Scientific Inference in Qualitative Research*. Princeton, NJ: Princeton University Press.

Kuran, Timur. (1998). "Ethnic Norms and Their Transformation through Reputational Cascades," *Journal of Legal Studies* 27 (S2): 623–659.

Kydd, Andrew and Barbara F. Walter. (2002). "Sabotaging the Peace: The Politics of Extremist Violence," *International Organization* 56 (2): 263–296.

Lacina, Bethany. (2006). "Explaining the Severity of Civil Wars," *Journal of Conflict Resolution* 50 (2): 276–289.

Laitin, David D. (2000). "Language Conflict and Violence: The Straw that Strengthens the Camel's Back," in Mats Bredal and David M. Malone, eds., *Greed & Grievance: Economic Agendas in Civil Wars*. Boulder, CO: Lynne Rienner Publishers, pp. 531–568.

Laitin, David and Daniel Posner. (2001). "The Implications of Constructivism for Constructing Ethnic Fractionalization Indices," *APSA-CP* 12 (1): 13–17.

Lake, David. (1993). "Leadership, Hegemony, and the International Economy: Naked Emperor or Tattered Monarch with Potential?" *International Studies Quarterly* 37 (4): 459–489.

Lake, David A. and Donald S. Rothchild. (1996). "Containing Fear: The Origins and Management of Ethnic Conflict," *International Security* 21 (2): 41–75.

Lake, David A. and Donald S. Rothchild, eds. (1998). *The International Spread of Ethnic Conflict: Fear, Diffusion and Escalation*. Princeton, NJ: Princeton University Press.

Lawrence, Adria. (2007). *Imperial Rule and the Politics of Nationalism*. PhD dissertation, University of Chicago.

Licklider, Roy. (1995). "The Consequences of Negotiated Settlements in Civil Wars, 1945–1993," *American Political Science Review* 89 (3): 681–690.

Lieberman, Evan. (2005). "Nested Analysis as a Mixed-Method Strategy for Comparative Research," *American Political Science Review* 99 (3): 435–52.

Lipset, Seymour Martin and Stein Rokkan. (1967). "Cleavage Structures, Party Systems and Voter Alignments: An Introduction," in Lipset, Seymour Martin and Stein Rokkan, eds., *Party Systems and Voter Alignments: Cross-National Perspectives*. New York: Free Press, pp. 1–64.

Lounsbery, Marie Olson and Alethia Cook. (2011). "Rebellion, Mediation, and Group Change: An Empirical Investigation of Competing Hypotheses," *Journal of Peace Research* 48 (1): 73–84.

Lyall, Jason. (2009). "Does Indiscriminate Violence Incite Insurgent Attacks? Evidence from Chechnya," *Journal of Conflict Resolution* 53 (3): 331–362.

Lyall, Jason. (2010). "Are Co-Ethnics More Effective Counter-Insurgents? Evidence from the Second Chechen War," *American Political Science Review* 104 (1): 1–20.

Lyall, Jason and Isaiah Wilson III. (2009). "Rage against the Machines: Explaining Outcomes in Counterinsurgency Wars," *International Organization* 63 (1): 67–106.

Mason, David T., Joseph P. Weingarten, Jr., and Patrick J. Fett. (1999). "Win, Lose or Draw: Predicting the Outcome of Civil Wars," *Political Research Quarterly* 52 (2): 239–268.

McLauchlin, Theodore and Wendy Pearlman. (2009). *Out-group Conflict, In-group Unity? Exploring the Effect of Repression on Movement Fragmentation*. Paper presented at the annual meeting of the American Political Science Association, Toronto, Canada, September 3–6.

Mearsheimer, John J. (2001). *The Tragedy of Great Power Politics*. New York: W.W. Norton.

Migdal, Joel. S. (1988). *Strong Societies and Weak States: State-Society Relations and State Capabilities in the Third World*. Princeton, NJ: Princeton University Press.

Miguel, Edward and Mary Kay Gugerty. (2005). "Ethnic Diversity, Social Sanctions, and Public Goods in Kenya," *Journal of Public Economics* 89 (11–12): 2325–2368.

Montalvo, Jose G. and Marga Reynal-Querol. (2005). "Ethnic Polarization, Potential, Conflict and Civil Wars," *American Economic Review* 95 (3): 796–816.

Mueller, John. (2000). "The Banality of 'Ethnic War,'" *International Security* 25 (1): 42–70.

Narizny, Kevin. (2003). "The Political Economy of Alignment: Great Britain's Commitments to Europe, 1905–39," *International Security* 27 (4): 184–219.

Nilsson, Desiree. (2010). "Turning Weakness into Strength: Military Capabilities, Multiple Rebel Groups and Negotiated Settlements," *Conflict Management and Peace Science* 27 (3): 253–271.

Oren, Ido. (1995). "The Subjectivity of the 'Democratic' Peace: Changing U.S. Perceptions of Imperial Germany," *International Security* 20 (2): 147–184.

Pearlman, Wendy. (2009). "Spoiling Inside and Out: Internal Political Contestation and the Middle East Peace Process," *International Security* 33 (3): 79–109.

Petersen, Roger D. (2001). *Resistance and Rebellion: Lessons from Eastern Europe*. Cambridge: Cambridge University Press.

Petersen, Roger D. (2002). *Understanding Ethnic Violence: Fear, Hatred, and Resentment in Twentieth-Century Eastern Europe.* Cambridge: Cambridge University Press.

Petersen, Roger D. (2003). *Identity, Rationality, and Emotion in the Processes of State Disintegration and Reconstruction.* Unpublished Manuscript.

Petersen, Roger D. (2011). *Western Intervention in the Balkans: The Strategic Use of Emotion in Conflict.* Cambridge: Cambridge University Press.

Platteau, Jean-Philippe. (1994). "Behind the Market Where Real Societies Exist," *Journal of Development Studies* 30 (3): 533–578.

Popkin, Samuel. (1979). *The Rational Peasant: The Political Economy of Rural Society in Vietnam.* Berkeley: University of California Press.

Posen, Barry. (1993). "The Security Dilemma and Ethnic Conflict," in Michael Brown, ed., *Ethnic Conflict and International Security.* Princeton, NJ: Princeton University Press, 1993, pp.103–124.

Posner, Daniel N. (2004). "The Political Salience of Cultural Difference: Why Chewas and Tambukas are Allies in Zambia and Adversaries in Malawi," *American Political Science Review* 98 (4): 529–545.

Posner, Daniel N. (2005). *Institutions and Ethnic Politics in Africa.* Cambridge: Cambridge University Press.

Powell, Robert. (2006). "War as a Commitment Problem," *International Organization* 60 (1): 169–203.

Przeworski, Adam et al. (2000). *Democracy and Development: Political Institutions and Well-Being in the World, 1950–1990.* Cambridge: Cambridge University Press.

Pye, Lucian. (1956). *Guerrilla Communism in Malaya: Its Social and Political Meaning.* Princeton, NJ: Princeton University Press.

Rasler, Karen. (1983). "Internationalized Civil War: A Dynamic Analysis of the Syrian Intervention in Lebanon," *Journal of Conflict Resolution* 27 (3): 421–456.

Regan, Patrick M. (1996). "Conditions of Successful Third-Party Intervention in Intrastate Conflicts," *Journal of Conflict Resolution* 40 (2): 336–359.

Regan, Patrick M. (1998). "Choosing to Intervene: Outside Interventions in Internal Conflicts," *Journal of Politics* 60 (3): 754–779.

Riker, William H. (1962). *The Theory of Political Coalition.* New Haven, CT: Yale University Press.

Risse-Kappen, Thomas. (1996). "Collective Identity in a Democratic Community: The Case of NATO," in Peter Katzenstein, ed., *The Culture of National Security: Norms and Identity in World Politics.* New York: Columbia University Press, pp. 357–399.

Roemer, John E. et al. (2007). *Racism, Xenophobia, and Distribution: Multi-Issue Politics in Advanced Democracies.* New York and Cambridge, MA: Russell Sage Foundation and Harvard University Press.

Rogowski, Ronald. (1989). *Commerce and Coalitions: How Trade Affects Domestic Political Alignments.* Princeton, NJ: Princeton University Press.

Rokkan, Stein. (1999). *State Formation, Nation Building, and Mass Politics in Europe: The Theory of Stein Rokkan Based on His Collected Works.* Peter Flora, Stein Kuhnle, and Derek Urwin, eds. Oxford: Oxford University Press.

Sambanis, Nicholas. (2001). "Do Ethnic and Nonethnic Civil Wars Have the Same Causes? A Theoretical and Empirical Inquiry," *Journal of Conflict Resolution* 45 (3): 259–282.

Sambanis, Nicholas. (2002). "A Review of Recent Advances and Future Directions in the Literature on Civil War," *Defense and Peace Economics* 13 (2): 215–243.

Sambanis, Nicholas. (2004a). "Using Case Studies to Expand Economic Models of Civil War," *Perspectives on Politics* 2 (2): 259–279.

Sambanis, Nicholas. (2004b). "What Is Civil War? Conceptual and Empirical Complexities of an Operational Definition," *Journal of Conflict Resolution* 48 (6): 814–858.

Sambanis, Nicholas. (In press). *The Organization of Political Violence, Self-Determination, and Civil War.*

Sambanis, Nicholas and Ibrahim Elbadawi. (2000). "External Intervention and the Duration of Civil Wars," *World Bank Policy Research Working Paper* No. 2433.

Schelling, Thomas C. (1960). *The Strategy of Conflict.* Cambridge, MA: Harvard University Press.

Schelling, Thomas C. (1978). *Micromotives and Macrobehaviors.* New York: Norton.

Schweller, Randall L. (1994). "Bandwagoning for Profit: Bringing the Revisionist State Back In," *International Security* 19 (1): 72–107.

Selznick, Philip. (1952). *The Organizational Weapon: A Study of Bolshevik Strategy and Tactics.* New York: McGraw-Hill.

Skarpedas, Stergios. (1992). "Cooperation, Conflict, and Power in the Absence of Property Rights," *American Economic Review* 82: 720–739.

Smith, Alastair. (1996). "To Intervene or Not to Intervene: A Biased Decision," *The Journal of Conflict Resolution* 40 (1): 16–40.

Snyder, Jack and Robert Jervis. (1999). "Civil War and the Security Dilemma," in Walter, Barbara F. and Jack Snyder, eds., *Civil War, Insecurity and Intervention.* New York: Columbia University Press, pp. 15–37.

Staniland, Paul. (2010). *Explaining Cohesion, Fragmentation, and Control in Insurgent Groups.* PhD dissertation, Massachusetts Institute of Technology.

Starr, Harvey. (1992). "Democracy and War: Choice, Learning, and Security Communities," *Journal of Peace Research* 29 (2): 207–213.

Stedman, Stephen John. (1997). "Spoiler Problems in Peace Processes," *International Security* 22 (2): 5–53.

Tajfel, Henri, M. G. Billig, R. P. Bundy, and C. Flament (1971). "Social Categorization and Inter-group Behavior," *European Journal of Social Psychology* 1 (2): 149–178.

Toft, Monica Duffy. (2003). *The Geography of Ethnic Violence: Identity, Interests and the Indivisibility of Territory.* Princeton, NJ: Princeton University Press.

Toft, Monica Duffy. (2010). "Ending Civil Wars: A Case for Rebel Victory?" *International Security* 34 (4): 7–36.

Valentino, Benjamin. (2005). *Final Solutions: Mass Killing and Genocide in the Twentieth Century.* Ithaca, NY: Cornell University Press.

Valentino, Benjamin, Paul Huth, and Dylan Balch-Lindsay. (2004). "'Draining the Sea': Mass Killing and Guerilla Warfare," *International Organization* 58 (2): 375–407.

Van Den Berghe, Pierre L. (1981). *The Ethnic Phenomenon.* New York: Elsevier.

Van Evera, Stephen. (1994). "Hypotheses on Nationalism and War," *International Security* 18 (4): 5–39.

Van Evera, Stephen. (2001). "Primordialism Lives!" *APSA-CP* 12 (1): 20–22.

Wagner, R. Harrison. (2000). "Bargaining and War," *American Journal of Political Science* 44 (3): 469–484.

Walt, Stephen M. (1987). *The Origins of Alliances.* Ithaca, NY: Cornell University Press.

Walter, Barbara F. (1997). "The Critical Barrier to Civil War Settlement," *International Organization* 51 (3): 335–364.

Walter, Barbara F. (1999). "Designing Transitions from Civil War," in Barbara Walter and Jack Snyder, eds., *Civil War, Insecurity and Intervention*. New York: Columbia University Press, pp. 38–69.

Walter, Barbara F. (1999). "Introduction" and "Conclusion," in Walter, Barbara F. and Jack Snyder, eds., *Civil War, Insecurity and Intervention*. New York: Columbia University Press, pp. 1–12 and 303–307.

Walter, Barbara F. (2006). "Information, Uncertainty, and the Decision to Secede," *International Organization* 60 (1): 105–135.

Waltz, Kenneth N. (1979). *Theory of International Politics*. New York: Random House.

Warren, T. Camber and Kevin Troy. (forthcoming). "The Logic of Intra-Ethnic Conflict: Group Fragmentation in the Shadow of State Power," *Journal of Conflict Resolution*.

Wedeen, Lisa. (1999). *Ambiguities of Domination: Politics, Rhetoric, and Symbols in Contemporary Syria*. Chicago: University of Chicago Press.

Weinstein, Jeremy. (2007). *Inside Rebellion: The Politics of Insurgent Violence*. Cambridge: Cambridge University Press.

Wilcox, Richard M. (1999). *The Politics of Transitional Anarchy: Coalitions in the Yugoslav Civil Wars, 1941–1945 and 1991–1995*. PhD dissertation, Massachusetts Institute of Technology.

Wilkinson, Steven. (2001). "Constructivist Assumptions and Ethnic Violence," *APSA-CP* 12 (1): 17–20.

Wilkinson, Steven. (2006). *Votes and Violence: Electoral Competition and Ethnic Riots in India*. Cambridge: Cambridge University Press.

Wimmer, Andreas. (2002). *Nationalist Exclusion and Ethnic Conflict: Shadows of Modernity*. Cambridge: Cambridge University Press.

Wimmer, Andreas, Lars-Erik Cederman, and Brian Min. (2009). "Ethnic Politics and Armed Conflict: A Configurational Analysis of a New Global Dataset," *American Sociological Review* 74 (2): 316–337.

Wohlforth, William et al. (2007). "Testing Balance-of-Power Theory in World History," *European Journal of International Relations* 13 (2): 155–185.

Zartman, William. (1998). "Putting Humpty-Dumpty Together Again," in Lake, David A. and Donald Rothchild, eds., *The International Spread of Ethnic Conflict: Fear, Diffusion and Escalation*. Princeton, NJ: Princeton University Press, pp. 317–336.

Zartmann, William. (2000). "Ripeness: The Hurting Stalemate and Beyond," in Bredal, Mats and David M. Malone, eds., *Greed & Grievance: Economic Agendas in Civil Wars*. Boulder, CO: Lynne Rienner Publishers, pp. 225–250.

Index

Abdić, Fikret, 162, 179, 186–189, 194, 249, 262, 276
Abdullah, Abdullah, 247
Afghanistan, x, 1, 3, 14, 19, 26–28, 30, 46, 57–62, 64, 67, 69, 73, 84, 86, 94–96, 98–101, 103, 213–215, 219, 224, 230, 231, 233, 237–241, 243, 247, 248, 251, 257, 259
    1978–1989 jihad, 15, 27, 149, 222, 239, 261, 271, 275, 283, 286
    1992–1998 intra-mujahedin war, 5, 15, 27–29, 42, 47, 54, 149, 239, 262, 271, 275, 283, 286
    2002–present war, 16, 31, 222, 228, 239, 262, 271, 275, 286
Agha, Mawlvi Akktar Mohammad, 143
Akbari, Mohammed, 60, 62, 67, 69, 73, 85, 89–94, 100, 226, 247, 259, 260, 275
Al Qaeda, 6, 233–238, 267, 279, 289
Algeria, 219, 262, 271, 272, 275, 283, 286
alliance portfolio volatility, 216, 221–224, 228
Amin, Hafizullah, 115, 116
Anbar, 16, 31, 233–238, 251
Angola, 219, 262, 272, 275, 276, 283, 286
Army of Bosnia and Herzegovina (Armija BiH – ABiH), 153–159, 161–163, 170, 172, 173, 176–178, 182, 185, 187, 188
Army of the Serb Republic (Vojska Republike Srpske – VRS), 153, 154, 159, 162
Atta, Nur Mohammed, 247
Austria, 219, 262, 272, 276, 283, 286

Autonomous Province of Western Bosnia, 162, 185–189
Azerbaijan, 66

Badakhshan, 59, 71, 73
Badghis, 71, 97, 98
Baghlan, 71, 96
Bagram, 68, 257
Balkh, 30, 60, 72, 125, 127, 128, 130–132, 134–137, 139, 140, 142, 248, 257
Bamyan, 69, 93
bandwagoning, 20, 34, 45, 50, 52, 53, 76, 111, 138, 215, 232, 236
Banja Luka, 165, 202, 205
Battle of Sutjeska, 208
Bhutto, Benazir, 73
Bihać, 166, 185–188, 202, 208
bin Laden, Osama, 230
Boban, Mate, 156, 172, 177, 179, 182–185, 195, 284
Boras, Franjo, 181
Bosnia and Herzegovina, 3, 14, 26–28, 213–215, 224, 233, 237–241, 243, 247, 249, 251
    1941–1945 civil war, 16, 27, 30, 102, 196, 220, 222, 239, 275, 283
    1992–1995 civil war, 16, 27–30, 145, 219, 221, 228, 239, 262, 272, 276, 284, 286
Burundi, 219, 262, 272, 276, 284, 286, 287

Cambodia, 219, 222, 263, 272
Carrington-Cutileiro Agreement, 163
Cazinska Krajina, 162, 185, 187
Central Intelligence Agency, 113, 116, 160, 162

Printed in Great Britain
by Amazon.co.uk, Ltd.,
Marston Gate.